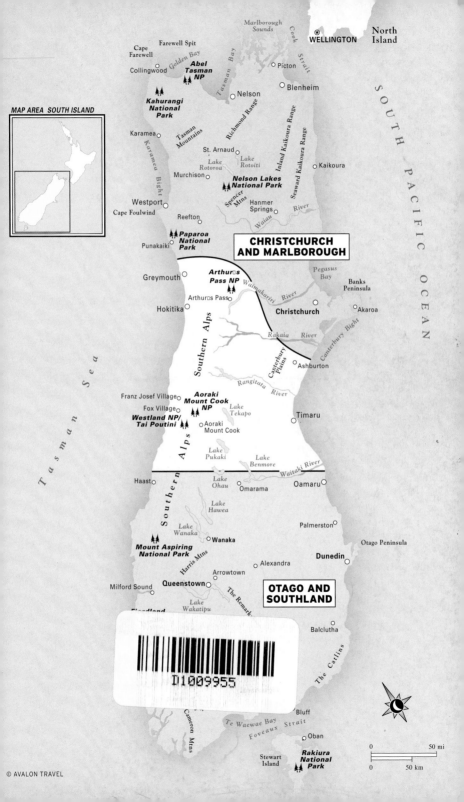

MAP AREA SOUTH ISLAND

North Island

WELLINGTON

Marlborough Sounds

Cook Strait

SOUTH PACIFIC OCEAN

Farewell Spit

Cape Farewell

Collingwood

Golden Bay

Abel Tasman NP

Picton

Blenheim

Tasman Bay

Nelson

Kahurangi National Park

Richmond Range

Karamea

Tasman Mountains

St. Arnaud

Lake Rotoroa

Lake Rotoiti

Inland Kaikoura Range

Seaward Kaikoura Range

Kaikoura

Murchison

Nelson Lakes National Park

Spencer Mtns

Hanmer Springs

River

Westport

Cape Foulwind

Karamea Bight

Reefton

Waiau

Paparoa National Park

Punakaiki

CHRISTCHURCH AND MARLBOROUGH

Greymouth

Arthur's Pass NP

Arthur's Pass

Waimakariri River

Pegasus Bay

Banks Peninsula

Hokitika

Southern Alps

Christchurch

Akaroa

Canterbury Bight

Rakaia River

Canterbury Plains

Ashburton

Rangitata River

Franz Josef Village

Aoraki Mount Cook NP

Fox Village

Lake Tekapo

Timaru

Westland NP/ Tai Poutini

Aoraki Mount Cook

Southern Alps

Lake Pukaki

Lake Benmore

Waitaki River

Haast

Lake Ohau

Omarama

Oamaru

Tasman Sea

Lake Hawea

Palmerston

Lake Wanaka

Otago Peninsula

Mount Aspiring National Park

Wanaka

Harris Mtns

Alexandra

Dunedin

Arrowtown

Milford Sound

Queenstown

OTAGO AND SOUTHLAND

Lake Wakatipu

The Remark

Fiordland

Balclutha

The Catlins

Cameron Mtns

Bluff

Te Waewae Bay

Foveaux Strait

Oban

Stewart Island

Rakiura National Park

0   50 mi
0   50 km

© AVALON TRAVEL

Contents

WITHDRAWN

LIVING ABROAD
NEW
ZEALAND

MICHELLE WAITZMAN

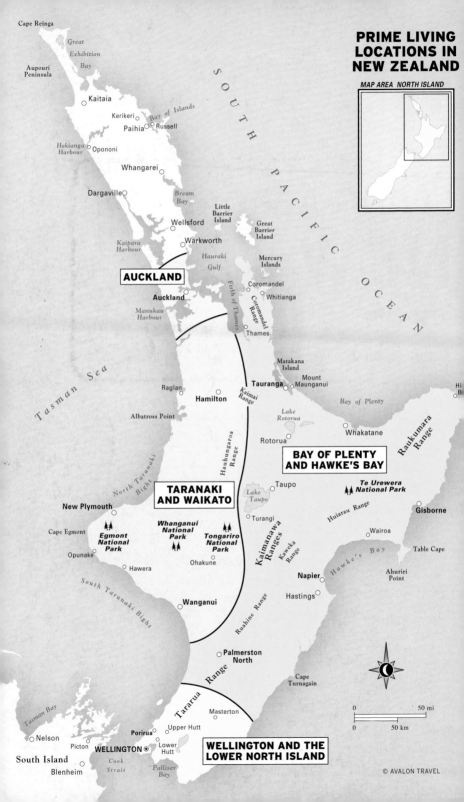

Why New Zealand? That was the question I was asked most often as I prepared to move there from my home in Toronto. The answer is not a simple one. This country calls out to many of us, for a variety of reasons. For me, it was the clean air, scaling back to a smaller city, and enjoying a healthier, more active lifestyle. For others, it's an escape from the rat race or a safe place to raise their children. Whatever the specific reasons are, people usually move to New Zealand for a lifestyle change.

New Zealand's first immigrants came from Polynesia. The Maori settled in this cool, southern land they called Aotearoa (The Land of the Long, White Cloud). For centuries they had the place to themselves, until European whalers and sealers arrived and made themselves at home, too. So began the long and tenuous coexistence of New Zealand's two domi-nant cultures—British and Maori.

Kiwis, as the New Zealanders call themselves, are generally a very friendly bunch. People here value humility and resourcefulness. When you're this isolated from the rest of the world, you've got to help each other out. That's what being a Kiwi is all about.

Living in New Zealand has many advantages. The unemployment rate is low, it's a comparatively safe country to live in, and there is a great at-titude toward finding balance in your life. On top of that, the scenery and recreational opportunities are unbeatable! Mountains, beaches, forests, lakes, rivers, glaciers, and even active volcanoes make this a fascinating country to explore.

Urban lifestyles in New Zealand are also more laid-back than in larger countries. With just one city of over a million people, this is not the height

of cosmopolitan living, but there are plenty of shops, cafés, theaters, and restaurants in the main centers to keep you busy. You'll have everything you need, even if you can't necessarily find everything you want.

Moving to New Zealand probably won't make you a millionaire or propel you up the corporate ladder. Instead, you'll find yourself eventually slowing down to the rhythms of the South Pacific. It's a place where one person can still make a difference, and people are willing to give just about anything a try, especially if someone says it can't be done.

Without a doubt, moving to New Zealand changed my life. It allowed me to go for a hike in the bush without getting into a car first. I stopped having pollution-induced headaches. I paid more attention to when local produce was in season, instead of relying on imports from thousands of miles away. And perhaps most importantly, I fell in love with another immigrant who was looking for the same lifestyle change as I was. By most accounts, my immigration story was a success.

Your story will be different from mine, but with a bit of luck and the right attitude, you can also find your happy ending.

Clockwise from top left: Maori carving, Lake Rotorua; horses on pasture; Cardboard Cathedral in Christchurch; aerial view of Queenstown.

▶ WHAT I LOVE ABOUT NEW ZEALAND

- Going for a hike in the bush without driving anywhere first

- The tui, a bird that sounds like R2D2

- Skiing on an active volcano

- Having friendly conversations with complete strangers

- Not hearing about "smog warnings"

- Going to the beach on Christmas Day

- Seeing people walk through town in bare feet

- Watching the All Blacks perform a *haka* before every rugby match

- Sir Edmund Hillary (the first person to climb Mount Everest) is on the $5 note, not a politician.

- People politely asking where I'm from, because they don't want to insult me by guessing wrong.

- Even though it is a small country with little international influence, its leaders are not afraid to take an unpopular stand on an issue, even if it contradicts their closest allies.

- Every time there's a warm, sunny day, everyone goes outside, no matter what.

- There are cities where 15 minutes in the car is considered a "long commute."

- Seeing dolphins or penguins in the harbor now and then

- Stopping at the local dairy for an ice-cream cone after a "tramp" in the woods

- The national animal is a bird that sleeps all day and can't fly.

- Kids are still allowed to climb the trees in the schoolyard.

- Your boss would find it strange if you didn't use all four weeks of your vacation time each year.

- It will take me many, many years to try all of the local wines and decide which ones I like best.

WELCOME TO
NEW ZEALAND

INTRODUCTION

Ask people what they picture when they think of New Zealand and you'll be surprised by the range of answers: from rugged, snowcapped mountains to rolling green fields full of sheep; from tattooed Maori warriors to Peter Jackson; from a British colony to a South Pacific paradise. New Zealand is a land of contrasts, and a country with a very enviable lifestyle. This diverse land of just 4.5 million people (a little more than half the population of New York City) encompasses a variety of landscapes that you'd be hard-pressed to find in such a small area anywhere else in the world. Mountains and pastures, yes, but also rugged coastline, boiling mud, lush rainforest, and awe-inspiring fjords. Add to that a Pacific culture with a thousand-year history and a modern Western society that boasts two of the top 12 cities in the world for quality of life, according to a 2014 Mercer Human Resources Consulting survey. It's a land of surprises where cutting-edge technology is developed and widely used, but highway traffic can be stopped in its tracks by a herd of sheep crossing the road.

If you're open to new experiences, New Zealand will take your breath away. Making the move requires a big leap of faith, but soon you will be able to count yourself among the fortunate few who call this beautiful, tiny nation their home.

New Zealand is a beautiful country, but moving to the bottom of the world is not for everyone. Perhaps the first thing to take into consideration is the isolation you may

feel in New Zealand. If you are close to your family or friends back home, it may be difficult knowing that you will not be able to see them very often. Bear in mind that flying from Auckland to Los Angeles or Vancouver takes about 12 hours, and to get almost anywhere else you will have to take connecting flights from there. On the other hand, if you are looking to get away from everyone and start with a fresh slate, New Zealand is a dream come true!

While New Zealand was colonized by the British and is now a multicultural Western society, its original Pacific culture is still present and highly visible. Unlike many other marginalized indigenous cultures, the Maori are still an integral part of New Zealand society. Maori is an official language in New Zealand, and many common Maori words and phrases have slipped into everyday speech among Kiwis of every race. Maori traditions, art, and culture have maintained a strong influence all over the country (although they are more prominent on the North Island); anyone who plans to live in New Zealand should look to accept and respect this culture.

You will also have to leave behind a lot of the products you may be used to when you move to New Zealand. You won't find any Gap stores or Krispy Kreme doughnuts once you move (at least not yet), although North American fast food has become a fixture in most cities. If you crave McDonald's, Pizza Hut, Domino's, KFC, Subway, or Burger King, you should be in luck, as long as you don't live in a rural area.

That being said, New Zealand has a lot of advantages to tempt you, such as a healthy economy, high quality of life, and a laid-back and tolerant society. Its relatively small size means it doesn't take long to get to beaches, parkland, or golf courses from just about anywhere in the country. Outside of Auckland you're unlikely to spend much time stuck in traffic, and most people have a short drive to work, if they bother to drive at all. It's a place where neighbors drop by to say hello and civil servants will actually try to help you. You may feel like you've stepped back in time, until you video chat with your friends across the world on your smartphone.

So if you think you may be ready to scale back a little and enjoy a smaller, simpler life, you will like what New Zealand has to offer.

The Lay of the Land

New Zealand tends to be pictured in the world's eyes as a couple of islands just off the coast of Australia. In truth, Australia is more than 1,200 miles away, or a three-hour flight. Almost as far away are the nearest countries of the South Pacific, such as Tonga and Fiji. There is no doubt that New Zealand is geographically isolated from the rest of the world, and the first European settlers must have truly felt like they had arrived at the end of the earth! In today's global village, communication with the rest of the planet is much easier, but the country remains physically distant from even its closest neighbors.

New Zealand's two main islands, the creatively named North Island and South Island, cover roughly the same area of land as the United Kingdom, or slightly more than Japan. Stewart Island lies south of South Island. It is small, housing only 400 full-time residents, and is often forgotten even by New Zealanders. The Chatham

© MICHELLE WAITZMAN

New Zealand has enough mountains to provide a lifetime of exploring.

Islands, several hundred kilometers to the east, also belong to New Zealand. If you truly want to live at the end of the earth, the Chatham Islands will fit the bill nicely.

Located toward the top of the North Island is Auckland, New Zealand's largest city and the only city in the country with more than half a million residents. The Auckland region is home to over 1.4 million people, almost one-third of the national population. The vast majority of new immigrants settle in Auckland because of the work opportunities, which makes it the most ethnically diverse city in the country as well.

The North Island has an active geothermal area in its center. Boiling mud, hot springs, geysers, and active volcanoes are just some of the results of this underground heat. New Zealanders have put this natural source of steam to good use as a power generator. It's one of the country's many sources of "clean" electricity, combined with hydroelectric power and wind turbines.

The Hawke's Bay region on the east side of the North Island is some of the most fertile land in the country; many of New Zealand's fruit crops are grown in the region, and it's home to a number of wineries with international reputations. Just north of Hawke's Bay lies the easternmost city in New Zealand, Gisborne, the first city in the world to greet the new day.

The southern end of the North Island is home to New Zealand's capital city, Wellington. Wellington is also the main transportation link to the South Island with flights and ferries leaving several times a day.

The northern regions of the South Island are prized agricultural land and home to some of the most successful wineries in the country. The island's main geographic feature is a string of mountains running almost all of the way down its center. They are known as the Southern Alps and have rugged, picturesque peaks and spectacular glaciers. The South Island also features the only significant plains in the country, in the Canterbury region to the east of the Alps. The far south is home to a small but hardy population who put up with the country's coldest conditions. Said to be similar in climate to Scotland, the far south attracted Scottish immigrants from the earliest days of European settlement.

Stewart Island is cool, rainy, and often covered in mud. The island is trying to turn itself into a popular holiday destination by attracting ecotourists with promises of unspoiled wilderness and rare wildlife.

COUNTRY DIVISIONS

The main way New Zealanders divide up their country is by island: North Island, South Island, and Stewart Island. But there are official government divisions that break things down further.

The country is divided into regions, run by regional councils. There are 11 regional councils plus 5 unitary authorities (which function as both regional and local governments) in New Zealand. These are more or less the New Zealand equivalent of states or provinces. They are the political boundaries that divide the country into manageable bits. The regional councils (going roughly from north to south) are Northland, Waikato, Bay of Plenty, Hawke's Bay, Taranaki, Manawatu-Wanganui, Greater Wellington, West Coast, Canterbury, Otago, and Southland. The unitary authorities are Auckland, Gisborne, Tasman, Nelson, and Marlborough.

Regional councils are responsible for a number of local resources, including air and land (such as controlling building permits and zoning). They manage regional coastal areas, rivers, and other freshwater sources, and take responsibility for flood, erosion, and pollution control. They are also in charge of regional transportation planning, including the contracting of public transit services and harbor safety. In the event of a natural disaster, another regional council responsibility is regional civil defense preparation.

Regions are further broken down into local authorities, each with its own local council. There are 12 city councils and 54 district councils representing every part of the country.

National maps rarely show the regions marked as boundaries, instead highlighting natural features and specific towns and cities. It seems Kiwis are not all that interested in regional identities, unless there's a rugby team involved! This may seem strange to anyone who grew up memorizing his or her state motto, state bird, and state flower, but bear in mind that New Zealand is small, and most of these regions have populations under half a million, with the smallest (West Coast) coming in at just over 30,000 residents.

However, as a potential immigrant you may find these regions useful in helping you to understand the differences between various parts of New Zealand, not to mention knowing where to go if you need to deal with regional government.

GEOLOGY

For such a small country, New Zealand has an awful lot of variety in its natural features. Much of this stems from its placement on the planet. New Zealand is part of the "Pacific Rim of Fire," and it also sits atop the border between two tectonic plates. These factors both give the islands a very active landscape that keeps local geologists on their toes. From active volcanoes to thousands of (mostly unnoticeable) earthquakes per year, there's an awful lot happening under your feet here.

A Fishy Tale

According to science, New Zealand split off from the prehistoric supercontinent called Gondwanaland. In Maori legend there is a different story for how this land came to be. It revolves around a demigod named Maui, who liked to cause trouble.

One day, Maui's two brothers were planning a fishing trip, but they refused to take Maui with them. Not being one to take no for an answer, Maui stowed away on their canoe until they had reached their fishing spot. He then cast his line into the water, using a hook made from his grandmother's jawbone. With this hook he pulled the entire North Island out of the water, clearly topping any catch his brothers made that day.

The Maori call the North Island "Te Ika a Maui," which means Maui's fish. Looking at a map, you can see that the island's shape does actually resemble a fish, with Wellington at the head. The South Island represents the brothers' canoe, "Te Waka a Maui," while Stewart Island is their anchor stone, or *punga*.

Mountain Ranges

The tallest mountains in New Zealand are part of the Southern Alps mountain range. The range was created when the two tectonic plates that run beneath the island became compressed, forcing one to rise up above the other. This happened about 10 million years ago, so the mountains are quite a lot smaller now than they were at the time. The highest peak of the range is Mount Cook/Aoraki at 12,342 feet.

The mountains on the North Island are not as impressive as the Southern Alps, but they still dominate many areas. There are a number of smaller ranges, beginning at the south end of the island with the fairly tame Rimutaka Mountains. Then heading north, the next range is the Tararuas, then the Ruahines. All of these mountains were created by the movement of tectonic plates millions of years ago, and you can see that they follow more or less a straight line from southwest to northeast, all the way from the bottom of the Southern Alps to the top of the Ruahine Mountains.

Volcanoes and Geothermal Areas

There are a number of impressive mountains on the North Island that don't belong to any of the ranges I've mentioned. These mountains are volcanoes, some extinct and others still steaming away. The four highest peaks on the North Island are all volcanic, including the iconic trio of Mount Ruapehu, Mount Ngauruhoe, and Mount Tongariro in the center of the North Island. Out toward the west, Mount Taranaki stands alone. The area around Auckland is home to a large number of extinct volcanoes, creating great recreational opportunities in areas like the Waitakere Ranges. While some of these volcanoes could erupt in the near future, there is little risk to life and limb. The government keeps close tabs on any peak that seems a bit too active, and the 1995 and 1996 eruptions on Mount Ruapehu took place with no injuries or deaths. In 2007, a lahar (which is when the crater lake overflows) injured a man camping close to the crater of Mount Ruapehu.

All of the steamy underground activity that causes volcanoes makes the center of the North Island a real "hot spot" for geothermal activity. Hot springs, steaming vents, and geysers show evidence of a lot of heat below the surface. Some of that heat gets put to use for power generation in the area near Taupo.

Fault Lines

Earthquakes are very common in New Zealand, so don't be alarmed if you feel something moving beneath your feet. Instruments record somewhere between 10,000 and 15,000 earthquakes in New Zealand every year, but only 100 or so are strong enough to be noticed by nearby populations. Unfortunately, two destructive quakes hit the city of Christchurch in late 2010 and early 2011 (measuring 7.1 and 6.3 on the Richter scale, respectively). The second was responsible for 180 deaths and toppled the spire of Christchurch's famous cathedral. This has led officials to look again at the already stringent building standards in New Zealand to prevent any similar loss of life in the future.

There are many fault lines in different parts of the country, but the largest is the Alpine fault that runs along the Southern Alps—in fact, the fault created them. This boundary between two tectonic plates has the potential to create a very large earthquake and has done so four times in the last 900 years. Luckily, with the fault line lying along the sparsely populated mountain range, even a large quake wouldn't be likely to cause a major disaster.

The other danger associated with earthquakes is a tsunami, or tidal wave. Warning systems are in place for coastal cities around New Zealand in case an offshore earthquake triggers a large wave.

© GERHARD PRETORIUS

New Zealand's weather can change quickly, especially in the mountains.

WEATHER

Parts of New Zealand boast that they can offer "four seasons in one day." That may sound a little daunting, but for the most part New Zealand weather is temperate and influenced mainly by the ocean air currents and the mountains.

It's important to remember that New Zealand is in the Southern Hemisphere. This means that its seasons are opposite those in the United States. Spring goes from September to November, summer from December to February, autumn from March to May and winter from June to August. Being in the southern hemisphere also means that the warmest areas of the country are in the north and the coldest areas are in the south. The seasonal differences have more to do with temperature than rainfall, as New Zealand doesn't really have dry or wet seasons like more tropical countries do.

North Island

The far north of the country has a subtropical climate. Summer days tend to hover in the high 70s to low 80s, and even over the winter the temperatures are generally pretty comfortable. The region gets lots of sunshine and is a favorite vacation spot. The rest of the North Island is more moderate, with average temperatures only varying by about 15°F between the warmest and coldest months. Snow is only common in the mountains over the winter, and in summer it's rare to see the temperature top 85°F.

South Island

The top of the South Island gets the most sunshine of any region in the country, with an annual average of over 2,300 hours. Again, the temperatures are moderate and snow is very rare.

The west coast of the South Island is affectionately known as the "wet coast," as the prevailing winds from the west blow clouds into the Southern Alps mountain range, causing them to dump their moisture on coastal inhabitants. This makes the areas to the east of the mountains, such as the Canterbury Plains, some of the driest land in the country. The mountains themselves have extremely changeable weather; overzealous hikers are often caught unprepared in sudden cold snaps or unseasonable snow.

As you head south the weather does grow colder. Frost and snow are common in the Otago and Southland regions over the winter, and the area around Queenstown gets some of the best skiing and snowboarding conditions in the southern hemisphere. Overnight temperatures often dip below freezing even in coastal cities like Christchurch and Dunedin. In summer the south is generally mild and occasionally hot, but not often humid and sticky.

Stewart Island

Overall, the climate on Stewart Island is not that different from other parts of the country. What sets it apart is the fact that it can be very unpredictable. Being a small island, any change in wind direction can bring in a different weather system almost instantly. So while you can expect comfortable summer days in the 60s and 70s and cool winter days in the 40s or 50s, you have to be ready for any weather at any time.

As you can see, it's important to be prepared for anything when you plan a day out in New Zealand. While the average conditions are easy to handle, things can change

A Fruit by Any Other Name

Kiwifruit evolved from the Chinese gooseberry.

Kiwifruit has become as much a symbol of New Zealand as the bird for which it is named. So it may come as a surprise to learn that this healthy green fruit is not actually native to New Zealand.

Early Chinese immigrants brought with them the Chinese gooseberry, a plant that bore green fruit a bit larger than a grape. The plants grew well in New Zealand, and some farmers began selectively breeding them to produce larger fruits. Eventually the crops were producing enough to consider exporting some to other countries. In a moment of marketing genius, the growers renamed them kiwifruit, because their fuzzy brown skins looked like New Zealand's famous national bird.

The fruits became a worldwide success thanks to their convenient size, delicious flavor, and high levels of vitamin C. In fact, a kiwifruit contains about 150 percent of the vitamin C in an orange.

quickly with a shift in wind direction, and you may just get to experience those four seasons in one day, ready or not!

FLORA AND FAUNA
Native

Back before humans showed up in New Zealand, the islands were isolated from contact with any other landmass for millions of years. This gave the native wildlife time to develop in some unique ways. New Zealand has only one kind of native mammal, a bat. On the other hand, there was once a huge variety of bird species thriving in the predator-free country, many of them having evolved into flightless birds because they had no need to fly away from attackers. This left them defenseless once the predators arrived.

When the first Maori settlers arrived and introduced animals from other Pacific Islands, many of the native species began to disappear, hunted into extinction by either human or beast. The arrival of European immigrants made the situation even worse. They brought their pets with them, not to mention farm animals like sheep and cows, as well as game animals to hunt. Today the native species continue to struggle against introduced pests such as the possum (originally brought over to farm for fur), the rabbit, and the rat. In fact, the possum population has gotten so out of hand that they actually outnumber sheep. The government has declared war on these fuzzy, unwanted immigrants, using specially targeted poisons in forests with large possum populations.

Some of the unique New Zealand species that have managed to survive the onslaught (so far) include the flightless brown kiwi, which has become the national symbol; the world's largest parrot, called the kakapo; and the world's heaviest insect, the weta. New Zealand remains a great location for whale-watching, and its waters are also home to orcas (killer whales), several kinds of dolphins, fur seals, sea lions, and the adorable little blue penguin.

Another icon of New Zealand wildlife is the paua. Paua is a kind of abalone found in New Zealand, and the seaweed and algae on which it feeds give it a vibrant blue and green mother-of-pearl shell. The shells were traditionally used by the Maori to decorate wood carvings, but now they are popular for making jewelry and are sometimes referred to as "sea opals." The meat of the paua is prized as well and often made into fritters.

The native flora of New Zealand has also taken a beating since humans arrived. The Maori burned native bush to help them hunt the large (and now extinct) flightless bird called the moa. Europeans cleared huge areas to create pastures for their farm animals. Native trees like kauri and rimu were harvested extensively for building materials and furniture.

Despite all of that, there are still many areas of lush, green parkland in New Zealand. Cabbage trees and tree ferns such as the ponga have become as emblematic of the country as the kiwi itself. Ferns can be found just about everywhere, with over 160 species native to New Zealand. Over one-third of the country is now protected as national

The *takahe* is an endangered native bird, once thought extinct.

Sheep, More Sheep, and Cows

© MICHELLE WAITZMAN

Cows in New Zealand are usually pasture raised, or in this case beach raised!

People all over the world are aware that New Zealand's economy has long centered on sheep, whether from it's woolly sweaters or legs of lamb. The early settlers from Britain brought sheep to their new home, for food and clothing. To say that the population took off would be quite an understatement. Conservative estimates put New Zealand's sheep population around 40 million: That's about 10 sheep for every person in the country. Historically, the proportions were even more impressive. Back in 1966 there were more than 21 sheep for every person in New Zealand.

Thanks to the profitability of dairy farming in recent years, cows are now having their own population explosion. In late 2010, the number of dairy cows in New Zealand had surpassed the number of people, reaching 4.4 million.

parks or forest parks. The Department of Conservation oversees the use of these areas, so any logging or clearing has to be specifically approved.

The government takes protection of the country's ecosystem very seriously. It has strict biosecurity measures aimed at preventing new species of just about anything from entering the country and posing a threat to the native wildlife. This applies to plants, and fines are routinely issued to people who try to enter the country with something as seemingly innocent as a piece of fruit or a sandwich. So remember not to pack too many snacks when you fly into New Zealand.

Imported

New Zealand's relatively small population of native animals allowed imported species to thrive. Unfortunately this has turned many of them into pests, threatening the native species and even destroying forests and farmland. The biggest threat to forests is the possum, whose numbers are estimated to be 30 million. They can strip trees of their leaves, leaving birds with no food or shelter. Rabbits wreak havoc on farms, getting into the crops. Deer were once found in the forests all over the country, destroying the habitat of native birds. An extensive culling operation has brought their numbers down, but hunters are still encouraged to go looking for deer in the woods.

Some introduced species are not so despised. Sheep and cows were for many years the backbone of the New Zealand economy, and they still play a large role. Exports of wool, lamb, and dairy products are some of the country's biggest industries.

One thing the Kiwis have managed to keep out of the country is snakes. While Australia is home to some of the deadliest varieties in the world, New Zealand is happily snake-free. The deadly species of spiders found in Australia have also been successfully prevented from crossing the Tasman Sea.

Imported plant species have been controversial in New Zealand since the first settlers arrived. The first imported plants were brought over by the Maori, who introduced kumara (sweet potato) to the islands. But the Europeans didn't just bring food crops with them. They also planted large areas of pine forest so they could harvest the lumber. This is still the main source of New Zealand's timber industry, especially since many of the native trees are slower-growing and have been seriously depleted.

The Europeans also brought over ornamental plants to set up traditional English gardens in their new home. Some of these plants have spread into the wild and become real pests. One of the most noticeable is gorse, a thorny shrub with yellow flowers. This prickly invader has taken over entire hillsides and pushed aside native growth.

Social Climate

New Zealanders are generally a good-natured bunch. They enjoy a climate of social tolerance and political stability, but they also enjoy a good debate and love to complain about their elected leaders as much as the rest of us.

New Zealand is a decidedly classless society for the most part. Anyone who puts on airs of superiority is quickly brought down to earth, and even the most powerful members of society are pretty accessible. This is not to say that everyone has the same lifestyle. There are very rich Kiwis and very poor Kiwis, but the vast majority have a comfortable, modest lifestyle. In some areas you may manage to find a bit of snobbery where things like which school you attended matter. Overall these leftover attitudes from the British old boys' club are ignored or actively discouraged. To gain respect in New Zealand you have to be someone who has worked hard and overcome the odds to succeed.

While fiercely proud of their country, Kiwis still suffer from a kind of inferiority complex. They are somewhat overwhelmed by the big guys "across the ditch" in Australia. Their self-image is one of the underdogs, the little guys struggling to prove their worth to both themselves and the world at large. Kiwis love a local success story, but sadly, they tend to only celebrate their own heroes once their achievements have been recognized outside of New Zealand. When a Kiwi does accomplish something that garners international attention, the whole country takes ownership of that achievement, whether it's the All Blacks winning the rugby World Cup or director Peter Jackson winning an Oscar.

When it comes to internal affairs, there is continuing conflict between government and Maori leaders over land, resources, and other details of the original treaties drawn up when the British colonized the country. These conflicts are generally political in nature, and although they may involve public protest, they almost never lead to any kind of violence. In fact, New Zealanders love a good protest. Farmers will march on parliament to protest trade restrictions, parents will protest the closure of a school, and if anything appears to threaten the cherished landscape or protected areas, there will be protests galore! Again, these tend not to escalate into violence; as often as not the two sides will end up drinking in the same pub later that evening.

To the average American, the politics in New Zealand will lean further to the left than you may be used to. It was one of the first countries in the world to come up with a pension plan for seniors and has many other government-funded social programs. The main areas of political debate are taxation, education, and health care, so you will probably feel at home hearing leaders argue those issues.

You may also find social attitudes in New Zealand more liberal on average than in the United States. When it comes to their attitude toward homosexuals, Kiwis, like many other nationalities, have a wide range of views. These views were widely debated in 2005 as the government introduced "civil unions," which gave gay or lesbian couples a way to register their relationships to receive some of the same benefits as marriage in New Zealand, and again in 2013 when same-sex marriage was legalized. For the most part there is a very live-and-let-live attitude toward gays and lesbians, with the loudest dissent coming from the Christian right and some rural communities. A gay Kiwi actor or politician is unlikely to make headlines because of his or her sexuality, and being openly gay or lesbian does not necessarily close doors professionally in New Zealand.

Despite their isolation, Kiwis consider themselves good global citizens. The country is committed to participating in worldwide efforts to address global warming. New Zealand also sends troops to join UN peacekeeping forces. It currently has soldiers deployed in Africa, the Middle East, the Solomon Islands, South Korea, and Afghanistan, among other locations. Kiwis love to travel, and many of them decide to live in another country for at least a little while—they call it OE (overseas experience). Many go to Australia, where they can live and work without a visa, and a good number of others move to the United Kingdom, especially London. So while they are from a small country, the people of New Zealand generally have a good understanding of the larger world in which they live.

Kiwis have a healthy sense of humor when it comes to their country and their culture, although they take more kindly to self-mocking than they do to being mocked by outsiders. They are quick to have a go at their stereotypes, and like the British they prefer a dry, sarcastic, and slightly over-the-top brand of humor. Their favorite target is their closest neighbor, the Australians, with the British (or "Pommies") coming in a close second. Americans may also take a bit of good-natured ribbing for being a "Yank." It's just the local way of bringing you down to earth, so don't take it personally.

NEW ZEALAND AND FOREIGNERS

A couple of generations ago the population of New Zealand was overwhelmingly of European (mostly British) descent. Otherwise, only the Maori minority and a handful of immigrants from other islands of the South Pacific were to be found.

In the last few decades, the face of New Zealand has changed significantly. The

New Zealand Public Holidays and Anniversary Dates

There are a number of public holidays in New Zealand when most people are not expected to work, and schools and most businesses are closed. Some fall on specific dates, while others vary slightly from year to year. Here are the major public holidays:

PUBLIC HOLIDAYS

Holiday	Date
New Year's Day	January 1
Day after New Year's	January 2
Waitangi Day	February 6 (marking the signing of the Treaty of Waitangi)
Good Friday	The Friday before Easter (late March or early April)
Easter Monday	The Monday after Easter (late March or early April)
ANZAC Day	April 25 (a national day of remembrance for war veterans)
Queen's Birthday	The Monday after the first weekend in June
Labour Day	The last Monday in October
Christmas Day	December 25
Boxing Day	December 26

population, particularly in major cities, has become diverse and multicultural. Immigration from India, the Philippines, China, South Africa, Korea, and other countries has helped to balance out the number of Kiwis who leave their own shores to seek their fortunes in the United Kingdom or Australia.

The good news for you is that New Zealand is actively looking for immigrants. If you possess the skills and experience to be a productive member of society, you are more than welcome. In fact, the government has even started a New Zealand Now website and Facebook page to encourage more Americans to apply for visas! (Find contact details in the *Resources* section.) Due to the relatively low rate of unemployment in New Zealand, there is not a lot of resentment toward immigrants who find good jobs. The locals are generally curious about other cultures, and you're likely to be welcomed into

REGIONAL ANNIVERSARY DAYS

In addition to these 10 national holidays, each region has an Anniversary Day. These are usually on a Monday or Friday to create a long weekend. Most calendars sold in New Zealand will have these days marked on them.

Some restaurants that remain open on public holidays charge an extra 15 percent on top of their normal prices to help them cover the additional cost of paying their staff holiday rates. Many restaurants simply don't open on holidays.

Anniversary Day	Date
Southland	mid-January
Wellington	late January
Auckland	late January
Nelson	early February
Taranaki	mid-March
Otago	late March
Canterbury (South)	late September
Hawke's Bay	late October (Friday before Labour Day)
Marlborough	late October/early November
Canterbury	mid-November
Westland	early December
Chatham Islands	early December

the community warmly and enthusiastically. Kiwis are keen to show newcomers what living in New Zealand is all about.

Immigrants to New Zealand are not faced with a "melting pot" where they are expected to immediately blend in and take on all of the typical Kiwi characteristics. The country's diverse immigrant groups are encouraged to hold on to their own traditions and incorporate those into their new lives. While everyone is expected to learn English and abide by the laws and morals of New Zealand, there is plenty of room for different backgrounds and ideas.

LIFESTYLE

New Zealand offers a lifestyle that is generally more relaxed and balanced than life in big American or European cities. Outside of Auckland, long commutes to work are unusual and traffic gridlock is practically unheard of. People have leisure time to spend with their families, and neighbors actually get to know each other.

While the urgency of American life may seem to be missing, New Zealanders get things done their own way—with quiet determination and a steely commitment to do whatever it takes. They call it "mucking in," and it's as much a part of New Zealand life as beer and rugby. You'll rarely hear the phrase "that's not my job," as people here are not hung up on those details. Instead they will focus their efforts wherever they are needed most and get on with it. This attitude applies both in the working world and in the community, where people often fix their own homes and take on other community projects.

As with other Western countries, people in New Zealand are marrying later and having fewer children than they have in the past. At the same time the number of single-parent families is increasing, as is the number of unmarried couples living together. The number of married couples without dependent children is also on the rise, mostly due to baby boomers whose kids have grown up and moved out.

Kiwis take full advantage of the natural features of their country. They have a very high rate of participation in a range of outdoor activities including hiking (which they call tramping), mountain biking, skiing/snowboarding, boating, surfing, and gardening. Team sports like rugby, cricket, and netball are also popular at a grassroots level. You won't find many couch potatoes in New Zealand.

Even in the big cities, the great outdoors are easy to access. Auckland is practically surrounded by water and boasts one of the highest rates of boat ownership in the world. It's easy to see why they call it "The City of Sails." Sailing is popular all over the country, from the local hobbyist to the Olympic level. Auckland played host to the 2000 America's Cup yacht races, taking its place among the sailing capitals of the world.

While people in New Zealand may be laid-back in their daily lives, they have also garnered a reputation for going to extremes when it comes to entertaining themselves. It is the birthplace of bungee jumping, with a variety of jumps now available all over the country. New Zealand is also a hot spot for other extreme activities like jet-boating, skydiving, and white-water rafting. The latest invention for the thrill-seeker is "Zorbing." A Zorb is a huge, bouncy plastic ball that you can crawl inside of and roll your way down a hill, becoming totally disoriented. Kiwis may seem to have gone a bit over the top with this stuff, but remember it was a New Zealander, Sir Edmund Hillary, who first made it to the summit of Mount Everest with Sherpa Tenzing Norgay back in 1953. Hillary is New Zealand's idea of a national hero, someone who sees a goal that others consider impossible and goes for it anyway—a true trailblazer!

Surfing, snowboarding, skateboarding, and mountain biking may not be considered extreme by comparison, but they are all popular among New Zealand's youth. Even the grown-ups are reluctant to stop participating in the sports they grew up with, so don't be surprised if some of the surfers you see are sporting a few gray hairs!

When it's time to sit back and relax, the average Kiwi will head to the local pub. Once almost exclusively the territory of men, particularly in rural areas, pubs now welcome women, although they may still be outnumbered. In the not-so-good old days pubs used to close at 6pm, causing a dangerous bout of binge drinking after work. The early closing laws have been abolished, but the problem of binge drinking remains one of New Zealand's biggest social challenges. Drinking and driving is also a problem, particularly in smaller towns and cities where there is no reliable public transportation late at night.

Buying alcohol outside of pubs and bars is also quite easy. Even your local movie theater can provide you with your favorite drink to enjoy during the film, although the combination of wine and popcorn may take some getting used to! Shops and supermarkets are able to sell wine, beer, and sometimes premixed drinks. So if you run out of beer in the middle of the big game, you only have to pop over to the corner store, or "dairy," to restock. For spirits and a larger selection of wines, you will need to head to a "bottle shop" (liquor store). If you're eating out, it may be worthwhile to check if the restaurant is "BYO"; if it is, you can bring your own bottle of wine and for a small corkage fee they will serve it to you there. You can save a few dollars compared with buying wine from the restaurant, and you'll be able to choose any bottle that you like. The legal age to purchase alcohol in New Zealand is 18, but parents and legal guardians are permitted to provide alcohol to minors under their care.

If the phrase "New Zealand cuisine" doesn't bring anything to mind, that's not surprising. The country is not known for its culinary style. The Maori stayed well fed historically by hunting birds for meat, fishing, and eating kumara. When the British came, they brought their own brand of bland, meat-and-potatoes cooking with them. Until very recently, the staples of the Kiwi diet were meat pies (just called pies here), fish-and-chips, and of course lamb. With the influx of immigrants from other cultures, there is now more to choose from at the supermarket. Indian and Asian ingredients are easy to find in the major cities, and ethnic and fusion restaurants serve up some distinctive dishes. A wide range of imported fruits is now available in stores, although they can be expensive. Locally grown fruits and vegetables are of excellent quality, but you'll have to pay attention to what is in season at which time of year.

New Zealand's strong dairy industry means that fresh milk, cheese, yogurt, and ice cream are widely available and of excellent quality. You won't find a lot of imported cheese, but you will be able to find the domestic version of all the most popular overseas varieties including cheddar, mozzarella, brie, blue, feta, edam, and Colby jack. Ice cream is popular all year long, and domestic brands like Tip Top and Kapiti are sold alongside international names such as Mövenpick and Cadbury.

So what will life be like for you in New Zealand? That answer is as individual as you are. Whether you're off to become a banker in Auckland, a student in Southland, or a farmer in Marlborough, there is a good chance you can find a lifestyle that suits you. Hopefully, as you make your way through this book, you will be able to form a clearer picture of what lies ahead once you make the move Down Under. There's no doubt that any move of this size will be a shock to your system, but it may be just the shock you've been looking for. It's a small country with a big heart, so open yourself up to a new world and a new life in New Zealand.

HISTORY, GOVERNMENT, AND ECONOMY

If you don't know much about the history of New Zealand, you aren't alone. This is a small country that has, for the most part, been quietly going about its business for the last century and a half, attracting little interest from the outside world. Prior to colonization, there was even less happening. New Zealand's story is mostly about the here and now. It's about leaving behind its European roots and forging something unique and new.

What has emerged is a nation where those old ties to Britain are evident, but they have been adapted to suit this very different country. While other colonized countries have marginalized or even wiped out their indigenous populations, New Zealand's Maori continue to be partners in the management of this land and its people. New Zealand's story is one of struggle and compromise, resulting in a proud, independent nation with a growing economy.

Comparisons to the United Kingdom and Australia are unavoidable, but New Zealand certainly has a history and a national identity of its own. Being so geographically isolated has resulted in a very independent spirit and weakened some of the links that bind it to other nations. New Zealanders are not afraid to go their own way, with

© NATHANIEL BEAVER

their own values, politics, and lifestyle based on their cumulative experience of living in this unique corner of the planet.

History

New Zealand spent millions of years isolated from other landmasses, with no human habitation at all. The first humans to arrive did so about a thousand years ago, on voyages of exploration from other islands of the South Pacific. The Maori eventually settled on the islands and had them all to themselves for several hundred years, until European explorers like James Cook and Abel Tasman started poking around to see if there was anything of interest to their homelands on these remote shores. While neighboring Australia was first colonized to house convicted criminals, New Zealand's first European settlers were there by choice. They were a long way from home, and their pioneering spirit can still be felt today.

PRE-EUROPEAN SETTLEMENT

There is some disagreement about who first made New Zealand their home and when. For many years, a group of Pacific Islanders called the Moriori were officially the first human residents. Now there are various theories around, but in any case it was travelers from the South Pacific who first settled the country. Their most likely departure points were the Cook Islands, according to some, or the Marquesas Islands, according to others. The Maori claim a place called Hawaiki as their homeland, but it cannot be pinpointed on a map. Some theorize that this homeland is a Hawaiian island, due to the similarity in names and the languages spoken by Maori and Hawaiians.

The first Maori to visit New Zealand, according to legend, was an explorer named Kupe. He is thought to have landed on the shores of Northland and made his way to several parts of the country before going home to tell others about this promising new land. However, several generations passed before anyone migrated to New Zealand.

The mass migration of Maori to New Zealand goes back roughly 700 years. There were fleets of traveling canoes, called *waka hourua,* which made the journey to New Zealand carrying Maori settlers. Many of today's Maori can still trace their ancestry to the canoe that brought them here. They named their new home Aotearoa, which means "the land of the long, white cloud." It is a name that endures.

The various *iwi* (tribes) settled on both islands. They survived by fishing, growing vegetables, and hunting local birds, many of which were flightless and quite easy to catch. There were land skirmishes between different *iwi,* and no one group dominated. Like other residents of the South Pacific, Maori had a warrior culture. They displayed courage in the face of the enemy and protected their people and their land with ferocity and dedication. They built fortified buildings called *pa,* which were surrounded by fences and trenches, making them easier to defend. These were often situated on hilltops, so the enemy could be seen approaching from far away.

Despite the competition for the best land and water, the Maori did very well in their new home. By 1800, their population had reached around 100,000. They had faced no interference from the outside world for hundreds of years.

CULTURE CLASH: EUROPEANS AND MAORI

Abel Tasman was the first European to set eyes on New Zealand in 1642, but after three of his crew were killed by Maori, he took the hint and left. It was James Cook's circumnavigation of the islands in 1769 that literally put New Zealand on the map for Europeans. Though a few incidents transpired wherein several Maori were killed by gunshot, relations between Cook's crew and coastal Maori eventually warmed and trading began. There was still a lot of caution in the air, but no outright attacks. Those tentative first encounters led to early settlement some years later, mostly by whalers, sealers, and missionaries. It was the missionaries who began to learn the Maori language and create a writing system for what had been a strictly oral culture up to that point.

The migration from Britain to New Zealand started off slowly, and by 1839 there were only about 2,000 Europeans living there. European missionaries were having some success in converting Maori to their religion. But overall, the European influence was minimal at this stage. It was not until the British government decided to create an official colony in New Zealand in 1840 that things started to heat up.

Queen Victoria ruled over the impressive British empire at the time and wanted to ensure that her subjects could confidently settle in New Zealand and make use of its resources. The queen dispatched a lieutenant governor, Captain William Hobson, to the country in order to draw up an agreement with the chiefs of the Maori tribes that would allow the British to govern New Zealand. This agreement has shaped the politics of New Zealand ever since that time, and the controversy surrounding it is always high on the political agenda.

The Treaty of Waitangi and the Land Wars

The Treaty of Waitangi is named for the small town in Northland where it was first signed by the queen's representatives and a few local chiefs. Later, copies of the treaty were widely circulated around the country so that chiefs from all regions could be urged to sign. It was eventually signed by over 500 Maori leaders.

Why is the Treaty of Waitangi so controversial? It has a lot to do with the language barrier. In an effort to ensure that the chiefs from the various *iwi* understood what they were signing, the treaty was translated into Maori, and then the Maori version was translated back into English. The two latter versions were used, so that in theory they were as close as possible to literal translations of each other. Over time, however, the Maori version has been shown to have small but significant differences in meaning from the English version.

One of the main points of contention is a phrase in English that promises the Maori continued possession of their lands. The Maori translation, *tino rangatiratanga,* suggests something closer to unlimited authority over their lands. So the Maori chiefs assumed they would still be able to govern in their own country with the British offering protection, while in reality the British were claiming sovereignty over the land.

The problems didn't take long to begin. In 1844, Hone Heke, a chief who had signed the treaty, repeatedly cut down the flagpole the British had erected in the town of Russell. In an effort to centralize power, a number of *iwi* joined forces under one "king" in 1858. They saw this as having a local leader to complement the faraway British ruler, but the British saw it as a rebellion against their authority.

© MICHELLE WAITZMAN

Europeans built new settlements when gold was discovered on the South Island.

By 1860, skirmishes and disagreements over landownership broke out into wars. The Maori were fierce in protecting their homes, but over the course of five years they were gradually worn down by the sheer numbers of British soldiers, who were also better armed. After the wars, the fair land purchase principles laid out in the Treaty of Waitangi were pretty much ignored and land was taken from the Maori without compensation. Legal battles over some of this land continue even today.

FORMING AN IDENTITY

Thanks mostly to the efforts of the New Zealand Company's campaign to encourage immigration, the population of British settlers in New Zealand grew to around 28,000 by 1852. These people were promised free land and assistance with the cost of the long voyage.

Around 1860, another important event changed the face of the country: Gold was discovered on the South Island's west coast. There was an instant influx of immigrants hoping to cash in on the gold rush. This brought more British settlers over, as well as New Zealand's first Chinese immigrants.

New Zealanders were fast becoming a strong, independent people with their own sense of right and wrong. Many were more than happy to have escaped the entrenched class system in the Old World and proud of what they were able to achieve by abandoning the industrial revolution and getting back to basics.

In 1893, New Zealand did something considered unthinkable at the time. It became the first country in the world to give women the right to vote. Kate Sheppard led its suffrage movement, tirelessly fighting for temperance and women's rights. She presented parliament with a petition signed by 32,000 New Zealanders, demanding that women be granted the vote. Sheppard has now been immortalized on New Zealand's $10 bill.

On Top of the World

Sir Edmund Hillary has been called a lot of things: a hero, the greatest modern explorer, a humanitarian—but to Kiwis he is simply Sir Ed.

Hillary grew up in a small town outside of Auckland, terribly shy and not very good at sports. But after discovering a love of mountaineering in his teens, he set his sights high—as high as you can go! In his early 30s, he finally joined a British team on an expedition to Mount Everest with the hopes of reaching the elusive summit. Others had tried, but nobody had yet conquered the world's highest peak.

When Hillary and Sherpa Tenzing Norgay set foot on the summit in 1953, they became instant celebrities. It had been over 40 years since humans first reached the South Pole, and Everest was considered that last great, unreachable place on Earth. Hillary informed the rest of the party of his achievement with a typical Kiwi lack of ceremony: "Well, we knocked the bastard off."

Shortly after, Edmund became *Sir* Edmund and a hero was born. While some would be content to ride on an achievement of that size, Hillary wasn't ready to settle down yet. In 1958 he went to Antarctica and traveled to the South Pole. He also returned to the Himalayas for another half dozen ascents on various mountains.

But perhaps what most made Hillary a real hero was his tireless effort to improve the lives of the Nepalese. Following his victory on Everest, Sir Ed set up a trust that has helped to build schools, hospitals, and medical clinics in Nepal. It has also funded two new airstrips that have made it easier to move supplies high into the mountains. Even well into his 80s, Hillary flew to Nepal on a regular basis to oversee projects the trust had undertaken.

Sir Ed was the epitome of a Kiwi kind of hero. He shied away from the spotlight, unless his fame could help a good cause. He was most proud of his accomplishments in charity work, not his moment on top of the world on Everest or at the bottom of the world at the South Pole. He was humble, committed, and hardworking. Sir Ed passed away in January 2008. His death was mourned by the entire nation, but his iconic status is not diminished by his absence.

While forging their own identity, New Zealanders remained loyal to their British heritage and fought alongside their Commonwealth colleagues in both World Wars. They combined with the Australian armed forces to become known worldwide as the ANZACs (Australia New Zealand Army Corps). Every year in New Zealand, February 25 is celebrated as ANZAC Day, a memorial to the troops much like Veteran's Day in the United States. The date was chosen to commemorate the beginning of the tragic landing of ANZAC troops in Gallipoli during the First World War. Terrible losses were sustained in that battle, including 2,721 New Zealanders and 8,500 Australians.

By the end of the Second World War, Kiwis were feeling proud and optimistic. They followed the news with pride swelling in their hearts as one of their own compatriots, Edmund Hillary, became the first climber to stand atop Mount Everest in 1953, with Tenzing Norgay. At that moment, a national hero was born, the beacon to which all New Zealanders have since been compared. Sir Ed, as he became affectionately known, had a huge influence on the country after his victory over Everest. He was a key player in New Zealand's ongoing role in Antarctica and promoted sports for children around the country. Sir Ed passed away in 2008 but remains an iconic Kiwi hero.

NEW ZEALAND TODAY

New Zealand is still a very small country, as far as the rest of the world is concerned. But New Zealanders have never let that stand in the way of having their own beliefs and their own way of doing things. The Kiwis have shown on numerous occasions that they're not afraid to stand up to the big guys.

This was never clearer than in the 1980s, when this small country was making all kinds of large noises. It began with the South African rugby team, The Springboks, coming to play on a tour against New Zealand's All Blacks. With opposition to South Africa's apartheid system growing, the controversial move of bringing its team to New Zealand ignited protests all around the country. Everywhere, Kiwis were making it known that the South Africans were not welcome.

There was only so much New Zealand could do to affect the internal politics of South Africa, but another issue loomed worldwide during the 1980s thanks to the tensions of the Cold War. The nuclear arms race was in full swing, and nuclear power generation was also becoming commonplace in many countries. For many Kiwis, the thought of bringing that level of risk to their shores was unacceptable. In 1984, the government instituted an antinuclear policy that remains in place to this day. No nuclear power, weapons, or vessels are allowed within New Zealand or its territorial waters. It was a bold move at the time, but it helped to define New Zealand as an independent nation that would not be cowed.

New Zealand and United States Relations

One of the immediate results of the antinuclear policy was a strain in relations between New Zealand and the United States, which wanted to be able to shelter nuclear submarines in New Zealand. Official relations were very cold between the two countries for a number of years. Some have suggested backing down on the policy to pave the way for a free trade agreement between the two nations, while others believe the issue is long forgotten by the U.S. government.

Generally speaking, Americans are welcomed in New Zealand and treated with respect. But as you have probably figured out by now, the Kiwis are a vocal and opinionated bunch. Once they find out where you're from, you're likely to hear everyone's opinion about U.S. politics, foreign policy, and any number of other issues. Bear in mind that this isn't directed at you, people are just sharing their point of view.

Official relations between New Zealand and the United States have improved lately, including high-level meetings between leaders and foreign ministers.

Rainbow Wars

New Zealand is generally regarded as a safe and peaceful place to live, and the country hasn't seen armed warfare on its shores since the Maori land wars of the 19th century. But there is one bloody stain on New Zealand's shoreline, which created international friction for many years.

New Zealand's official stance against nuclear weapons and power put it at odds with several nations during the Cold War, including the United States and France, who were both proud of their nuclear arsenals. In 1985, the French government was about to carry out some nuclear testing in the South Pacific. The Greenpeace ship *Rainbow Warrior* was planning to sail out to the testing area to disrupt the tests. Prior to its voyage, the Greenpeace ship was docked in Auckland.

Late on the night of July 10, 1985, when the crew members were supposedly all ashore, two bombs exploded on the hull of the ship. It quickly sank, and the one crew member who had been onboard, a photographer named Fernando Pereira, drowned. Two French secret service agents were arrested a few days later, accused of bombing the ship.

The French government originally denied any involvement in the attack, but eventually the truth was uncovered. France's defense minister had ordered the attack to prevent any disruption to the planned nuclear testing and had planned for the ship to be unoccupied at the time of the bombing. The death of the photographer was an unfortunate accident.

France's reluctance to take responsibility for the attack, and the fact that it had been carried out on New Zealand soil, strained relations between the two countries for many years. In 2005, as the incident's 20-year anniversary approached, the French government officially apologized for the bombing.

To this day, the *Rainbow Warrior* has a special place in New Zealanders' collective conscious. Greenpeace is very active in the country, and Kiwis still take it very personally that another country's government had so little respect for them.

Government

If you're used to dealing with an essentially two-party system, the government in New Zealand can be a bit dizzying. Trying to sort out the coalitions, the "minor parties," and the seemingly endless time it takes to accomplish anything in parliament, makes it a bit tempting to ignore the whole thing. However, understanding the government is an important step in deciding to immigrate to a new country. If you can't trust the leaders or don't believe that the system is fair, you might think twice about choosing to live in such a place.

Queen Elizabeth II is officially the head of state in New Zealand, but that is not terribly relevant to the daily lives of the country's residents or even its politicians. The relationship is strictly arm's length, and the system of government is democratic and representative.

MAJOR POLITICAL PARTIES

At the time of writing, the ruling political party in New Zealand is the National Party, a slightly right-of-center party led by Prime Minister John Key. It has been in power since 2008. The party tries to balance being business-friendly with a commitment to education, economic growth, and international trade.

The other main party is the Labour Party, which leans more to the left. Its followers prefer to focus more on providing for the less fortunate and supporting families. Since the mid-1930s, only the Labour and National Parties have held the seat of power in New Zealand.

A number of other parties also have representatives in parliament, and their cooperation is often needed by either the ruling party or the opposition in order to create a majority vote on an issue or bill. I won't bother describing the additional parties that have no elected members at this point, since they have no real influence on the government of the country.

New Zealand First is a party that relies heavily on the personality and reputation of its longtime leader Winston Peters. They are a nationalist (anti-immigration) party and fight for the rights of seniors.

The Green Party has a relatively strong presence in New Zealand. Its main agenda is obviously protecting the environment; its other policies tend to be left-leaning. The Greens, as the members are commonly known, usually side with the Labour Party on major issues.

The Maori Party is a relatively new player on the political scene, having formed in 2004. Its policies center on the concerns of the Maori people and their place in New Zealand society. While there are Maori members in other parties, this is the only party that puts their issues front and center at all times.

United Future is a small party with a "family values" focus and a strongly Christian background. They have only one representative in the current government.

ACT also calls itself the Liberal Party, which may seem confusing as its principles are very different from what would be called "liberal" in other countries. The party is in favor of free enterprise and minimal government interference. It also has only one representative in the current government.

SYSTEM OF GOVERNMENT

Originally, New Zealand modeled its government on the British system. In many ways it still reflects that original system, but over time it has changed and adapted.

There is only one house of representatives in New Zealand, the parliament. This means that there are no senators, elected or appointed. Members of parliament (MPs) hold all of the power when it comes to making legislation.

Since 1996 the system used to elect members to parliament is the MMP, or mixed member proportional system. The way it works is that voters get to cast two votes in a federal election. One vote helps to choose the local representative, and voters can only choose from the candidates selected to represent their electorate. The other vote is for the party of their choice. So even if their favorite party has no candidate running in their area, voters can still cast a vote toward putting that party into power. Of the 120 seats in parliament, 62 are elected as representing an electorate, 7 are from the Maori electorates, and 51 are determined by the party vote.

Seven seats in parliament are specifically set aside for Maori representation. This ensures that no matter how small the Maori population becomes, its role as one of the founding cultures of New Zealand gives Maori people a say in every decision made at parliament. People with Maori ancestry (they don't have to be full-blooded Maori) can choose to either be on the general electoral roll or the Maori roll. Only those on the Maori roll can vote for the candidates for these seven seats.

LOCAL AND REGIONAL GOVERNMENT

Local and regional government take care of a wide range of things in New Zealand: local road repairs, garbage pickup, water supply, building regulation, parks and gardens, and a myriad of other local concerns. So if you are planning renovations to your house, need a permit to sell alcohol, or want to find out where the nearest landfill is located, you'll be turning to the local council. Also, while the source of funding and national policies on health care all come from the federal Ministry of Health, the actual provision of services (hospitals and clinics, for example) is run by regional District Health Boards.

Your local government will include both local and regional councils. Councillors are elected every three years. All cities and towns have a mayor taking charge of local issues, with a council working under him or her.

Economy

In New Zealand's early days as a British colony, it served as a kind of offshore farm. Exports of lamb, wool, dairy products, and beef, along with timber from the old-growth native trees, made the country a good investment as far as the motherland was concerned. The agriculture and forestry industries have remained at the heart of New Zealand's economy to this day and continue to play an important role is the country's exports.

Today's economy is more complex than in the colonial days, however. In addition to agriculture and forestry (now using pine plantations rather than native trees), New Zealand is involved with manufacturing, biotechnology, information technology, service industries, and tourism. It is a robust, market-driven economy that depends on trade with other countries such as Australia, Japan, China, the United States, and the United Kingdom. New Zealanders enjoy a standard of living on par with other developed countries.

INTERNATIONAL TRADE

New Zealand is a member of the OECD (Organisation for Economic Co-operation and Development), an international group of 34 nations working together for improved trade relationships and stable economies. Membership in the group gives New Zealand an international economic presence and provides a measure for how the country is performing compared with other member states.

Having such a small population, New Zealand does rely on imports for a lot of its manufactured goods. For example, there are no car manufacturing plants in the country. The main sources of car imports are Japan and Europe. If you're looking for an American car, you're likely to find some Fords on the market, but few others. Most appliances and computers are also imported, and even "local" goods are often manufactured overseas in countries like China and Indonesia, where wages are much lower.

The major exports include the agricultural ones, such as dairy products, lamb, beef, wool, and fruit, plus both treated lumber and untreated logs from the forestry industry. Some specialty items are manufactured in New Zealand for export, such as electronics and certain car components. Plastics are also a bit of a specialty item.

More and more, exporting services has also become a significant business for New Zealand. Overseas clients find it cost-effective to have New Zealand researchers carry out studies for them, particularly in agricultural or biotechnology fields, or to have their software written by Kiwi programmers. Hollywood studios may have their special effects created by specialists in Wellington. It's a small piece of the export pie right now at around $4.5 billion, but for services in a small market like New Zealand, bringing in overseas clients is often the only way for New Zealanders to grow their business significantly.

Tourism also plays a large role in New Zealand's economy. In addition to boosting the food and beverage industry, tourism attracts a large number of immigrants. Visitors from all over the planet come and spend nearly nine billion dollars per year exploring New Zealand's cultural and natural treasures. So while it's not exactly an export, tourism does bring foreign money into the country. International students are another major source of foreign income into New Zealand.

SAVING AND SPENDING

At the start of this century, Kiwis had become consumers on an unprecedented level. Once a nation of down-to-earth and thrifty people, a strong economy and a strong dollar spurred on Kiwi shoppers. Big-screen TVs, the latest cell phones, and even investment properties were driving New Zealanders further and further into debt. Although the global recession slowed spending, Kiwis are still pushing the limits of what they can afford. It has reached a point where the government is concerned about the effect it will have on inflation and whether people are carrying more debt than they can ever hope to repay. Rather than stashing away their pennies for a rainy day, Kiwis are still buying gadgets and taking holidays.

In an effort to encourage more people to save for their retirement, the government introduced a savings system called Kiwisaver. It is essentially a plan to deduct a small percentage of workers' wages every time they are paid and place the money in a savings plan they can't access until retirement age. This is a relatively new scheme in New Zealand, introduced in 2007, but well over a million people have signed up.

IMPORTS AND CARBON IMPRINTS

Being located at the bottom of the world means that no matter how "green" New Zealanders want to be, every import or export travels a long way and uses huge amounts of fuel. In this era of climate-change awareness, it's a big challenge for the country to cut back its carbon imprint on the global scale.

New Zealand was one of the first countries in the world to implement an "Emissions Trading Scheme." The ETS puts a price on greenhouse gases to provide an incentive to reduce emissions and to encourage tree planting. It is being introduced in stages so that key industries are better able to prepare for the implications.

One of New Zealand's biggest environmental challenges is one that you might not expect—farm animals! With so many sheep and cows all over the country, a huge amount of methane gas is created by their digestive systems. Methane is a greenhouse gas, which contributes to global warming. To counter this, the government is encouraging more reforestation of the land.

Power suppliers in New Zealand are also facing the challenge of coming up with cleaner ways to produce electricity. The country is fortunate to have a number of ways to generate clean power, including hydroelectric dams, geothermal power, and wind turbines. But despite all of this, the power grid is still partly dependent on coal and gas. More wind farms are planned, however, which should decrease the country's dependency on coal as time goes on.

PEOPLE AND CULTURE

The people of New Zealand often define themselves by what they are not. They are *not* British, and they are *not* Australian. As a nation, New Zealanders view themselves as the underdog, the little guy who fights twice as hard to prove he's equal to the big boys. This is easiest to spot as it relates to sports, but Kiwis are also constantly pushing to be taken seriously in the business world and the international political scene.

The Maori may now be a minority group in their own country, making up about 15 percent of the population, but they are in no way accepting a supporting role in the New Zealand story. Integration with the *Pakeha* (European) population has been a matter of compromise, not surrender. Not long ago, those two groups told pretty much the whole story. These days, an increase in immigration from other Pacific islands, Asia, and India has added a new element to New Zealand's culture. The country is becoming more multicultural, and this will likely continue to become even more evident.

COURTESY OF WHITIREIA PERFORMING ARTS

Ethnicity and Class

New Zealand's main ethnic groups are the Maori, other Pacific Islanders, and Europeans (which includes all those of European descent, whether they are currently coming from Europe or not), who are sometimes referred to using the Maori word *Pakeha*. Thanks to the Treaty of Waitangi, the Maori enjoy certain privileges not available to other ethnic groups, such as guaranteed representation in government. It is, in a sense, a racist policy in that not all New Zealanders are treated equally, but it is a policy designed to protect the original inhabitants of the country. Most people respect the Maori right to special treatment to some extent.

New Zealanders are decidedly classless, with little regard for titles and birthrights. Kiwis value success through hard work and determination, rather than being born into privilege. In fact, they openly resent anyone who expects to command respect without having done anything to earn it first. This attitude can take some immigrants off-guard, especially in the workplace.

MAORI AND PACIFIC ISLANDERS

Most Maori and Pacific Islanders in New Zealand lead similar lives to other Kiwis. They live in the same cities, usually attend the same schools, and compete for the same jobs. Socially, some Maori and Pacific Islanders have chosen to retain some of the elements of their traditional lifestyle that they consider important. Often this includes a more communal way of living, incorporating their entire *whanau* (extended family). They are more likely to pull together in times of crisis and offer support to one another.

There are some social problems that are more common among Maori and Pacific Islanders than other New Zealanders. Violence in the home is one that never fails to make headlines. Both spousal and child abuse seem to occur more frequently among the Maori. It has been difficult to address the problem while still respecting Maori cultural norms, but within Maori communities the taboo is slowly being broken and there is some hope that progress will be made. There are also larger numbers of Maori and Pacific Islanders among the unemployed, and they are statistically less likely to complete their education. About 40 percent of Maori don't finish high school, compared with a national average of 25 percent.

NEW IMMIGRANT GROUPS

New Zealand has been working hard to attract immigrants for many years. Traditionally, the bulk of them came from Britain. Today, however, immigrants are coming to New Zealand from all over the world. China now provides the largest overall number of immigrants, followed by India and then Britain. This has certainly changed the ethnic mix in New Zealand.

Other large, but less visible, immigrant groups include South Africans, Russians, Romanians, and Dutch. People from the United States and Canada total about 5 percent of all immigrants.

People of African origin living in New Zealand tend to stand out, because there aren't many. Outside of the largest cities it's extremely rare to run into someone of

Kiwi Stereotypes

Kiwis love to poke fun at themselves—or more often each other—so people from different parts of the country get ribbed about their stereotypical behaviors. This will give you a bit of a head start on your Kiwi stereotypes, so you can be in on the joke too.

Auckland: You'll often hear Aucklanders referred to as JAFAs. That's an acronym for "Just Another F-ing Aucklander." People from other parts of New Zealand tend to think of Aucklanders as self-obsessed, fashion-conscious, and materialistic. Since Auckland is the biggest city, it breeds the most resentment in the rest of the country.

Rotorua: This hot spot for Maori culture (and geothermal heat, too) is nicknamed "Roto-Vegas" by Kiwis due to its ability to bring in the tourists, both by cashing in on Maori culture and coming up with new activities, like Zorbing, to part visitors from their cash. It lacks the flash of the real Vegas, but the sulfur fumes in the air do smell a bit like a sweaty casino!

Wellington: If you ask anyone outside of Wellington, they'll tell you to hold on tight when you visit "Windy Welly." Wellingtonians roll their eyes at the stereotype that every day sees gale-force winds ripping through the city. But you'll notice that even in heavy rain, almost nobody bothers to carry an umbrella. Why? They'd get blown away!

Christchurch: The biggest city on the South Island has a personality of its own—and not everyone paints a flattering picture of it. Christchurch, with its very English atmosphere, has a reputation for being more class-conscious than the rest of New Zealand. Children must attend the "right" schools, and many an old boy finds his way into the old boys' club. Immigration is starting to shake things up in the Garden City, but stereotypes take a long time to fade away.

Invercargill: Most Kiwis think you'd have to be a bit nuts to live way down south in Invercargill, so the stereotype of this southernmost city is a bit colorful to say the least. This is where Burt Munro of *The World's Fastest Indian* fame came from, and he personifies the eccentric, resourceful, and good-humored Southlander to perfection. These are people who will try to fix anything with a bit of number eight fencing wire and a crescent wrench—and will often succeed.

African descent. The resulting stares can be rather unnerving, but most people are simply curious. It's almost impossible to say how many people of African descent live in New Zealand because this ethnicity is lumped together with Middle Eastern and Latin American on the census.

Most Kiwis have formed their opinions of African people based on what they have seen on TV and in the movies, so stereotypes are bound to be a bit of an issue. But there is generally no assumption that a person of this ethnicity is more likely to be a criminal or start a fight. African Americans may face less discrimination in New Zealand than they do in the United States, simply because their numbers are so few.

RACISM

For the most part, Kiwis are very welcoming to different races. But there is a minority who feel threatened by the change in the country's ethnic makeup, and visible minorities do face some instances of discrimination. Racial violence is not common, but there have been attacks on Asian people by young men. There was some minor backlash against Middle Eastern or Muslim New Zealanders after 9/11, but that died away quickly. There have also been occasional anti-Semitic incidents such as desecrating Jewish graves.

Overall, it is easier to be a visible minority if you live in a major city like Auckland, Wellington, or Christchurch. In small towns, you may find yourself garnering unwanted attention simply because you are unusual. But on the whole, most people find they are well treated in New Zealand and able to integrate without any trouble.

It's illegal to discriminate based on race, so if you feel you've missed out on a job or an apartment because of your race, religion, or nationality, you can complain to the Human Rights Commission.

Customs and Etiquette

Kiwis are quite proud of their national identity, and they will appreciate you embracing their ways as a newcomer. You won't be expected to leave all of your old values and customs behind, but you should respect the way things are done in New Zealand, including recognizing the bicultural elements of New Zealand culture involving the Maori.

Kiwi culture is very informal. If you want to fit in, the best thing you can do is relax and try to have some fun. Friendliness and humility are two of the most important virtues to Kiwis, and new residents most often run into trouble when they fail to embrace these values. What you may consider professionalism or politeness, locals will more likely see as an attitude of superiority. A smile is almost always welcome.

THE KIWI WAY

In many ways, Kiwis still see themselves as pioneers. It probably comes from being so isolated: This has led them to be very resourceful. They tinker in sheds to fix and build things, they do work on their own homes, they sell sausages in front of shops to raise funds. New Zealanders don't like asking outsiders for help if they think they can work things out for themselves. You might find them a bit stubborn, especially if you're used to calling in an expert whenever it seems logical, but it's a big part of the Kiwi identity.

The other thing you'll immediately notice about Kiwis is the importance they place on their lives outside of work. Sure, they work hard, but they play just as hard. Whether they spend their weekends tramping up a mountain or playing rugby, they make time for recreation and family.

Dining

Sadly, the British exported a lot of their eating habits to New Zealand. Many diets are based on a constant stream of fish-and-chips and meat pies. Chinese takeaways and curries round out the unhealthy convenience-food regimen that too many Kiwis are following. Other favorites include sausages on white bread and lots of ice cream. Their favorite "fancy" dessert is pavlova, a layer of meringue topped with whipped cream and fruit. This dessert is so much a part of their culture that Kiwis often just call it "pav" to save time.

But things are slowly (very slowly!) starting to change. People are realizing that healthy eating is important and vegetables are not just for decorating your plate. The

© MICHELLE WAITZMAN

New Zealand is known for its fresh seafood, such as mussels and oysters.

increased diversity in New Zealand's population has also helped to broaden the food choices. More Asian foods can now be found in supermarkets, along with Indian and European items. Families are also being encouraged to eat together more often. Just like in North America, busy lifestyles have led to family members grabbing food on the go at different times.

The most dining choices are found in the major cities, where there are also more immigrants. Out in the rural areas, it's harder to find a wide range of products and restaurants.

If you're invited to a party at someone's home in New Zealand, it's appropriate to bring a bottle of wine, some beer, or food with you. If the host asks you to "bring a plate," that means the party is a potluck and guests are expected to bring some food and drink to share.

Drinking

Drinking culture in New Zealand can be problematic. Not so long ago, the government tried to force folks to behave themselves by shutting down the pubs at 6pm. This created a culture of binge drinking, where people would throw back as many drinks as possible between work and closing time. The enforced hours are now long gone, but the binge drinking remains. A blasé attitude toward drunk driving compounds this problem, particularly in smaller towns where public transit is not an option. If you think someone has been drinking, do not accept a ride with that person.

Getting drunk isn't just a male problem, either. Women are almost as likely to overindulge on a night out. You may feel some pressure in social situations to keep up with the hard drinkers. Use your own best judgment in these situations. You may get some ribbing for being a "lightweight," but chances are your drunk friends won't remember the evening anyway.

Tattoo You

Moko, or tattooing, is an important part of Maori culture. Over the years it had begun to disappear, particularly among women, but it is rising in popularity again as Maori culture becomes better understood and widely accepted.

Traditionally, the *moko* was created using hand tools, basically chiseling lines and shapes into the body and face and using black dyes to ink them in. Patterns identified the Maori's *iwi*, or tribe, and also expressed his accomplishments. Putting *moko* on the face was a mark of pride in your heritage, since you would not be able to cover it up. While men often wore *moko* covering their backs, buttocks, and legs, as well as their entire faces, women usually had a more subtle version. Most women's *moko* covered only the chin and lower lip, although some also decorated the forehead, nose, and throat.

Early British settlers found the tattoos intimidating, accentuating the Maori image as "savage warriors."

If you are fond of tattoos, it's tempting to copy the traditional designs. Maori do not believe any non-Maori can be said to have a *moko*. When their traditional patterns are used on people of other ethnic backgrounds, they call it *kirituhi*, or writing on skin.

Tattoos are widely accepted in New Zealand due to this long-standing tradition. No matter what your race, age, or gender, you will hardly get a second look simply because you are sporting a tattoo. If you decide to get a tattoo in New Zealand, ask around to be sure the artist you choose is skilled and the conditions are sterile.

Harden Up and Muck In

Part of the Kiwi spirit involves putting up with discomfort. "Harden up," they'll tell anyone who complains about the weather or the hard work they're doing. If you're a real Kiwi, it seems, you'll just put your head down and get on with whatever needs to be done.

This flows into the tradition of "mucking in." That means helping out whenever help is needed. If there's been a disaster in a community, or even if there's a need to fundraise, you are expected to get involved without any benefit to yourself. This shows a dedication to community, that Kiwi virtue of humility, and a good work ethic.

RESPECTING MAORI CULTURE

Today's Maori constantly struggle between preserving the past and embracing the future. Traditions and cultural rituals are very important to many Maori, and it is expected that other cultures will recognize the special relationship the Maori have with New Zealand.

Te reo Maori, the Maori language, is the most obvious way in which the culture is being preserved. It became an official language in New Zealand in 1987 and is now taught as part of the school curriculum to some extent. Parents who want their children to speak *te reo* fluently often send them to extra classes or to a special Maori immersion school.

Genealogy is extremely important to the Maori, and many can trace their ancestry right back to the *waka* (canoe) which brought their ancestors to New Zealand.

Maoritanga

Maoritanga is literally Maori culture. It includes the legends that are the basis for Maori explanations of how things came to be. A variety of gods and demigods are involved with the Maori oral tradition. Many stories are also captured through wood carvings and woven panels.

Many places in New Zealand have names relating to the Maori myths of their creation. Where the British came in and renamed something, you will often see two official names these days. Both the original Maori name and the British name are given equal billing. Hence you'll often see things written as: Aotearoa/New Zealand or Aoraki/Mount Cook.

Maori Etiquette

On ceremonial occasions, Maori etiquette is often used by the government. This is most common when foreign dignitaries or heads of state visit New Zealand.

Otherwise, Maori etiquette is generally only observed on a *Marae*, a Maori courtyard and complex of buildings including a meeting house. There is a strict protocol for entering someone's *Marae*, and if you have the occasion to do so, you will be briefed on what to expect.

Maori funerals are also quite different from what you may be used to. There is a three-day *tangi*, or mourning period, before the burial. This is a time for family and friends to get together on the *Marae* (or in a home) to share their grief and say goodbye.

Gender Roles and Sexuality

One of New Zealand's points of pride is that it was the first country in the world to grant women the right to vote. Ever since that moment in 1893, New Zealand's reputation for equality of the sexes has been world-famous. That hasn't prevented a wage gap from existing here, like everywhere else. Nor has it put women at the heads of many multinational corporations. But with two female prime ministers already, New Zealand has made some inroads to gender equality.

On the other hand, the macho "Kiwi bloke" image has not gone away. New Zealand men are expected to be good at working with their hands and interested in sports and beer. Men who don't fit this description have always found the going a little tough in New Zealand. In the major cities, however, you can find a burgeoning "metrosexual" crowd.

WOMEN IN NEW ZEALAND

There's a lot of good news when it comes to being a woman in New Zealand. The country has twice been run by women, and they've been able to vote since 1893, but the good news extends beyond politics. More than half of the students enrolled in tertiary (college and university) education are female. So Kiwi women are at least as educated as their male counterparts. In fact, 87 percent of Kiwi women complete the highest level of high school, compared with 67 percent of men.

Generally, women are well treated and respected in New Zealand. Discrimination on the basis of gender is illegal. Open harassment is unusual (except perhaps in a pub full of extremely drunk men), and in most places it's safe for women to walk the streets alone, even at night. Common sense should always prevail, however, and accepting rides from strangers carries a certain risk.

Women in Power

Being the first country to grant women the right to vote back in 1893, New Zealand features women in a lot of powerful roles. The country is doing well on the equality front by global standards: According to the United Nations, New Zealand ranks fifth in the world for equality for women. This includes areas like education and pay rates.

WOMEN IN POLITICS
Two women have held the position of prime minister so far in New Zealand, and around one-third of parliament is female.

Wellington is now on its third female mayor, Celia Wade Brown. She took over from Kerry Prendergast, who held the position from 1995 to 2010. Fran Wilde started the trend in Wellington: She was mayor from 1992 to 1995.

Other female mayors around the country include Lianne Dalziel in Christchurch, Annette Main in Wanganui, and Julie Hardaker in Hamilton.

WOMEN IN BUSINESS
Ann Sherry—the first female CEO of a bank in New Zealand—ended her reign at Westpac Banking in 2007. Banking is still a pretty good place for women, with ASB Bank choosing Barbara Chapman as CEO. Theresa Gautting spent seven years at the head of Telecom (now called Spark), New Zealand's major telecommunications provider. However, in the private sector women are still underrepresented on boards of directors, making up just 12 percent in private companies in New Zealand. The public sector is doing better, with their boards sitting at 42 percent female.

The picture isn't all rosy, though. There are still problems with violence against women in New Zealand, particularly domestic violence. Police calls for family violence (which would include spousal abuse and child abuse) average about 200 per day.

Women are also at some disadvantage in the workplace, particularly if they have children. Most women in New Zealand work outside of the home. Some do take time to raise their children without working, but fewer and fewer families can afford to get by on one income. The government does provide some subsidies for families with children under the "Working for Families" scheme. Most families still rely on the mother to take primary responsibility for raising children, often at the detriment of her career. Many women compromise by working part-time while their children are young, coincidentally during their prime earning years. Mothers also have more difficulty getting executive positions, since they are unable to devote as many hours to the workplace. Of course, none of this is news to women from the United States or Canada, who face many of the same challenges.

GAY AND LESBIAN CULTURE
From the rugged stereotype of Kiwis, you may think that New Zealand is a hard place to be a gay man or a lesbian. In reality, there is an overall live-and-let-live attitude in most places. Of course, the bigger the city, the more likely there is to be a gay and lesbian "scene" and a community support system. In more rural areas, it may be harder to fit in, and gay men and lesbians may find some resistance from locals. In

small towns, the attitude appears to be closer to "don't ask, don't tell" than outright acceptance or exclusion.

It's difficult to find any official statistics, but in a 2004 study of lesbians and gay men in New Zealand, about 18 percent of men and 9 percent of women had been physically assaulted because of their sexuality. Verbal abuse results were much higher, with over 75 percent of men and about 64 percent of women reporting verbal attacks at some point.

Gay and lesbian residents will find the most support and social opportunities in Auckland, followed by Wellington and Christchurch. Most universities have a group for gay and lesbian students, too, which can be helpful in Hamilton, Palmerston North, or Dunedin. Other clubs can range from social and sports get-togethers to special units of Alcoholics Anonymous. What you won't find in New Zealand is "gay neighborhoods"; there are no concentrated areas where gay men and lesbians are clustered in any city although there are some areas of Auckland where the gay population congregates. That can make it difficult to find the local gay and lesbian bars and clubs, or to meet other gay men and lesbians. That's why the social clubs and support groups are so valuable, especially for new immigrants.

Officially, sexual acts between consenting men were decriminalized in 1986 (it was always legal for women), as long as both people are at least 16 years old. It is illegal to discriminate against anyone on the basis of sexual orientation.

Marriage and Civil Unions

In 2013 New Zealand joined the list of countries making it legal for same-sex couples to marry. This gives them rights equal to straight married couples in every legal sense. Couples can also choose to be joined in a civil union, which is a recognized relationship with full legal rights similar to marriage. Either of these options will allow same-sex partners to have shared parental rights and to have contracts and wills legally recognized between them. You have to be at least 16 to marry or enter into a civil union (with permission from a parent or guardian until you are 18), and you must not be married or in a civil union with another partner at the time. The Department of Internal Affairs can supply you with a list of official celebrants who can perform these ceremonies, and yes, mixed-sex couples can also choose the civil union instead of marriage.

Also, there is a Property Act in New Zealand, which states that after a couple has been together for at least three years (whether same-sex or mixed-sex), their property should be divided equally if they break up. This applies even if you are not married or in a civil union. So if you are involved in a long-term relationship in New Zealand, the law forces you to diving your belongings equally if things don't work out, unless you draw up a legal agreement that states otherwise.

Sports and Games

New Zealand is a sporting nation in many ways. Kiwis love to both watch and play a wide variety of sports. The country turns its most successful athletes into national heroes, more trusted than newscasters and more respected than scholars. The biggest rival for New Zealand's sports teams is Australia, whose success in international athletics is hugely frustrating to Kiwis.

Getting involved in sports here, either as a participant or a spectator, can take some adjustment. The major sports are not the ones you're probably used to. While you can find places to play basketball and softball, the main attractions in New Zealand are rugby, cricket, and netball.

Motor sports are also very popular in New Zealand, with both car and motorcycle races getting a lot of TV coverage. In fact, it's hard to find anything else on TV on Sunday afternoons! Horse racing and dog racing are also well watched, with a lot of betting taking place.

Golf is another widely practiced sport. There are public courses all over the country, and greens fees are generally reasonable. While most courses are fairly laid-back, you should not wear jeans or shorts when you go golfing. Some courses require shirts with a collar, too.

Of course, New Zealand is also well known for more extreme sports. After all, this is the home of bungee jumping. Adventure racing, mountain biking, trail running, and other wild outdoor pursuits bring out huge numbers of Kiwis and visitors. And for those who prefer to take in the outdoors at a slower pace, tramping (hiking or backpacking) is a favorite weekend activity.

RUGBY

If you asked most Kiwis what the nation's main religion is, they'd answer "rugby." It's more than a game here, it's a national obsession and a source of pride. When the All Blacks have a big game, the nation stops to watch. There are also regional teams, who play against each other and Australian teams. This is called "Super 15" rugby, as there are 15 teams in the association. Rugby is often called football or footy by New Zealanders.

Rugby is a tough game, with all of the full-on contact you'd find in American football and none of the padding or helmets! The ball is a similar shape to a football, but slightly larger. Games are 80 minutes long, divided into two halves. (You'll often hear people call rugby "a game of two halves.") The object is for your team to score by carrying the ball over the opposing team's end (a try) or kicking it through their goalposts (a drop goal). But unlike American football, you can only pass to a teammate who is behind you on the field.

There is a related but slightly different kind of rugby played, called "rugby league." It tends to be a more violent game. The main type of rugby in New Zealand is called "rugby union." When kids learn rugby at school, they play with touch rules, rather than tackling. Often community teams also play touch, even among adults.

Back in Black

New Zealand's national rugby team adopted the name All Blacks back in 1905 on its first tour of England. The name came from the team's black uniforms. The huge international popularity and success of the All Blacks has led to New Zealand adopting the color as its own, using it for national team uniforms at almost all events, including the Olympics.

Other sports team names have also taken their cue from the All Blacks. Some of the other "Black" teams in New Zealand and their sports:

- Black Sticks—(field) hockey

- Tall Blacks—basketball

- Black Caps—cricket

- Black Sox—softball

- Black Cocks—badminton

COURTESY OF EDUCATION NEW ZEALAND

Black is the unofficial national color of New Zealand.

NETBALL

Netball is an extremely popular women's sport, although it is also played by men. It looks similar to basketball, but there are no backboards behind the nets, so shots need to be more precise. It's also a noncontact sport, so a lot of the physical side of basketball is stripped away. Dribbling is also not allowed, which makes this mainly a game of passing and shooting. Despite these rules, it is very fast-moving when played by skilled athletes. New Zealand's national netball team, the Silver Ferns, are among the best in the world.

SAILING

Since New Zealand is surrounded by water, it should not be a surprise that its residents are fond of sailing. Everything from casual cruising to top-level competition takes place down here. Boat ownership is very high among Kiwis; many of them learn to sail as small children.

On a competitive level, Kiwis are on par with the world's best sailors in many divisions. They are often in the running for Olympic medals, as well as the America's Cup. Every coastal city will have opportunities to learn how to sail and participate in races if you wish.

You Call That a Bat?

Local cricket players enjoy a weekend match.

To most North Americans, the rules of cricket are rather mysterious. A game can run anywhere from an afternoon to several days, and one player can score over a hundred runs in the course of a game! Here's a brief overview that may help you follow the conversation in the local pub:

Innings: In cricket the teams do not switch between offense and defense throughout the game. In most cases, there are only one or two innings per team. That is the team's turn to score runs. So one team scores all of its runs for the match, then the other team tries to score more runs when its turn comes up. An innings (even the singular form ends with s) ends when 10 out of the team's 11 batsmen are out, or "dismissed." The batting lineup does not repeat as in baseball.

Bowler: There is no "pitcher" in cricket. The person who throws the ball is a bowler. He must throw overhand and his arm must be straight when he releases the ball. Usually the bowler bounces the ball off the pitch, because this makes it harder to hit.

CRICKET

Cricket can be an intimidating sport if you haven't grown up with it. After all, a single match can last for five days! But playing can be good fun, and even watching might enthrall you after you've figured out how it all works.

There are different types of professional cricket matches, with some running as one-day events and others as five-day events. New Zealand's team is generally among the 10 best in the world, but they're not quite at the top of the list.

The basic skills needed in cricket are similar to those in baseball. You have to hit the ball with a bat when you are on the scoring side and be able to throw and catch the ball on the defensive side. However, the bats are a different shape, and there are no padded gloves.

Overs: When a bowler has thrown six legal pitches, this is called an over. At this point he has to let another bowler take over. The new bowler stands at the opposite end of the pitch from his predecessor, and he bowls to the other runner. Bowling usually rotates between two players, and they can be relieved and replaced when they become tired.

Scoring Runs: Two runners are playing at any one time. One is the batsman (the one batting at the time) and the other is a nonstriker. They stand at either end of a long strip of earth with a wicket at each end. This is called the pitch. When the batsman hits the ball, the two runners will both run, exchanging places at either end of the pitch. If they reach the opposite ends, a run is scored. If they manage to run back and forth several times, they can score multiple runs on one hit. Runs can also be scored by hitting the ball to the boundary of the playing field.

Wicket: This is a set of three wooden stumps, topped by two crossbars called bails. The batsman stands in front of his wicket to bat. If the bowler gets the ball past the batsman and knocks over the wicket, the player is out. There are no "three strikes" in cricket! When the defensive team gets a batter out, by any means, they are said to have "taken a wicket." If a wicket is knocked over while the runners are still running, the player who was supposed to arrive at that end will be "run out." The wicket can be knocked over by the ball, or by a player's hand holding the ball.

Fielding: The 11 fielders are placed around the elliptical field to catch the balls after they are hit. One is placed behind the wicket, and he is known as the wicket keeper. Only the wicket keepers can wear gloves to protect their hands when catching the ball. All other fielders use bare hands. The bowler is the only other player with a set position. The other nine fielders may position themselves anywhere on the field (with certain restrictions).

Game Timing: There are two ways for cricket matches to be set up. One involves limiting the time each team plays. The other is to play for a specific number of overs.

Test Matches: In first-class international cricket competitions, matches are played over five days, with each day broken into three two-hour sessions. There is a lunch break between the first two, and a tea break between the second and third. Each team has two innings to play each day. If the last day's innings aren't finished by the end of the allotted time, the match is called a tie, even if one team was significantly in the lead! Finally, everyone wears white so the red ball is easier to see.

KAPA HAKA

Kapa Haka is not a sport, but a cultural competition. It's based on traditional Maori songs and dances, including *haka* and *poi*. Teams from all over the country work hard to preserve the Maori heritage and create amazing performances in groups sometimes several-dozen strong. There are many *Kapa Haka* groups formed in schools, but adults are also big participants. Obviously it is most popular among Maori, but many other New Zealanders enjoy learning this challenging form of dance and song and participating in competitions.

Haka

Anyone who has caught the beginning of an All Blacks rugby match has seen the team perform a ritual dance before the game. This is called a *haka*, and it is a traditional Maori form of dance.

The *haka* has many variations and uses. It is performed for visiting dignitaries as a welcome and a show of respect. It can also be used, as the rugby matches illustrate, to lay down a challenge to an enemy and try to intimidate. The people performing the *haka* believe that it helps them to connect with the spirits of their ancestors; additionally, it gets them charged up for battle.

Haka can be performed with or without weapons in hand. Most *haka* feature the men out front, with women sometimes supporting from behind.

Haka consist mainly of choreographed stomping of the feet, forceful arm movements, and facial expressions. The facial expressions are meant to show ferocity and courage, expressed by bulging out the eyes and showing the tongue.

Haka is also accompanied by chanting in Maori. Here are the lyrics to the *haka* usually performed by the All Blacks in English and Maori:

LEADER
Ringa pakia
Uma tiraha
Turi whatia
Hope whai ake
Waewae takahia kia kino

English Translation:
Slap the hands against the thighs
Puff out the chest
Bend the knees
Let the hip follow
Stamp the feet as hard as you can

TEAM
Ka Mate! Ka Mate!
Ka Ora! Ka Ora!
Tenei te ta ngata puhuru huru
Nana nei i tiki mai
Whakawhiti te ra
A upane ka upane!
A upane kaupane whiti te ra!
Hi!!

English Translation:
It is death! It is death!
It is life! It is life!
This is the hairy person
Who caused the sun to shine
Keep abreast! Keep abreast!
The rank! Hold fast!
Into the sun that shines!

Religion

New Zealand does not have an official religion, and it has separated church from state. The dominant religion in the country is Christianity, representing nearly half of New Zealanders who claim a religious affiliation. The largest Christian group is Catholics, followed by Anglicans and then Presbyterians. There are also Maori-specific forms of Christianity, which developed early in the 19th century as missionaries tried to reconcile traditional Maori beliefs with the Christian faith. Just under two million New Zealanders identified themselves as Christians on the 2013 census.

Of the non-Christians, there are significant numbers of Hindus, Buddhists, and Muslims, and much smaller numbers of Sikhs and Jews. It is illegal to discriminate against anyone based on his or her religion. Most people find that they are free to practice any faith they choose, but there are occasional incidents where certain religious groups are targeted. This was most evident following 9/11, when some Muslims found they were being treated unfairly because of an attack that happened half a world away. But generally, there is a lot of religious tolerance in New Zealand.

More Kiwis are labeling themselves as nonreligious than ever before. In the 2013 census, 42 percent of the population claimed to be nonreligious. Some people in New Zealand feel that their religious beliefs, or absence of them, are nobody's business. In 2013, more than 173,000 Kiwis refused to answer the census question regarding their religion.

The Arts

New Zealand does value the arts, particularly when it comes to government funding. Everything from visual arts to fashion to film is given monetary support. And New Zealand prides itself on being the little country that could, so whenever a local artist, band, or designer makes it big on the world stage, the whole country likes to take credit. When he won an Academy Award, director Peter Jackson thanked everyone in New Zealand, and it's a good thing, because they would have been insulted if he hadn't!

While New Zealand's arts scene is not "world class" when it comes to its orchestras, ballet, opera, and so on, all these are at least available in the biggest cities. Theater is also widespread, although major Broadway-type spectacles are rare. International music artists come into New Zealand fairly regularly for concerts, but many only play one show in the entire country. So it's not unusual for New Zealanders to plan a trip to Auckland or Christchurch just to catch a show.

TRADITIONAL ARTS

Maori art has become iconic to New Zealand, and few visitors leave the country without a bone or greenstone carving, or a wood sculpture of some kind. The popularity of these items has helped to preserve the knowledge of the arts passed down through generations. Carving wood and bone, weaving flax, and other traditional arts were once disappearing in New Zealand, but with renewed interest, they are likely to survive for many more generations.

MADE IN NEW ZEALAND

Everything from fashion to film can be a source of Kiwi pride. New Zealanders love to see their artists recognized internationally. Sometimes, unfortunately, it can be hard for them to find the support they need to make it at home. Many go overseas to get their careers off the ground, becoming well known in New Zealand only after they have left. But some, like Peter Jackson, have made a point of staying home and making it work for them.

Some of New Zealand's favorite homegrown artists include the opera diva Dame Kiri Te Kanawa, pop superstar Lorde, *Lord of the Rings* and *Hobbit* film director Peter Jackson, and *True Blood* actress Anna Paquin.

INTERNATIONAL INFLUENCE

With the influx of immigrants from various parts of the world on the increase, international art forms are becoming more common in New Zealand. The arts of the Pacific Islands, like Fiji and Samoa, are the most common because so many people from those countries now live in New Zealand.

There have long been immigrant populations from Italy, Germany, China, and other countries adding their influence on the arts scene as well. Arts festivals centering on ethnic events, like Diwali and the Chinese New Year, have given Kiwis a chance to experience traditional dance and music from other countries.

PLANNING YOUR FACT-FINDING TRIP

Visiting New Zealand as a potential immigrant is very different from visiting as a tourist. Many of the top tourist destinations in the country are simply not practical places to live. Their natural beauty may amaze you, but trying to find work in a small coastal town is no easy feat! So you'll have to put away the glossy brochures, leave the bungee jumping for later, and look at New Zealand the way New Zealanders do. Be realistic about where you are most likely to settle down. Much of the country is very rural, and even many of the cities have populations of less than 50,000. Can you continue your career outside of a major city? Do you want a rural lifestyle, or would you miss the conveniences of city life? How far away will your children have to travel to get to school? Reading about a place can help, but it's only by seeing it for yourself that you'll really get an idea of whether it could feel like home.

It's best to plan for at least a two-week trip if possible. It can take a long time simply to fly to New Zealand and back, especially from the eastern side of North America, which can account for three or four travel days out of your total time. If you are already sure which city you're interested in, you can get away with a quick, one-week visit. Otherwise, you won't have time to get enough of a feel for your options. Ideally,

CAUTION
NEXT 5 km

Movie Magic

Even before you arrive in New Zealand on your fact-finding trip, you can do some research about the landscape on screen. Movies shot in New Zealand make a great introduction to the stunning landscape and may even give you some cultural insights.

The Lord of the Rings and *The Hobbit* trilogies feature some of the most beautiful scenery New Zealand has to offer. From the snowcapped Southern Alps to the shocking blue rivers to the rolling, pastoral hills, you can see an awful lot of the country over the course of these epic films. Unfortunately, it's all cleverly disguised as Middle Earth, so it's difficult to tell what you're looking at.

A road movie is always a good introduction to the landscape, and one of New Zealand's classic road stories is *Goodbye Pork Pie*. This 1981 comedy follows two mates who drive the entire length of the country (from Kaitaia in Northland to Invercargill in Southland) in a yellow Mini. A little dated, perhaps, but it's a national tour in one go.

Whale Rider features some wonderful rural scenery and coastline. You'll also get a bit of insight into Maori culture and traditions in this moving story of a young girl fighting to prove that she is destined to be a leader.

The less glamorous side of Maori life in New Zealand is shown in *Once Were Warriors*, where the seedier Auckland suburbs play host to a troubled family. A teenager named "Toot" living under the motorway is a harsh example of the lifestyle of New Zealand's poorest citizens.

you should take even longer than two weeks if you want to consider several places. Three weeks will give you a good look around, and a month will afford you some sightseeing time, too.

Preparing to Leave

You won't have to do much to prepare for your trip. Americans and Canadians can enter New Zealand for up to three months without a visa, but you will need an up-to-date passport. Remember that you are going to the opposite season from the one you are leaving, so you need to bring the right seasonal clothing. Hotel bookings and rental cars should be organized well in advance if you are visiting during the busy summer season, between December and February.

WHAT TO BRING
Currency
New Zealand dollars can be bought at many international currency traders in North America, but always research where you can get it rather than assuming it will be readily available. As long as you have a credit card and/or debit card with you, your cash needs should be pretty minimal. Taking large amounts of New Zealand currency is unnecessary and adds the risk that you will lose it or have it stolen. Exchange rates can fluctuate quite a lot, so keep an eye on them and choose a good time to exchange your money. Bear in mind that if you change too much and want to change it back after your trip, you may be getting an entirely different exchange rate.

Tips on Tips

If your average trip involves handing out tips left, right, and center, you'll have to adjust to a new attitude toward tipping when you get to New Zealand. Tipping is generally not part of the culture here, and good service should not depend on receiving any kind of bonus.

The no-tipping rule applies pretty much across the board. Restaurants do not expect you to tip the servers, although some cafés do have tip jars by the cash register where they're happy to take any change you don't want. You should not be expected to tip the concierge at a hotel either, nor the taxi driver who took you there. Sometimes people round up taxi fares, giving the driver a bit of spare change, but tipping as a percentage of the fare is not common practice.

I used to get "sticker shock" every time I ate at a restaurant in New Zealand, because the prices on the menu seemed high for the type of food I was ordering. But when I remembered that I was not going to be adding sales tax to those prices or leaving a 15-20 percent tip on top of the bill, I realized that those extras contribute significantly to the total cost of eating out in North America. So a meal out in New Zealand is actually quite reasonable because of the no-tipping policy and the fact that taxes are included in the menu price.

While nobody in New Zealand expects you to hand them extra cash, you can feel free to offer a tip when service has been exceptional. For instance, I have occasionally been offered a tip when working as a tour guide. You may find that your offer is refused, but rest assured that you have still made that worker's day.

You will be able to charge your car rentals, hotel rooms, and other major expenses on your credit cards. Most shops and restaurants will also accept major cards like Visa and MasterCard. Some also accept American Express. You'll be able to change travelers checks at some banks and hotels, if that's your preferred form of payment. They are used less and less these days, though, since plastic is so convenient.

Clothing

New Zealanders are very casual, so you will not need a great deal of dressy clothing for your trip. If you are planning to meet with potential employers, you may wish to bring a suit or other clothing appropriate to the type of work you are looking for. Outside of the office environment, jeans are acceptable almost everywhere, even in relatively nice restaurants. You may want to bring one dressy outfit if you plan to splash out now and then on a fancy dinner or something.

Comfortable footwear will be important, as you'll be spending a lot of time walking around to get a feeling for each place you visit. The sun in New Zealand can be very strong, so good sunglasses, sunscreen, and a hat are recommended in summer.

Job Search Materials

A fact-finding trip is an excellent opportunity to make contact with potential employers. The Kiwis are pretty approachable and will generally make time to see you if they can. Making a good impression in person will give you a big advantage over a résumé that arrives in the mail.

Bring copies of your résumé or CV with email and telephone contact information. (See the *Employment* chapter for details of what to include on your CV.) If you have personal business cards, these might also be useful. If you suspect that your current or

© MICHELLE WAITZMAN

Avoid visiting during public holidays and major events that bring large crowds.

previous employers may not be well known in New Zealand, it wouldn't hurt to bring some materials that explain what your company does. You may also want to provide contact details for current or former employers you'd be happy to use as references.

WHEN TO GO

If you're bringing the whole family along and you have school-age children, you'll be tempted to make your trip during the summer holidays. Don't forget that this will be the middle of winter in New Zealand! On the bright side, you'll get a realistic picture of what the worst weather conditions will be like. If you're hoping to explore the outdoors during your trip, it may be a better idea to visit over spring break (in March or April), when the weather will still be summery.

Visiting New Zealand over Christmas and New Year's should be avoided if you're on a serious fact-finding trip. Most Kiwis take vacation at this time of year and won't be in their offices. The entire month of January can be challenging if you are trying to make contacts. You will also find the hotels and car rentals at their busiest at this time of year, which will make bookings more difficult and expensive.

Other public holidays can also interrupt your plans. Check the list of public holidays in the *Introduction* chapter to be sure that you are prepared. You will find some shops closed on these days, as well as banks and the post office. Restaurants generally charge 15 percent more on public holidays, to cover the cost of paying their employees overtime.

School Holidays

In addition to the summer holidays, which last from late December to the first week of February, New Zealand schools have three other holiday periods. If you arrive during these periods, tourist activities and hotels will be busier than usual. You will also find it difficult to check out potential schools for your children during any holiday period.

The first term usually begins in early February. There are two-week breaks between school terms in mid-April (this break often begins on Good Friday), early July, and early October. The exact dates vary from year to year and are slightly different for different levels of schooling.

Arriving in New Zealand

Expect to be sleepy and disoriented by the time you reach New Zealand. Most people traveling from North America have to deal with connecting flights and a number of time zones by the time they arrive. Then you'll have to find your luggage, get through customs, and possibly take yet another flight if your final destination is not the city where you've entered New Zealand.

To arrive at your best (considering the circumstances), try to get some sleep, or at least rest, on your flight. Stay well hydrated by drinking water or juice several times during your journey, and avoid too much coffee or alcohol. Get up out of your seat now and then and walk down the aisle, or do some stretches in your seat if you can. All of this will help to combat jet lag later.

VISAS AND PASSPORTS

If you have a Canadian or U.S. passport, you'll be able to enter New Zealand without any special visas for a three-month period. You will have to have a return ticket, to show that you are not planning to stay in the country indefinitely. If your passport is from another country, you may need a visitor's visa. Check with New Zealand Immigration before your trip to see if you need one. If you have a British passport you can stay for up to six months, and if you have an Australian passport you can stay indefinitely. In any case, your passport has to be valid for at least six months after the date you are planning to leave New Zealand.

You may face some serious questioning if you look as though you're coming to New Zealand on a tourist visa and looking for work. Customs and immigration are concerned about people entering the country illegally. If you are carrying copies of your résumé to give to potential employers or real estate listings, you may arouse suspicion. Be sure to explain clearly that you are on a fact-finding trip and are definitely returning to your home country before attempting to move to New Zealand. If your immigration paperwork is already in progress, they will be able to confirm this.

CUSTOMS AND BIOSECURITY

New Zealand is famously picky about what can and can't come into the country. Biosecurity is tight, so anything that might introduce foreign pests to the country is a big no-no. Avoid carrying food in your baggage, including all fruits, vegetables, meat products, and dairy. Sweets and chocolate are OK, but honey is banned. You may also be asked to have any dirty footwear disinfected, to be sure there are no unwanted

© MICHELLE WAITZMAN

Renting a motor home is a popular way to get around New Zealand.

microorganisms hanging out in the dirt. This mainly applies to people who have been on farms or out camping recently.

Aside from biosecurity concerns, there are other items you can't import into New Zealand. This includes weapons and firearms, products made from endangered animals, utensils for smoking cannabis (and any illicit drugs themselves), and pornography. There is a duty-free limit of 50 cigarettes, 4.5 liters of beer or wine, and three bottles, no larger than 1,125 milliliters each, of spirits.

TRANSPORTATION

The way you choose to get around the country will depend on the amount of time you have, your budget, and your level of comfort in driving on the left. If you are planning to see several cities in a short time, domestic flights are the fastest way to get from place to place. All of New Zealand's main cities have airports, although only Auckland and Christchurch have extensive international connections.

If you have some time to spare, taking trains or buses between the cities will give you a more leisurely view of the countryside.

Driving will offer you the most flexibility by far. If you want to check out a city's suburbs or explore some of the more rural communities, you will almost certainly need to rent a car. Even in Auckland, having your own wheels will give you the freedom to set your own schedule and also have a realistic idea of how long the driving times are from place to place.

Renting a Car or Caravan

Your driver's license from home will be acceptable for driving a rental car or caravan. A caravan, also known as a motor home, will allow you to travel around the country without needing to stay in hotels. These are available in a variety of sizes and styles and are popular with tourists. If you're planning to move around a lot on your trip, this might be a good choice.

Renting a car will give you a lot of freedom. Make sure you're familiar with the rules of the road before you head off. (See *Driving* in the *Travel and Transportation* chapter.) Driving times are much longer in New Zealand than similar distances in North America, because there are not many multilane motorways and the main highways pass directly through towns and cities, causing them to slow down considerably. There are car rental companies at all international airports, and you can often arrange to drop off your rental at a different place than where you picked it up (for a fee).

Sample Itineraries

If you are only considering one city as a potential home, then one week may be enough to investigate real estate options and job opportunities. Otherwise, count on at least two weeks to get familiar with the major cities, longer if you plan to drive from place to place.

ONE WEEK

With only one week plus a weekend on either end for your trip, including travel time, you'll actually have about five or six days at the most to do your fact-finding. This pretty much limits you to one city. I'll use Auckland as the example, because it is the biggest city and the one that attracts the most immigrants.

Days 1-2

Travel to Auckland. Pick up a rental car at the airport and find your hotel. Sleep off the jet lag. Buy a copy of the *New Zealand Herald* newspaper, and look through the real estate and employment sections. Make appointments with potential employers, schools, and real estate agents for later in the week. To avoid traveling back and forth between suburbs, try to plan your time so that your real estate and school appointments are in the same suburbs on the same days. Likewise, you should do your explorations of the city center on the same days that you are meeting centrally located potential employers.

Using a rental car to get around will make fact-finding easier and more efficient. However, if you are not planning to use a car when you move to Auckland, I recommend taking public transit (both buses and trains are run under the Auckland Transport system) while you do your research. This will help you discover whether you'll be happy with the transportation services available or whether you'll find it too slow or limited.

Days 3-4

Explore the Central Business District (CBD) to get a feel for Auckland's business hub. Meet with potential employers in the city center. A trip up the Sky Tower is a touristy thing to do, but I recommend it in this case because it will give you an overview of Auckland and help you to get your bearings. Back on the ground, wander into various stores to get an idea of prices and selection for different items you might need, like electronics, appliances, and furniture. And check out some of the inner suburbs like Parnell and Ponsonby for a taste of Auckland's character. Cafés in New Zealand are not just places to buy coffee, but often become full-service restaurants in the evening. While you are in Parnell or Ponsonby, have dinner at a café and see what you think, as this will be typical restaurant fare for New Zealand.

If you're up for a late night, stay in the city to experience some of Auckland's nightlife. Most of the nightlife scene is in the city center near High Street and Vulcan Lane, and along Karangahape Road. If your clubbing days are behind you, you can pop into a pub instead for a more laid-back night out. Another nightlife option is SkyCity Casino, right in the heart of Auckland.

Days 5-6

Time to leave the city and discover the suburbs. Read the neighborhood descriptions in the *Prime Living Locations* section and choose two areas that interest you. For example, go to Henderson in the west on one day and Howick in the east on another day. Note how long it takes to drive to each suburb from the city. Visit a suburban supermarket, such as New World or Countdown, to see the range of products and prices. Visit local schools if you have children. You can have a real estate agent show you properties if you are thinking of buying right away, or visit some rental properties to get a good idea of what you can expect at various price levels. Look for free property-advertising booklets in racks at shopping malls or outside of real estate offices. These are magazine-sized booklets full of homes for sale and contact information for the real estate agents. To find rentals in the area, check the classified section of the *New Zealand Herald* or the rental property section on the **Trade Me website** (trademe.co.nz).

© UNA HUBBARD

A hotel room with a view can help you take in the city.

Day 7

Take some time to check out Auckland's leisurely side. Go to a nearby beach, such as Takapuna or Piha. Or take a walk up a volcano like Mt. Eden to admire the view. Lifestyle is important to New Zealanders, so it's worth taking a day to see how they play, now that you've got an idea of how they work.

Days 8-9

Return your rental car and head for the airport, leaving at least two hours for check-in and security before your departure. You'll have lots of time on your flight home to go through the information you've gathered. This is a perfect time to make detailed notes about what you liked or didn't like, whom you met with, and so on. You'll be surprised how fast you forget the details once you're back home. Once you are back, it's a good idea to follow up with thank-you notes to people who took the time to see you, especially potential employers. This will make them more likely to remember you fondly later when you apply for work.

TWO WEEKS

Within two weeks you can check out New Zealand's three major cities to decide which one fits best with your expectations and lifestyle. I'm going to assume you'll fly between the cities to save time, but if you plan to drive, you'll have to put aside a full day to get from Auckland to Wellington (assuming you don't stop off along the way to check out other cities). It will require another, even longer day to get from Wellington to Christchurch, since you'll need to take the three-hour ferry ride into consideration.

Days 1-2

Travel to Auckland. Pick up a rental car and find your hotel. Now that you're in the country, try to call around and confirm any meetings you've been planning with potential employers, schools, and real estate agents. Pick up a copy of the *New Zealand Herald,* which is the main Auckland newspaper, and see if you can also find a copy of the *Dominion Post* (Wellington) and *The Press* (Christchurch), which may be available at your hotel or at large bookstores such as Whitcoull's. Each newspaper will have a section of employment, real estate, and rental listings for their own city. Weekend editions are the best for these listings. By scanning through all of the papers, you may find more potential employers to contact or properties you'd like to see. While you're at it, flip through the front section of each newspaper to see what Kiwis are talking about in the news.

Days 3-6

Explore Auckland, using the one-week itinerary to guide you. Start with the inner city, meeting with potential employers and browsing various shops to get a feel for the products available in New Zealand. Focus on the essentials for setting up your home, such as furniture, electronics, appliances, and home furnishings. Eat at a café or restaurant in the city, or the inner suburbs like Parnell or Ponsonby. Try out the New Zealand beers and wines on offer. This is your chance to see if the size and pace of Auckland are a good match for you and your family.

Next, explore the suburbs where you are most interested in living. You can base your choices on the descriptions in the *Prime Living Locations* section. Take the bus or train to see how accessible the suburbs are. Or drive there in your rental car and try to wrap your head around the traffic flow and how long your daily commute would be. Stop at the local supermarket, such as New World or Countdown, to see what the selection and prices are like. Decide which neighborhoods meet your needs for schools and shopping, and what neighborhood's offerings are most line with your budget.

Days 7-10

Fly to Wellington and pick up a rental car. Wellington has a very compact CBD, so you can wander around it on foot to get a better feel for the city. If you don't already have a copy of the *Dominion Post* newspaper, pick one up and look through the employment, real estate, and rental listings. Try to meet with some potential employers

© MICHELLE WAITZMAN

Stay in a residential neighborhood, such as this one in Wellington, to get a feel for living in the area.

while you're in town. If you're interested in working in Wellington's large public service sector, visit the website jobs.govt.nz to find out which government departments have openings in your field.

Take some time to visit Te Papa, the national museum. It will give you some historical and cultural insights into New Zealand. Take your car or a bus up to the Mount Victoria Lookout. This will give you an excellent overview of the city and inner suburbs. You'll be able to see a lot of residential areas from here, and compare the real thing with a city map. Have dinner in or around Courtenay Place and take in the city's nightlife.

On one day, drive out to the Hutt Valley or up to Porirua and the Kapiti Coast to see the more suburban housing options. You can visit properties with a real estate agent to get an idea of values and what's on the market. And if you have children, make some time to visit schools in the areas where you are thinking of settling. Prices for food, furniture, and appliances are pretty consistent throughout the country, so if you checked these out in Auckland, there's no need to do it again in Wellington or Christchurch.

Days 11-13

Fly to Christchurch and pick up a rental car. This is your third city, so you've got the routine down now. Check out the city center to get an idea of how the rebuild from the quakes of 2010 and 2011 is progressing. Then move out to the suburbs to see what the housing and schools are like. Pop into one of the malls around the city's outskirts to see what's available and check out the city's mall culture. Riccarton Mall is very popular, and the largest shopping center on the South Island.

Canterbury's natural attractions are also a reason to consider living in Christchurch, so if you're visiting in winter, you may want to check out the ski hills, and in summer try the Banks Peninsula or other hiking spots. Talk to a real estate agent about the areas that are expected to grow in the coming years, and try to see some different suburbs to get a feel for them. Would you prefer an older suburb with homes with character like Cashmere or somewhere newer and more modern like Rolleston?

Day 14

Time to collect your thoughts as you depart for home. You may be able to fly out of New Zealand directly from Christchurch, or you may need to catch a connecting flight in Auckland, depending on your route.

While you are on your way home, take a pen and paper and write some notes about the different cities you have seen. How do they stack up in terms of job opportunities, schools, lifestyle, transportation, and housing? Are there any places you fell in love with? Any you would no longer consider moving to? It's important to write this stuff down while it's fresh in your mind. By the time you get home, memories will begin to blur and one suburb may become indistinguishable from another.

When you return home, write a thank-you note to anyone who took the time to meet with you during your trip. This will leave potential employers and other contacts with positive memories of your visit, and hopefully they'll be happy to hear from you again after you immigrate.

ONE MONTH

Over the course of a month you can really get to know what New Zealand is like. Drive from town to town and take in the countryside. Stop at a few tourist destinations to see where you might spend your holidays. Get a firsthand experience of the difference between urban life and rural life.

You should plan your trip to cover the country either north to south, or south to north. I'll outline a possible route starting in Auckland, but you could always reverse it.

North Island

Auckland is the most popular choice for immigrants, so be sure to give yourself a few days to wander around and let the city's atmosphere sink in. Get an idea of the distances between the suburbs and downtown, and the different types of neighborhoods. Find out if any of the potential employers you are considering in Auckland also have offices in other parts of the country. Take a few moments to relax as you're running around the city, and have a coffee outdoors to do a bit of people-watching.

Before you leave the north, a weekend trip to the Bay of Islands will be a great way to recharge your batteries and enjoy some time on the beach before your big journey south begins.

Heading down State Highway 1, you'll arrive at Hamilton, New Zealand's fourth-largest city. You'll probably need just a day or two here to decide whether it's the right match for you. Despite its reasonably large size, Hamilton can feel quite rural because agriculture is so dominant in the surrounding areas.

After Hamilton, you'll have to choose between heading east or west. The eastern route will take you to the Bay of Plenty and Hawke's Bay, while the western route is the way to New Plymouth and the Taranaki region. I'm going to follow the eastern route, as it passes more of the cities where you might want to live.

Make your way to Tauranga on the Bay of Plenty, then follow State Highway 2 to Gisborne, before continuing south to Napier and Hastings. These are all coastal cities with very different personalities, so if living by the ocean is your thing, use your time to compare the lifestyles. You may also want to take a couple of days to check out some of the Hawke's Bay wineries or sample the fresh produce if you're there for summer. If you have extra time, head from Tauranga to Rotorua before you go to Gisborne. Rotorua is one of the top spots for tourism and is well known for presenting Maori culture to visitors, as well as geothermal sights.

Unless you are planning to attend Massey University, or have another specific reason to stop in Palmerston North, I suggest passing it by and heading straight into the Wairarapa. Again, unless there is something specific you want to look into here, you should probably drive straight through to Wellington.

Give yourself a few days to explore the capital and the surrounding region. This is the place to look into public sector employers. They hire immigrants into New Zealand's public sector all of the time, so you shouldn't worry about the fact that you are just moving to the country. There are also a range of other potential employers in Wellington, including the creative sector, information technology (IT), and finance. Check out the national museum, Te Papa, while you are in Wellington. It has a lot of great information about New Zealand's natural and social history.

South Island

From Wellington, it's off to the South Island. It's often cheaper to return your rental car in Wellington and rent another in Picton than to pay the fees for taking the car on the ferry. After your arrival in Picton, head off to Nelson and spend a day or two exploring Marlborough.

On your way from Nelson down to Christchurch, you may want to stop off in Kaikoura. This is a big ecotourism center, with whale-watching, dolphin encounters, a seal colony, and other wonders of nature. It's on the way, anyway, and it breaks up an otherwise long journey. If Kaikoura doesn't interest you, you can check out the rural life around Blenheim instead. Blenheim is a lot farther north, though, so it doesn't break up the trip quite as well.

Christchurch is the biggest city on the South Island, so give it a few days. The city center is quite small, but you'll need some time to explore different suburbs if you are seriously considering a move here. You may also want to take some time to meet with potential employers to see how your odds stack up.

Continue south to Dunedin, the fifth-largest city in the country and one of the oldest. You'll sense its Scottish roots right away in the architecture and the residents' down-to-earth attitudes. The university campus is worth a visit, even if your student days are over. Dunedin is facing slow population growth, so the city is keen to attract both immigrants and other New Zealanders.

If time permits, you can make your way through Southland and visit Invercargill. The population is quite low down at this end of the country, and you may feel even more isolated living here than in other parts of New Zealand. But if you've got that pioneering spirit, and especially if you love oysters, it might work beautifully; this is one of the most affordable places to set up house in the country.

Practicalities

Once you arrive in New Zealand, try to stick to your planned itinerary and not get distracted by visiting tourist destinations. Remember, you'll have time to see the sights after you move. Most of your destinations will have no shortage of accommodations and food options. But if you are traveling during the summer, especially during late December and January, hotel rooms can be scarce. Booking ahead is a good idea at those times.

The information I've given here for hotels and dining is by no means comprehensive, but these details will keep a roof over your head and ensure you don't starve. I encourage you to check things out for yourself, and try out restaurants recommended by locals you meet or that simply look appealing when you walk by. Also, if you enjoy bed-and-breakfast accommodations, pick up a New Zealand bed-and-breakfast guide and try to stay in more residential areas, as this will give you more of a feeling of what living in that city is like.

If you're checking out cities or towns that I haven't listed here, you may want to use a tourist guidebook like *Moon New Zealand,* which will have more accommodations and restaurant listings.

AUCKLAND
Accommodations
City Life Apartments (171 Queen St., tel. 09/379-9222, www.heritagehotels.co.nz, $159-559) lets you choose between a standard hotel room and a two- or three-bedroom suite with a kitchen if you will be in Auckland for a while and want to settle in. If you're on a tighter budget, the **Princeton Apartments** (30 Symonds St., tel. 09/950-8300, www.princeton.net.nz, $89 for a two-bedroom apartment) may be a good pick, with family rooms that include kitchenettes. If you'd prefer to be slightly removed from downtown, the **Great Ponsonby Arthotel** (30 Ponsonby Terrace, tel. 09/376-5989, www.greatpons.co.nz, $245-400 d) offers bed-and-breakfast-style accommodations in a restored 1890s villa in the fashionable Ponsonby neighborhood.

Food
There are certainly no problems finding a restaurant in Auckland. If you want to have a special dinner one night, try **Vivace** (50 High St., tel. 09/302-2303, www.vivacerestaurant.co.nz) for a tasty meal and a massive wine list. In Ponsonby, **Prego** (226 Ponsonby Rd., tel. 09/376-3095, www.prego.co.nz) offers Italian dining of high quality, and you don't need a reservation. For a quick lunch or dinner option, **Burger Fuel** (291 Queen St. plus 38 other New Zealand—mostly North Island—locations, tel. 09/309-0660, www.burgerfuel.com) is New Zealand's homegrown gourmet burger chain, using only grass-fed beef or free-range chicken and offering several vegan options too. If your kids are picky eaters and want something familiar, there are five locations of **Denny's** (51 Hobson St. plus 4 other Auckland locations, tel. 09/309-90220, www.dennys.co.nz) including a 24-hour location right near the Sky Tower.

Bring Your Own Wine (BYO)

Some restaurants in New Zealand have a special liquor license that allows them to operate a BYO service. In addition to offering its own range of alcoholic drinks, the restaurant allows customers to bring in their own bottles of wine to drink on the premises.

BYO restaurants usually have this marked on their windows or front doors. Otherwise it will be stated on the menu. You can only bring wine, so leave the bottle of whiskey back at your hotel. The restaurant will charge a "corkage fee" for serving your wine. This fee is usually just a couple of dollars per person or around five or six dollars per bottle, but it can be higher in fine dining restaurants where selling wine at $15 per glass contributes a significant portion of the profits.

Bringing your own wine to a restaurant can have several advantages. The most obvious is price, with the cost of a bottle marked up significantly in restaurants. Another advantage is that you can bring along a wine you really love instead of having to choose from a limited selection at some restaurants. BYO can also help you keep track of how much you've had to drink. If your two bottles of wine are empty, you'll know it's time to switch to water. Ordering by the glass, it's easy to lose track of just how many glasses you've gone through, especially if you're having a long, leisurely meal with friends.

If you aren't sure whether a restaurant is BYO or not, ask when you reserve a table. That way you'll know whether to visit a bottle shop or supermarket before dinner to pick up some wine.

TARANAKI AND WAIKATO
Accommodations

In New Plymouth, the **Landmark Manor Motel** (72 Leach St., tel. 06/769-9688, www.landmarkmanor.co.nz, $130-150 d) offers a convenient location, and some rooms have cooking facilities and spa baths. If being central isn't so important, try the **Egmont Eco Lodge YHA** (12 Clawton St., tel. 06/753-5720, www.mttaranaki.co.nz, $37.50-125 d) just outside of town. It is a backpackers' lodge, but there are some double and family rooms. The bush setting will give you a more rural experience.

In Hamilton, you can find a string of motels on the road from Auckland, including **Bella Vista Motel** (1 Richmond St., tel. 07/838-1234, www.bellavistahamilton.co.nz, $135-155 d), which has the bonus of a spa bath and cooking facilities in some suites. Or for a more luxurious experience, the **Novotel Tainui Hamilton** (7 Alma St., tel. 07/838-1366, www.novotel.co.nz, $159-255 d) is located on the banks of the Waikato River in the heart of the city adjacent to the SkyCity Casino.

Food

New Plymouth has some decent dining options, although you won't find the range here of the bigger cities. Try **Arborio** (65 St. Aubyn St., tel. 06/759-1241, www.arborio.co.nz) in the Puke Ariki Museum for an Italian menu that keeps locals coming back. Everything from brunch to dinner gets good reviews here. You'll find European fare and a $10 kids menu at **The Ugly Duck** (601 Devon St. East, tel. 06/789-2084, www.uglyduck.co.nz) in the New Plymouth suburb of Fitzroy.

In Hamilton, the city center offers lots of options. The **Furnace Restaurant Bar & Nightclub** (150 Victoria St., tel. 07/839-9099, www.furnacebar.co.nz) offers a range of options including pizzas, salads, and pastas. For a quick breakfast or lunch try **The**

River Kitchen (237 Victoria St., 07/839-2906). They raise the bar for cafeteria-style food including a unique "breakfast salad."

BAY OF PLENTY AND HAWKE'S BAY
Accommodations

In Tauranga, the **Cobblestone Court Motel** (86 Chapel St., Otumoetai, tel. 07/576-9028, $135-155 d, $175 3 bdrm. unit) will keep the kids busy with a heated pool. You can stay in a studio unit or a family unit that sleeps up to seven people. If you're looking for a room with a view, try the **Hotel on Devonport** (72 Devonport Rd., tel. 07/578-2668, www.hotelondevonport.net.nz, $157-270 d). It's a business-style hotel with an upmarket feel.

Gisborne has motels overlooking the harbor that all offer similar rooms and rates. The **Captain Cook Motor Lodge** (31 Awapuni Rd., tel. 06/867-7002, www.captaincook.co.nz, $145-225 d) offers one- and two-bedroom options, and it's close to the beach and the city center.

Down in Napier, Marine Parade is lined with small hotels facing Hawke's Bay. In the town center, the refurbished **Masonic Hotel** (at Marine Parade and Tennyson St., tel. 06/385-8689, www.masonic.co.nz, $169-299 d) is an art deco landmark that offers a convenient location. For a less touristy experience, try basing your stay in Havelock North, just south of Hastings. The **Havelock North Motor Lodge** (7 Havelock Rd., tel. 06/877-8627, www.havelocknorthmotorlodge.co.nz, $140-190 s/d) will accommodate you in the middle of town so you can see what local life is like. They also have a two-bedroom apartment available for families.

Food

In Tauranga, you'll be spoiled for choice if you take a walk along The Strand. One good option is **The Phoenix** (67 The Strand, tel. 07/578-8741, www.thephoenixtauranga.co.nz). Their menu is full of comfort food and bar and grill favorites. They have a $10 kids menu for smaller appetites, and it even comes with a sundae for dessert.

Gisborne is less of a foodie town, but a surprise find is the French fine dining at **The Marina Restaurant** (Marina Park, Vogel St., tel. 06/868-5919, www.marinarestaurant.co.nz). They offer a bistro menu on the terrace Thursday to Saturday for more affordable meals. For reliable, economical family meals try **Breakers Café and Bar** (6 Reads Quay, tel. 06/867-7311, www.breakerscafebar.co.nz), which also has locations in Mt. Maunganui, Napier, Hastings, and New Plymouth. It's not fancy, but it will keep the kids and burger lovers happy.

Napier has most of the restaurant business around Hawke's Bay, since it attracts the most visitors. Seafood is a popular choice for special occasions. **Pacifica Restaurant** (209 Marine Parade, tel. 06/833-6335, www.pacificarestaurant.co.nz) is a unique experience, featuring two $50 tasting menus. For something homier, **The Rose Irish Pub** (at Marine Parade and Tennyson St., tel. 06/385-8689) is housed in the famous Masonic Hotel. Try pub favorites like fish-and-chips or beef and Guinness pie.

WELLINGTON AND THE LOWER NORTH ISLAND
Accommodations

The **Bay Plaza Hotel** (40 Oriental Parade, tel. 04/385-7799, www.bayplaza.co.nz,

$120-207 d) has rooms with a great harbor view in one of Wellington's most sought-after neighborhoods. The **Duxton Hotel** (170 Wakefield St., tel. 04/473-3900, www.wellington.amorahotels.com, $160-240 d) is conveniently located near Te Papa museum and the waterfront. Rooms are very comfortable, and with 192 rooms it usually has space available. If you're looking for a suite with kitchen and laundry facilities, **Quest Apartments** (corner of Lambton Quay and Hunter Sts., tel. 04/916-0700, www.questwellington.co.nz, $147-249 d) has serviced apartments right downtown in a historic art deco building. Two-bedroom apartments are also available. If you need to keep your budget in check, try **YHA Wellington** (292 Wakefield St., tel. 04/801-7280, www.yha.co.nz, $75-133 d). It's one of the top-rated youth hostels in the country. Twin and double rooms are available, and there's a supermarket right across the street.

Food

Central Wellington is packed with restaurants, so if you're the adventurous type, try out a few different places. Malaysian and Indian restaurants are abundant. Courtenay Place and Cuba Street are the main areas for nightlife and dining, but wherever you are, there should be something nearby. **Chow** (45 Tory St., tel. 04/382-8585, www.chow.co.nz) has Asian fusion cuisine in a casual setting with lots of gluten-free, dairy-free, and vegan options. For a high-end experience on the waterfront, **Shed 5** (Queen's Wharf, tel. 04/499-9069, www.shed5.co.nz) offers fresh New Zealand seafood in a historic 19th-century building. If you consider dessert the main attraction, head to **Strawberry Fare** (25 Kent Terrace, tel. 04/385-2551, www.strawberryfare.co.nz). It serves full meals but is famous for its enormous, decadent desserts, so save lots of room! The restaurant is BYO wine, so you can bring your own bottle if you wish. To rub elbows with Wellington's alternative crowd, try **Midnight Espresso** (178 Cuba St., tel. 04/384-7014) on upper Cuba Street. The atmosphere is all grunge, but the breakfast, desserts, and coffee are delicious.

CHRISTCHURCH AND MARLBOROUGH
Accommodations

Just north of Christchurch city center you'll find **Centre Point on Colombo** (859 Colombo St., tel. 03/377-0859, www.centrepointoncolombo.co.nz, $160-220 d). They offer both standard rooms and apartments with kitchenettes. The **Randolph Motel Apartments** (79 Papanui Rd., tel. 03/355-0942, www.randolphmotel.co.nz, $170-210 d) are fully self-contained apartments, some of which have the added benefit of spa baths to ease away your fact-finding tensions. To get an idea of what life in the suburbs might be like, you can stay outside the town center at **Fyffe on Riccarton Motor Lodge** (208 Riccarton Rd., tel. 03/341-3274, www.fyffeonriccarton.co.nz, $140 double-studio units, $190 two-bedroom spa units). All of the units have kitchen facilities, some have spa baths, and there are spacious two-bedroom units for families available.

Nelson is a good place to stay while exploring Marlborough and Tasman, since it has a large range of accommodation choices. For a modern comfort just outside the city center, **The Sails** (7 Trafalgar St., tel. 03/546-6463, www.thesailsnelson.co.nz, $159-245) is earning top reviews. If you prefer the motel option, try **Apartments Paradiso** (corner Tasman and Weka Sts., tel. 03/545-7128, www.paradisoapartments.co.nz, $99-149 d), which features kitchenettes and a swimming pool.

Food

To enjoy locally raised lamb and other Greek favorites in Christchurch try **Costas Taverna** (478 Cranford St., tel. 03/352-3232, www.costastaverna.co.nz). It's a short taxi ride north of the city center. If you're exploring Riccarton, you can enjoy a meal at **Dux Dine** (28 Riccarton Rd., tel. 03/348-1436, www.duxdine.co.nz), a local favorite that has relocated from downtown. **BASE Woodfired Pizza** (Re:START Mall, Cashel St., tel. 022/182-1921, www.basepizza.co.nz) is cooking pizzas in a wood oven, all inside a shipping container! If you're browsing the Re:START Mall or in the city center, check it out.

If you're looking for tasty vegetarian options, make your way to **East Street Vegetarian Café** (335 Trafalgar Sq. East, tel. 03/970-0575) in Nelson. For a nice seafood experience, try **The Boat Shed Café & Restaurant** (350 Wakefield Quay, tel. 03/546-9783). It's even open for breakfast on weekends.

OTAGO AND SOUTHLAND
Accommodations

In Dunedin, **Manor Motel** (22 Manor Pl., tel. 03/477-6729, www.manormotel.co.nz, $95-160 d) offers units for any size family, some sleeping up to six people. All have kitchenettes, so you can keep breakfast and snacks handy. Even more central is **97 Motel Moray Place** (97 Moray Pl., tel. 477-2050, www.97motel.co.nz, $120-140 d), right near The Octagon. Rooms and family studios are available.

Food

As a student city, Dunedin is a bit short on fine dining, but it has lots of café-style restaurants near The Octagon that serve good lunches and snacks. For a nice Italian meal, **Etrusco at the Savoy** (8A Moray Pl., tel. 03/477-3737, www.etrusco.co.nz) offers delicious pastas at reasonable prices. To get a big taste of down-home Dunedin culture, dine at the **Speight's Ale House** (200 Rattray St., tel. 03/477-9480) at the Speight's Brewery. Although there are other locations in this upscale pub chain, this is its home.

DAILY LIFE

MAKING THE MOVE

Moving across an ocean can be complicated, to say the least. But the great thing about immigrating to New Zealand is that if you meet their requirements, Immigration New Zealand would rather bring you in than keep you out. So you'll find that the various officials you deal with along the way are usually both friendly and helpful. It certainly makes for a more pleasant experience than New Zealanders encounter when they try to move to the United States! Paperwork aside, you'll face a lot of decisions when you make the move Down Under. What type of visa do you need? How long are you planning to stay? Should you ship all of your possessions or start fresh? It's enough to make your head spin.

The logistics of moving your household across an ocean can be overwhelming. I've tried in this chapter to provide information about which of your belongings will be helpful in your new life in New Zealand, so you can start creating that "garage sale" pile and only ship the things you'll actually need.

The more of your immigration paperwork you can do before your move, the easier it tends to be. You'll have a much harder time getting your hands on things such as birth certificates and police certificates that prove you do not have a criminal record once you're outside your home country. Employers are also more interested in immigrants who have already shown the initiative to start applying for a visa. It tells them

that you are serious about moving to New Zealand, and that considering you as an employee is not a waste of their time.

Immigration and Visas

There are many different options for people wanting to come to New Zealand. Depending on your situation and how long you plan to stay, you can narrow down the options to those that apply to your circumstances. Young people have the most options, since they can enter on student visas or working holiday visas. Older people will have to qualify for work visas, business visas, or residency. The rules for visas and residency are constantly changing to suit the country's needs. So don't rely solely on the information in this book, as it could be out of date by the time you read this. The best source for up-to-date information is the **Immigration New Zealand website** (www.immigration.govt.nz), where all of the rules, fees, and latest news are available.

IMMIGRATION ADVISERS

For some people, the logistics of moving to another country can be overwhelming. This is especially true if the application is not in your first language or if you are very busy. That's where immigration advisers can help. They can provide you with assistance in preparing your applications, searching for work, and even arranging your move.

New Zealand only allows licensed immigration advisers to provide immigration advice. This regime was introduced to ensure that immigrants were not being scammed or given incorrect advice. The Immigration Advisers Authority (IAA) manages this licensing system and their website includes a list of licensed advisers in New Zealand and other countries. Even advisers based in the United States or Canada should have a license from the IAA.

You will be able to find an adviser based in your home country or in New Zealand. There are advantages to each. An adviser in your home country will be able to provide a more personalized service in the early stages, like walking you through the paperwork. However, a New Zealand-based adviser is likely to have better employment and housing contacts and more likely to give you ongoing support after you enter the country.

If your application is straightforward, you may not need any kind of outside assistance with it (I didn't). But if you prefer to have someone with specialized experience help you out, a licensed immigration adviser can take away a lot of the pressure and possibly improve your chances of getting the visa or permit you're after. There are a couple of options listed in the *Resources* section at the end of this book, or you can check the **IAA website** (iaa.govt.nz).

STUDENT VISAS

If you want to study in New Zealand for longer than three months, you will need a student visa. (If your course lasts less than three months, you can enter the country on a visitor visa instead.) To qualify for this visa, you will need to meet health and character requirements. This includes proving that you do not have a criminal record and having an up-to-date medical examination. Your medical examination should include a complete medical history, blood and urine tests, and a chest X-ray to screen for tuberculosis. You will need to have your doctor fill out the form provided by Immigration New Zealand, and it must be filled out in English. You'll also need to show that you've been accepted at an approved school. Finally, you need evidence that you have sufficient funds to support yourself while you study, since you are not allowed to work full-time. You must have access to at least $15,000 per year.

Student visas are granted for up to one year at a time, so if you are planning to study in New Zealand for several years, you need to reapply for your student visa each year. In most cases, you need to be a full-time student to qualify for a student visa. You can be a part-time student if you are enrolled in a course that requires you to complete a certain amount of work experience. Once you have finished studying, you must either leave the country or apply for a job search visa, a work visa, or a residency permit.

It's important to arrange for proper medical insurance while you are in New Zealand on a student visa. International students are not covered by the public health care system, and you will be asked for proof of your insurance as part of your visa process.

Students are allowed to work part-time on a student visa, up to 20 hours per week, if enrolled in a student exchange program lasting at least one year or a tertiary level program lasting at least two years. You can also work full-time over the summer holiday period.

Once you have been granted a student visa, you must attend classes full-time and get passing grades. If you decide to stop taking the course you were approved for and enroll in a different subject or at a different school, you will need approval from Immigration New Zealand or your visa could be revoked.

If you want your partner or children to come to New Zealand with you while you study, they will have to apply for visitor visas. These last only three months, so they will need extensions if you are staying longer.

WORKING HOLIDAY VISAS

A Working Holiday Visa is a great way to live in New Zealand for a limited period of time, generally one year, and be able to pay for your stay by working. Working holiday programs are available to citizens of 42 countries, between the ages of 18 and 30. Although this visa allows you to do temporary work while in the country (you are not eligible for permanent jobs), you must have at least $4,200 available to show that you will be able to fund your trip. Most visitors on working holidays get seasonal work on farms, do temporary office jobs, or work in the tourism industry. You will have to register with the Inland Revenue Department and pay tax on your income, just like any employee.

Working Holiday Visas do not allow you to bring children with you, and your passport must be valid for at least three months after your planned departure date from New Zealand. Once you have been to New Zealand on a Working Holiday Visa, you can't apply to do it again, even if you are still under the age limit. Both the United States and Canada have unlimited spaces available for Working Holiday Visas, so there is no deadline for applications.

WORK VISAS
Work to Residence Visa

Work to Residence Visas are one of the most common ways to immigrate to New Zealand. They give you the opportunity to gain valuable experience inside the country for up to two years, which then helps you to gain residency later on if you want to stay. In addition to fulfilling the usual health and character requirements, you will need a job offer from a New Zealand employer for a duration of at least six months to qualify for a work visa. You won't be able to apply for a visa with just any job offer, though. New Zealand has certain vocations where there are skill shortages, and immigration officials are focused on filling those shortages rather than letting in anyone with the ability to hold down any job. There are three categories your job offer can fall under to qualify for a work visa:

- Your job is on the Long Term Skills Shortage list, which is regularly updated.

- Your potential employer has been accredited to recruit workers from overseas.

- You have a recognized talent in the arts, culture, or sports (e.g., coming to New Zealand to star in a film or play for a professional sports team).

If you have come to New Zealand on a tourist visa and want to apply for a work visa while you are in the country, you are permitted to do so. But having an application in process doesn't automatically extend your stay, so be sure to apply for a tourist visa extension before yours expires or be prepared to leave the country until your work permit is granted.

If you have a partner, he or she will have to apply separately for a work or visitor visa. The fact that you have been granted a work visa does not automatically permit your partner to remain in the country with you. However, once you have a visa, your partner and children should be able to apply under the Family stream, which takes into account whether you have a family connection in New Zealand who can help support you.

Temporary Work Visa

If you are not planning to make a permanent move, you can apply for a Temporary Work Visa instead of a Work to Residence Visa. Your visa will be connected with a specific type of work. It is a good option if you are coming to New Zealand for a specific event where you will be working (such as a trade show or film shoot) or you are joining a partner who is in New Zealand to study or work. If there is any chance that you'll want to stay permanently in New Zealand, however, it's better to try for a Work to Residence Visa so that you can transition to permanent residency more easily.

Silver Fern Visa

In 2010, Immigration New Zealand introduced a new visa category to attract young, skilled immigrants. The Silver Fern Visa allows people to enter New Zealand for nine months to search for skilled employment if they have a degree or trade qualification in their field. There is a limit of 300 places per year. To be eligible for the visa, you must currently live outside of New Zealand, be aged 20-35, and have at least $4,200 to support yourself during your stay. Once you find a job, you can secure a visa for two years under this policy.

Long-Term Business Visa

If you are planning to start your own business when you move to New Zealand, you'll need to apply for a Long-Term Business Visa, also known as an Entrepreneur

DAILY LIFE

Helping to Smooth the Move

On Arrival is a relocation service that mainly works with New Zealand employers to help their overseas hires to settle in New Zealand successfully. The company's managing director, Dan Casagranda, moved from Calgary, Canada, to Wellington, New Zealand, in 1986 after being hired by Telecom New Zealand. His experience was so difficult that he set up On Arrival so that other new arrivals wouldn't have to struggle as his family did.

Eve and Don Casagranda, owners of On Arrival

© LISA CASAGRANDA

What challenges did you face in your own relocation?
First, no one was there to meet us at the airport (as they had mixed up our arrival time), so we booked two taxis to our motel—my wife and I and two daughters with our 8 suitcases. It was a one bedroom unit that had no closets, no cooking facilities, no table and chairs, no washing facilities; it was like going back into the 1950s.

I was the first of the international recruits to arrive in Wellington, and the HR/Personnel department had no concept of the needs of expats arriving in a new country. I started work the second day after arrival, so my wife and daughters had no way of getting around. Trying to find a place to rent was a challenge, as real estate companies had no rental divisions in 1986. We then had to get our daughters registered in school and set about "discovering" where to register with a doctor, find a dentist, the local shops, and other outlets.

How did you get started, and how has your business grown over the years?
In 2000, I decided that I needed a change from the corporate environment, and our

Visa. This visa allows you to be self-employed for up to three years to establish your business. First, if you have a good business plan, have at least $100,000 to invest in your business, and meet the health and character requirements, you will be granted a work permit for 12 months. This will allow you to get your business set up and running before you apply for the long-term visa. If you can show that your business is established and viable, you should be granted the Long-Term Business Visa for two additional years. You'll need to show proof of your business, audited accounts, GST (goods and services tax) records, and other business documents. Your Long-Term Business Visa can be used as a step toward gaining residency under the Entrepreneur category. You can apply for residency as an entrepreneur after two years of successfully running your business or after six months if you have invested at least $500,000 into the business.

Renewing Your Visa

If you have been in New Zealand on a work visa for two years and wish to stay longer, you have two options: You can apply for permanent residency or for an extension of daughter, who had just finished her master's degree in marketing, suggested my wife Eve and I should consider starting our own relocation/resettlement company. We created On Arrival as a resettlement service which would focus on the needs of families, not just on finding a house for new arrivals as other companies were doing.

To find prospective clients, we visited all of the recruitment companies and many corporate organizations and government departments that were advertising internationally, and we went to a "Working In" expo in London. Over the next few months we recruited our initial consultants in Auckland, Hamilton, Christchurch, and Dunedin. All of our consultants have gone through an international move themselves, so they have empathy with incoming families.

In the next year we grew from a Wellington-based company to full national coverage, and we now have 25 consultants in 14 locations throughout New Zealand.

What types of services does On Arrival provide to newcomers?
On Arrival works alongside our clients' HR teams to help resettle new employees and their families. Our core services include pre-arrival, arrival and orientation, home search, school selection, community orientation, and spouse and family support services. We have formed alliances with several organizations that provide additional "value add" services for our clients, such as immigration and visas, furniture removal, setting up bank accounts, international funds transfer, mortgage financing and insurance, IRD registrations, purchasing furniture, and car purchase.

How long does it take most people to feel "settled in" after they move?
It generally takes two years. In the first year they are missing friends and family, they tend to compare everything to "back home," and realize how far New Zealand is from their home. If the family does not settle and establish a support base quickly, this becomes the major reason for their returning home.

We have been here 29 years now, and New Zealand is an amazing country in which to live and raise your children.

your work visa. Either way, you will need to begin this process well before your original visa expires so that your new visa or permit has time to be approved before you find yourself in the country illegally.

RESIDENCE FROM WORK

If you have been in New Zealand on a Work to Residence Visa and want to become a permanent resident, you can use the Residence from Work stream to apply. To qualify, you must have worked full-time in New Zealand for at least 24 months with a work visa. Depending on your category of work, you will also have to show that your base salary is at least $45,000-50,000, and that you will continue to work in a field that requires more employees. Again, the government only wants new residents who can fill in shortages in the workforce that New Zealanders aren't filling. You'll also need to meet English language requirements under this category, but that shouldn't be a problem for most North Americans. Applying under Residence from Work should be slightly more straightforward and faster than applying for residency from scratch. You can also apply for residency after two years of running your own business under the

Entrepreneur category. If you have invested at least $500,000 in your business, you may be eligible for residency after just six months.

RESIDENCY PERMITS

For certain people, it is possible to skip the work visa period altogether and apply for permanent residency right away. If you've decided that permanent residency is for you, you'll need to go through quite a stack of paperwork, which is easier to accomplish if you start it in your home country. Acquiring police certificates that prove you do not have a criminal record, for example, is much more straightforward if you are there to be fingerprinted in person.

But for many seeking residency, you will already have been in New Zealand for an extended period on a student or work visa. Be prepared for several months of effort to gather everything you need for your residency application, and be patient. As a permanent resident, you can stop worrying about conditions for getting a job or having to work in a specific field, and after your first year, you'll be eligible to vote in New Zealand elections. After your first two years as a permanent resident, you can spend as much time as you like outside of New Zealand and always be considered a resident when you return.

Skilled Migrant Category

This category allows Immigration New Zealand to prioritize who they will grant residency to, based on how well they fit the current workforce needs of the country. Applicants are assessed using a points system based on a number of factors. These include age (you must be under 55 to apply), type of work experience, type of qualifications, work experience and/or work offers in New Zealand, whether you have family living in New Zealand, and your partner's ability to also meet eligibility requirements.

The application process happens in two stages. First, you must complete an Expression of Interest, which is then entered into the application pool for up to six months. If your application is not selected after six months, you must apply again to remain in the running. At this time, the minimum number of points needed to have your application considered is 100. However, your application will automatically move forward if you have at least 140 points. Currently, an offer of skilled employment in New Zealand will earn you 50-60 points, an undergraduate degree will earn you 50 points, and a postgraduate degree will earn you 60 points. Your work experience in skilled employment can earn you 10-30 additional points depending on how long you've been working. You'll get 10 bonus points if your job is going to be outside of Auckland (to encourage more even settlement of the country). Even your age is worth points (you earn more points if you are over 20 and under 55). You can earn bonus points if you work in a field where there is a shortage of skills, or if your job is in Canterbury and on the Canterbury skill shortage list. When you are ready to assess your chances of getting approved, go to the Immigration New Zealand website to check on the latest point tables, because they can change at any time.

The cutoff levels are adjusted fortnightly (every two weeks) depending on the number of applications in the system and how many the immigration officials want to let through. There is an Expression of Interest fee when you apply, $510 if you apply on-line and $650 if you apply on paper. This dissuades people from applying if they aren't really committed to immigrating.

Once you have been selected from the pool, you will be asked to submit an application for residency within four months. This is where most of the paperwork comes in, including medical certificates, police certificates, and a birth certificate that names both of your parents. There is an interview as part of the application process, which will either be held in person (if you are in New Zealand or somewhere with a New Zealand Immigration office) or over the phone. There's another fee to pay with your final application, which is currently around US$2,400. On top of that, if your application is successful, you'll be charged a tax of $310 per person.

If your residency is approved, you will be granted a permanent resident's visa and a returning resident's visa. The returning resident's visa allows you to reenter the country after you leave. It expires after two years and you will have to apply for a new one at that time. If you have not spent at least 183 days in New Zealand during each of your first two years as a resident, you may be denied a new returning resident's visa.

Investor Category

If you have a large amount of capital and want to invest in your new home country, there is a residency category for investors. The Investor and Investor Plus categories were introduced to encourage investors to use their funds to help New Zealand businesses. The requirements for these two categories are:

- Investor, for those investing at least $1.5 million and having a minimum of three years of business experience. You must also have an additional $1 million in settlement funds (money to live on). Applicants must be under 65 years old and have an IELTS (English test) level of at least three. Additional points are given for younger applicants, those with more money to invest, and those with more business experience and better English skills.

- Investor Plus, for immigrants investing at least $10 million. There are no age or English-language requirements for this category, but applicants must invest their money in assets other than those meant for personal use, such as residences or vehicles.

Entrepreneur Category

If you have been operating a business successfully in New Zealand for at least two years (probably under a Long-Term Business Visa), then you may be eligible for residency under the Entrepreneur category. You will need to own at least 25 percent of the business and to have worked at that business for at least two years. In addition, you will be judged on your level of business experience, and you must still be in the same business for which you were granted your original visa. The Entrepreneur category has no age limit, so if you are over 55 this may be a good way to achieve residency in New Zealand.

Family Category

If you have family members in New Zealand who are New Zealand citizens or permanent residents, you may qualify for residency under the Family category. Each year the government sets a particular quota of places available under this category, and applications are selected by ballot. In some years, there are no places at all, so check with Immigration New Zealand before you count on this option.

Before you can apply, your New Zealand family member has to sponsor you, which means that they must be in a position to take financial responsibility for you for at least two years after you arrive. Your sponsor must have been a resident of New Zealand for at least three years before you apply.

In order to act as your sponsor, your family member must be one of the following: your parent, your adult child, your adult grandchild, or your adult brother or sister. If you have an appropriate sponsor with the resources to offer support, your partner and children can also be included on the application.

Partner Visa

If you've fallen madly in love with a Kiwi, or a New Zealand resident, and want to live happily ever after Down Under, your partner can sponsor you for residency. In order for this to happen, you must both be 18 or older and have been in a genuine, stable relationship for at least 12 months. It does not matter whether this is a relationship between partners of the same gender or different genders.

To sponsor you, your partner must be able to support you financially for at least two years after you gain residency. You'll also have to provide evidence that your relationship is genuine and stable, such as records showing that you live together and statements from friends and family.

If your partner is not a New Zealand citizen, he or she will have to have been a resident for at least three years before sponsoring you.

RETIRING IN NEW ZEALAND

People who have visited New Zealand often dream of retiring there. The laid-back lifestyle, uncrowded beaches, affordable golf courses, and great outdoors provide a wonderful opportunity to enjoy your golden years. However, New Zealand is more interested in attracting young, productive immigrants than retirees. To immigrate after your working days are over requires, to be frank, a lot of cash in your bank account. If you don't qualify under either of the categories below, your other options are the Investor Category (if you are under 65 years old) or the Investor Plus Category (at any age) described earlier in this chapter.

Temporary Retirement Visa

Immigration New Zealand responded to the demand for a way for those over 65 to live in New Zealand by creating the Temporary Retirement Visa. As the name suggests, this does not allow you to stay in New Zealand permanently. The two-year visa can be granted to those aged 66 and over who invest at least $750,000 in New Zealand for a minimum of two years. You must also have at least $500,000 in "maintenance funds" to support yourself while in New Zealand and purchase comprehensive health insurance to cover your stay.

You can stay for longer than two years by reapplying for the visa before it expires. Immigration New Zealand does not specify how many times you may reapply for the

© GERHARD PRETORIUS

Becoming a New Zealand citizen is a proud moment for immigrants.

visa, so it's possible that you could just keep getting a new visa every two years for as long as your money holds out.

Parent Retirement Category

If you have an adult child who is a New Zealand citizen or permanent resident, you can apply for residency under the Parent Retirement Category. Again, this option is only open to people with money to invest. You will need to invest at least $1 million in New Zealand for a minimum of four years to qualify.

On the bright side, since this category makes you a permanent resident, you will qualify for public health care in New Zealand and receive all of the other benefits of residency.

BECOMING A CITIZEN

If you have made the decision to live in New Zealand permanently, you may wish to eventually become a New Zealand citizen. As a citizen you will be able to obtain a New Zealand passport. Citizenship applications go through the Department of Internal Affairs.

You can apply for citizenship after living as a permanent resident in New Zealand for at least five years. You will have to have spent at least 240 days of each of the five years in New Zealand in order to qualify. New Zealand allows multiple citizenships, so you will not be asked to renounce your original nationality in order to become a New Zealander. However, some countries do not allow multiple citizenships and will no longer consider you a citizen if you hold citizenship in another country. Both the United States and Canada allow multiple citizenships, as long as you do not renounce your former citizenship when you become a New Zealand citizen.

Moving with Children

Many immigrants come to New Zealand because they want their children to grow up here. It may be different from home, but your children are likely to adjust to New Zealand life even faster than you do. Children are naturally curious and accepting of new things. The older your children are, the more likely it is that they will experience culture shock and homesickness. You can help by preparing them for the move and allowing them to keep some ties with their friends back home.

BABIES AND PRESCHOOL-AGE CHILDREN

In many ways, the youngest children are the easiest to move. They have not had the time to get attached to their homes and forge deep friendships. To make the transition as smooth as possible, bring some items from home that will give your baby or pre-schooler a level of comfort. Familiar toys, blankets, and the like will take away some of the fear of the unknown.

Once you arrive in New Zealand, you will be able to make use of Plunket resources. Plunket runs offices all around the country that offer advice to new parents, rent out approved car seats, run toy libraries, and have local information about playgroups, day care, and other new-parent needs. Plunket also has a toll-free phone line where parents can speak to a registered nurse for advice about their children.

Kids will have plenty of fun at events like this Medieval Festival.

© MICHELLE WAITZMAN

DAILY LIFE

SCHOOL-AGE CHILDREN

Try to prepare your children for the move by teaching them about New Zealand before you leave home. Show them on a globe where they will be living, and tell them about the unusual animals that live there. Using the Internet, find pictures of the city where you are planning to settle. The more your kids know, the less anxiety they will have about moving.

Starting school in a new country will be stressful, but New Zealanders are used to having immigrants appear at any time during the school year. Most schools are happy to provide extra support for foreign students, even if English is not a problem. If you are concerned about your children getting confused by a midyear move, try to arrive in New Zealand in January so your kids can start the new school year in February with all of their classmates.

TEENAGERS

Teens may be the most reluctant to immigrate. They will have friends they don't want to leave behind, and perhaps romantic relationships as well. Hopefully you can get your teenagers excited about the adventures that await them in New Zealand. If they are skiers, hikers, or enjoy other outdoor activities, you may be able to dazzle them with New Zealand's natural wonders.

One way to encourage your teenagers is to embrace their generation's passion for social networking. Have them find Kiwis on the Internet by using Facebook, Twitter, YouTube, and other popular sites. They may even have made friends by the time they arrive!

Your teens may feel a bit left out at school until they get up to speed on topics that interest Kiwi kids, such as rugby and the latest episode of *Shortland Street* on TV. But given a bit of time and a lot of understanding, they will likely settle in and enjoy their new home.

Moving with Pets

It's hard to say goodbye to a pet, but it can be very complicated to immigrate with one. Before you make a decision about bringing your pet with you to New Zealand, take all of the issues into consideration. You'll need to start the process up to six months before you move, ensuring that your pet has the proper medical clearance. The long journey could be very hard on some animals, particularly older ones, and then they are going to be stuck in quarantine for a month after arriving in New Zealand. All in all, moving your dog or cat to New Zealand is likely to cost several thousand dollars.

Before you even consider moving your dog or cat, a visit to the vet is necessary. Your pet will need up-to-date rabies shots, a microchip, and certain blood tests required by New Zealand. The Ministry for Primary Industries is in charge of animal imports and can give you all of the forms and details. A rabies test must be taken at least six months before the animal comes to New Zealand, and the test will be repeated before the animal can leave quarantine.

There are only five approved quarantine facilities in the whole country, so you'll have to arrange a place for your pet and pay the boarding fees, which run $15-50 per day depending on the facility and the size of your pet. Because of this quarantine rule,

© MICHELLE WAITZMAN

Moving with your pet is expensive and complicated.

your pet will be met at the airport by a ministry official and taken directly to quarantine. You'll be able to visit with your pet during the 30 days of quarantine, but this can still be a pretty traumatic period for a dog or cat to endure.

Certain breeds of dog have been banned in New Zealand, and if your pet is one of these, you will not be allowed to bring it into the country: American pit bull terrier, Dogo Argentino, Japanese tosa, and Brazilian fila. Crossbreeds containing those breeds are also banned.

DANGERS TO YOUR PET

Your pet should be quite safe in New Zealand. Rabies and other diseases are well controlled here. Keeping your pet's shots up to date should take care of most major diseases. Your pet may occasionally suffer a bout of fleas, but this is easily treated.

Many dog owners in New Zealand allow their dogs to walk off leash. This is not officially encouraged, but it is not often prosecuted unless there is an attack of some kind. This means that your dog is always in some potential danger from other, aggressive dogs. If your cat is an outdoor cat, it will also be exposed to more aggressive animals.

One major danger to dogs in the bush and parkland areas is a poison used to control the possum population. The poison is called 1080, and it takes the form of green pellets. If your dog eats any of these pellets or tries to eat a dead possum that has been poisoned, it can be fatal. There is no antidote to 1080, so keep a close eye on pets in the wilderness.

BUYING A PET IN NEW ZEALAND

Keeping pets is common in New Zealand, so you'll have no trouble finding an animal companion for your family after you settle in. Dogs and cats are the most common pets. Buying from reputable breeders is the best way to be sure you're getting a healthy, well-bred pet. Animal shelters, like the SPCA, have dogs and cats waiting for adoption. Puppy mills do exist in New Zealand, so it's best to avoid buying a dog or cat from an unknown breeder or pet shop.

Cats are often allowed to wander outside, but it is up to you whether you would prefer to have an indoor cat. With the way people drive in New Zealand, I'd be pretty keen to keep my pets off the streets! Along with dogs and cats, you will be able to purchase birds, fish, and other popular companions. Snakes are not permitted in New Zealand.

Dogs must be registered annually, which costs anywhere from $50 to over $100. Registration is done at the regional level, so check with the regional council where you live for its fees and regulations. Domestic dogs must also get microchipped. Rules and fees differ for working dogs on farms and for special needs dogs.

What to Take

A lot of your possessions will do you absolutely no good in New Zealand, because the electricity here is on a different voltage. So before your pack up all of your appliances, electronics, and computer hardware, make sure that you know what will be involved in making them function Down Under. You may find that it's not worth the expense of having them adjusted.

Your nonelectrical possessions are another story. Shipping to New Zealand can be quite expensive. Shipping a whole household of furniture can cost several thousand dollars, depending on where you live and how much you own. If you are paying your own moving costs, have a good think about how much your possessions are worth to you. If your house is full of antique oak, you will likely want to keep it. If your furniture all came from Walmart or is made of chipboard (particleboard), it may be easier to just buy new furniture after you move. Also consider how long you plan to live in New Zealand; if you know you'll be returning to your home country after a year or two, you may not want to bother with moving all your things twice. Renting a storage unit for your belongings can be a good option.

APPLIANCES AND ELECTRONICS

New Zealand's electricity is on a 240-volt system. Most North American appliances will not work here. Unless your appliance is specifically designated as dual-voltage, you would be advised not to try using it in New Zealand.

Large Appliances

Your washing machine, dishwasher, stove, fridge, and other large appliances from North America are not compatible with New Zealand's electrical system. If you are planning to return to North America after a stay in New Zealand, you may wish to put these appliances into storage. Otherwise, you might as well sell them. New appliances are easy to buy in New Zealand, and if you are staying in the country for a limited time, you can rent them instead of buying. Over the long term, however, it is more economical to buy than to rent.

Stocking the Pantry

Once you arrive in New Zealand, you'll want to get some food onto those empty shelves in the pantry or the fridge as soon as possible. Your first trip to the supermarket in a new country can be a bit daunting. It's harder to find what you're looking for than you might expect. Some things are simply not found in New Zealand, such as frozen juice concentrates or corn syrup. Other items go by different names than you're used to. Here are some common items you may be seeking at the local supermarket, translated into their Kiwi names:

- green or red pepper—capsicum

- zucchini—courgette

- eggplant—aubergine

- sweet potato/yam—kumara

- chili powder—chilli seasoning

- whole milk—full-fat milk

- skim milk—trim milk

- ketchup—tomato sauce

- mild cheddar—mild cheese

- sharp/old cheddar—tasty cheese

- kiwi—kiwifruit

- Jell-O—jelly

- jelly—jam/preserves

- cookies—biscuits

- granola bar—muesli bar

- oatmeal—porridge

- breaded (meat/fish)—crumbed

Small Electric Appliances

Some small appliances, such as hair dryers, razors, and battery chargers, are designed to work with multiple voltages. Check the original manual from your appliances to see if this is the case before you bring them to New Zealand. If they are indeed dual-voltage, you will only need to buy a plug adapter in order to use them in New Zealand. Adapters for Australia and New Zealand are the same, with two flat prongs angled inward. Some have a third flat prong for grounding.

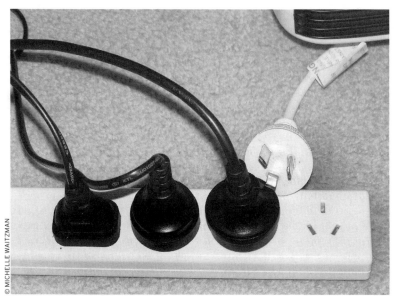

DAILY LIFE

New Zealand and Australia use flat, angled plugs.

If you are attached to a small appliance that does not take multiple voltages, you can purchase a transformer, which will make the appliance comply with a new voltage. These can be expensive, around $200-250, so you wouldn't want to buy one for each of your small appliances. But if your appliance would be very expensive to replace, the transformer may be a worthwhile purchase.

Battery-Powered Appliances

Anything that runs on batteries will not be a problem when you move to New Zealand. All of the same standard batteries are widely available in New Zealand, including lithium-ion batteries for cameras. You should decide whether to bring battery-powered items along based on the space they take, how much you use them, and how expensive they would be to replace.

COMPUTERS AND TELEPHONES

Phone systems differ from country to country, and New Zealand's can be a bit confusing. What was until recently a Telecom monopoly is now fragmented. New technology is opening up more possibilities for both landlines and cell phones. There's a possibility you can use your old phone here, but it may be best to wait until you arrive and buy the phone that works best with the provider you choose.

As for your computer, you should be able to ship it down to New Zealand and have it work, as long as you are able to get an appropriate power supply.

Converting Your Computer

Computers from North America will be running on a 110/120V power supply. Some will have switches that allow you to convert to a 220V or 240V power supply, in which case all you will need is a new plug adapter. If your power supply does not adjust, you can buy a new one when you get to New Zealand. This will be much cheaper than buying a whole new computer. Many laptop computers now come with variable voltage power supplies; if yours says something like 100-240V on it, you will be able to use it in New Zealand with only a plug adapter.

Tablets and e-readers from anywhere in the world should work in New Zealand as long as you have a variable voltage charger. If necessary, you can buy a new charger in New Zealand.

Remember that if you are bringing a laptop computer or tablet with you as carry-on baggage when you move, you may have to turn it on for airport security. Make sure the battery is charged before you head off.

Telephones with Power Supplies

Regular phones that plug into a wall jack should be usable in New Zealand. The wall plug is slightly different, but electronics shops can sell you an inexpensive cord or adapter that should work with your phone. If your phone also has a power plug, as many cordless phones do, it will need a transformer like other small appliances. You will probably find it is not worth the cost of converting these phones and just buy a new phone when you arrive in New Zealand. Some Kiwi phone service providers are starting to use IP (Internet protocol) technology to deliver their phone services, in which case your old phone won't work anyway.

Cell Phones

A lot of factors affect whether your cell phone will work in New Zealand. Some companies put a "lock" on their phones so you cannot use another company's SIM card in them. This makes them useless unless you want to continue paying high roaming rates for every call.

If you have an unlocked phone, you will need to determine whether it works on any of New Zealand's providers' systems. Vodafone uses GSM, UMTS, HSDPA, and LTE networks. Spark uses HSDPA UMTS, and LTE networks, and 2degrees uses GSM, UMTS, and LTE networks. If all of this sounds completely confusing to you, it may be easier to just buy a new phone after you move! Bear in mind that the "free phone" offers you may be used to from North American providers are rare in New Zealand, so be prepared to fork out anywhere from $90 for the cheapest phones to over $1,000 for the latest smartphones. You can choose either monthly call plans or "pay as you go" options.

SHIPPING OPTIONS

Once you have decided what to bring to New Zealand, the next decision is how to ship it. Shipping over the entire Pacific Ocean can be a slow process, so make sure you have packed enough essentials in your luggage before you go. Carry a wide range of clothing, plus your job search materials and other important paperwork, with you. If your shipment is held up for any reason, it could be months before you see the contents again.

Moving or relocation companies are most often used to ship household contents. There are many of these companies around, so get several quotes before you choose and check around to see if their reputations are good. Some will require you to pay for an entire shipping container, even if you don't fill it. Others will charge by weight or volume of goods.

Ask a lot of questions before you choose a shipping company: Will the company pack your items? Is there an extra charge for packing materials and boxes? How much will insurance cost and what will it cover? Will the items be delivered door-to-door, or will you have to make special arrangements to retrieve things from the port in New Zealand? What company will you be dealing with at the New Zealand end? How long will it take for your shipment to arrive? All of these factors are just as important as price.

For those who like to take matters into their own hands, you may be able to skip the hiring of a relocation company and simply rent a container from a shipping company. That will leave you the tasks of arranging to have the container brought to your home, packing it yourself, insuring the contents, having the container brought to the port, and having it brought from the New Zealand port to your home there. It's a lot more work, but it could save you thousands of dollars.

Biosecurity

When your goods arrive in New Zealand, they will have to be approved by the Ministry for Primary Industries, as well as customs, before you can claim them. The paperwork involved is not onerous if you are organized (it took me half a day), but it will help if you keep detailed packing lists for all of your boxes.

For any items that have been used outdoors (tents, boots, gardening equipment), you should detail how they were cleaned before packing. The ministry will require you to have dirt-contaminated items treated at your expense if they were not well cleaned before entering the country. Plants and most animal products will not be allowed in, so give away your houseplants before you move.

HARD-TO-FIND PRODUCTS

You should be able to find everything you need to set up a household in New Zealand. However, if you are very brand sensitive, you may want to stock up on some items from home. Some clothing labels, like Gap and Banana Republic, haven't made their way to New Zealand yet. Clothing and footwear are generally more expensive in New Zealand, so you should bring all you can with you.

Sometimes the little things are what you miss the most. I tend to stock up on solid antiperspirant when I go back to North America, as most Kiwi shops only stock sprays and roll-ons.

FIREARMS

Pistols, military-style assault rifles, and automatic weapons are not allowed to enter New Zealand. For permitted firearms, you will need to have a permit to import issued by the New Zealand Police. New immigrants are encouraged to leave their firearms in their home country until they have gained residency in New Zealand. At that point, you will be eligible for a permit to import firearms and a firearms license, which is necessary to own a firearm in New Zealand.

Unless you are strongly attached to your current firearms, it may be more convenient to sell them before you move and buy new firearms once you are a New Zealand resident. Before you can own a gun in New Zealand, you will need a firearms license. You must be 16 years old or older to get a license, as well as provide three pieces of identification, a passport-sized photo, and contact details for two references, one of whom is your next of kin. The current fee for a license is $126.50 and it is good for 10 years. If you want to buy a pistol or a semiautomatic weapon, you will need a special endorsement on your license.

CARS

Bringing your car to New Zealand is an expensive choice. To begin with, it can cost around $3,000-4,000 to ship a car from overseas. If you are coming from North America, remember that cars in New Zealand are right-hand drive. There is no point in bringing a left-hand drive (North American) vehicle to a country where it won't be deemed roadworthy. In most cases, you will need to have your car converted to right-hand drive before you are allowed to drive it. This is a very expensive process—thousands of dollars—and not all cars can be converted. Unless your vehicle is a one-of-a-kind collector's model, it would be more cost-effective to buy a car when you arrive.

HOUSING CONSIDERATIONS

You'll sometimes hear Kiwis refer to the "quarter-acre dream." That's because residential areas in most New Zealand towns and cities were originally divided into quarter-acre lots, and the dream was to have your own family home on one of those lots. Until quite recently, this was a dream that came true for the average New Zealander. But over the past 15 years or so, a real estate boom put home ownership out of reach for some and created a larger market for condominiums and rentals. The recession of 2009 put an end to the boom in most cities, but unless prices actually drop significantly, it will take the average income a while to catch up with the cost of home ownership.

As a newcomer, you'll have to decide whether buying a home in New Zealand is the right choice for you. Interest rates are higher in New Zealand and house prices can be daunting in some areas. On the other hand, owning a home is a big part of being a true Kiwi and, generally, investing your money in real estate pays off. Having your own little piece of New Zealand can also help you to feel more settled, giving you some roots in your new home. It's a chance to really say something about yourself, whether you choose a 19th-century cottage or a modern high-rise.

Housing Terms in New Zealand

Reading a real estate listing can sometimes seem like trying to crack a secret code. Here are some common terms and abbreviations you're likely to come across.

HOUSING TERMS

- cottage—small house with 1-3 bedrooms, usually older

- villa—old Victorian house, more spacious than a cottage

- bach—holiday home (sometimes also called a "crib" on the South Island)

- apartment—condominium unit in a multiunit building, usually a high-rise

- unit—part of a multiunit dwelling, usually low-rise or semidetached

- carport—a covered parking spot for a car, not a garage

REAL ESTATE ABBREVIATIONS

- ac—air conditioning

- BBO/BEO—buyer's budget over/buyer enquiry over (minimum asking price)

- bir—built-in closet (the "r" here stands for "robe," short for wardrobe)

- bv—brick veneer

- det—detached

- elhws—electric hot water service

Renting

Renting a home was traditionally a student-only lifestyle in New Zealand, but has gained popularity as house prices have increased. It's a good way to limit your commitment to a particular city or neighborhood when you first arrive, so you can take your time deciding where you would like to live in the long term. It can also give you some more time to improve your credit rating in the country so you will qualify for a bigger mortgage. In major cities, the rental market has been growing by leaps and bounds as property investors rent out their investment houses and city dwellers put ownership on the back burner for the time being.

Renting in New Zealand has its own set of laws and assumptions, which differ from the situation in North America. Be sure you understand the conditions of your rental before you sign a tenancy agreement.

When choosing a rental property, it's always preferable to visit in person before

- ens—ensuite bathroom

- f/furn—fully furnished

- gge—garage

- ghws—gas hot water service

- GV/QV—government valuation/quotable valuation

- ldr—lounge/dining room

- neg—negotiable

- osp—off-street parking

- pa—per annum

- pmth—per month

- pw—per week

- rf—roof

- s'out—sleepout cabin

- tf—timber frame

- ww crpt—wall-to-wall carpet

deciding. Remember that most New Zealand homes are not centrally heated, so the amount of sunshine a home sees is quite important. Good rental properties can disappear quickly, so if you like a place, don't wait too long to apply for it.

LEASES OR TENANCY AGREEMENTS

When you rent, you will be asked to sign a Tenancy Agreement. This can cover any period of time but is usually between three months and one year. Some agreements are for a set period, after which, if both parties agree, the tenancy will continue on a month-by-month basis. This is called a periodic tenancy, and in this situation the landlord must provide 60 days' notice before raising the rent. If either party wants to end a periodic tenancy, they are required to give 21 days' notice.

Your rent will usually be stated as a weekly amount. Often you will be asked to make rent payments either weekly or fortnightly (every two weeks) rather than monthly. This may be negotiable if, for instance, you are only paid monthly. You'll probably be asked to pay one or two weeks' rent in advance when you move in, on top of your bond payment. The landlord cannot ask for more than two weeks' rent in advance. If a rental agency is in charge of the leasing, you may also be asked to pay an agency fee at the beginning of your rental. Ask about this up front, because agencies can charge anywhere from one week's to four weeks' rent as a fee.

Bond is an amount set aside when you begin your tenancy to cover any damage that you do to the property (known as a security deposit in the United States). It can also be used to compensate the landlord for rent you haven't paid. This bond amount is usually 2-4 weeks' rent, but it cannot exceed four weeks' rent. So be prepared for that extra expense when you start a new lease. Your landlord cannot hold on to the bond money, but must give it to the Tenancy Services agency of the Ministry of Business, Innovation and Employment. When you end your tenancy, you will apply to get your bond payment returned. The landlord must then justify any claims against it, such as repairs needed because of something you did. In the case of disagreements, Tenancy Services has a dispute resolution service.

It's important to inspect the property carefully when you move in, making sure that you take note of damage and inform the landlord. Put it all in writing so that your landlord cannot claim later that you caused the damage. When you move out, the landlord will inspect the property to make sure everything is clean and undamaged.

Your tenancy agreement will probably have details about the property you are renting and what you are allowed to do. It may state whether you can have pets, whether you can smoke inside, and how many people are allowed to live in the property.

Renting Appliances and Furniture

Many rentals come with only a cooktop (stove) and oven. This leaves you in need of

As inner-city living gains popularity, new apartment buildings are being built to keep up with demand.

Leaky Liability

Generally speaking, the newer a house is, the less likely it is to need major repairs. However, this generality doesn't always apply to houses and apartments built in New Zealand between 1990 and 2005. During this time, a combination of factors allowed faulty building materials to be approved without proper testing. Poorly treated timber was used in framing; it subsequently allowed moisture to penetrate the wood, which has caused rotting frames and leaky buildings.

This was a widespread problem—some estimates put the number of affected homes at over 15,000. The government introduced a resolution service for people affected by the problem, through the Ministry of Business, Innovation and Employment.

If you are considering buying or renting a house that may have been built during the affected period, check carefully for signs of moisture damage on the walls, ceilings, and floors. Ask the agent or landlord whether there have been any leaks, and if you are buying, check the land information memorandum (LIM) to see whether any claims have been lodged or repairs have been done. If you are buying an apartment, check with the body corporate to see if there have been reports of leaks, and if they have been repaired. Ask what the repairs cost and how owners were charged. If new problems arise, does everyone pay an equal share, or does the affected owner pay his or her own costs?

Not only are leaky homes expensive to fix, they can also ruin your possessions and make the house unlivable. The faulty materials have since been taken off the market, so anything built now shouldn't have these issues. Anything built before 1990 or after 2005 should also be fine, although many older homes suffer structural damage eventually. With so many homes affected, however, owners are keen to dump these problem properties, so buyer beware.

a refrigerator at the very least, and possibly you'll also want a washer and dryer, dishwasher, and other appliances. If you're not staying in New Zealand long enough to justify buying all of these things, you can rent them instead. This can also be a good option if you think you will be moving often and don't want to have a truckload of household items to haul around. In fact, you can also rent all of your furniture and simply give it back when you move.

Over the long term this is more expensive than buying, so if you are planning to stay for two years or more, you may want to purchase your furniture and appliances.

SHARED FLATS

Flatting, or sharing a flat, has been popular with students for many years. It helps keep expenses down by sharing the rent, electricity bills, and other household expenses. In New Zealand, shared flats can range from splitting a two-bedroom apartment with another person to living in a six-bedroom house with a bevy of flatmates. If you are looking to flat with others, check the local newspapers for ads, as well as flatmate websites, and coffee shops and supermarkets that may have notice boards.

Flatting opportunities are most abundant near universities, but with house and rental costs rising, even young professionals are continuing to share flats. Many homeowners also rent rooms in their houses to help them cope with high mortgage payments.

TENANT RIGHTS

When you enter into a Tenancy Agreement, you have certain legal rights. Landlords who want to inspect the property (they can do this as often as every four weeks, but annually or semiannually is more common) must give you 48 hours' notice. If they are coming in to fix something, or sending someone to fix it on their behalf, you must be given 24 hours' notice.

Your landlord is responsible for fixing things that he or she owns, such as the plumbing, electrical wiring, and any appliances that are part of the property. You must let the landlord know immediately when something needs fixing and give reasonable time for the work to be done. But if the landlord ignores necessary repairs, you can ask Tenancy Services to intervene.

If you are late paying your rent, your landlord can give you a notice that allows you 10 working days to pay what you owe. After that, the landlord can apply to have your tenancy terminated.

During the time set out in your Tenancy Agreement, the landlord cannot raise the rent. However, when the agreement expires, you may be asked to renew at a higher rent. This can make it a good idea to agree to a longer-term rental, locking in your rent for a longer period of time.

COUNCIL FLATS AND STATE HOUSING

For those who are struggling financially, both the national and local government bodies can assist with low-cost housing. As you can imagine, there is a long waiting list for these homes, especially in major cities. The national waiting list has over 5,500 people on it.

To qualify for assisted housing, you must be a permanent resident and be able to show that you cannot afford to pay market rent. For national state housing, you must apply through Housing New Zealand. Many city councils have their own subsidized housing, for which you can apply through the council.

Your chances of getting a low-cost rental depend on your level of need, whether you are considered a good tenant, and how many others have applied.

Buying a Home

Owning a home is a point of pride for New Zealanders. So is doing your own renovations, so look out for shoddy, amateur work when you're checking out potential homes. There are a lot of things to consider when choosing a home to purchase in New Zealand, and you can't always count on real estate agents for a straight answer. It's "buyer beware," so be sure to do your homework before you sign on the dotted line.

New Zealand is no exception to the "location, location, location" rule of real estate, so learn about the neighborhoods where you are considering buying a home. Is it close to shops and schools, public transport, hospitals, and any other conveniences that are important to you? Does the area suit your lifestyle? What are the plans for the area in the future? The same house in different parts of New Zealand can vary in price by hundreds of thousands of dollars. So settling on a city or suburb is your first major decision.

House location is also important in determining whether it is likely to be a cold, damp home or a warm, airy one. Properties that get a lot of sun are more valuable than sheltered ones. The age and state of the house will also affect its value. Many homes in New Zealand are aging and in need of expensive upgrades to make them safe and comfortable. Find out the age of the wiring and plumbing, and whether any insulation has been added to the house. These upgrades can cost thousands, so you should factor these expenses into your offer price.

You can get a good idea about the value of a property by looking at its Ratable Value (RV), often quoted in real estate listings. This can also be listed as Quotable Valuation (QV) or Government Valuation (GV). This is the value placed on the property for tax purposes. However, properties can sell for considerably more or less than their listed values, depending on market forces.

TYPES OF PROPERTIES
Houses

Most homes in New Zealand are detached houses. In fact, the country is dominated by the three-bedroom bungalow. Most of these have one bathroom, and only some have a garage. Basements are rare. This is the standard in New Zealand, but there are many other housing options available. Many two-bedroom "cottages" remain from the Victoria era and can make lovely homes for couples or small families. Larger homes with four or more bedrooms are becoming more common, particularly in the affluent suburbs around Auckland, Wellington, and Christchurch. The closer you are to a city center, the less likely it is that your home will be on a quarter-acre property. As populations have increased, many properties have been subdivided and infill housing is the norm.

Apartments and Town Houses

If you are buying an apartment (condominium) or town house, you will probably be joining a "body corporate" as well. This is a board that looks after the common property associated with these kinds of dwellings. Find out what fees you will need to pay the body corporate and whether they are likely to increase regularly. Look into the activities and financial situation of the body corporate before you buy a property. If the common expenses are not managed well, it could become a nightmare for you in the future.

Lifestyle Blocks

If the rural lifestyle is what you're after, you may be interested in purchasing a lifestyle block. These are small farm properties, usually divided up after the sale of a larger farm, for those who want to live in the country but not own a working farm. Lifestyle blocks are popular with older people, who no longer need to commute into the city for work each day. This option allows you to have a large property without a huge price tag.

WORKING WITH REAL ESTATE AGENTS

Most home sales in New Zealand go through real estate agencies. Sellers use agents to get more exposure for their homes and hopefully a higher purchase price. In exchange for their efforts, agents usually charge a commission on the selling prices of the property (currently about 4 percent plus GST) and often an agency fee as well.

Sellers will usually be asked to sign an agreement stating that a specific agency will

DAILY LIFE

Half a Property?

Traditionally, New Zealand houses were built on quarter-acre lots so that everyone had a large garden to enjoy. But as cities have become more densely populated, the demand for housing has inspired many homeowners to subdivide their lots into two sections using a cross-lease (or X-lease), so that a second house can be built on what was once the backyard.

These subdivided properties create "in-fill housing." This means that although an area has been completely developed, new properties are built in the leftover spaces, increasing the population. Living in one of these homes means sacrificing a backyard, and often living very close to your neighbor.

If you are buying a larger property, it is a good idea to find out whether you would be allowed to create two sections from it, as this can raise the value of your purchase.

Some properties can be subdivided into two.

The local council determines where it will allow these divisions, and on which sections.

If you are buying a property on a section that has already been subdivided, apply to the local council for a land information memorandum (LIM), which will tell you whether the division was legally done. If not, you could run into a legal ownership nightmare later on. If you are buying the cross-leased portion of the section, you are actually buying a 100-year leasehold on the land, rather than a freehold title.

The closer to a major city you live, the more likely you are to find sections that have been split this way. If every section on the street has been subdivided, you might find that traffic is heavier than the street was designed for, or that there are a lot of cars parked on the road. These factors will all affect the value of your home in the long run.

be the only one trying to sell their home for a fixed period of time. This means that if they are not performing as well as you'd hoped, you will have to wait for that agreement to expire before replacing them with another agency. Read the fine print on your agency contract before you commit to an agent.

As a buyer, your main concern is resisting any bullying tactics from agents. They will sometimes try to pressure you into deciding quickly and paying the highest price they can squeeze out of you. Go into any negotiation with a clear idea of what you are willing to spend, and stick to your guns. It's easy to get carried away and find yourself with a huge mortgage to pay.

Agencies use a few different methods to sell homes, depending on what they think will fetch the highest price. The main options are selling by negotiation, where the agent deals individually with potential buyers to get the best possible price; by auction, where potential buyers all gather on one day to bid on the property and it is sold to the highest bidder that day (if the owner's minimum price is met); and by tender, which is more like a silent auction where interested buyers submit the price they will pay and the highest offer by a certain date will be accepted. For buyers, tender is probably the most frustrating way to deal with property sales. You'll have no idea how much other people have offered for the property, and the agent will try to convince you that there is a lot of demand.

Extra Charges

Often, real estate agents in New Zealand charge their clients more than just their agent's fee and commission. You may be asked to pay for advertising your property in glossy magazines, putting up signs in front of your house, and having an evaluation done. Be sure that you have talked to the agent about these extra fees before you sign up to let them sell your home. And I can't stress this enough: get everything (including the amounts of these fees) in writing.

PRIVATE SALES

With real estate agents taking a big chunk of cash from vendors, some prospective buyers are turning to private sales instead. If you are interested in buying from a private vendor, keep your eyes on the listings in newspapers, on the **Trade Me website** (www. trademe.co.nz), and even on local notice boards. If no real estate agency is named, you may be dealing with a private sale. Call and ask the vendors if they are selling privately.

The advantage to a private sale is that the vendor may be willing to sell at a lower price, since there are no commissions to pay. The disadvantage is that you will have to be sure you are dealing with all of the legal details properly. Make sure you use a legal agreement for the purchase, and check the land title to be confident that the vendor is the legal owner of the property.

INSPECTIONS AND EVALUATIONS

Before you agree to buy a property, you should get it professionally inspected. This is often a condition on the offer of purchase. That way, if you suddenly discover that the roof needs replacing or the wiring is likely to start a fire, you can walk away from the purchase. While real estate agents can't legally lie to you about any problems with the house, they are under no legal obligation to disclose problems. This is why an inspection is so important.

Often, the vendor's agent will recommend an inspection company. Remember that the agent is trying to get the sale done, and his or her inspector may not be looking out for your best interests. It's a good idea to ask around among friends or colleagues to see if anyone knows of a reputable inspector. Even choosing one from the phone book is better than accepting the first inspector the agent offers to you.

Be sure that your inspector covers all of the bases, including the roof, insulation, floors, electrical wiring, plumbing, windows, and any possible leaks or rotting timber. You can also have the house examined for pests, such as termites or cockroaches.

LEGAL DETAILS AND INSURANCE

A licensed conveyancer or property lawyer can be a good safeguard when you purchase a home, especially when you are new to the country. These professionals can help with things like checking the legal title on the property, ensuring that your purchase agreement is legal and includes everything you want included, drawing up transfer of ownership documents, arranging the financial settlement, and even negotiating the price and details of the purchase.

Whenever a property changes ownership in New Zealand, it must be registered with Land Information New Zealand. This requires a transfer document, which is usually supplied by your lawyer or conveyancer. The title certificate the vendor supplies will not only tell you whether that person is the rightful owner of the property, but also whether any mortgages have been taken out on it and if there are legal issues with the title.

For other detailed information about the property, you can get a land information memorandum (LIM) report from the local council. This costs a few hundred dollars, but will give you a complete history of the property, including major renovations done and how many owners it has had.

Insuring your property is important. Once you have purchased a home, arrange for property insurance that begins the day you take possession.

TAXES AND FEES

Happily, New Zealand does not charge a land transfer tax when you buy a property. There is also currently no tax on the capital gain when you sell property, as long as you have owned it for at least two years.

But the good news has to end somewhere, and it's with the local government. City and district councils get most of their funding from "rates," or property taxes. Your rates are based on the value of your home (according to the council, not the price you paid for it) and are evaluated annually. Rates differ from place to place, so they are another factor to consider when deciding where to settle. A general average would be in the $800 per year range.

Building or Renovating

Having your home built new is the surest way to get what you want, but it doesn't come cheap, and it can be very stressful. Finding a reliable builder, getting the proper consents from your local council, and purchasing a vacant lot in a good area can add up to a huge cost. Delays are always to be expected, and so are cost overruns. Renovating an older home is another option. Kiwis have always been big on fixing up old places, so the expectation is that you'll do some handiwork yourself. Finding a contractor to do it all for you can be a challenge in some areas.

BUYING LAND TO BUILD A HOME

The first step to building your own home is finding a vacant lot, or "section." The easiest place to find land is in newer suburbs, but sometimes parcels of land are available in more established neighborhoods, too. If an older home is on its last legs, you may get a good enough price to buy the property and demolish the existing house. If the area where you want to live is densely populated, this may be the only way to make room for a new house.

There are several large companies in New Zealand that specialize in building homes from scratch. They can make the process cheaper, because they already have standard designs available and can make bulk purchases of building supplies and finishing materials like flooring and tiles. They may also be able to guide you through all of the

© MICHELLE WAITZMAN

Building a house from scratch can give you exactly what you want.

building consents that are needed before you can begin. This is the easiest way to have a home built, but it won't allow you as many options as hiring your own architect to design your dream home from scratch.

Hiring an architect and builders gives you the chance to get everything you want in your new home, but it is the most expensive way to get a house. You may also face long delays if you are ordering fixtures and materials from overseas. You'll also need to coordinate all of the various tradespeople who need to work on the house at different times, such as electricians, plumbers, and plasterers. If you're handy, you may be able to save money by doing some work yourself, but for jobs where safety is an issue, like electrical wiring, a licensed professional must do the work.

Kitset Homes

A kitset home provides you with a set of plans and materials to build your own house. These are less expensive than custom-designed houses because they are premade based on standard designs. If you purchase a kitset home, you can either hire builders to put it all up for you or do a lot of the construction yourself if you are very ambitious and handy. You will also have to get someone to pour a concrete slab for you to build on.

You can get anything from a cottage to a barn to a two-story house as a kitset. It's a good idea to see some samples put together before you commit, to be sure you like the materials and the designs. And before you choose a design, make sure that it will work with the dimensions and layout of your section. Some homes, for instance, won't work if your section is on a hill.

Moving a House

Maybe you've found the perfect house, but it's in the completely wrong neighborhood.

Building a Dream House

California architect Michael and his wife Roslyn built a stunning home on a rural section in Martinborough on the North Island while they were still living in the United States. In 2012 they made their permanent move to New Zealand to take up residence in their dream home.

How did you go about finding a section of land to purchase?

In 2006, we passed through Martinborough in the Wairarapa on vacation and unexpectedly fell in love with the area. On a whim, we visited a local estate agent to see what kinds of properties were available. One of the properties was a 5-hectare (12-acre) section that a local farmer had recently subdivided. What appealed to us was that more than 90 percent of the property was native or regenerating bush, with a flat, cleared area that was a perfect homesite. We decided to purchase it within 10 days of seeing it. Two years later, we had a finished house.

How much red tape is involved in building consents and other construction paperwork?

The red tape was identical to what we experience in California. We did have to learn some new vocabulary, but nothing too strange ("consents" instead of "approvals," for instance). In our case the planning review process was pretty simple. Even with Michael being an architect, we worked with a local building designer as a consultant, and this helped tremendously with specific code and detailing issues.

How did you identify the best contractors for your build?

We interviewed three builders in the local area, toured some of the projects they'd done and checked references. The one we selected was a midsize construction firm with a stellar reputation. It helped that they were very familiar with the area and had good Internet communication skills.

What's different about the processes and materials in New Zealand as opposed to the United States?

The caliber of New Zealand builders and tradesmen was higher than what Michael was used to in California; probably the strong apprenticeship system in New Zealand fosters this high level of quality. In California just about anyone can call himself a builder. As for materials, most materials come in metric dimensions. The common use of corrugated iron was refreshing. The use of steel straps for cross bracing instead of sheathing the entire structure in plywood as we do in California was a little disconcerting at first.

Were you happy with the quality of the work and materials in the end?

Very happy except for a few electrical and plumbing things. When it came to these issues we found that the standard New Zealand "Master Builder" guarantee is as good as a handshake—that is to say, don't bother considering this a real factor in hiring anyone. We ended up paying extra to fix problems that should have been covered by the company. Still, the issues were fairly small, so we aren't too upset.

© MICHAEL MCKAY

Michael and Roslyn's dream house in Martinborough, on the North Island

Are there "American" expectations that people need to leave behind when building in New Zealand?

There are fewer people, fewer choices, fewer materials and products that are readily available, but you have to be pretty picky or very wealthy before these become a talking point. For most of us the choices are still overwhelming.

Now that you've had your house for a while, how are you feeling about the experience and the end result?

We are overwhelmed with the feeling of rightness about the house and the land. The best thing about the whole process was the relationships we formed. We have great rural neighbors, have become friends with all sorts of local people, our neighbors, distant neighbors, our builders, and people in town. We never expected this to happen so quickly; it probably wouldn't have unless we'd taken the big risk of building our house.

Any advice for other immigrants planning to build a home in New Zealand?

Spend time on your property, camp out, spend time with neighbors, and experience the property in all seasons before you build. We made some good assumptions and did well, but we may have been lucky.

Not a problem, as Kiwis often move entire houses on the back of a truck. Since most New Zealand homes do not have a basement, they can simply be lifted off their foundations and moved to a new location. It's not cheap, but it's certainly cheaper than building a whole new house.

HIRING BUILDING PROFESSIONALS

There are a lot of unscrupulous builders and tradespeople around, so try to get personal recommendations from people you trust. If possible, see samples of their other work, or ask for the names of former clients and check these references, before you sign them on.

Get quotes in writing for the work you need done, and make them as specific as possible. There should be definite time frames outlined as well, preferably with penalties for the builder for going past the scheduled deadlines. You can ask several builders to tender for the contract to build your house, and choose the one that comes in with the best combination of price, schedule, and services offered.

Make sure that anyone working on your wiring or plumbing is licensed to do so. If one guy claims he can do everything, he's probably doing it without a license.

DIY REGULATIONS

DIY (do it yourself) is a huge industry in New Zealand. Fixing your own home is a point of pride for Kiwis, and everything from decks to new kitchens are built over many weekends. This is something to be aware of as a home buyer, since DIY was not well regulated in the past. Shoddy work in older houses (and some not-so-old houses) can cost you thousands in repairs.

The government has recently tightened the rules about what homeowners can and can't fix for themselves. Any electrical work needs to be carried out by a licensed electrician, or at the very least checked over by one before the power is switched on. The same goes for anything connected to the water supply or gas mains. Installing your own cabinets, flooring, insulation, and the like is perfectly acceptable.

BUILDING REGULATIONS

You will need building consents from your local council before you can begin any building project. This ensures that you are using approved building materials, you have the right to build on that parcel of land, you are using licensed professionals, and there are no outstanding issues with your land, such as environmental concerns.

Getting the official paperwork done can be a significant cost, easily totaling a few thousand dollars. You'll need to acquire a project information memorandum (PIM), a building consent, have various stages of work inspected by an authorized inspector, and get code compliance certificates for the electrical work and gas fitting.

RENOVATING YOUR HOME

Renovating an existing house can be a good alternative to building from scratch. Older homes are often in need of updating to current standards, and adding new rooms can increase your property's value and improve your lifestyle.

Major renovations need to go through a consent process with your local council, just like building a new home. Consents are required for any major work, including additions, alterations, replacing pilings, demolition, plumbing, installing a wood-burning furnace or fireplace or an air-conditioning system, and even some kinds of decks and fences.

If you hire contractors to do your renovations, get their quotes in writing and make sure they detail what is included in the price. Also, try to get them to commit to a finishing date. Contractors often have several jobs on the go at once, leaving anxious clients with half-done renovations for weeks on end.

Insulation and Heating

New Zealand homes are notoriously cold and damp. Until very recently, there were few regulations in place regarding minimum standards for insulating homes. New homes are now forced to use insulation in the roof and under the floors, and windows must be double-glazed. But if your home was built before 2007, you cannot count on these features. In fact, you can pretty much guarantee they won't be there.

Adding insulation to your home will keep it warmer and drier during the winter. It will generally cost $3,000-5,000 for a whole house to do the roof and under the floor. Insulating the walls of an older house can be very expensive, and sometimes impossible. The government has introduced a subsidy to help more people upgrade their home insulation. For those who qualify, one-third of the cost of floor and ceiling insulation will be funded, up to a maximum of $1,500. Details are available from the Energy Efficiency and Conservation Authority (EECA).

Heating your home is another factor to think about when you decide what to buy. Central heating is rare in New Zealand, although it is starting to increase in popularity. Most older homes, if they have any built-in heating, have a wood-burner. These must be up to current standards because the older ones create too much pollution. Gas or electric wall heaters were built into many homes in the 1960s and 1970s. Now, heat pumps are being installed in many new homes and some older ones. Installing a heat pump is one of the most efficient ways to heat and will cost about $5,000.

If you live in a warm area, or don't mind a colder home, you can get away with using small electric or gas heaters that warm up one room at a time.

Household Expenses

Household expenses can run quite high in New Zealand, especially in older homes that are poorly insulated (or more often not insulated at all) and drafty. Electricity is provided by a number of companies, but rates are not particularly competitive. Keeping your home warm and dry, and your appliances running, will be one of your key expenses in New Zealand.

HEATING AND COOLING

As few homes in New Zealand are centrally heated or air-conditioned, your heating and cooling needs will probably be met with electrical or gas-powered appliances. Gas is generally more cost-effective than electricity in New Zealand, but because you pay a base fee for having your house connected to the gas mains, this savings is less than you might expect.

You can get your gas and electricity from the same company in some cases, or source them separately.

POWER

If everything in your home is run on electrical power (including your hot water, appliances, and heaters), then you can expect to pay around $2,000-2,500 per year. If you are using gas to heat your hot water and gas heaters or wood to warm your home, you may be able to cut your electricity costs significantly.

Gas can be a money-saver for households that use a lot of hot water and other gas-powered appliances. Overall, however, the average price of household utilities is only about $200 cheaper per year if you use a combination of gas and electricity, as opposed to electricity only. If you use mostly electricity and maintain a gas connection as well, your expenses will be even higher than electricity only.

Of course, energy prices fluctuate quite a lot, so it can be difficult to predict the most efficient power source in the future. Providers also have different charges depending on where in New Zealand you live, so do some careful comparison shopping. Many providers also give you a choice between a fixed daily charge or a variable charge based on your monthly use. So there are even more options to consider even after you choose a provider.

OTHER EXPENSES

Rates (property taxes) are your biggest additional expense as a homeowner in New Zealand. These will cost most families between $1,400 and $2,400 per year depending on where they live and the size of the property.

Other expenses to factor into your budget include telephone, Internet, and satellite or cable TV services. These can easily add another $1,000 per year or more to your household budget. (See the *Communications* chapter for more information on these services.)

LANGUAGE AND EDUCATION

You may think that language barriers are the one thing you won't have to worry about in New Zealand. After all, everyone speaks English, right? Yes and no. It's English, all right, but New Zealanders have their own brand of the language that takes some getting used to. For instance, what would you make of this sentence: "My mate's bub was at kindy and they had feijoa ice blocks for morning tea, and when my mate found out, she spat the dummy." So how much Kiwi English did you understand? Let me clarify the sentence for you: "My friend's child was at preschool and they had feijoa (a locally grown tangy fruit) popsicles for a snack. When my friend found out, she had a fit!" If you were a bit lost, don't worry. You'll catch on to Kiwi English soon enough.

Once you get into the swing of things, you'll catch on to all of the subtle differences in language, and probably even pick up a few words of Maori that get tossed around in everyday speech. But being new to the country, there's no shame in asking people to explain an unfamiliar word or phrase, or to repeat something if you can't understand their accents. (I admit that I heard a radio ad for a mattress company three or four times before I understood that they sold "beds" and not "beads"!)

If you have kids, you will probably find that they pick up the local slang pretty

quickly once they start going to school. There's no need to find "international" schools when you move your children to New Zealand. The curriculum at the schools is quite similar to North American systems, and your kids will be able to study and socialize with their Kiwi peers to help them integrate quickly.

Understanding Kiwi

As an English-speaker, you are at a great advantage over other immigrants to New Zealand, but sometimes you may question whether you're really speaking the same language. Getting used to spelling the British way takes time for folks from the United States, and there are a lot of phrases Kiwis use regularly that you will not have heard before. Then there are the Maori place-names, which may seem unpronounceable at first.

One common slang practice for Kiwis is to shorten words. Kindergarten becomes "kindy," sandwiches become "sammies," and sunglasses become "sunnies."

BRITISH SPELLING

Spelling in New Zealand follows British rules, which are also very close to Canadian rules. In fact, the only difference I've seen between Kiwi and Canadian spelling is that Canadian cars have tires, and Kiwi cars have tyres.

A few simple rules will offer most of the spelling clues you need if you are unfamiliar with British spelling. Most words that end with "er" in the United States end with "re" in New Zealand. For example: theatre, centre, metre. Many words ending with "or" in the United States end with "our" in New Zealand. For example: colour, harbour, labour, favour. Kiwis use double consonants when adding suffixes. For example, travelling and counselling. And when you go to the bank, you'll be asked whether you want a chequing account, not a checking account.

In the computer age, the easiest way of dealing with the differences is to switch your computer's spell-check to English (New Zealand) and run it on all of your correspondence before you send it to anyone.

MAORI WORDS

Most New Zealanders are not fluent, or even conversational, in te reo Maori (literally, the Maori language). Although it is an official language in New Zealand, it is only spoken by about 157,000 people out of the total population of 4.5 million. However, there are a few Maori words that most New Zealanders know and many use in their normal, English conversations.

Words of greeting, including *kia ora* (hello), *haere mai* (welcome), and *ka kite* (see you), are all commonly used. Other common terms include *whanau* (extended family), *iwi* (tribe), *hangi* (earth oven), and *koru* (spiral shape representing ferns). The other frequent use of Maori is in place-names. The Maori name Aotearoa is often used side by side with New Zealand to refer to the country. Many cities are known only by Maori names, and many mountains and other natural features have both English and Maori names in use. These include Aoraki/Mount Cook and Taranaki/Mount Egmont.

You won't have to learn any Maori to get along in New Zealand, but learning to

Sweet As! How to Sound Like a Kiwi

Although New Zealanders won't have any trouble understanding your accent, you can blend in more quickly by starting to use some typical Kiwi phrases when you speak. Here are a few things you can throw in to your everyday conversations to make you sound more like you belong.

- Sweet as!—Great, cool

- Good on ya—Good for you, way to go

- How ya going?—How are you?

- She'll be right—It'll be all right

- Mate or bro—Pal, buddy

- Spit the dummy—Have a fit, lose it

- Sausage sizzle—A fundraiser selling barbecue sausages

- Bring a plate—Potluck

recognize some of these commonly used words will make life easier. Of course, in some government jobs it would be necessary to learn some Maori language and customs, but those positions are relatively few.

Children attending school in New Zealand will likely learn a certain amount of te reo Maori as part of the curriculum, although it is not compulsory, but are unlikely to become fluent unless they participate in extra classes or attend a special immersion school (there are several around the country) where most classes are taught in te reo Maori.

Education

Education is a big priority for New Zealanders. Most children attend state-run schools, although private schooling is available as well. Your children could find things in New Zealand a bit different from what they're used to. Some high schools are single-sex, and most require students to wear uniforms.

There are national curriculum standards, so where you live should not greatly influence the quality of education your children receive. College and university programs cover pretty much every subject you'd expect, but in some cases enrollments are quite limited.

EARLY CHILDHOOD EDUCATION

For children between two and five years old, there are several choices if you want to get them started on their schooling (or just need a safe place for them while you're at work).

A Sign of the Times

In 2006, New Zealand added a third official language to English and Maori: New Zealand Sign Language (NZSL). This gives deaf New Zealanders the right to receive government services in their own language and also means that sign language skills have become part (albeit a small part) of the state school curriculum.

New Zealanders weren't always so keen to give different languages official recognition. Despite being the first language spoken in New Zealand, Maori was not an official language until 1987. But te reo Maori has made a comeback: There are now Maori language schools, Maori radio stations, and even a Maori TV channel.

It remains to be seen whether NZSL rises to those heights. It would seem unlikely given the small number of people who use it, but official recognition is the first step toward teaching more New Zealanders how to communicate with their deaf compatriots.

If you're able to stay home with your child but want to participate in some socialization and group learning for your child, you can join a playcentre or playgroup. These are community-based groups where parents and children come together at set times and places for learning through play. Usually there are fees involved to fund the rental of the space and the purchase of toys and other materials. The main difference between playcentres and playgroups is that playcentres are licensed and belong to the national New Zealand Playcentre Federation, which provides parent education programs. These programs give parents and caregivers training to help them enrich the children's activities.

There is also home-based care available, where a caregiver looks after a small group of children in a private home. This is a viable option for parents who can't stay home to look after their children but want them to be in a small, cozy group.

Education and care centers are licensed services that provide either all-day or part-day care. They can be community-owned or privately run. They may be based at the local church, at your workplace, or in child care centers. Teachers at these centers must be registered and hold a diploma in early childhood education. Other staff at the centers may have different qualifications. Each center will have its own rules about what age of children it accepts, but some will take infants. Fees vary depending on the center, your children's ages, and how long you are leaving them in care.

Kindergarten, or kindy, is different in New Zealand compared to the North American version. This is a type of preschool service run by qualified teachers, and most take children 2.5-5 years old. Most children attend half-day sessions, either morning or afternoon. Most kindergartens ask for a fee or a parent donation.

The government subsidizes kindergarten fees for three-, four- and five-year-olds. This is supposed to be enough to provide parents with 20 hours per week of free preschool education for their children, but in reality some schools charge an extra fee on top of the subsidy.

LEVELS AND SCHOOL TERMS

All children in New Zealand are required to attend school from their sixth birthday through their 16th birthday. However, children can start school as soon as they turn five (and can remain in school until they turn 19), and most do. There's no need to wait until the beginning of the next school year or term, as the schools will take your child at any time after his or her fifth birthday.

The school system in New Zealand is structured similarly to those in the United States and Canada. Your child will attend a primary school for the first 6-8 years, followed by intermediate or middle school for two or three years, then secondary school up to year 13. Secondary schools are often called colleges, but don't confuse these with university-level (tertiary) schools. The years are simply numbered 1-13, with year 1 being the equivalent of kindergarten in North America. Year 13 would be the equivalent of grade 12.

Your child will be assessed by the school to make sure he or she is put in the right academic level when he or she starts attending a New Zealand school. In most cases, the school will try to place your child with other kids of the same age, even if it means providing extra help to catch up in some areas. Most children from North America find that they are able to keep up with their Kiwi peers without too much help transitioning, though local history and geography could be problem areas.

Physical punishments such as hitting or caning are not allowed in New Zealand schools. If your child is punished, it will likely mean doing extra work or staying after school for a detention. In cases where more severe punishments are needed, a child may be suspended from school.

Children generally attend classes between 9am and 3pm in primary school and 8:45am and 3:15pm in intermediate and secondary schools. Some schools provide before- and after-school supervision for working parents at an extra cost. Most children will have to complete homework as part of their schooling. The amount and difficulty of their homework will vary from school to school and generally increase as they move into higher levels.

If you have the choice, it may be easiest on your children to plan your move so they begin school in New Zealand at the beginning of a school year. The first term starts during the first week of February. The New Zealand school year is divided into four terms. Each of the first three terms is followed by a two-week vacation period, and the final term is followed by a six-week Christmas/summer vacation.

Graduating from the New Zealand school system involves receiving a National Certificate in Educational Achievement (NCEA) qualification. This is like getting a high-school diploma in the United States or Canada. There are three levels of NCEA qualification, depending on what you require for your further education. Level 1 is roughly the equivalent of grade 10, level 2 is like grade 11, and level 3 is like grade 12. There are specific requirements for the number and type of credits a student must earn in order to qualify for university entrance (plus individual schools and programs may have additional requirements), so make sure that your child is taking everything that is required if you want to leave your options open. The Ministry of Education website has an overview of the system, or you can ask the school's guidance counselor to explain how it all works.

STATE SCHOOLS

Most children in New Zealand attend state-run schools. These are government-funded and do not charge tuition fees, although sometimes parents will have to pay

New Zealand School Calendar

The school year in New Zealand does not match up with the school year in the Northern Hemisphere. Summer holidays Down Under coincide with Christmas and New Year's. It can be a bit confusing during that first, transitional year, but once your children get used to their new system, they'll be back on track at their proper level.

Here is a list of the school terms in New Zealand. The dates are approximate because they vary from year to year and can also be slightly different depending on the school your children attend.

- Term 1: Early February to mid-April

- Term 2: Late April to early July

- Term 3: Mid-July to late September

- Term 4: Mid-October to mid-December

Each of the first three terms is followed by a two-week holiday. Then the final term is followed by approximately six weeks of summer vacation, from mid-December until early February. Schools are also closed on public holidays.

for uniforms and other extra items or activities. Ask the school's principal what extra charges or donations will be expected of you.

Most state schools are coeducational (boys and girls together) at the primary and intermediate levels. Some state secondary schools are also coeducational, while others are single sex for boys or girls. The state school your children attend will almost always be the closest one to where you live, although you are entitled to enroll them in any other school as long as there is space available. Preference will be given to students who live in the school's area.

There is also a category called State Integrated Schools. These are schools that were once private but have now been brought under the state system. Most of these schools are affiliated with a particular religious belief, and members of that specific group may be entitled to first right of entry to the school. Because the property these schools are on is not state-owned, you may be asked to pay "attendance dues" to cover the cost of maintaining the school property.

PRIVATE SCHOOLS

Also known as independent schools, private schools offer a similar range of subjects as the state schools. However, they may offer a wider choice of subjects or have smaller class sizes, which give the students more individual attention. Some independent schools also offer advanced instruction in specialties like music and the performing arts.

Some private schools are created very much in the image of British prep schools. The idea is to prepare young people to be the leaders of their generation. These schools may have very high entry standards and are sure to charge the highest fees, too.

Sending your child to a private or independent school will set you back some cash.

COURTESY OF EDUCATION NEW ZEALAND

Private schools sometimes offer extra resources and subjects.

Fees vary greatly, but the range is generally between $8,000 and $20,000 per year for tuition only; you may also pay for uniforms, enrollment fees, and/or building levies.

Boarding Schools

Boarding school is a concept that never really took off in North America, but it is alive and well in New Zealand. Around a hundred state and independent schools throughout the country offer boarding options. This can be a good opportunity for children whose parents live in very rural areas where attending the "local" school would involve a long commute each day. Some parents board their children at school so they can attend the best school possible, while others simply feel that a boarding-school experience is good for children, helping them to gain independence and maturity.

There are fees for boarding your children at a school, on top of whatever tuition fees may apply at private boarding schools. Some schools allow the kids to stay seven days a week, while others only board on weekdays and the students return home each weekend. The average cost of boarding at a school is around $10,000-12,000 per year.

UNIVERSITIES, POLYTECHNICS, AND PROFESSIONAL TRAINING

Any additional schooling after the secondary school level is called tertiary education. This includes universities, polytechnic colleges, and other professional training institutions. According to Statistics New Zealand, over half of New Zealanders aged between 25 and 34 have a tertiary qualification.

If you are thinking of coming to New Zealand to study, you're not alone. There are thousands of international students in New Zealand attending universities and other schools around the country. Some come for the experience of living in New Zealand, while others are looking for specific programs that New Zealanders do well. Some of the areas where Kiwi universities and schools excel are agriculture, biotechnology, and outdoor education. Studying in New Zealand requires a student visa (see the *Making the Move* chapter) unless you are a permanent resident or citizen.

Residents and citizens may qualify for interest-free student loans and will pay lower tuition fees than international students on student visas. Tuition for New Zealanders is subsidized by the government, so the student pays around $5,000-8,000 per year for most courses. International students pay in the range of $15,000-25,000 per year, depending on the school and the program of study.

College, as I mentioned earlier in this chapter, is a word Kiwis use to refer to secondary schools. So if you are looking for the equivalent of a community college, you will probably find what you're after among the polytechnics and institutes of technology. These schools offer a range of certificate and degree courses that focus on practical skills. These schools also have subsidized tuition for New Zealand citizens and residents, with higher fees for international students.

Other schools offering career training are run commercially and can charge whatever course fees they can get students to pay. These are not closely regulated, so you will have to do some research about their reputations and instructors before you invest in training courses at one of these places. They will likely have lower entrance requirements than the universities, institutes, and polytechnics, so they may be a good option for people who don't have a secondary school diploma.

Technology is becoming more integrated into the New Zealand curriculum.

Universities

New Zealand has universities spread around the country that offer courses in subjects from fine arts to medicine. Selecting a university program involves choosing the course of study for the career you'd like to pursue and taking into account factors like campus location, faculty and professors, class sizes, and other details. If you can, it's best to visit the campus before making a final decision.

The eight universities in New Zealand are (from north to south) University of Auckland, Auckland University of Technology, University of Waikato (Hamilton), Massey University (Palmerston North, Auckland, and Wellington), Victoria University (Wellington), University of Canterbury (Christchurch), Lincoln University (Christchurch), and University of Otago (Dunedin). Each university has a different range of course offerings at the undergraduate, master's, and PhD level. There is no clear "best" university in the country, as some might consider Harvard or Oxford. Each has its own merits.

When you attend classes at a New Zealand university, you choose certain "papers" toward your degree. These are the courses. Most papers will involve attending lectures, as well as smaller tutorials with a group of 10 or so students. Class sizes in lecture courses vary greatly depending on the subject and the university.

A degree from any New Zealand university should be recognized without question if you move to another country or return home. All of them meet international standards, and are monitored by Universities New Zealand.

Institutes of Technology and Polytechnics

If a traditional university doesn't seem practical to you, there are other options. New

Institutes of Technology like Wintec offer degree programs that focus on practical learning.

Educational Climate Change

U.S. student Melanie Harsch studied abroad for a year in New Zealand, and then returned to take on a PhD researching climate change through its effect on the tree line. She lives in Christchurch with her Kiwi husband, Malcolm.

What attracted you to studying in New Zealand?
New Zealand is a world leader in conservation biology. The overseas program I found in my undergraduate studies emphasized the opportunity to meet and work with biologists, government agencies, and community groups across the country.

**How difficult was the process of applying to the university
and getting your student visa? What advice would you
give other students who are about to do this?**
I found the process of applying for the visa for my undergraduate and PhD studies to be very easy. Read the instructions and start early, and if all else fails, call Immigration New Zealand. My biggest concern is the conflict between visa length and PhD length. The student visa is easily renewed after one year for two more years while studying here. After three years in New Zealand, you will need a new permit, which requires more (expensive) medical exams and police records. Most campuses have a staff member whose job is to assist international students with any questions they may have about their visas. But I have also found that when you go into or call Immigration New Zealand, you can get several different answers to the same questions.

**How do you think student life in New Zealand compares to student life
in the United States? What are the pros and cons of studying here?**
First, there is very little competition here until after one leaves the education system, and the graduate work environment is relaxed. This means that if you are self-motivated and know what you need to do, then New Zealand can be a great place to build confidence and achieve a lot with minimal stress. But it also means you need to know what you want to get out of your time here and how to do that, especially if doing a master's or PhD.

Zealand has a number of polytechnics and institutes of technology that specialize in giving students the practical skills they need to succeed in the working world. These institutions can offer undergraduate and some postgraduate degrees, as well as various kinds of certifications recognized by the New Zealand Qualifications Authority (NZQA). The subjects covered in these schools are wide-ranging, from engineering to nursing to journalism to hairstyling.

Tuition fees are generally a bit lower than at universities. Again, you will pay much more if you are not a New Zealand resident or citizen. If you are a resident, you can get some real bargains. The Southern Institute of Technology (SIT), with its main campus in Invercargill, offers a program with no tuition fees at all. This is part of a huge effort to attract more New Zealanders to Southland, the idea being that if they enjoy going to school there, perhaps they'll stay and settle down in the south.

Training Academies

There are a myriad of training academies and professional schools all over New Zealand

How did experiencing life in New Zealand change your attitude or perceptions when you returned home?
Going back to the United States was a significant culture shock. I found that people talked quickly, moved quickly, wore very little clothes and lots of makeup. I found that America was far more conservative and blinded by propaganda than I had previously realized.

Why did you decide to return to New Zealand for your PhD?
When I was in New Zealand the first time, I fell in love with the country and the man that would become my husband. So, halfway through my master's degree, we decided to get married and live in one country, together. Initially we looked at programs in the States, but Malcolm read that Landcare Research, a crown research institute, had just won a grant for climate change research. I quickly approached them and received a very positive response. It became obvious that New Zealand would give me access to a higher-caliber supervisory team than in the states, interactions with government agencies, and more freedom.

What would you tell other U.S. students thinking about coming to New Zealand to attend university?
Be prepared. Know what you want to do with your career before getting here and what you need to do to be competitive when you get back to the States. Take every opportunity that comes up and make opportunities, be your own advocate. Be proud of but do not boast about your achievements. I really recommend reading about the "tall poppy syndrome" before you get here. Don't be afraid to take vacations; your supervisors most likely will believe you need some time off—they do. Finally, try to get in contact with someone living in the city or working in the lab you want to join before you arrive; they can help you find a house, good stores to get the foods you enjoy, and explain what lollies are.

What are your plans after you complete your PhD?
Studying in New Zealand has been very beneficial. I made the most of every opportunity available and came out with a very competitive degree. I am very happy here, but would like to go back to the States if the right position in the right area came up.

in such diverse fields as information technology, hospitality, film, and child care. These schools vary in quality, and their qualifications may or may not be recognized by employers. Before you choose a course from one of these schools, find out what kind of qualification you will get at the end, and check with the NZQA to see if the institution has passed quality checks. Most qualifications are monitored and recognized, but it pays to be sure.

Warnings aside, a quick course at a training academy may be all you need to get trained for a new career, without wasting several years on a full degree or certificate program. Try to visit the school before you sign up, and ask if you can sit in on a class to see what the level of instruction is like. Ask questions about the experience and qualifications of the tutors and lecturers.

APPRENTICESHIPS

New Zealand has a skills shortage in most trades. So if you are interested in working with your hands, you're likely to be very welcome in New Zealand. Training for trades

Victoria University has several campuses in Wellington.

in the building and automotive industries usually requires a term of apprenticeship to give you firsthand experience. Even less traditional areas are starting to use apprenticeship programs; printing, communications, and hospitality are all areas where hands-on training can give you a head start on your career. Your school should be able to help set up an apprenticeship for you.

Apprentices often work part-time while studying their trade. This helps with the tuition fees as well as letting you graduate with valuable New Zealand work experience under your belt. Apprenticeships can last anywhere from a few months to four years.

HEALTH

It's pretty easy to stay healthy in New Zealand. The food and water are safe, there are few dangerous diseases to worry about, and as long as you remember your sunscreen, the environment is not too harsh. Of course, sometimes you do need help to stay well, and health care in New Zealand is in many ways walking the middle ground. You won't find the top surgeons in the world here, but you won't have to mortgage your house to pay your medical bills, either. Most health care needs are subsidized by the government, so the average person can afford to see a doctor, take medications, and get the treatments needed.

While New Zealand has a publicly funded health care system, it works differently from the public system in Canada and from Medicare in the United States. Every country has its own formula for where to spend those precious health care dollars, and in New Zealand the focus is on making sure that those most in need get the most help.

It's open for debate whether New Zealand is finding the right balance. With such a small population, resources are scarce. Finding the latest equipment and treatments can be difficult, if not impossible. So while staying healthy is easy, getting cured when you're not healthy is often a frustrating process. This is definitely a place where an ounce of prevention is worth several pounds of cure.

© MICHELLE WAITZMAN

Public Health Care

New Zealand's publicly funded health care system doesn't translate into free care for everyone all of the time. There simply isn't enough money in the system for that. Instead, each part of the country gets a portion of the health budget paid to its District Health Board (DHB) to be used for providing services in that region. Certain types of coverage are dictated at a national level, while other care is supplied as the DHB sees fit.

Accident-related care is covered by the Accident Compensation Corporation (ACC), so if you are injured in an accident, whether at work, at home, or somewhere else in New Zealand, your care will be paid for. Other health problems requiring care in the hospital (for instance, cancer treatment or an organ transplant) are covered by the public health care system. Most laboratory tests, such as blood and urine tests, and X-rays, are also fully funded.

Other types of medical costs are subsidized but not fully covered. This includes going to see your family doctor. You'll pay a fee for each visit, but it is not the full cost of the doctor's time. Children and seniors get a larger subsidy for this than adults. Prescription medications are also subsidized, but not all drugs are covered.

To qualify for public health care in New Zealand you will need a work visa that is valid for at least two years unless you are a permanent resident or citizen. People on short-term work or student visas will be required to have private health insurance to pay for their medical expenses.

ACCIDENT COMPENSATION CORPORATION

The ACC was introduced as a way of making sure that all New Zealanders receive the treatment they need following an accidental injury. It also ensures that the court system is not bogged down with personal injury claims. Everything from treatment at an emergency ward to follow-up visits to a doctor to X-rays to lost income compensation is paid by ACC.

When you arrive in the country, you are immediately covered. There is no need to enroll. Your ACC levy is paid by your employer, or if you are self-employed, you'll be sent an invoice for your dues after you file your first tax return. Your levy is based on the risk level of the job you perform. So if you are a skydiving instructor, you will have a higher ACC levy than an office clerk, since you are more likely to be injured.

If you are prevented from working because of your injury, you will get a weekly payment from ACC to help you get by, but this takes quite a lot of paperwork and doesn't pay the full amount you would earn if you were working. If you are permanently unable to return to work, you may also be paid a lump sum by ACC to compensate you for the total loss of income.

Unlike public health care, ACC is available to you no matter what type of visa you have. Even tourists are covered for accidents that occur while in New Zealand.

LOW-INCOME AND HIGH-USE ASSISTANCE

If you are struggling to get by, there are government programs in place to help you with your health care expenses. Low-income earners can qualify for a Community Services

Lawyer's Nightmare

The Accident Compensation Corporation (ACC) in New Zealand ensures that if you are injured in an accident—whether at home, at work, at school, or in the middle of the wilderness—your medical expenses will not have to come out of your own pocket.

One side effect of this system is that it leaves very little opportunity for people to sue for personal injuries. What has become an entire branch of law in the United States is virtually nonexistent in New Zealand. In fact, individuals are not allowed to sue for a personal injury.

The one area where lawyers do get involved is when a workplace injury happens. The ACC has agreements with employers, who pay the cost of ACC coverage for their workers. Employers can lower the cost of those ACC levies by taking more responsibility for workplace injuries, but this opens the door for legal action between ACC and the employer over whether the workplace caused the injury in question.

As the injured party, however, you shouldn't have to worry about any of that. As long as you can show that your injuries were caused by an accident (which includes things like being shot or stabbed), you will have your medical care paid for. But if you're a personal injury lawyer, you might want to consider a change of specialty before you move to New Zealand.

Card. (You'll have to be a resident for at least two years before you can apply for this.) The card entitles them to higher subsidies for doctor's visits (a $15 discount for adults and $20 for children) and prescription medications.

People who use the health care system more than usual (over 12 doctor visits per year) are given a High Use Health Card. This also entitles them to higher subsidies on both doctor's services and prescriptions.

CHOOSING A DOCTOR

You are free to choose whatever doctor you wish for your medical care in New Zealand. It is most convenient to find a doctor near your home or work, and there are clinics in many different areas of most cities to suit the residents' needs. Most people stick with one general practitioner (GP) for most of their medical care, although you are free to switch any time you like.

Not all doctors charge the same amount for a visit, so ask before you go if you're concerned. While most appointments for children under six are free, some GPs charge a small fee. There are also subsidies for those 6-24 years old, and those 45 and over. People age 25-44 can expect to pay up to $70 to see a doctor, although the average cost is usually $45-60.

Doctors in New Zealand must meet national standards and be registered with the Medical Council of New Zealand. This means that doctors not trained in New Zealand (which is about half of all doctors in the country) must either come from a country where the training meets New Zealand standards, or they must complete additional training and testing before they are allowed to practice in New Zealand.

Choosing the right doctor for you and your family is a highly personal decision. Ask around among friends, family, and colleagues for recommendations. If you can't find anyone to make suggestions, GPs are listed in the front section of the phone book under "registered medical practitioners."

Many GPs belong to a primary health organization (PHO), which means that they work cooperatively with a team of doctors. This helps to provide better service by giving patients the choice to see another doctor if theirs is not on duty, and to reduce costs by sharing overhead. PHOs receive government funding based on need, so poor areas have better-funded PHOs.

Specialists

Specialists who work at public hospitals are part of the publicly funded system. If your GP refers you to a specialist, you should be able to see the specialist free of charge. However, as in many other places, there are too few specialists for the number of patients. This can mean a long waiting list to see some doctors.

For those who have the means and prefer not to wait, you can see a private specialist. This is a doctor who does not rely on government subsidies for payment. By paying for the treatment yourself, you can receive care more promptly. The level of care from public and private specialists should be equally good, so seeing a private specialist is only better in that you get to "jump the queue."

HOSPITALS

The New Zealand health care system includes both public and private hospitals. Public hospitals are funded by District Health Boards, and most necessary treatments are free to the patients. But resources can be stretched to the limit, especially in areas where there are fewer facilities. For this reason, some people prefer to use private hospitals, which are less crowded. If you have private health insurance, you may be covered for some procedures at private hospitals. Otherwise, your care will be at your own expense.

While there are hospitals in all areas of the country, they are not all equally funded

© MICHELLE WAITZMAN

The emergency number in New Zealand is 111.

or equipped. The bigger the city, the more services will be available at the hospital. So patients in need of specialized equipment often find themselves traveling to a major center, like Auckland, Wellington, or Christchurch, to get the treatment they need.

If you have severe health problems and are likely to need hospital care often, you should think twice about settling in a very rural area. Emergency treatment is also more available in larger cities.

Auckland has the only dedicated children's hospital in the country, although all hospitals will treat children. Starship Hospital specializes in treating children and offers extra support to their parents. Several other hospitals have children's wards that specialize in treating young patients.

AMBULANCE SERVICES

The ambulance services around New Zealand are community-based, nonprofit services. Most are operated by St. John's Ambulance. Although some of the cost is subsidized by the government and donations, there is a charge every time you require an ambulance call-out, as much as $90. Wellington, however, runs a free ambulance service.

Ambulances usually have a local dispatch phone number, found in the front of your phone book, but can also be reached by calling the emergency number, which is 111. This is the number to call for ambulance, fire, and police emergencies.

The farther you live from a major city, the scarcer ambulance and paramedic services will be. Many areas are so understaffed that their vehicles only have one person in them, both driving and providing the medical care. Often, rural ambulance drivers are volunteers.

Private Health Care

Waiting lists and limited resources can make the public health care system too frustrating for some people. If you have the means, you may be able to bypass the public system and use private health care.

Private health care, including hospitals and clinics, is available in many areas. Many people choose to supplement their public health care with private facilities for elective procedures, such as cosmetic surgery. Others prefer to use private health care even for procedures that would be covered by the public system, but may involve long waiting lists, such as heart bypass surgery or a hip replacement. These costly operations can be done much faster if you have the option of using private facilities.

If you are likely to use private medical care, it is probably in your best interest to buy extra health insurance to cover some of the costs.

HEALTH INSURANCE

Many New Zealanders are happy to rely on the coverage they receive automatically from the public system and ACC. However, if you are going to use private health care, or if your employer is offering insurance as part of your employment package, it's good to know what you can get covered.

Most comprehensive policies will cover your hospital costs if you seek treatment in a private hospital. They may also cover the cost of seeing a specialist in a private clinic and getting tests done that are not normally covered by the public system.

The cost of your insurance will vary significantly depending on the level of coverage you want, your age, and how much you'd like your "excess" to be. Excess is what you may know as a "deductible." It's the amount of your bill that you will be required to pay before your insurance covers the rest. The higher your excess, the less your insurance will cost. For example, a family of four (with two adults in their 30s and two children under 21) might pay around $1,600 per year for basic coverage with no excess, or $1,350 per year for the exact same coverage with a $500 excess.

Another variable that can affect your premium is the waiting period that applies to any "income protection" payments. These are payments you receive if you are unable to work due to an illness or disability (although if this is the result of an accident, you may also receive payments from ACC). By making your waiting period before the first payment two months rather than one month, for example, you could save around $300 per year.

If you have preexisting health issues, they will generally be excluded from your insurance coverage. You may be able to arrange a policy that offers some coverage of a preexisting condition, but it will increase your insurance premiums substantially, and you may face a waiting period before you can file claims for treatment of that condition. Read the fine print on your policy carefully. If you have a preexisting condition and are unhappy with the waiting times or treatments available under the public health care system, you will most likely be out of pocket for your private treatment.

Many policies have the option of adding extras like dental, vision, and GP cover (so you don't pay for appointments with your general practitioner). Take a good look at the cost of these extras before you sign up, as they can cost more than the average user will pay for the services themselves.

PRIVATE HOSPITALS

If you are on a waiting list for treatment for a non-life-threatening condition, you may want to consider using a private hospital to get your treatment sooner. If you are covered by an insurance policy or can spare the money, private hospitals allow you to bypass a lot of frustrating waiting and bureaucracy.

There are private hospitals in all regions of New Zealand, offering a range of services from face-lifts to heart surgery. Some specialize in certain procedures, so look into the hospitals in your area carefully before you decide where to go for treatment or surgery.

There is no real reason to believe that the doctors working at private hospitals are any better than those at public hospitals, or that you will receive better care there. In individual cases this may be true, but really these hospitals are simply operating on a different funding model than public hospitals. Some will be better than others. If you have the opportunity, visit the hospital before deciding to have a procedure or surgery done there, and make sure that you are comfortable with what you see. If possible, get firsthand reports about the quality of the doctors and the patient care.

Pharmacies and Prescriptions

Prescription drugs are dispensed through pharmacies, or chemists. Many medications are subsidized by the health care system, but not all.

If you are prescribed a fully subsidized drug, you will have to pay a dispensing fee of $5 to the pharmacist. If the drug is only partially subsidized, or is not subsidized, you may have a much higher cost to pay. When your doctor prescribes a medication, he or she should tell you whether it is subsidized; if not, make sure you ask.

You'll find pharmacies generally as their own storefront, not incorporated into supermarkets or other stores. Most pharmacies also sell other related nonprescription items including over-the-counter medications, first-aid products, hair care products, contact lens care supplies, and cosmetics. They do not, however, carry as wide a range of products as many drugstores in other countries. You will not find stationery supplies or diapers, for example, at a pharmacy.

If you are on prescription medication when you immigrate, the brand name of your drug may be different in New Zealand, so check with a doctor or pharmacist to be sure you are taking the same thing as before. Many over-the-counter medications also go by different names here. Always ask the pharmacist if you aren't sure what to buy.

PHARMAC

The agency that regulates drug subsidies is called Pharmac. Pharmac decides which medications to subsidize and which brands will be offered under the subsidy. It tries to best divvy up the total amount of funding for prescription medications under the health care budget, based on what is needed and what is most effective.

The list of subsidized medications changes as Pharmac tenders supply contracts to various drug companies. There is always a struggle between wanting to include the newest drugs available, and not wanting to drop any of the old ones that are still useful. Like the rest of New Zealand's health care system, Pharmac tries to work with limited resources and is not always successful. However, if a medication you are determined to use is not funded, you can apply for funding under exceptional circumstances, or simply pay for the medication yourself. Of course, you will not be able to purchase any medication that has not been approved for use in New Zealand.

Having a Baby

Many immigrants come to New Zealand because they believe it will be a good place to raise a family. It is safe, clean, and friendly, with good schools and lots of opportunities. But it can be very stressful having children when your family and friends are far away.

In New Zealand, the government makes an effort to ensure that you aren't left to figure it all out on your own. Although I haven't had a baby myself, all of the immigrant parents I've talked to about having their babies have had good things to say about their own experiences. For the average parents there is very little cost involved in pregnancy and delivery, the level of care is good, and the level of follow-up support is exceptional.

Abortion is legal in New Zealand; if approved by your doctor, the cost may even be covered by the public health care system. Of course, it's a better plan to avoid getting pregnant in the first place if you don't want children, so oral contraceptives are fully funded by Pharmac, and condoms are widely available at supermarkets and pharmacies.

PREGNANCY AND CHILDBIRTH

Once they have discovered they are pregnant, most parents contact a midwife as their first step. In New Zealand, midwives provide the majority of pregnancy care, rather than obstetricians. Unless you are at risk (e.g., older or have a preexisting

New parents are well supported in New Zealand through the nonprofit Plunket.

medical condition), you'll most likely find the care provided by a midwife to be excellent. Those who prefer to see an obstetrician are free to do so, but they will have to pay for their appointments. If your general practitioner refers you to an obstetrician due to any risk factors, your appointments will be paid for by the public health system. Your appointments with your midwife are fully subsidized and will cost you nothing if you are a New Zealand resident. For those who don't qualify for free health care, a hospital birth will cost around $4,000.

The midwife will first meet with you to go over your situation. After the initial assessment, you will probably see the midwife monthly at first, with increasingly frequent appointments as your delivery date gets closer.

It is up to you whether you wish to deliver the baby at a hospital or at home.

DAILY LIFE

Kiwi Kids

Until 2006, pretty much any baby born in New Zealand was automatically registered as a New Zealand citizen. The only exceptions to this rule were children born to diplomats serving in New Zealand posts. This meant that if you were in New Zealand temporarily, say on a vacation or a study visa, and gave birth while you were in the country, your child would have the right to live in New Zealand at any point in his or her life.

In 2003, claims were made that some women were coming to New Zealand solely to have their babies, so the babies would have New Zealand citizenship by birth. This would give the parents the opportunity to apply for citizenship as immediate family members, bypassing the normal immigration process. It was a loophole in the immigration and citizenship laws that needed to be closed so the government could control who was allowed to live in the country.

In 2005, the Citizenship Act was amended to state that any child born after January 1, 2006, is a New Zealand citizen by birth only if at least one parent is a New Zealand citizen or entitled to reside in New Zealand indefinitely. That means if one of the parents has permanent residency, the child will be a Kiwi by birth, but if both are in the country on temporary visas, such as work or study visas, the child will not be a New Zealand citizen automatically.

If the pregnancy is risky in any way, you would be better off at a hospital, where it is easier to respond to medical emergencies. Most women spend two or three days in the hospital following the birth. Staff will want to see that you are able to breastfeed effectively before you go home. (Breastfeeding is very much the preference in New Zealand. You may meet with a lot of resistance if you are not planning to breastfeed.) If your delivery was by cesarean section, you will likely stay in the hospital for three to five days.

INFANT CARE AND SUPPORT

Once your child is born, Plunket takes over as the main source of support. Plunket is a nonprofit society that promotes the care of children under five. It has been operating in New Zealand for over a century, helping new parents to cope and providing information and support.

A Plunket nurse will visit you at your house weekly for the first six weeks after you bring your baby home. The Ministry of Health will provide you with a *Well Child Health Book,* where you can record things like immunization dates for your child's first five years.

After your home visits are finished, you can always go to your neighborhood Plunket office if you have any concerns. They can help to connect you with local playgroups, child care, used toys, car seat rentals, and other parental needs. Plunket even has a phone line for emergencies, or if you are having trouble coping.

Dental Care

For most adults, dentistry in New Zealand is not covered by the public health care system. It may, however, be included in your private health insurance if you have a policy through work or that you've arranged for yourself. When choosing a dentist, it's best to ask around among your friends and colleagues for recommendations. All dentists in New Zealand must be qualified and registered, but quality and price can vary quite a lot. As a basic guideline, you can expect to pay between $80 and $120 for a basic checkup and cleaning appointment.

Your local District Health Board should be able to help you find a list of dentists in your area, or you can look in the phone book.

Cosmetic dentistry and denture-making are also widely available, at least in the main cities. If you are looking to make your teeth whiter, straighter, or just fill in some gaps, you can expect to pay similar prices to the United States or Canada for these procedures.

CHILDREN'S DENTISTRY

For children, there is a government subsidy that aims to pay for necessary dentistry. Children can attend dental clinics at their schools or go to a private dentist. If you are bringing your children to a private dentist, find out whether you will have to pay for the visit. Some dentists do not participate in all of the available government programs, so they may charge a fee for services, even for patients under 18.

Preventive Measures

The New Zealand government is catching on to the fact that it's cheaper to prevent people from getting sick than to treat them after the fact. Many vaccinations and other preventive measures are funded by the health care system. Alternatives to mainstream medicine, however, are usually not funded, so if you want acupuncture, therapeutic massage, or other nontraditional treatments, you will probably be footing the bill. The exception to this is therapies recommended by a doctor following an accident, which may be subsidized by ACC.

ALTERNATIVE THERAPIES

Alternative medicine is not widely used in New Zealand. Unless you live in Auckland or Wellington, your access to things like acupuncture is going to be limited. Massage therapists and occupational therapists are somewhat easier to find. The phone book is a good place to start if you're looking for a local practitioner, or try an Internet search using the type of therapy you are after, plus the name of your nearest city.

Traditional Maori medicine is seeing a bit of resurgence among Maori in New Zealand. This mostly involves using native plants for their medicinal qualities.

How Sweet It Is

Manuka honey is a sweet treat created in New Zealand. It is different from other honey because the bees that make it use pollen from the flowers of the manuka plant, native to New Zealand. It has long been used for medicinal purposes, but modern science has finally backed up the claims of manuka advocates with hard facts.

Manuka honey has been touted as having antibacterial properties that made it helpful for people with gastrointestinal problems, such as ulcers, as well as being good for external wounds. The active ingredient was dubbed "Unique Manuka Factor" or UMF, which you will see on the labels of some products.

It was a team of German researchers who finally determined what this unique ingredient was. It is called methylglyoxal (MGO). Now that medical professionals know what makes the honey so special, they can find other uses for it. There is a possibility that it may actually help in the treatment of some cancerous tumors. Not bad for something you were just going to stir into your tea.

When you are looking for manuka honey in New Zealand, be aware that the special ingredient that makes it beneficial to your health is not active in all products. If it doesn't specifically state that it contains UMF, then it's just the same as other kinds of honey. Some products include measurements of how much UMF is present in the honey. In theory, the higher the number, the more of the beneficial active ingredient is in there. However, these products are not well regulated at present, and there is no way to substantiate the claims that any particular honey may be making.

VACCINATIONS

Vaccinations are provided free of charge for all children under five. The government has also started providing a vaccination program of Gardasil, which is given to adolescent girls to prevent cervical cancer later.

Free flu vaccinations are offered for pregnant women, those over 65 years old, and others who are at high risk of dying if they get influenza. This includes people with asthma, heart disease, and other illnesses that affect the immune system. People who don't qualify for a free flu shot can get one for a fee from their GP.

NUTRITIONAL SUPPLEMENTS

Nutritional supplements, or vitamins, are popular among New Zealanders (who aren't exactly famous for eating their veggies). There is currently no regulation over these supplements, so quality and effectiveness can vary a great deal. It's "buyer beware," as far as the government is concerned. You can find supplements in supermarkets, pharmacies, and health food stores, as well as special stores carrying health and fitness products.

Multivitamins are popular among many Kiwis, and herbal supplements such as echinacea, Saint-John's-wort, and many others are readily available. Calcium and iron supplements are also common.

SEXUALLY TRANSMITTED DISEASES

Sexually transmitted diseases are a concern in all countries, and New Zealand is no exception. The rates of infection for HIV and other STDs are not particularly high in this country, with chlamydia being the most common and genital warts coming in second. HIV is diagnosed in around 150-200 people in New Zealand each year, although many of them acquire the infection while outside the country. For example, refugees arriving from countries with high rates of infection (such as sub-Saharan Africa) make up a significant number of those diagnosed. The highest rates of transmission remain among males who engage in sexual activities with males, but an increasing proportion of HIV diagnoses are among the heterosexual population, in part due to the number of infected refugees. Still, it is important to be vigilant and take all possible precautions. Condoms are available at most supermarkets and can help to prevent the spread of sexually transmitted diseases.

Environmental Factors

New Zealand's environment is generally a healthy one. It has fewer problems with pollution than most developed countries, thanks to the lack of large-scale manufacturing and the fact that, as an island nation, the air is constantly moving. Natural disasters are not common, but they do happen. The most common are floods, although potentially the most dangerous are earthquakes and volcanic eruptions.

EARTHQUAKES AND FLOODS

New Zealand is located on many fault lines. Earthquakes happen all of the time, but most are too small to notice. When a major earthquake does happen, however, it can be devastating. It's important to be prepared for an earthquake at any time. Keep a supply of clean water and canned food at home, along with a flashlight, candles, and first-aid supplies. An earthquake could cut you off from assistance for several days, so make sure you'll be able to get by.

Floods are a problem in low-lying towns and river valley areas. Heavy rains can cause flash floods and sometimes landslides that cut off access on major roads. If you are living in a flood-prone area, make sure that you have a plan in place in case you need to evacuate quickly. Have a bag that is always packed with some clothing, sleeping bags, and other essentials. Flooding can also damage the local water supply, so it's a good idea to have some bottles or jugs of drinking water standing by in case of emergency.

DAMP AND COLD HOMES

New Zealanders have long lived under a mass delusion that their climate is warm—so warm, in fact, that they needn't bother to properly heat or insulate their homes. This has led to most New Zealand houses getting damp and cold during the winter. The dampness causes condensation on the windows and allows mold to breed. This can cause health problems, such as asthma.

The government has finally stepped in and created new guidelines for builders requiring a certain level of insulation and double-paned windows. But unless you are living in a brand-new home, you'll likely have to deal with the earlier problems.

If you buy a home that is underinsulated, invest in upgrading the insulation. It will make a big difference in how much heat stays inside the house. While most houses

© GERHARD PRETORIUS

Sun protection is vital in New Zealand.

have a wood-burner, gas heaters, heat pumps, or electric heaters, some still have no built-in heat at all.

SUN PROTECTION

One of the biggest dangers to New Zealanders is the sun. There is a hole in the ozone layer over Antarctica, which allows more UV radiation to penetrate the atmosphere in New Zealand than in the Northern Hemisphere. Skin cancer is a very real concern here. Even if you have always been a sun worshipper, be prepared to increase the level of protection you use. Sunscreen is essential if you spend time outdoors in the summer, and a hat and sunglasses are important, too.

EXPOSURE AND HYPOTHERMIA

One of the wonderful things about living in New Zealand is the access you have to the great outdoors. With mountains all over the country, it's very tempting to throw on some hiking boots and hit the trails. But the weather in New Zealand can change very suddenly, especially in the mountains. Never go on a hike, even a short one, without some warm and waterproof clothing to put on if the weather changes. Getting lost in the woods won't kill you, but getting cold while you're lost can.

SMOKING

Smoking is no better for you in New Zealand than it is anywhere else. The government has set up a "quit line" phone service to help smokers who want to stop. Medical aids, such as nicotine patches and gum, are available too. Ask your doctor about the options.

If you do smoke, you'll have to refrain from doing it in most public places. Smoking is banned in public buildings, including restaurants and pubs.

FOOD AND WATER SANITATION

Tap water in New Zealand is safe to drink. The Ministry of Health is responsible for the overall health of the country's water supply, but regional governments each look after their own regional water processing. The water can come from rivers, reservoirs, or wells, and in many cases there is fluoride added to the supply, although not in all areas. Large cities like Christchurch, Nelson, Napier, and Tauranga do not currently add fluoride in their water supply. However, Auckland, Hamilton, New Plymouth, and Wellington do add fluoride. You can find out whether your tap water is fluoridated from your local council. In rural areas it can be a challenge to monitor all of the small water sources, but outbreaks of illness due to contaminated water are rare.

On the other hand, it is not advisable to drink untreated water directly from lakes, rivers, or streams, even way out in the wilderness. Water that looks pristine can be contaminated with nasty bacteria and viruses if there are animals grazing anywhere upstream. If you are camping, you should filter, treat, or boil your water before drinking it, or use the rainwater collected at most backcountry huts.

Food sanitation is generally good in New Zealand, although a number of people do get ill each year from eating chicken and other fresh meats that have high levels of bacteria. It's important to cook meat properly, and store it in a cold fridge or freezer. Sanitation standards in most restaurants are good, but if the place looks unclean, it may be better to avoid eating there.

Disabled Access

New Zealand does not have a great track record when it comes to people with disabilities finding decent employment and integrating into mainstream society, but the country is working on it. It has made New Zealand Sign Language the country's third official language, showing that it respects all members of society. A telephone relay service is available to deaf New Zealanders, to help them communicate with the hearing world.

People with disabilities are protected from discrimination when it comes to employment, housing, education, and so on, but there is no specific policy in New Zealand that would equate with the Americans with Disabilities Act. Nothing is forcing employers to accommodate workers with disabilities or local councils to make sure that the streets are wheelchair-friendly. Nor is there any requirement for public transit to be wheelchair-accessible.

The government has a New Zealand Disability Strategy, designed to improve access and make sure that disabled Kiwis have the same opportunities as others. This strategy is delivered by the Office for Disability Issues within the Ministry of Social Development. But mostly this is a case of the government trying to lead by example and hoping private businesses will follow.

Children with disabilities may be able to attend school with the general population, if the school is able to provide the necessary access and support. More severely disabled children will be admitted to "special needs" schools, where there is more opportunity for individual help.

Personal Safety

For many immigrants, one of the things that draws them to New Zealand is the belief that it's a safe, nonviolent place to live. For the most part, this is true. Almost everywhere in the country, you can feel safe in your home and out on the streets. But New Zealand isn't perfect, and you can't make the assumption that nobody will try to hurt you. Whether it's a brawl in the local pub, an armed robbery, or a sexual assault, bad things do sometimes happen in New Zealand.

It's important to stay alert to dangerous situations and make sure that you don't become a victim. Try to avoid walking around alone at night, don't accept rides from strangers (even if they seem well-meaning), and don't let your children wander too far from your sight. If you wouldn't do it where you live now, don't do it in New Zealand. It's better to be overcautious than to end up hurt.

VIOLENT CRIME AND THEFT

Now that I've got you all worried, I have to be clear that muggings and other violent crimes don't happen that often in New Zealand. If you avoid getting into scraps with young troublemakers who have had too much to drink, you are unlikely to be attacked out of the blue.

Occasionally, foreigners are targeted by thieves because tourists are often carrying cash and make easy prey. There are rare incidents of racially based attacks against visible minorities, but these are few and far between. You're more likely to be targeted because your car is worth stealing than because of where you're from.

Gangs

There are a few gangs operating in New Zealand. They are involved in organized crime and can be violent (although mostly against one another rather than the general public). The gang names you will hear most often on news reports are "Mongrel Mob" and "Black Power." If there is a lot of gang activity in a particular neighborhood, it can affect all of the residents. Recently, gang-related problems have most often surfaced in South Auckland and Whanganui.

DOMESTIC VIOLENCE

While the streets of New Zealand are generally safe, it would seem that the homes often aren't. Police respond to a domestic violence call an average of 200 times per day in New Zealand. It's a shocking statistic for such a small population, and the government is trying hard to turn this around. They have introduced tougher laws against child abuse, making it an offense to give a child more than a minor smack for misbehaving. Violence against women is troublesome, too. A mixture of alcohol abuse and a history of using violence to control family situations has made this a particularly hot issue for Maori and Pacific Islanders, but other cultures have domestic violence problems as well, both Kiwis and immigrants from overseas.

If you get into a relationship with someone in New Zealand and it becomes violent or abusive, seek help immediately. There are women's refuges for those who need a place to escape. The police can help if you fear that your partner may pursue you. Don't be drawn in by any claims that domestic violence is acceptable behavior in New Zealand.

EMERGENCY SYSTEMS

If you find yourself in need of help in an emergency, the first thing to do is call 111, the emergency number. This will connect you with a local dispatcher who can send ambulance, police, or fire services to help you. The farther you are from a major center, the longer it will take for help to arrive. If you are in a rural area, be as self-sufficient as you can. Take a first-aid course and keep some supplies in your home and your car.

On a larger scale, New Zealand has emergency plans in case of major earthquakes, volcanic eruptions, and tsunamis. Having a battery-powered radio is a good way to keep yourself connected to what is happening during an emergency, since you may lose power connections to your home.

EMPLOYMENT

The success of your move to New Zealand is likely to hinge on whether or not you can find employment. The country has a moderate unemployment rate (5.7 percent at the end of 2014), which means that most qualified people are able to land a job without too much trouble. And you no longer have to be a sheep farmer to work in New Zealand (although there's always room for one more). Whether you're a professor, a plumber, or a graphic artist, you're in demand. And for the more ambitious, it's also possible to set up your own business once you move.

On paper it looks like a very promising situation, and for those in the right fields of work it will be smooth sailing. For people in other fields, however, it can be a real challenge to find work. Employers must legally prove that there is no New Zealander who can fill their vacancy before they go looking for a foreign worker to bring in. And even if you are a resident, there is a certain nervousness about hiring people with no "New Zealand experience" on their résumés. It's a paradox in this land where importing skilled people is so crucial, and yet there remains a resistance to putting those imported skills to use in the workforce.

High-Demand Industries

New Zealanders are very aware that their country suffers from "brain drain." Many of their best and brightest leave the country for better pay or bigger opportunities elsewhere, mainly the United Kingdom or Australia. This leaves openings for immigrants in a lot of key areas. If you are willing and able to work in a field with a skills shortage, you will find yourself very much in demand.

Immigration New Zealand keeps track of which areas require the most new workers, and potential immigrants in those fields are given priority when it comes to getting work visas and residency permits. These priority lists are broken down into three categories: Immediate Skills Shortages, Long-Term Skills Shortages, and Future Growth Areas. This gives them the ability to choose those who will fill the most urgent needs first, then those whose skills are likely to be in demand, although the situation may not yet be as desperate.

All of the lists are updated on a regular basis, so while I can give you an idea of what is on them at the time of writing, they will have changed somewhat by the time you are applying for a visa. Check the **Immigration New Zealand website** (www.immigration.govt.nz) for the current lists.

IMMEDIATE SKILLS SHORTAGES LIST

These are the areas where there is an immediate need to bring in new, skilled people to fill positions. If you work in one of the areas identified on this list, your visa application will be given higher priority. The list is regional, so you will have to be willing to live and work in the area where your skills are needed, but many jobs are repeated in several regions.

Some of the main areas featured on the current lists include most health care workers (doctors, nurses, physical therapists, dentists, etc.), agricultural managers, builders, mechanics, oil and gas workers, engineers, bakers, winemakers, and, believe it or not, skydiving and snowboarding instructors.

This is not a complete list, and it does change often. If you do find your profession on the list, note that you'll need a recognized qualification in that field, plus in some cases a certain number of years of experience, in order to be considered a good candidate to fill that shortage.

LONG-TERM SKILLS SHORTAGES LIST

Long-Term Skills Shortages are on one national list. These are the areas where there are simply not enough New Zealanders qualified to fill the number of vacancies now, and the situation is not likely to improve in the next few years.

Most of the jobs on the list fall into the areas of health care (general practitioners, surgeons, nurses, midwives, pharmacists, etc.), horticulture/agriculture, science, engineering, IT, electrical trades, construction management, chefs, university lecturers, and veterinarians.

This list is updated as needed but isn't likely to change as much as the Immediate Skills list, since these are ongoing shortages. Again, you'll need to be qualified to New

Zealand standards in your field in order to be considered as an immigrant who could fill a long-term shortage.

CANTERBURY SKILLS SHORTAGES LIST

Christchurch and the surrounding area are experiencing a construction boom thanks to the large number of buildings damaged in the 2010 and 2011 earthquakes. If you have the skills to help them rebuild, you will certainly be welcomed. To this end, Immigration New Zealand has created a Canterbury-specific skills shortages list. This is likely a temporary measure, but it should be around for the next couple of years at least.

As you would expect, most of the jobs on this list involve construction, engineering, and trades. Truck drivers are also included. Compared with the other skills shortages lists, the level of experience or education required to qualify for some of these roles is lower. If you are interested in living in Christchurch and have trades experience, you should definitely have a look on this list to see if your skills are listed.

FUTURE GROWTH AREAS LIST

This list looks at areas where there are likely to be more vacancies in the future, and not enough New Zealanders with the right qualifications and experience to fill them. These are areas where New Zealand would like to see more growth because they can be expected to boost the economy. There are three broad areas now identified as Future Growth Areas, but these could be changed or expanded at any time so check with Immigration New Zealand to see if you can use your skills to prioritize your visa application.

The three current Future Growth Areas are biotechnology, information communications technology (IT), and creative industries. This leaves a lot of room

DAILY LIFE

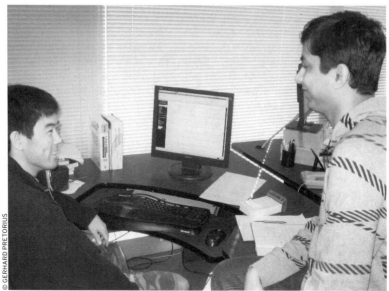

© GERHARD PRETORIUS

New Zealand offices are generally casual and friendly.

for interpretation (especially "creative industries"), so if you are unsure whether your area of work falls under one of these categories, check with Immigration New Zealand.

The Job Hunt

Despite the moderate unemployment rate and skill shortages, many newcomers to New Zealand find it quite difficult to get that first job. Employers are nervous about hiring people with no local experience, particularly if the companies on their résumés or CVs are not familiar.

Thanks to the Internet, your job search can begin long before you arrive in New Zealand. Either on your own or using recruitment agencies, you can make yourself known to potential employers. This is crucial for those who need an offer of employment to be granted a visa.

You may find you hit a catch-22 at some point, where you can't get a work visa without lining up a job offer, but you can't get that job offer without being able to show that you've already applied for a visa. This can be a frustrating stage in the immigration process, and all you can do is try to keep your sense of humor and persevere. There are employers who understand how the system works and why you are trying to find a job before you move. Others who haven't had much experience with immigrants may not want to deal with the extra paperwork.

It all comes down to finding the right match between your skills and the employer's needs. Whether you use an agency or you do it yourself, it's a process that can take several months. Those who line up a job quickly are the lucky few and usually work in the high-demand areas covered by shortages lists.

Not only can finding your first job in New Zealand take longer than you would like, you may also have to consider the possibility that you won't find a job at the same level as you were working at before. You may need to take a step backward to secure a job, then work your way up again once you have that precious "New Zealand experience." On the flip side, don't sell yourself short. If you're a qualified architect, you shouldn't need to take a job at a building supply store. Try to give yourself time to find your place in the workforce.

JOB LISTINGS

If you choose to head up your own job search, you'll need to find out where the vacancies are. Job listings appear in a variety of places. New Zealand newspapers can be a good starting point if you are already in the country. Everything from major dailies like the *New Zealand Herald* and the *Dominion Post* to community weeklies usually carries employment ads. In the big dailies they run on certain days, generally Wednesday and Saturday. Trade journals can also carry vacancy ads for their specific fields.

If you aren't on New Zealand shores yet, access to local papers could be a big problem. In that case, you're better off using job search websites. In fact, even for those in New Zealand, the websites are more frequently updated and tend to list a wider range of vacancies. There are a number of employment websites listed in the *Resources* section

Recruitment Agencies and Your Job Search

AN INTERVIEW WITH RECRUITER DANIZA GALINOVIC

If you're looking for work in New Zealand, a recruitment agency can help by matching up your skills and experience with the right iemployers. There are recruitment agencies in New Zealand for a variety of fields, including IT professionals, trades, construction, administration, public service, and hospitality.

Daniza Galinovic, an immigrant from Chile, works with The Johnson Group, a recruitment agency for the public service. I asked her about how new immigrants can use recruitment agencies to find work.

**When should someone hoping to immigrate contact a recruiter
or employer–before or after starting the immigration process?**
When they have real evidence that they want to move to New Zealand, such as visa application in process (this demonstrates motivation and genuine interest) or they have a valid work visa. There are some exceptions: when you have specific technical skills and your profession is part of the Immigration Skills Shortages List. In this case you can contact employers regarding the possibility of sponsorship.

**What do New Zealand employers worry about
when they consider hiring immigrants?**
Will they fit in? This involves culture, traditions, and language barriers among other variables. Also what is the risk of them and their families not settling, and consequently returning to their home country?

What do New Zealand employers look for on a résumé or CV?
They look for the experience that matches the vacancy that they have; usually the last 5-6 years of experience are the most important. The CV needs to be clear and simple, highlighting the relevant experience for the job that they are applying for.

**What mistakes do immigrants often make when
they approach agencies or employers to find a job?**
They approach employers or agencies with insufficient preparation or research. Consequently they may not create a very good impression. Also, immigrants need to understand that recruiters cannot act as immigration consultants.

**What other job search advice do you have
for people immigrating to New Zealand?**
Prepare yourself, study the market, and research your professional area before applying. To make the most of your time and the employer's or recruiter's time, be totally sure that you want to move to a new country. You need to demonstrate a genuine interest and motivation.

of this book. It also pays to go to the websites of individual companies that interest you, since many list job vacancies right on their websites.

Large employers are the most likely to advertise their vacancies this way, but there are thousands of small businesses in New Zealand with 10 employees or fewer. These are the companies it can be a challenge to reach from abroad, and yet they make up a large portion of the workforce. If you want to be considered by a small business, you'll have to find it first. Find the company's contact details in the phone book, or see if it has set up a website, then make contact to explain who you are and why you should

Don't Call Me Mister

One of the main differences in a New Zealand office compared to those in other countries is the casual atmosphere. Kiwis don't like to stand on ceremony, and they certainly don't tolerate a lot of strict hierarchy. So almost without exception, people are addressed by their first name, regardless of their relative positions in the company.

This attitude extends beyond the first-name basis. Colleagues in New Zealand workplaces are normally encouraged to socialize together. They often have a weekly morning tea or Friday afternoon drinks to give people a chance to get away from their desks and have a pleasant chat with workmates. While serving alcohol to employees during office hours would be unheard of in a lot of places, it is considered quite normal in New Zealand.

Some companies also encourage their employees to socialize outside of work hours. They may sponsor sports teams of their employees or set up occasional off-site social events like Christmas parties, quiz nights, and the like.

If you're used to getting automatic respect as a manager, the Kiwi system can take some time to get used to. Your employees are likely to voice their opinions, even if they contradict yours. They'll respect you for what you do, but not because of your title. And if you swoop in and make a bunch of "improvements" right away, they may think you're full of yourself and give you a hard time. So if you want to get along with your employees and peers in New Zealand, remember to be humble, friendly, and willing to participate in a bit of office fun.

be hired from overseas. It's a hard sell, because most people running a small business have little time to spend on immigration forms.

RECRUITMENT AGENCIES

Many immigrants use recruitment or employment agencies to assist them in finding a position in New Zealand. This can help break down some barriers, because if an agency recommends you as a good match for a position, the employer is less likely to dismiss you out of hand just because you're an immigrant.

There are a wide variety of agencies around the country. Some are large, generalized firms that can place people in any number of fields, while others are more specialized. Before you send your résumé to every agency you can find, take a moment to investigate what they do. If an agency only places office workers and you are a crane operator, it won't be much help to you. By targeting the best agencies for your field, you can improve your chances. They will have contacts with the major employers in their area and be able to give you a realistic idea of what kind of job you would be considered for, based on your qualifications and experience.

RÉSUMÉS OR CURRICULUM VITAE

Your résumé, or curriculum vitae (CV), is the main document that represents you to a potential employer. If it doesn't sell you, your chances of getting a job are very slim. The most important things your résumé should do are present your qualifications, outline the jobs you've done, and highlight your skills and achievements so far in your career. When the people reading the résumé are not familiar with the companies you've already worked for (because they're in a different country), your previous positions may need more explanation than usual.

Brain Drain

New Zealand and Australia have a very close relationship when it comes to their citizens. If you are a New Zealander, you can work and live in Australia for as long as you like, without any visa or permit; it works the other way for Australians wanting to live and work in New Zealand, too.

Many Kiwis see moving to Australia as a step up. It's a bigger country with a bigger population. There are higher rates of pay available for the same jobs in Australia. And to top it all off, many New Zealanders would prefer to move to the warmer Aussie climate.

In fact, an awful lot of New Zealanders consider living in another country, either temporarily or permanently, a rite of passage. Young Kiwis finishing school call it OE (overseas experience), and most either head for Australia or the United Kingdom to get some work experience in the larger world and to experience life outside their own borders.

With all of these people leaving New Zealand, it creates a bit of a "brain drain" problem. The best and brightest seem to head overseas seeking fame and fortune. But that's where you come in! Immigration is the easiest way to counter the "brain drain" by importing new talent from other countries. Those who grew up in New Zealand may be anxious to see the world, but there are plenty of people from other countries (like you) just as anxious to live in New Zealand and who are more than happy to take their places.

Every résumé or CV you send to a potential employer should be accompanied by a cover letter. This is where you can really explain why you are the right person for the job. You can also explain how far along the immigration process you are and when you plan to be in New Zealand. Make sure you target each letter for the specific job, rather than using a form letter. Employers want to know that you are actually interested in their company. Find out the name of the person to whom you should send the résumé, and use his or her name on your letter—and double-check the spelling.

References are often used to let the employer find out what kind of employee you will be. It's not necessary to put your references right on your résumé, but you should have at least three ready to present if you are asked. These should be people you have worked for in the past, preferably people who worked directly above you who can say firsthand what it's like to work with you.

Calling your references is often the last step before an employer decides whether to hire you, so make sure those people are going to help your application. It's important to warn them ahead of time that they may be contacted and give them the opportunity to decline if they are not comfortable talking about you. In New Zealand, references can also be called referees, so don't be confused if you see that on the application. Most employers won't ask for personal or character references.

Because New Zealand workplaces tend to value social contact among their employees, they will be looking for clues that you will be a good fit. So although it may have nothing to do with your job, you should include some personal information about yourself on your résumé, such as hobbies, volunteer work, and other interests. This gives employers a more complete picture of you as a person, not just a set of skills. Most résumés are between two and five pages long, depending on the type of work you do and your level of experience. Don't expect an employer to be impressed by a 20-page autobiography. Instead, make the information needed clear and easy to find.

Serving up a Taste of America

A PROFILE OF ROSS PALMER, OWNER
OF UNCLE MIKE'S KANSAS CITY BBQ

Ross Palmer and Sharon Oxley moved to Wellington with their son Pierson in 2005. Working originally in government jobs, they moved to the Queenstown Lakes district on the South Island in 2008 when Ross was offered a role as CEO of Snow Sports NZ. Sharon's brother Michael ("Uncle Mike") Oxley, a culinary professional, also moved to New Zealand and worked in Wellington restaurants. The three decided to open an authentic Kansas City-style barbecue restaurant in the tourist town of Wanaka, then moved the business to Petone, near Wellington, two years later.

Why did you decide to move the family to New Zealand?

Well, other than the fact that English is spoken in New Zealand, no developed democracy on earth could be more different than today's United States in so many important ways. Those differences are a powerful lure. The Bush reelection was the straw that broke the camel's back for us after 9/11, the sniper in the trunk of the car in DC (remember that?), and we felt the general environment for raising a child was poor.

What do you like about living in New Zealand?

It just feels safer and a bit geared back from the relentless pace of life to which we had become accustomed. It's not all about chasing the dollar. Here, it's about the journey. Employers are family-friendly. Family always comes first, pretty much no matter where you work. For the most part the air and water quality are great. The education system is in good shape, and university costs, while increasing, are far from the obscene sums at U.S. universities.

In order to get the quality food we eat every day, you'd have to shop at premium supermarkets in the United States, and even then you might not be able to get what we can get here. The meat, dairy, fruit, and veggies here, while relatively expensive, are so much better than typical fare in the states. Part of the reason we pay more at the till is that these industries are not subsidized here as they are in the states. There are no true factory farms here, for example.

How did you come up with the idea for Uncle Mike's BBQ? What made you believe that an American-style BBQ restaurant would appeal to Kiwis?

We were inspired by Michael's background in the restaurant business, Sharon's awesome culinary skills, their combined knowledge of authentic Kansas City BBQ processes (slow smoking at low temperatures, etc.) and recipes, and our combined business sense.

We offer the only authentic American BBQ in New Zealand, and of course the only Kansas City-style BBQ in New Zealand. We had a strong hunch it would be popular after introducing some of the cuisine to friends and also through informal market research.

What was the process of setting up your restaurant like? Did you hit any roadblocks?

The biggest roadblock was sourcing a smoker big enough for the job. Lucky for us, a Kiwi had imported a large smoker that holds more than 500 pounds of meat. His business idea of smoking and packaging ribs to be sold wholesale to supermarkets wasn't successful, so we happened to find it for sale online, barely used.

DAILY LIFE

© ROSS PALMER

Michael "Uncle Mike" Oxley, Sharon Oxley, Pierson Palmer, and Ross Palmer

The term barbecue also has a slightly different meaning to some down here. The iconic Kiwi barbecue is simply sausages on what amounts to a skillet-style barbecue (not open flame) without a cover. Part of our challenge has been educating Kiwis on how what we do is different to this. What we have found, though, is that once people try our fare, they get it and they love it.

There were no other major roadblocks other than those common to anyone opening a restaurant, such as finding the right location. Getting the liquor license and other permits is relatively easy and inexpensive here.

Did you have any mentors or support in New Zealand to help you out?

We received advice from many corners, including from those Mike had worked with in the restaurant business in Wellington. We did not tap into the NZ Hospitality Association at the start, but probably would have if we had it to do over again, if only for a few tips and tricks we would have picked up along the way.

How is running a business in New Zealand different than running a business in the United States?

The primary difference in our business is cost. There is a higher cost of doing business here compared to the United States. Many basic products, including wholesale meats and other staples, are slightly or sometimes significantly more expensive. One of our biggest costs is employees—and this is where it's very different to the United States—we pay above minimum wage to all employees. The minimum wage is $14.25 per hour here, and while that's not a lot, it's much higher than what waitstaff earn in the states. There's no tipping here, so service staff have to be paid a living wage.

What advice would you give to immigrants who want to run their own businesses in New Zealand?

The cost of doing business can be high, but it depends on what business you're in. If something has caught on in the United States and it's not here yet, it's an opportunity worth exploring.

The important thing to keep in mind is that this is ultimately a small market. Total population: four million. One million of those people are in Auckland. The South Island has a total population of one million. If you're a bricks-and-mortar business, Auckland, Wellington, and Christchurch are your best bets, simply due to population density.

10 Franchise Tips

This list is extracted from the article "Emigrating to NZ – The Franchise Option." The full article and other information on franchising for immigrants can be read at www.franchise. co.nz. Some things to consider if you're thinking of buying a franchise:

- Only consider franchises that fit with your skills and experience. Learning to operate a business is enough of a challenge without having to learn new techniques and skills at the same time.

- Never sign anything until you have taken the advice of an accountant and a lawyer with experience in franchising in New Zealand.

- Spend at least one day "doing the rounds" with an existing franchisee—see exactly what is involved in the day-to-day business.

- Find out exactly how the business is marketed most efficiently—personal selling, advertising, or word-of-mouth referrals.

- Do the sums. Prepare your own cash-flow forecast and budget for the business and remember to allow for the capital or loan costs of the franchise. The franchisor's figures will be a good starting point, but every business has its own costs and expenses. Do your own figures!

- Think about the unique possibilities and competitive advantage you hold by being a member of an immigrant community. Are there ways of marketing specifically to your own communities?

If you have a name that Kiwi employers might find unfamiliar or difficult, it may be a good idea to include a pronunciation guide so they do not feel embarrassed when they meet you. And if your name could be either male or female, make it clear by using a term such as Mr., Mrs., or Ms., or by referring to your gender in the cover letter. Don't give them an excuse to take your application out of the pile because it makes them feel awkward.

INTERVIEWS

Job interviews can be stressful at the best of times, but when you're conducting them over the phone with someone who speaks in an unfamiliar accent, they can be even worse than usual. If you are looking for jobs before you move, chances are you will have to interview by phone. Be as prepared as possible before the call comes. Have your résumé or CV and a copy of the cover letter in front of you, because the employer may refer to things you've written. Remember to stay on topic and not go off on a tangent. You won't be able to see if you've lost the interviewer's attention over the phone. Pay careful attention to the questions and answer what you are asked, rather than having a prepared speech. It's OK to have a few answers to expected questions ready, but make sure you don't sound rehearsed, as this will not go over well with Kiwis.

If you are already in New Zealand and going to job interviews, you should be just as prepared. Dress as you would if you were doing the job (unless it is a construction job).

- Remember that having an accent can be a good talking point to develop rapport with a client. Never get tired of answering the question, "Where do you come from?"

- Use your recent arrival in New Zealand as a positive factor. Tell your clients you are keen to grow your business in New Zealand and need their help with referrals.

- You may have a choice of buying a franchise business starting up in a new area or one which is being resold by an existing franchisee. If it is being resold, check the figures carefully. An established business should offer an immediate cashflow, which may be attractive; although setting up a new business may be a little riskier, it offers greater opportunities for capital growth.

© FRANCHISE NEW ZEALAND

Simon Lord of *Franchise New Zealand* magazine

- Be clear about your personal competitive advantages. Don't rely on the franchise image and advantage to do it all for you.

Most offices in New Zealand have a more relaxed dress code than their counterparts in North America or Europe, but it's still a bad idea to present yourself in a T-shirt and shorts unless you're absolutely certain it's appropriate. For kayaking instructors it's fine, but for IT professionals, try something a bit more conservative for that first impression.

Being flexible is important to New Zealand employers. If you seem set in your ways or reluctant to do duties that you think are beneath you, it will make a bad impression. You may also want to resist the urge to tell them that you will use your experience from another country to fix everything the company is doing wrong. People don't like an outsider to come in and tell them their way of doing things is wrong. In New Zealand, you're likely to be labeled a "tall poppy," which is someone who thinks rather too highly of himself or herself. To Kiwis, that's a mortal sin.

QUALIFICATIONS

There are many jobs in New Zealand that require specific qualifications. These can be technical jobs, such as mechanics and electricians, or professions such as doctors and lawyers. The New Zealand Qualifications Authority (NZQA) is in charge of determining whether people from overseas have appropriate training in their field to be qualified in New Zealand. If the NZQA cannot confirm that your qualifications are at their standards, they may send out a representative to assess your skills.

In many areas, even after you have determined through NZQA that your qualifications are acceptable, you will have to register with a board representing your profession in New Zealand. These boards represent accountants, architects, barristers and solicitors (lawyers), dental technicians and surgeons, electricians and line mechanics, engineers, nurses, medical practitioners, occupational therapists, pharmacists, physiotherapists, plumbers, gas fitters and drain layers, real estate agents, surveyors, teachers, veterinarians, and one large body representing chiropractors, dietitians, opticians, medical laboratory technicians, radiation technologists, midwives, osteopaths, optometrists, podiatrists, and psychologists.

Self-Employment

Small business is the backbone of the New Zealand economy. Whether you're hoping to run your own farm or become a consultant, you won't be discouraged from doing your own thing here. Many immigrants successfully open shops and restaurants, practice trades and professions, and put their entrepreneurial skills to the test in their new home.

There are basically three types of businesses in New Zealand: sole traders, partnerships, and companies. Sole traders are people who work for themselves and do not have any employees. For example, as a freelance writer, I am a sole trader, and so is a plumber who works on his own. Partnerships are similar, but involve more than one owner. A company, on the other hand, is a legal entity separate from its owners and shareholders.

TAXES

Sole traders and partnerships pay tax using the same sliding scale of tax rates as individuals, based on their level of income. Companies, however, pay tax at a fixed rate of 28 percent regardless of their level of income.

In addition to income taxes, goods and services tax (GST) must be collected by any business with over $60,000 of income. This means charging your clients or customers an extra 15 percent for any service or product you provide. On the other hand, you will then be able to deduct the GST you have paid to suppliers from the amount of GST that you owe. You will need to register with the Inland Revenue Department (IRD) for a GST number.

STARTING A BUSINESS

Kiwis really respect those who take a good idea and run with it. Starting your own business is a risk in New Zealand, just like anywhere else, but it can also bring great rewards. One common mistake for immigrants is to forget how small the population of New Zealand is. If you are selling a product or service to the domestic market, remember that you're only dealing with four million people, and only a portion of those are potential customers. A carefully constructed business plan, based on the New Zealand market, is an absolute must.

You'll need that business plan anyway if you are looking to immigrate with a business visa or switch from a work visa to a business visa. Immigration New Zealand will want to know that you have done your homework before it allows you to start up a company in New Zealand. Your history and experience will also influence the decision, so if you've run a successful business before, you have better odds of getting that visa.

If you are a permanent resident or citizen already, you can start up your own business at any time. If it is a company, you must register it in the **Companies Register** (www.business.govt.nz/companies). You may be able to get help from your local **Chamber of Commerce and Industry** (www.newzealandchambers.co.nz), of which there are 31 around the country representing some 22,000 businesses.

Buying a Franchise

If setting up a business from scratch seems too daunting, you can still be your own boss by running a franchise of an existing business. There are hundreds of opportunities to buy a franchise, from fast food to real estate or housecleaning. By franchising, you get all of the knowledge and experience of the company behind you, and many provide complete training to those with no experience running a business. Not only do you get the company's proven system, but also the brand recognition that goes with its product, which can make it easier for your business to succeed in a competitive marketplace. The best resources for finding out about available franchises in New Zealand are *Franchise New Zealand Magazine* (www.franchise.co.nz) and the **Franchise Association of New Zealand** (www.franchiseassociation.org.nz), which runs franchise expos around the country.

Working as an Independent Contractor

An independent contractor is the same as a sole trader for tax purposes. Basically, people who make a living selling their own services are independent contractors. If you make over $60,000 as a contractor, you will have to register for a GST number just like any company.

Working as a contactor appeals to many people because of the freedom it allows. You can make your own hours, take vacation when it suits you, and work as much or as little as you need to. It is mainly people in trades who work as contractors, but this arrangement can also work for journalists, graphic artists, accountants, musicians, or anyone whose business revolves around their own skills.

AGRICULTURE

New Zealand began as a land of farmers (and whalers), and agriculture is still the largest industry in the country. The main agricultural products are dairy, meat, and wool, but there are also significant numbers of people growing fruit or vegetables and maintaining vineyards. Over 200,000 people in New Zealand work in agriculture, and that doesn't include some 25,000 unpaid family members who help out on family-run farms.

If you don't have a farming background, you may need to start as a farmhand or other low-level job until you learn enough to move into a management role. There are lots of courses available for those who want to learn about farming at universities, polytechnics, or private training academies. But nothing will replace firsthand experience on a farm.

If you do have experience running a farm before you move, you'll find it goes a long way in getting your work visa or residency approved. Farm management is one of the areas with a constant shortage of qualified New Zealanders. Other agricultural jobs in demand include viticulture specialists (winemakers) and sheepshearers.

Entrepreneurial types may even want to buy their own farm. Purchasing an established farm will cost more and involve lots of paperwork for non-Kiwis, but it will also start earning money right away. Setting up your own farm from scratch can take a lot of patience and is much riskier.

For those in New Zealand on a working holiday visa or other temporary work permit, a short-term job on a farm is a common way to make ends meet and finance your further travels. Picking fruit is a seasonal job where workers are always in demand.

Labor Laws

Knowing your rights is essential before you agree to take a job. Regulations and benefits are different in New Zealand than they were back home, so ask questions of your potential employer and don't make any assumptions.

When you are offered a job, there should be a written employment agreement. It should include your job title and a description of your duties, the salary you are to be paid, the hours of work, whether you will be paid extra for overtime work, and the number of vacation days you will receive.

You cannot be turned down for a job on the basis of your gender, race, religion, sexual orientation, disability, marital status, or whether you have children. Your employer is required to provide a safe working environment and to pay your Accident Compensation Corporation (ACC) levies in addition to your salary.

You will be required to apply for an IRD (Inland Revenue Department) number before starting a job in New Zealand so the government can keep track of your earnings and tax you accordingly.

UNIONS

Labor unions in New Zealand do not seem to pack the same punch as those in North America or Europe. Part of the reason is that individual workers cannot be forced to join the union that represents their peers. If there is a union-led collective agreement in place when you are offered a job, you will be given the option to join the union and be employed under the collective agreement or not join the union and negotiate your own employment agreement. There are advantages and disadvantages to each option, so if you work in a unionized area, have a close look at the collective agreement before you decide. Just remember that if you decide to do your own thing, the union will not back you up if problems arise.

MINIMUM WAGES AND BENEFITS

New Zealand currently has a two-tier minimum wage. For adults (18 and over) the minimum wage is $14.25 per hour. For 16-17 year olds, there is a starting-out minimum wage of $11.40 per hour for their first six months on the job. There is no minimum wage for employees under 16. There are *no* exceptions to the minimum wage, including waitstaff, home workers, and part-time workers. Everyone must be paid at least the minimum hourly rate. This is why tipping is not expected in New Zealand restaurants.

In addition to annual leave, employees are entitled to 11 public holidays, including 10 national holidays and one regional Anniversary Day (see the *New Zealand Public Holidays* and *Anniversary Dates* sidebars in the *Introduction* chapter for the list). If you are required to work on a public holiday, you are entitled to 1.5 times your usual pay. You are also entitled to an alternate day off in lieu of the holiday. If public holidays fall on a day when you don't normally work (such as the weekend), you will get an alternative day off (typically the following Monday).

Sickness and Bereavement

Sick leave is given to employees who are unwell or have a spouse or dependent (child) who needs care. Most people get five days of paid sick leave per year and can carry over unused days to the next year, up to a maximum of 20 days. Many employers require a doctor's note if you take more than two consecutive days of sick leave.

Bereavement leave is given to employees who lose an immediate family member or someone close to them. In the case of an immediate family member, they can take up to three days of paid leave, and they do not have to be consecutive days. For cases where the deceased is not an immediate family member, one day of paid leave is available if your employer is convinced that you have genuinely suffered a bereavement.

Parental Leave

Parental leave can be taken by either parent to care for a new baby. Paid parental leave can begin up to six weeks before the baby is due and lasts for a maximum of 14 weeks. The current maximum payment for parental leave is just over $500 per week. It's not much, especially if you're a single parent. You are also entitled to paid parental leave if you are adopting a child less than six years old.

After the 14 weeks of paid leave is up, parents can take up to 38 more weeks (a total of 52 consecutive weeks) to stay home and care for their child. At the end of this period, the employer must take the parent back at the same rate of pay as before the birth (although not necessarily in the same position). This unpaid leave can be divided between the two parents, but the total cannot be more than 52 weeks.

Annual Leave

After your first year of working for an employer, you are entitled to four weeks of paid annual leave. You and your employer must agree on the times for this leave to be taken, but you must be given the opportunity to take at least two weeks consecutively if you want to. In some cases you may be given the option to trade up to one week of annual leave for the equivalent in extra pay.

Many businesses in New Zealand close down over the Christmas-New Year's period, and employers are allowed to force their employees to take some of their annual leave to cover these closures. This generally amounts to five days at the most, over a period of two weeks. It does not include the days that are paid holidays already: Christmas Day, Boxing Day, New Year's Day, and January 2. Before you make plans for all of your annual leave, check with your employer to see whether there is an office closure to include in your calculations.

ENDING EMPLOYMENT

While you're more likely to be concerned with getting a job, it's good to know what the rules are when your job ends.

If you are dismissed (fired) from a job, there must be a good reason for it, and you must be treated fairly. You have the right to ask for an explanation from your employer for up to 60 days after you are dismissed. The employer can dismiss you for not fulfilling your duties in the employment agreement or if you have conducted yourself in a way that is damaging to the business or the workplace. Your employment agreement may include terms of dismissal, such as a notice period or payment, but it does not have to.

There may be an exception to the above if you have been in your job for fewer than 90 days. There is a law that allows employers to fire new employees within a 90-day "trial period" with no explanation if they feel things aren't working out. This can only be enforced if you agree in writing to a trial period. The job offer, however, may depend on you agreeing to this.

If you are made redundant (laid off) for business reasons, you aren't much better off. There is no requirement in New Zealand for employers to pay compensation to redundant workers. However, many collective agreements will have provisions for this, so make sure you know what your agreement says.

You may eventually decide you've had enough of the working life and choose to retire. Your government pension (superannuation) will kick in when you turn 65 if you qualify, but your employer cannot force you to retire at a certain age if you are still capable of doing your job competently.

FINANCE

Back in the 1990s, moving to New Zealand from overseas was a financial dream come true. The cost of living was comparatively low, and the exchange rates favored foreign currencies like the U.S. dollar and British pound. In fact, you could get over two New Zealand dollars for each U.S. dollar, and about three New Zealand dollars for a pound. I'm sorry to tell you that those days are over, at least for the moment. Rising real estate, food, and fuel prices have driven up the cost of living here, interest rates are higher than you would find in the United States, and the Kiwi dollar has been overvalued recently. At the time of writing a Kiwi dollar was worth roughly $0.70 in U.S. currency, but by the time you are changing your money, it could be at a very different rate.

Even though things are not as rosy as they used to be, getting by in New Zealand isn't all that difficult. As long as you are employed full-time, you should be able to afford life's necessities, and maybe even a luxury or two. Like anywhere, you can live cheaply or expensively in New Zealand, depending on your lifestyle. Not many people get filthy rich living here, but most people are comfortable, even though they may be carrying a bit more debt than they'd like.

© MICHELLE WAITZMAN

Cost of Living

The cost of living in New Zealand is comparable to other developed countries. Costs tend to be a bit lower than in the United States and Canada, but salaries are also lower so it pretty much balances out. Salaries range from around $28,000 per year for unskilled workers and salespeople, to over $75,000 for professionals and managers. Of course, there are people who make much more than that, and many high-level jobs will have six-figure salaries. Getting by at the lower end of the scale can be challenging, particularly if you are trying to support a family. The median salary for full-time work is around $44,000, but because many people do not work full-time, the average income is substantially lower.

Rent or mortgage payments will be your biggest expense. With inflated house prices and higher interest rates than many countries, some Kiwis are spending well over half of their income to pay their mortgages. The average house price in central Auckland sits at $738,000, while down in Dunedin it is a more affordable $290,000. If you're anxious to buy a home right away, you may want to settle in a smaller city where prices are still reasonable.

Renting a house or flat (apartment) when you first arrive can help you to keep your options open until you've settled in. It can also keep debt at bay for a while. As house prices have increased, so have rental prices, so that property investors can have their tenants help to pay off that huge mortgage. If you want a downtown flat with 2-3 bedrooms in Auckland or Wellington, you can expect to pay over $450 per week for rent. Moving farther from the city centers will bring down the weekly price to around $400 in the closer suburbs and $350 in more distant or less desirable suburbs. Again, living in a smaller city is more affordable, with rentals available in the $250-300 per week range.

Food is another major cost in your budget. New Zealand is fortunate in that many of the basic staples can be produced locally and don't have to be expensively imported. This includes dairy products, eggs, meat, and some fruits and vegetables. These local products are reasonably priced. Imported fruits and vegetables are brought in to supplement the local crops, both for things that don't grow well in New Zealand (like bananas and pineapples) and to continue providing items off-season. On average, you should count on spending at least $60 per person per week on groceries. Children will cost a bit less, and people who rely heavily on prepared foods will find their bills higher.

Eating out can also add up in New Zealand. Depending on the style of restaurant, main dishes can range from around $16 in some family restaurants all the way up to $50 for fine dining. Appetizers and desserts can add another $10-20 each. Even a basic food court meal will cost about $12 including a drink. While this may cause a bit of sticker shock at first, you can at least take comfort in the fact that tax is included in menu prices and you are not expected to leave a tip on top of the bill when you dine out.

Fuel costs have taken the same ride in New Zealand as they have in the rest of the world. Filling up at the pumps will cost around $1.95 per liter (which is roughly a quarter of a gallon), depending on how things are looking that week. If you have a diesel vehicle, your costs will be closer to $1.25 per liter.

Sample Monthly Budget

Your monthly expenses will vary a great deal depending on where you live and your lifestyle. This example is simply an average budget for a family of four paying off a mortgage and one car.

Expense	Amount
Housing (mortgage, taxes)	$3,000
Utilities (electricity, gas)	$250
Car (payments, fuel)	$600
Food	$1,000
Phone and Internet	$150
Entertainment	$400
Clothing	$150
Total	$5,550

INFLATION AND INTEREST RATES

The Reserve Bank of New Zealand is in charge of setting official interest rates, and the banks and other financial institutions take their lead. They would like to keep the inflation rate in the country under 3 percent, while stimulating the economy. They have been very cautious about raising interest rates, and at the time of writing the official cash rate was sitting at 3.25 percent.

Some homebuyers are currently facing mortgage interest rates ranging from 6 percent to over 8 percent depending on the type and duration. Interest on other kinds of loans and on credit cards is also higher in New Zealand compared to the United States, Canada, and the United Kingdom.

On the other hand, inflation is actually quite low once you eliminate housing and food from the equation. Things like furniture, clothing, and electronics have not seen big price increases, and in some cases the high New Zealand dollar value has brought the price of imported goods down. But to counter that, salaries haven't gone up much in recent years.

MANAGING DEBT

The high interest rates associated with mortgages and credit cards in New Zealand have made debt a real problem for a lot of Kiwis and immigrants alike. The government is concerned about this and has created a website called **Sorted** (www.sorted. org.nz), which offers information on debt, savings, retirement, and other financial matters.

The longer you're in debt, the more interest you'll have to pay. Some financial service providers can consolidate your various debts into one loan, so you have fewer payments to make each month. This is something to consider if you have a lot of high-interest debts from credit cards, personal loans, and other sources, but it's vital to read the fine print before doing so.

It's difficult not to get into the red when you've just arrived and need to set up a home, fill it with furniture and appliances, and buy a car or two. Try not to overextend yourself, and take the time to compare rates from various lenders before you borrow.

ASSISTANCE FOR LOW-INCOME EARNERS

There are a number of ways the government helps to support people who can't quite make it on their own. The most commonly used is the unemployment benefit, which is available for those who can't find work though they are actively trying to.

To qualify for unemployment benefits, you have to have been a citizen or permanent resident for at least two years and be over 18 years old. Payments are very small, currently ranging from $153 per week for people under age 20 living at home, to $335 for single parents. The payments are not based on your past earnings. If you've been collecting unemployment benefits for a full year, you will have to reapply to continue receiving them.

An Independent Youth Benefit is available for 16- and 17-year-olds who are supporting themselves while they look for work or attend a work-related course. The weekly payment is about $190, and you can't be living with your parents at the time. This is basically the junior version of the unemployment benefit.

There are other benefits available to people who are permanently unable to work due to a disability or illness, called the Invalids Benefit. There is also a Sickness Benefit, which provides temporary payments if you are kept from work by sickness, injury, or pregnancy. This is in addition to the ACC payments you may also receive for accidental injuries. (See *Public Health Care* in the *Health* chapter for details on ACC.)

People on benefits generally qualify for a Community Services Card, which gives them a discount on doctor's fees and prescriptions. The cost of doctor visits is discounted by $15 for an adult and $20 for a child.

Single parents and other caregivers may qualify for a Domestic Purposes Benefit if they need to stay home full-time to look after children or an elderly or disabled person. Some women over 50 may still qualify for this benefit, even if they have finished raising their children or caring for their sick relative. In addition, a Widow's Benefit is available for some women after their husbands or partners die. The rules are a bit complicated, but basically you have to have been married (or the equivalent) for at least 15 years and raised children.

The government also offers a tax credit for families with dependent children. Called Working For Families, it consists of a sliding scale of tax credits depending on your household income and the number of children you are supporting. Even people with a reasonably high income sometimes qualify for this, so check into it before the end of your first tax year in the country.

ASSISTANCE FOR SENIORS

New Zealand has a social security program for those over 65, which they call superannuation. You'll sometimes hear people just call it "super." In order to qualify for payments, you have to be a New Zealand permanent resident or citizen and have spent at least 10 years in the country since you were 20 years old.

However, New Zealand has reciprocal agreements with a few other countries, which may help you to qualify for payments if you previously lived in the United Kingdom, Ireland, Canada, Australia, Denmark, Greece, or the Netherlands.

Superannuation provides a flat weekly payment, which is roughly between $320 and $420, depending on whether you live alone or with someone, and whether that person does or does not also qualify for payments. The payment amounts are in no way connected to how much you earned while you were working and are not funded by a specific deduction from your paychecks.

You are allowed to continue earning money while you are collecting superannuation, but there are some cases where the amount of your benefit may be affected, so be sure to check the latest rules when the time comes. You may also qualify to get pension or social security payments from your home country even after moving to New Zealand. It's worth checking with your former home's government on the latest rules, as they can change from time to time.

Seniors qualify for other financial assistance, like lower fees for doctor visits and prescription medicine. Seniors also usually pay lower prices for things like movies, plays, and other ticketed events.

KIWISAVER RETIREMENT SAVINGS SCHEME

In 2007, the New Zealand government introduced a new program to encourage more Kiwis to put aside a bit of money for their retirement. The trend among New Zealand employers, as in other countries, is tending away from pension plans that help their former employees get along after retirement. More and more, it is up to the individuals to make sure their retirement will be comfortable. Though the government helps out with a small superannuation payment, it's not enough to keep most people living the way they are used to.

Kiwisaver allows employees to have 3, 4, or 8 percent of their gross wages diverted into a savings plan of their choice. The money is then locked away until they reach retirement age. There are some exceptions where money can be withdrawn from the scheme—to pay for a first home, for example. But the idea is that if you never see the money in your paycheck, you won't be tempted to spend it.

The government also provides tax incentives to people who take up this plan with a tax credit of up to $520 per year. Employers are also forced to contribute the equivalent of 3 percent of their employees' salaries per year to their savings plans. People who are self-employed can open a Kiwisaver account if they choose, but they obviously won't benefit from any employer contributions.

Banking

Banking in New Zealand is relatively modern and efficient. Most of the major banks are large companies based in Australia. They offer the kinds of services you'd expect, including a range of accounts, credit cards, debit cards, loans, mortgages, insurance, and investments.

Most people like to open a bank account right away after arriving in the country. Employers almost always use direct credit (called direct deposit in the United States) to pay employees, so you'll need an account when you start work. This will also enable you to apply for credit and debit cards, to make paying for things more convenient.

New Zealand's banks are run as businesses, so they are competitive with each other. They will also try to maximize their profits by charging fees wherever they can! It pays to compare banks, accounts, and fees so you don't end up wasting a lot of your money.

It is worth noting that New Zealand does not have a deposit insurance scheme for its financial institutions. This means that if your bank or investment company goes bankrupt, there is no guarantee that you will get any of your money back. This is unlikely to happen to a major bank, but some financial services companies have disappeared in the past, and customers' savings sometimes disappeared with them.

CURRENCY

New Zealanders use the New Zealand dollar as their currency. Since 1985, it's been a floating currency, which means that its value is in constant flux against other international currencies. It's a popular currency to invest in because of New Zealand's high interest rates. This has inflated (overinflated, according to many) the value of the currency, making exporters unhappy.

The New Zealand dollar is divided into 100 cents, just like the U.S. dollar. However, the government has done away with both $0.01 and $0.05 coins, so that the lowest cash denomination is now the $0.10 coin. The other coin denominations are $0.20, $0.50, $1, and $2. Notes are produced in $5, $10, $20, $50, and $100 denominations. Each note is a different size and color, and they are made of a plastic polymer that is more durable than paper money and can go through the washing machine undamaged. They're also harder to counterfeit than paper notes and contain a clear window that makes them impossible to photocopy. New, brighter-colored notes are being introduced between October 2015 and April 2016.

BANKS, ACCOUNTS, AND SERVICES

New Zealand has all of the modern banking services you'd expect in a developed country. Most people rarely have to show up at their branch, since there are cash machines on every street corner, plus banking services by phone, text message, and Internet. But be warned, many services from New Zealand banks come with hefty service fees, including monthly account fees just for the privilege of banking.

There are several large banks operating branches throughout New Zealand. Most of them are owned by Australian companies, with the exceptions of Kiwibank, which is owned by New Zealand Post, and TSB, which is also New Zealand-owned. The other main banks are ASB, Westpac, BNZ, and ANZ. Each has its own set of accounts with different features, fees, and limitations. All of the main banks have websites where you can compare accounts before you decide where to open one, so see what will work best for you.

The account you use for everyday banking is usually called a "current" account. This often includes checking, but if you don't need to write checks, you can get an account without that service and save on the fees. And remember, it's spelled *chequing* Down Under. Savings accounts are also available in all banks and usually offer a higher interest rate than current accounts, but with fewer services. They may also charge higher fees for withdrawals.

Opening a Bank Account

Most major banks in New Zealand will let you open an account before you even arrive in the country. You will have to provide proof that you'll be residing in the country for over six months, but having an account open when you arrive can make the transition much easier. The bank's website should have instructions on its process for approving new immigrant accounts and forms for you to fill in.

If you are already in the country, simply visit your local branch and bring some photo ID, your residency permit or work visa, and proof of your residence (such as a power bill or a copy of your tenancy agreement) to show. The bank should be able to set up an account for you right away.

When you open an account, you should also give the bank your Inland Revenue Department (IRD) number if you already have one. This number identifies your tax account with the government, so that when some of the interest is withheld on your bank accounts, it is applied to your taxes. If you cannot supply an IRD number, tax will be withheld at a fixed rate of 33 percent rather than the appropriate rate for your income.

Online Accounts

These days you can have a bank account without ever actually going into a bank. Online call accounts, as they're called in New Zealand, are gaining popularity. Because they don't have to support any branches, they can offer higher interest rates and usually lower fees than regular banks. In fact, some of the big banks are now offering online call accounts in addition to their usual accounts. The main difference is you can only do your banking online or by phone, not in person.

The main provider of online-only banking is RaboDirect. But Kiwibank was an early joiner from the mainstream banking world. Most of the big banks have also created similar accounts. Find out what restrictions are imposed (often you can only transfer funds to or from one other account), what interest rate is on offer, and whether there is a minimum balance requirement.

Moving Money Between Countries

Thanks to electronic transfers, it's quite easy to move money between bank accounts in different countries. Unless you're keen to close off your account before you leave for New Zealand, it's easiest to wait until you've set up a local account and have your money moved electronically. If you don't want to leave your old account open, you can

Who's on the Notes

Each denomination of bills, or notes, in New Zealand currency bears the picture of a person of either historical or current significance to the country. Of course you'll have no trouble telling the notes apart without memorizing the faces, since they are each a different size and color. But here's a quick introduction to the people looking back at you from New Zealand's money.

$5–SIR EDMUND HILLARY

Sir Ed has been a national hero to Kiwis since he became the first individual to successfully climb Mount Everest back in 1953. His lifelong charity work only added to his status in his home country, and the fact that he was chosen to grace the currency confirms his status as a New Zealand icon.

$10–KATE SHEPPARD

In 1893, New Zealand became the first country in the world to grant women the vote, thanks in large part to the tireless efforts of Kate Sheppard. Sheppard led the suffrage movement, which managed to compile a petition of 32,000 signatures to present to parliament, insisting on equal voting rights for women. She is a symbol of human rights and sexual equality in New Zealand, and a natural choice for the honor of appearing on a note.

$20–QUEEN ELIZABETH II

The reigning British monarch is the official head of state in New Zealand. Although the monarchy has little influence in the day-to-day lives of Kiwis, her symbolic presence is important to many. Before 1990, all New Zealand banknotes featured a portrait of the queen. Interestingly, she is now pictured on both the New Zealand $20 note and the Canadian $20 note, and both are green.

$50–SIR APIRANA NGATA

To honor the bicultural heritage of New Zealand, Sir Apirana Ngata was chosen to represent the importance of Maori to the country. He was the first Maori to graduate from a New Zealand university, in 1893, and went on to become a lawyer and eventually a member of parliament (MP). He served in parliament for 38 years, working tirelessly to bring about legislation that would benefit the Maori people. As a leader and role model for his people, Sir Apirana Ngata has earned a special place in New Zealand history.

$100–ERNEST RUTHERFORD

It may seem unusual to put a scientist on a banknote, but Ernest, Lord Rutherford of Nelson, certainly did his country proud. He is known as the "father of the atom" for his work on radioactivity and how it related to atomic structure. Rutherford received a Nobel Prize in 1908 for his research. In 1914, he was knighted. While Rutherford's work took him away from New Zealand quite early in his career, the country still claims him as one of its heroes.

always get a bank check for your entire account balance and keep it safe until you can deposit it in your new account, though this approach does involve some risk.

If you don't have a New Zealand account up and running when you enter the country, you can use your credit and debit cards from your bank account back home at most retailers and bank machines in New Zealand. There may be some hefty international transaction charges though, so try to make a few large transactions rather than a lot of small ones.

Banking on the Post Office

Almost every post office in New Zealand is also a bank branch.

New Zealand Post has a proud tradition of delivering service to even the remotest corners of the country. But with email and fax taking away a lot of the traditional mail business, there was a real possibility that a lot of the smaller post offices would be shut down. Rather than downsize, New Zealand Post decided to diversify, opening its own bank.

Kiwibank has been around since 2002, selling itself as the New Zealand-owned option for personal and business banking. Since most post offices double as bank branches, Kiwibank has close to 300 branches around the country. It offers all of the same services as other banks, including accounts, credit cards, loans, and mortgages. It also has ATMs all over the country and offers online banking.

So if you like the idea of being able to send packages, pay your bills, and withdraw some cash all in one stop, banking with the post office might be a good option for you.

You can open a foreign currency account at some New Zealand banks. This is handy if you want to keep some of your savings as U.S. dollars, euros, Canadian dollars, or another major currency. If you plan to return often to your home country, or to return permanently at some point, it can save you money on currency exchange. It's also a way of putting off converting your currency to New Zealand dollars if you think the exchange rate will improve later.

CREDIT CARDS

Kiwis rack up a remarkable amount of credit card debt, to the tune of over $2.5 billion charged every month. Plastic is king here, and all of the banks will try to get you on board with a variety of cards available. Visa is the most common card and widely accepted in shops and online. MasterCard is also widely used. American Express cards are not often carried by Kiwis and not accepted in a lot of shops, but you can get one from some New Zealand banks.

Interest rates on credit cards can have a huge range, so shop around if you tend to carry a large balance. At the time of writing, the lowest interest rates were around

13 percent, with the highest rates sitting around 25 percent. Over time, high-interest credit card debt can certainly add up.

When you get a credit card in New Zealand, you can sometimes choose between two security options. Either you can have your purchases authorized by signing the credit card slip whenever you make a purchase, or you can have a PIN (personal identification number) assigned to the card that you will have to punch in to authorize the purchase. Some cards will only offer one of these options. Ask the bank what kind of security it uses when you apply for a card.

DEBIT CARDS OR "EFTPOS"

The term "debit card" never really caught on in New Zealand. Instead, they use the tongue-twisting acronym EFTPOS, which stands for electronic funds transfer at point of sale. And Kiwis just love to use their cards to buy stuff! Even small purchases, like a cup of coffee, are often paid for by EFTPOS. It may not be a cashless society just yet, but in New Zealand it's closer than anywhere else I've seen.

Your EFTPOS card will be issued when you open a bank account, and you will have a security PIN that you need to punch in every time you use the card. If your card is lost or stolen, you should tell your bank immediately so it can cancel the card and issue a new one. It can take several days to get your card replaced, but most credit cards can also be used to access funds from bank machines.

DIGITAL WALLETS AND NEAR FIELD COMMUNICATIONS

Near field communications (NFC) is a system that allows communication between two devices without them actually touching each other. This technology is starting to revolutionize electronic payment, and may eventually replace traditional debit and credit cards.

In New Zealand, the most common use for NFC is public transportation. Some transit companies sell NFC-enabled cards that can be used to pay for fares by holding the card next to a reader. A few shops and cafés have also introduced NFC readers to allow payment for small purchases.

The next step will involve payments through a smartphone app. New Zealand's mobile providers and banks are currently working together to set up systems for customers to use NFC-enabled smartphones as a payment option. This will only be available with certain phone models, at least at first. It is hoped that eventually all smartphones will include NFC functionality to make digital wallets the norm.

LOANS AND MORTGAGES

If you're making any major purchases after you arrive in New Zealand, like a house or a car, you're probably going to need to borrow money. Mortgages, or home loans, come in all shapes and sizes at New Zealand banks. You can generally borrow up to 80 percent of the cost of your house, and either fix your interest rate for a certain term (usually between six months and five years) or choose a variable rate that changes over the course of your term. Many banks will let you know your credit limit ahead of time so that you don't look at houses you can't afford. This will also speed up the approval process once you do buy a house, since the bank will already have all of your details.

Loans and Mortgages for New Arrivals

Jason Liu is a private banking manager for ASB. He answered a few questions about how to improve your chances of getting the loan or mortgage you need, even if you're new to the country.

What's the first step for immigrants who want to borrow money in New Zealand?
Some New Zealand banks, including ASB, have a specialized Migrant Banking Division, experienced in dealing with the unique financial needs of new immigrants.

We welcome all new immigrants to New Zealand to visit a local branch to have a chat with our experts.

What will be required of them in order to qualify for a loan?
Customers will need to provide proof of employment with a company that is legally registered in New Zealand. We will need to confirm that the loan applicant is a full-time staff member of the company and require a pay slip and a bank statement to confirm income and ability to service the loan.

Are there any differences in New Zealand loans and mortgages compared to other countries?
Different countries have different rules and regulations for loan and mortgage requirements.

In New Zealand the general maximum lending ratio for nonresidents is in the range of between 50 and 70 percent loan to value ratio (meaning you would be required to have a 30-50 percent down payment). However, we assess all customers on their own individual circumstances and financial situation.

Do you have advice for building a credit rating in New Zealand?
We are happy to help any customers who have questions on how to build a good credit rating in New Zealand. Things that may help with this include paying all bills on time, including utility and credit card, and having a history of saving.

Any other advice for new arrivals who want to finance a home, car, or other large purchase?
A good credit rating will help new immigrants with any type of new loan including mortgages or smaller personal loans that may help with setting up life in a new country.

Personal loans are available for expenses like buying a car, going on a trip, or anytime you need a bit more cash on hand. These can be a good alternative to carrying a high balance on your credit card, because the interest rates are generally a bit lower. Be sure to compare, though, because some banks charge comparable interest on loans to their credit card rates.

University students (if they have been New Zealand residents for at least two years or are New Zealand citizens) can get interest-free government loans to help them pay for their education.

DAILY LIFE

Taxes

Moving to New Zealand will certainly not get you away from taxes. With a large government infrastructure to fund and relatively few people in the country to share the cost, taxes take a pretty big bite out of your earnings.

Income tax will account for the biggest chunk, but other taxes add to the burden. Almost everything you buy will have GST (goods and services tax) included in the price. This adds 15 percent to the cost of most items. Fuel, cigarettes, and alcohol are taxed at even higher rates. And if you own your home, you will also pay local "rates," which are local government taxes on your property.

Most taxes are collected by the Inland Revenue Department, more commonly called the IRD. It collects income tax and business tax from all individuals and companies in New Zealand. When you arrive in the country, you'll need to apply for an IRD number, which is like a Social Security number. This will help the IRD identify you when it comes to keeping track of taxes owed and paid.

INCOME TAX

Income tax is calculated in New Zealand based on a financial year that begins April 1 and ends March 31. This can be confusing if you come from a country where the tax year is the same as the calendar year. It is especially confusing during your first year in the country, when there can be crossover between taxes due back in your home country and in New Zealand.

On the bright side, many people in New Zealand don't have to fill in tax returns at all. If you earn a salary where tax is automatically deducted, and that is your only source of income, there is no need for paperwork. Even tax on your bank interest is automatically calculated and deducted on a monthly basis.

People with more complicated income sources, such as stock investors, contract employees or self-employed people, will be sent IR 3 (individual tax return) forms to work out their income tax each year. The forms are due in early July, along with any additional taxes that you owe. It's reasonably easy to fill out your own tax return, but if this sort of thing makes your head spin, there are professional tax agents who will file your return for you for a few hundred dollars.

Income is taxed at incremental rates depending on how much you earn. Your first $14,000 of income is taxed at 10.5 percent, the amount between $14,001 and $48,000 at 17.5 percent, the amount between $48,001 and $70,000 at 30 percent, and everything over $70,000 at 33 percent. Of course politicians love to change tax rates, so check with the IRD for the current rates when you start your first job in New Zealand.

PAYE Deductions

If you are earning a salary from an employer, your income tax will be automatically deducted from your pay. This is called PAYE, or "pay as you earn." For most people, this keeps their taxes nice and simple, and they have nothing further to pay at the end of the financial year.

Withholding Tax

Tax is automatically deducted from your interest payments on your bank accounts. It may also be deducted by employers if you are contracted to do work for them and you do not operate as your own business. These taxes are called withholding taxes, as they are held back from you and sent directly to your account at Inland Revenue.

Resident Withholding Tax is deducted at 33 percent (the highest personal tax rate) unless you make other arrangements. If you know that this is not the rate you're likely to owe based on your total income, you can ask your bank to deduct the correct rate for you to avoid working it out at the end of the year.

BUSINESS TAXES

If you are running a business in New Zealand, you will have to pay business income taxes. If your company is large, you may need the assistance of a professional tax agent or accountant to keep track of your paperwork. He or she will be able to ensure you get all of your forms filled out correctly and stay on top of any deductions and depreciation that can be written off. Your company will need an IRD number, separate from your individual number.

The tax rate for businesses is 28 percent. This applies to all companies except for sole traders and partnerships (companies where the owner is the only employee). If you are self-employed and have no employees, then your business income is taxed at the same rate as personal income tax.

Businesses that owed over $2,500 in unpaid taxes at the end of the previous year may need to make provisional tax payments throughout the year, using the previous year's earnings as an estimate of what you will owe, and paying a percentage of that in installments during the year. This avoids having a huge lump sum to pay at the end of the year. Provisional tax applies to both companies and sole traders/partnerships.

HIDDEN TAXES

GST, or goods and services tax, is added to almost every purchase you make in New Zealand. To make it more palatable, however, retailers tend to include it in the sticker price so you don't get any surprises at checkout. If you check your receipt, you will usually see the amount of GST included in your purchase as a separate figure at the bottom. This 15 percent tax applies nationwide. If you run a business that charges GST, you will be able to write off the GST you pay on business purchases throughout the year, so hang on to those receipts.

The taxes on fuel, alcohol, and cigarettes are also invisible to the naked eye, but they are quite significant. Fuel taxes total over $0.67 per liter. Over 70 percent of the cost of cigarettes is taxes, and the government is increasing this by 10 percent per year. Alcohol tax rates vary depending on the type of drink, but for a bottle of hard liquor, you can expect to pay over $19 in taxes even before you add on GST. And, yes, the GST is added to the after-tax price, so you're paying tax on tax.

FOREIGN TAXES AND DOUBLE TAXATION AGREEMENTS

Just because you have relocated to New Zealand doesn't necessarily mean you can forget about the tax authorities back home. If you are still earning income in your home country, you will be expected to pay tax on it. This includes income from properties, investments, dividends, royalties, and work done for companies based there. If you are staying in New Zealand for an extended period, you may be considered a nonresident in your home country and be taxed at a different rate.

On the bright side, you shouldn't have to pay two taxes on the same income. Double Taxation Agreements exist between New Zealand and the United States, the United Kingdom, Canada, Australia, and 35 other countries. If you can prove that a source of income has been taxed in another country, you won't be charged New Zealand tax on the same income. Read the fine print on your agreement, though, because there are some exceptions to this rule.

Investing

If you're in the happy position of having extra funds to invest in New Zealand, there are several options open to you. Of course, you're under no obligation to keep all of your money in the country. New Zealand does not place limits on funds you take out of the country, but the country you move them to may charge high taxes on investments from nonresidents.

If you are planning to keep your wealth within New Zealand, you'll have many choices, including simple savings accounts and other banking options, investing in the property market, or playing the stock market. Your own financial savvy and comfort with different risk levels will be the deciding factors in how you help your savings to grow.

SAVINGS ACCOUNTS AND TERM DEPOSITS

With interest rates higher in New Zealand than most countries at the moment, you can earn quite a good return simply by leaving your savings in a high-interest bank account. Banks are competing for your cash, so check the rates carefully if you have a significant deposit. Interest rates change quite frequently.

Term deposits often give you higher interest than a savings account, but you will not be able to access your money until the deposit matures. Again, different banks and financial providers will be offering a wide range of options, so it's important to shop around.

Be wary of any offer that seems too good to be true. You'll see a lot of advertising for very tempting investments from finance companies (not banks), and it's easy to get caught up in the hype and not read the fine print. The risk may pay off, or it may not, but check out the company's details before you commit. Several financial service companies have gone bankrupt in the past due to bad property development investments. This has left their investors in limbo about whether they will get any of their invested money back.

You may see the term PIE (Portfolio Investor Entities) advertised. These investments are taxed at a lower rate to encourage investment in New Zealand. The rates are based on your taxable income level, but are capped at 28 percent.

PROPERTY INVESTMENT

The property market in New Zealand went through a huge boom at the turn of the millennium. This turned a lot of average Kiwis into part-time property investors. With growth in some areas of up to 15 percent per year, it was hard to beat as an investment opportunity. With the property market finally leveling off (apart from Auckland) during the 2008 recession, however, this is no longer a sure way to make money.

Before you dive in, make sure you do your math. The rise in property values has slowed down, mortgage rates are high, and renting your investment property to tenants isn't likely to cover all of your costs. The investment isn't without risk, as you could be faced with costly home repairs or declining values.

On the other hand, a lot of investors have made hundreds of thousands of dollars over the past 15-20 years by buying multiple homes and reselling them after they increase in value. Fixing up and reselling older houses has also become a way for real estate investors to maximize profits.

NEW ZEALAND STOCK EXCHANGE (NZX)

Investing in the stock exchange carries similar risks and rewards in New Zealand as it does elsewhere. The NZX is based in Wellington and trades shares in all of the large, public companies in the country. You may want to wait until you've been in the country for a while before stepping into the market, so you can become familiar with the companies and their recent performance and plans for the future.

Some of the most popular companies traded on the NZX are Fletcher Building, Xero (software), Spark New Zealand, Fisher & Paykel Healthcare, Sky Network TV, and Contact Energy. Companies must be valued at no less than $5 million to be listed on the NZX.

DAILY LIFE

COMMUNICATIONS

With the Pacific Ocean lying between you and your friends and family back home, communicating with the rest of the world takes on new importance after you immigrate. Not so long ago, immigrants were left waiting for weeks to get letters from back home. Now, instant communication is not just possible, it's expected. Online chatting, text messaging, and cheap (even free) long-distance calling can make those faraway loved ones feel like they're right next door.

New Zealand media is still quite small-time compared with the United States or Britain, but local shows do entertain and inform. And to fill any voids, the networks buy programming from around the world, so you'll see not just New Zealand programs, but also American, British, Australian, and even a few Canadian shows. Radio stations cater to a variety of tastes but perhaps lack some of the extremes you might find in bigger cities. If your tastes are far from mainstream, you may have to make an effort to keep up with the latest releases, but the big hits from back home will almost always find their way to New Zealand airwaves.

All of these kinds of communication and media can help you to feel less isolated after you immigrate, whether it's because you can talk to your mother every night using Skype or because you never have to miss an episode of your favorite sitcom.

Telephones and Mobile Phones

The phone system in New Zealand is modern and reliable. Most people still have a landline, although more and more are choosing to rely on their mobile phones completely. In the past, having a home phone meant having a Telecom line; the government has broken that monopoly over the lines and more competition is emerging. Mobiles, as cell phones are more often called here, are very pervasive in New Zealand, despite having high charges compared with North America and Europe.

LANDLINES

Phone lines are laid to just about every corner of New Zealand, although if you buy a brand-new property in a previously undeveloped area, it can take the infrastructure several months to catch up with you. But for most, phone lines can be hooked up almost immediately.

There are now several providers of home phone service, including the former monopoly, Telecom, which is now called Spark New Zealand, Vodafone, and a number of Internet service providers. Others are also joining the competition as the industry moves forward. It's often worth comparing the prices and services offered by different providers, because a package deal combining your phone service with other things like Internet and mobile phone can sometimes save you money.

Phone numbers in New Zealand have seven digits, plus a two-digit area code. If you are calling a local number, you will not have to dial the area code. However, there may be places within your area code that are not local calls. If you are calling from overseas, using New Zealand's country code of 64, you have to drop the first digit (always zero) of the area code. If you are calling from another area of New Zealand, you will use both digits of the area code, but not the country code.

Toll-free numbers in New Zealand start with either 0800 or 0508, and this will be followed by a six- or seven-digit number. Any number starting with one of those prefixes will be free of charge, but the numbers will only work within New Zealand. Numbers beginning with 0900 are commercially operated and will add an extra charge to your phone bill.

Most phone plans include unlimited free local calls, but this does not extend to calling mobile phones. Extra features such as voice mail and call forwarding can be added for an additional charge. You can expect to pay $42-60 per month for basic phone service. Phone connections at the wall are a different shape than those in North America, so if you are bringing a telephone from home, you will need to buy an adapter to plug it in to a New Zealand phone outlet.

Phone Companies

Spark (formerly Telecom) still dominates the landlines thanks to its former monopoly, but its strength in the market is not what it once was. Spark's advantage is that it provides service throughout the country, while some of the others only service certain areas. There are a wide range of plans and packages available from Spark, depending on which services you want and whether you include a long-distance plan.

Vodafone is the other company with a big slice of the landline market. It has a number of plans, either with just phone service or combining it with Internet and/or cable TV services.

Several of the main Internet service providers in New Zealand also offer a home phone service. Your options include Orcon, Slingshot, Woosh, and Compass.

Domestic Rates

All of your local calls in New Zealand should be free (included in the cost of your phone line), and some of the new providers entering the market are also offering free national calls. When you sign up for phone service, ask how your local and national calls will be handled on the plan you've chosen.

Long-distance calls within New Zealand are usually charged by the minute. Each phone service provider can set its own rates and may offer special plans that allow you to call anywhere in the country for a set monthly fee. Depending on the provider and the plan, you should expect to pay around $0.20-0.50 per minute for domestic long-distance calls. Calling a mobile phone from your home line also costs extra, usually around $0.40 per minute.

International Rates

Toll rates for international calls can vary wildly depending on the provider, and how and when you make your calls. Going through your home phone provider, you may be able to get a calling plan that caps rates for calls to certain countries—for example, calling the United Kingdom for up to two hours for a maximum charge of $5. Other plans include minute-by-minute rates, which are different for every country.

Only a few pay phones still accept coins.

Calling cards are another way to get cheap long-distance rates. Available at shops and Internet cafés, these cards come from several different providers, and each has its own set of rates and charges. But the rate for calling the United States using one of these cards can be as little as 2.5 cents per minute, although there can also be a fixed connection fee. The companies providing this service use VoIP (Voice over Internet Protocol) technology. You call a local number for the service, and then they prompt you to enter the long-distance number you wish to connect to.

Many people trying to stay in touch with friends and family in other countries are forsaking their phones altogether and using their computers and mobile devices instead. Chatting programs like Skype and FaceTime cost nothing to use (other than your regular Internet or data charges) and can offer extras like being able to see the person you're talking to. They are easy to use and definitely giving the phone companies a run for their money.

MOBILE PHONES

Cellular or mobile phones come in all shapes and sizes in New Zealand. The simplest, cheapest phones can be had for under $100, while the latest smartphones can cost close to $1,000. Kiwis seem to love using their mobiles, with 4.7 million mobile connections in New Zealand. That's more than one for every Kiwi!

The main providers of mobile phone service in New Zealand are Spark, Vodafone, and 2degrees. Your provider will also determine your "area code." Rather than using the same area codes as landlines, New Zealand mobile phones have separate three- or four-digit prefixes that precede their phone numbers. Traditionally, Spark numbers begin with 027, 2degrees numbers begin with 022, and Vodafone numbers begin with 021, but providers are now allowing customers to keep their existing mobile number when they switch providers. This is followed by the individual's mobile number, which can be anywhere from six to eight digits long.

All three providers have good coverage in urban areas, but things can get spotty out in the sticks. If you live in a rural location, check the coverage for your area (by calling the provider or looking at coverage maps on its website) to see if you will get a signal. If you are planning to use your mobile phone to get broadband services, your coverage will be more limited still. The best way to find out if you will get good signals in your area is to ask locals which phone company they use and how well it works for them.

Mobile Plans

Paying for your mobile phone use comes down to two main options: monthly plans or prepaid service. A mobile plan involves paying a monthly fee to your mobile service provider, and getting a certain number of minutes, text messages, etc., included for that price (or at a discounted rate). A variety of plans are available, depending on when and how much you use your mobile. The base rates for most mobile plans are $30-100 per month. Some plans only provide free minutes of calling on evenings and weekends. Others also include some weekday minutes. Check the minutes and data amounts included in your plan, and take note of the additional costs once you go over those limits. Sometimes upgrading your plan can be much cheaper than frequently going over your limit.

Prepaid Mobile

For people who don't use their mobile very much, sometimes it's cheaper to avoid signing up to a plan. By prepaying for your calls, you only get charged for the time you use. Rates may be higher for each call, but you will save $30-100 per month on plan fees. There are prepay packages you can buy for $20-30 per month, and unused amounts should carry over. Incoming calls are free.

Prepaid mobiles can have their balance upped in several ways. You can call in and use a credit card, you can do the same over the Internet, or you can buy "top-up" (refill) cards from local shops. Any unused balance on your prepaid phone expires one year after you purchased it. However, any unused amounts for add-ons like bulk text rates or free weekends may expire each month, so read the terms of your agreement carefully.

International Rates

Making international calls from your mobile isn't really much more expensive than making domestic calls beyond your "included" minutes. With some plans, it can even cost exactly the same! On Vodafone prepay, for example, it costs $0.89 per minute to call a non-Vodafone mobile or a landline in one of 15 selected countries, including the United States and Canada.

Calling cards can also be used from a mobile phone, but there is usually an extra fee or a higher rate for this. Read the fine print (which is usually not on the card itself but on a brochure or website) before you get an unpleasant surprise.

Internet Services

Internet service is available from a large range of providers in New Zealand. Although use is high, the infrastructure supporting broadband in New Zealand is still in the process of getting updated to a fiber-optic network in many areas. If you're a big downloader and your area doesn't have fiber yet, expect frustrating waits. But for general use, the Internet in New Zealand is affordable and reliable.

If you get a home Internet connection, you can choose to connect using your phone line (ADSL), or in some areas a cable connection is available. Some of the most popular Internet providers include Spark, Vodafone, Snap, Orcon, Slingshot, Actrix, and Woosh. Most Internet plans include free web-based email addresses. The cost of your plan will be determined by the speed of your connection and the download limit. You can get a bare-bones package for $55 per month, but plans range up to about $100 per month for the fastest connections and the biggest limits.

High-speed Internet services are not available in all areas, so it's important to check that your address is in the provider's zone of coverage before you decide on anything. Those in rural areas may be stuck with slower service.

PUBLIC INTERNET ACCESS

If you want to access the Internet but don't have a connection at home yet, you have a few options depending on what devices you own and where you live. The main choices will be public wireless Internet spots, Internet cafés, and libraries.

Trade Me

When eBay took the world by storm some years ago, it missed out on setting up a New Zealand site. (I know, we're easy to miss, tucked away at the bottom of the world.) That left the door open for Kiwi entrepreneur Sam Morgan, who set up a New Zealand-based online auction site called Trade Me.

The site took off, and soon Kiwis were auctioning everything that wasn't nailed down. By 2005, it was the most popular website in the country.

In 2006, Morgan cashed in on the empire he had built. He sold Trade Me and its associate websites to Fairfax Media for $700 million.

From its auctioning roots, the company has expanded to include a variety of services: selling cars and real estate; listing flats, houses, and vacation homes for rent; online dating; advertising service providers; selling travel; selling insurance; matching up flatmates; and posting job opportunities. It's a real hub of online activity. With over 3.5 million registered users in 2014, Trade Me generates a huge percentage of New Zealand's Internet traffic.

Items being auctioned on Trade Me must be from New Zealand sellers, and most purchases are paid for by direct bank transfers into the seller's account, doing away with the need for credit card security or PayPal registration. Some items locally purchased can be paid for in cash and picked up in person. This is convenient for larger items like furniture or cars, where shipping is impractical. While things started off with individuals doing most of the selling, a large number of professionals have set up shop on Trade Me, selling brand-new merchandise.

So when you get to New Zealand, whether you're looking for a place to live, furnishings for your new place, or just a little something special for yourself, you will probably end up visiting Trade Me to see what's on offer.

DAILY LIFE

Public wireless access is becoming more available in New Zealand's cities and tourist hot spots. There are free hotspots in Auckland, Wellington, Rotorua, and Dunedin offered by the local government. In addition, some cafés and fast-food restaurants offer free wireless Internet as an incentive. There are some McDonald's locations, for example, where you can connect.

There are Internet cafés all around New Zealand, although their numbers are decreasing as public wireless Internet becomes more available. The main users are now gamers, who gather to play online games at all hours, but travelers still use them as well. These places have computers available for use by the hour, with rates ranging $2-8. Some have a minimum charge as well, so if you just pop in to check your email for five minutes you could end up paying for more. Many offer printing for an extra charge. This can be helpful during your job search if you don't yet have a printer at home.

All libraries in New Zealand have free wireless Internet available. You can bring your own device to use in the library, and most branches will also have computers available for those without devices of their own. There may be time limits for using the library's computers, and some websites may be blocked.

Postal Service and Couriers

New Zealand Post provides good service in the areas of traditional postage and courier services. Within the same city, it is not unusual to get a letter the day after it was mailed. Sending packages overseas can be incredibly expensive, however, and take a long time.

New Zealand Post Shops are abundant, located in towns and cities around the country. Pretty much every town has one, although the smallest towns may have them located inside another shop. These Post Shops offer a full range of postal services, from buying stamps to sending packages overseas, and most also function as the New Zealand Post-owned Kiwibank branches. You can send registered letters from any Post Shop.

You can mail your letters in postboxes, which are located on sidewalks, near shopping centers, and in other convenient places around town. Most boxes are picked up once or twice daily. There are often two boxes side by side. One of these is for standard mail and the other for Fastpost.

Sending a standard-sized letter anywhere within New Zealand costs $0.80 for regular service, or $1.40 for Fastpost, which will arrive a day or two faster. This two-tier pricing system also applies to larger envelopes and packages. You can pay extra to have your items delivered faster. For international shipping, you will have to choose between International Courier (ground shipping) or International Air (air mail). Often the difference is only a few dollars, and the delivery times can be quite a lot faster by air. Things

© MICHELLE WAITZMAN

a tiny rural post office in Arthur's Pass on the South Island

get a lot pricier, however, when you are sending a package. For example, a box weighing 2 kg (about 4.5 pounds) would cost almost $59 to mail to the United States using International Courier, and over $76 by International Air.

Almost everyone in New Zealand can have their mail delivered directly to their homes. In the cities, delivery is daily to your mailbox, Monday through Friday. If you are going to be away and don't want your mail to pile up, you can have New Zealand Post hold your mail for a fee.

If you live in a rural area, your mail will be delivered (and outgoing mail picked up) by a RuralPost owner/driver. You have to register for this service through New Zealand Post, and your mailbox must comply with certain standards.

New Zealand Post operates its own courier services. The same-day service is

Learning the Post Code

For a long time, New Zealand Post was happy to deliver any letter in the country, as long as it contained a street address and town. With New Zealand's low population, there were rarely any problems figuring out where the letter was meant to go.

As time has passed, there is more need to assign specific codes to areas of the country to help sort and deliver the mail efficiently. Post codes were first introduced in 1977 but mainly used within New Zealand Post itself to organize bulk mail lodgments. Kiwis were not expected to know the code for their area or to write codes on their letters.

In 2006, new post codes were introduced because growing populations, duplicated street and suburb names, and other confusing details were making sorting and delivering letters to the intended address more difficult. For example, there's a Cuba Street in downtown Wellington, and a Cuba Street in Petone, Wellington—if you forgot to write Petone, your letter could be delivered to the wrong Cuba Street. Therefore, four-digit codes have been assigned to all areas in New Zealand.

Problem solved, right? Well, not quite. First New Zealand Post will have to convince Kiwis to use the new codes. After so many years of not needing them, it's a hard sell. For the most part, letters without post codes are still faithfully delivered, hopefully to the right address. But in the future, a time may come when leaving off the post code means having your letter returned.

called Pace, and the next-day service is called Courier Post. Other courier companies do operate within New Zealand, including UPS, Fastway, FedEx, and Post Haste. If you have a lot of packages to send, it pays to shop around for the best deal.

Media

If you're used to getting 200 channels on your TV and having a choice of three or four daily newspapers in your city, you may find the media situation in New Zealand a bit lacking. Even full satellite TV subscriptions will only bring you up to about 70 channels, many of which are feeds from Australian channels. Newspapers are regional or local, and some don't even publish daily. But there is no lack of access to information in New Zealand, and using the Internet can keep you in touch with all of the happenings back home, too.

New Zealanders get most American movies in full release, although sometimes much later than they are seen in the United States. Your favorite sitcoms and dramas will probably be shown on New Zealand TV if they're popular enough, but again the episodes can be several weeks behind what is airing in North America or the United Kingdom. Some immigrants (and Kiwis) are so frustrated by this that they watch their favorite shows on the Internet or download episodes directly to their computers rather than waiting for them to make it to local networks (of course I only endorse legal downloads, such as via iTunes).

New Zealand-made movies and television are sometimes just as entertaining (or

Satellites and aerials are popular choices for television viewing, but streaming is also an option now.

informative) as the imports, although the budgets are often low. But watching Kiwi entertainment is a great way to get better acquainted with the culture, the Kiwi sense of humor, and the issues that are important to New Zealanders.

TELEVISION

The state-owned networks TV1 and TV2 are general-interest networks, much like the big U.S. networks. They air both local and international shows and use advertising to generate revenue, unlike PBS. TV2 is aimed at a slightly younger audience than TV1.

TV3 was the country's first foreign-owned network, started by the Canadian CanWest Global group. The network is now owned by a large New Zealand media company called Mediaworks. The network is another general-interest one, with news and a variety of local and foreign shows. The final general network is Prime, which is owned by Sky, the country's satellite TV provider.

In 2004, Maori Television began broadcasting, giving a national presence to Maori culture through a channel that is bilingual and partly owned by the government. This channel is free-to-air, like the main networks. Other free channels include Trackside TV, which broadcasts horse- and dog-racing events, and FOUR, which features dramas, comedies, and reality shows. Free digital channels include things like a Christian channel and a Chinese-language channel.

Some areas have local channels, although their content is not always local. Auckland has Face, which combines local public-access programming with international feeds from networks like Bloomberg TV, Deutsche Welle, Euronews, and PBS. Christchurch's local channel is CTV, and farther south, Invercargill is the home of

The American Stream

For viewers who are used to the wide range of online streaming offerings in the United States, it can be frustrating to find out that services like Netflix U.S. and Hulu are blocked outside of the country. Kiwis think this is pretty unfair, too. In fact, some Internet service providers in New Zealand have found a way to offer American streaming services to their New Zealand customers.

In 2014, both Slingshot and Orcon started offering something called Global Mode as part of their packages. This mode allows users to bypass the "geoblocking" that normally prevents people from using streaming services from other countries. The companies claim to be confident in the legality of this, although it may be challenged on the grounds that other services have paid for exclusive rights to offer some of that content in New Zealand.

Using Global Mode allows users to subscribe to any version of Netflix (there is a version for Australia and New Zealand, but it offers a different selection of titles from the U.S. service), Hulu, HBO Go, and other streaming services. Users still need to subscribe to the services themselves and pay the monthly fees for them.

This work-around has made competition extra tough for Kiwi streaming services such as Sparks' Lightbox and Sky TV's Neon.

educational channel Cue TV, also available nationally on Sky and Freeview. You may find it strange that there are no local newscasts to speak of in New Zealand, but the country is small enough that local stories often get covered on the national network newscasts, so there is no need for local news. My biggest complaint about this is having to listen to the weather forecasts for the entire country when I'm only interested in Wellington's.

Locally made shows vary quite a lot in quality. Newscasts are generally pretty good, although foreign stories are often feeds from U.S. or UK networks, and current affairs shows have some interesting content. Local dramas can be a bit cheesy, but some develop strong followings. Documentaries are popular, along with factual programs.

Free-to-Air TV

If you're not a big viewer, you may be perfectly happy to join the thousands of Kiwis who continue to receive TV programming from an aerial or dish on their roof. The main networks are all available as digital free-to-air signals, along with a variety of national and local offerings. In all, you may receive as many as 34 channels over the air depending on your location. Reception can vary depending on how far you are from the local transmitter and whether your home has a clear line of sight to it.

New Zealand has completed the transition to digital transmission of over-the-air signals. For those with an older TV that did not come with a digital tuner installed, there is an option called Freeview. It uses a satellite dish and digital receiver to deliver signals to your TV, but only carries free-to-air channels. That means that once you pay for the equipment and installation, the service itself is free. However, receivers start at around $100, and if you don't already have a satellite dish, you'll have to buy one of those and have it installed as well. There is reception of Freeview services via the rooftop TV aerial in certain areas, mainly in the major cities. This gives you the same digital reception without a satellite dish, but it will only work for people who have good line of sight to the transmission towers. Any new TV should be able to receive free-to-air signals without a receiver box, but you will still need a dish or aerial connected to your TV.

For those who want a little more than the free offerings, there is also a service called Igloo. This uses a digital box and a rooftop antenna, much like Freeview. However, you can choose to add to the free channels by subscribing to a package of 13 additional channels for around $20 per month, and you also have access to pay-per-view movies and sporting events.

Cable and Satellite TV

The most popular (because it's the most available) choice for Kiwis who want a wider range of channels is Sky satellite TV. Sky offers the only satellite subscription service in New Zealand. The basic package gives you about 50 channels for $50 per month. This includes international news from BBC World, CNN, CNBC, and Fox News, if you are concerned about keeping up with what's happening back home.

Additional packages of channels include movies, sports, arts, and interactive games. If you want the works, you can easily find yourself paying over $100 per month. There is a video-on-demand service that offers movies and events at an additional cost.

It costs $99 to have the system set up at your home, but the equipment remains the property of Sky, so you have to return the receiver and dish if you cancel your service. Sky is available to most people, although some may find that if there are large objects blocking the dish (trees, high-rise buildings, etc.) their reception will suffer.

Cable TV has not taken off in New Zealand the way it did in North America. Cable service is offered by Vodafone in limited areas around Wellington and Christchurch. Rather than offering their own range of channels, Vodafone offers its cable TV customers Sky TV packages or Freeview channels with an additional pay-per-view service.

Online Streaming Services

The new kid on the block for delivering media content is online streaming services. Spark New Zealand was first off the block with its Lightbox service. You can watch all you want for $15 per month with no commercials. At the time of writing there are plenty of popular shows available, but this may change as new services start to compete for rights.

Quickflix offers a monthly subscription for $13, but they also offer "premium" (which means newer) movies on a pay-per-view basis.

Sky TV has also joined the streaming party with their service, Neon. It launched in December 2014 for $20 per month. It currently has a deal with HBO, so it's the best place to find their shows at this time.

Netflix launched their service to Australia and New Zealand in March 2015. But don't expect this to be the same as Netflix in the united States. Different territories have the rights to different content, so the pickings could be slim compared with what you had before your move.

RADIO

Both AM and FM radio signals are broadcast in New Zealand, so you can enjoy a range of programming in your car, on your clock radio, or at your office. Many also broadcast digitally as well these days. Most radio stations are commercial and run by either independent companies or larger networks. Advertising is used to finance most of the stations.

A lot of the radio offerings in New Zealand are "branded" stations, where the same format is used by a string of local stations throughout the country to make a sort of network. Some of the more popular brands include The Edge, More FM, and ZM, which focus on pop music; The Rock, Radio Hauraki, and Classic Hits, which have a more old-school feel; The Breeze, for easy listening; and Kiwi FM, for New Zealand music. There are no regulations requiring radio stations to play a specific amount of New Zealand music, so local musicians must compete with superstars from around the world for airtime.

Urban and hip-hop music is mostly found on local Auckland stations, while country offerings are abundant in more rural areas. There are Christian stations dotted around the country, some aimed at younger listeners, while others are for the more mature. Newstalk ZB caters nationally to those who aren't looking for music at all. If the station you'd most enjoy isn't broadcasting in your area, see if it offers an Internet feed of its signal. A lot of stations offer a live feed, so you can listen to them from anywhere.

Maori stations are also located in various parts of the country, encouraging people to use the language more and get interested in Maori culture and events.

Several stations around the country are aimed specifically at immigrant populations. Pacific stations are the most common, for immigrants from Samoa, Tonga, Fiji, and other Pacific Islands. There is also a station for the Indian community.

Public Radio

Radio New Zealand is a state-owned company that broadcasts nationwide over three networks: Radio New Zealand National, Radio New Zealand Concert, and the AM network, which relays parliamentary proceedings. All of its broadcasts are commercial-free.

RNZ National is an FM network that carries news, current affairs, documentaries, dramas, Maori programming, and music. Talk shows make up about 60 percent of the schedule, and the music played is at least one-third Kiwi. RNZ Concert mainly plays classical music but also includes jazz, contemporary, and world music in its schedule.

NEWSPAPERS AND MAGAZINES

Print media is alive and well in New Zealand, offering everything from major dailies to small, community papers. The level of journalism in some of the smaller papers can be amateur, but the main news providers are reasonably reliable if not always impartial.

New Zealand being a quiet, stable country, the papers (and TV newscasts) often seem to blow stories out of proportion just to make things seem more dramatic. An event that would barely get a mention in other countries may be written about for days or even weeks here until something more interesting comes along. So sometimes you have to take the news with a grain of salt and put it into perspective on a more global scale.

International stories do receive coverage, but if you're really interested in what's happening back home, you may prefer to check websites or TV channels that originate in your home country. Only the biggest international stories will make it into New Zealand newspapers.

Major Newspapers and Magazines

The closest thing to a national newspaper in New Zealand is the *New Zealand Herald*, which is published in Auckland daily. While it covers news from around the country, as well as international news, its circulation is limited to the top half of the North Island. Subscribers outside that area have to sign up for postal delivery, which is quite expensive. The paper is sold in shops all over the North Island, however, and in Christchurch.

For those in Wellington, the newspaper most accessible to you is the *Dominion Post*. It has local Wellington stories, but still covers all of the national and international news. Subscriptions are delivered around Greater Wellington, and some shops stock it farther afield.

The Press is the daily paper in Christchurch and is read widely around the South Island.

Many of the newspapers (and magazines) in New Zealand are owned by a few large companies. The biggest owners are Fairfax Media and New Zealand Media and Entertainment (NZME).

Magazines are popular with New Zealanders and available on just about any topic imaginable. There are news magazines like *Time* and *New Zealand Listener,* fashion

A full range of local and imported magazines are available in New Zealand.

magazines, and magazines for every niche from fine cuisine to gardening to mountain biking. In addition to national magazines, there are international magazines available at most bookstores and magazine sellers. These are often Australian, but you can also find some popular U.S. and UK titles.

Local Newspapers

To find out what's happening in your corner of New Zealand, there are dozens of local newspapers. In bigger cities, these can be daily papers. In smaller communities, they are more likely to be weekly. Some community papers are delivered to all residents free of charge, with advertising paying all of their costs. These papers are good sources of information on what's happening around town, and local council issues. Stories that are too localized to make the bigger papers can often be found in your community newspaper.

TRAVEL AND TRANSPORTATION

Compared to the United States or Canada, New Zealand is a physically small country. It covers about the same area as Great Britain or Japan. That makes traveling around the country a good deal easier than you might be used to. Nobody lives more than a couple of hours away from a coast, and in a day's drive you can cover the entire length of the North Island. But even though distances are reasonable, the traffic doesn't go particularly fast. New Zealand's state highways are no match for the U.S. interstates or European freeways, but the average Kiwi does try to push the limits of safe speeds. If you want to travel around the country quickly, domestic flights can certainly speed things up, or for a more leisurely journey, you can enjoy some scenic train travel.

Despite the country's "green" reputation, most Kiwis own cars and use them daily to get to work, do their shopping, and, of course, drive themselves to the gym! This is partly because the quality of public transportation in New Zealand varies widely between different cities. The sprawling layout of Auckland has not been well served by its trains and buses, but the city is gradually improving the system. Wellington has had more success in getting commuters out of their cars, but is also struggling to replace aging trains and buses. Christchurch has an extensive bus network as well, yet its

© MICHELLE WAITZMAN

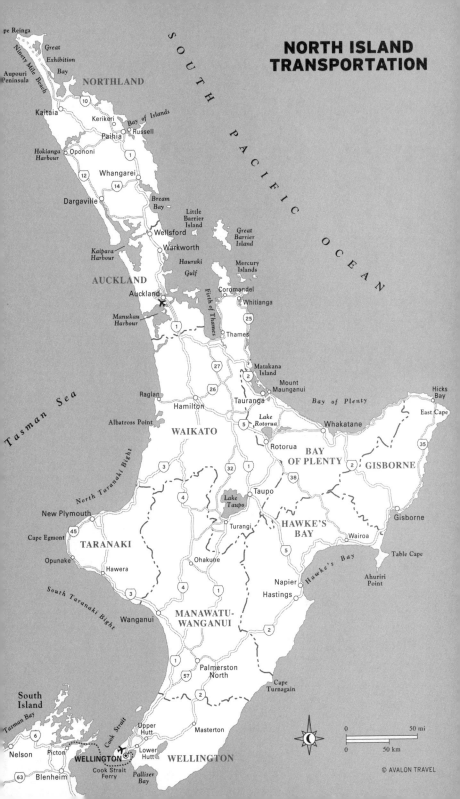

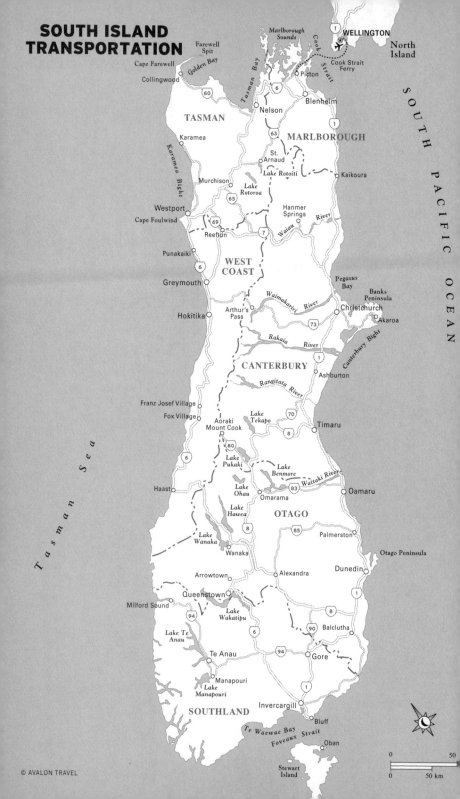

urban sprawl can make the distances daunting. Smaller cities have more limited public transportation options, and in many places it's nearly impossible to get by without a car.

Air

Living on an island nation means that your international travels will always require flying. New Zealand has several international airports, but flying to North America, Europe, or Asia generally involves heading out from Auckland or Christchurch, although Hamilton airport has a few long-haul flights to North America. The other international airports, including Wellington, Dunedin, Queenstown, Rotorua, and Palmerston North, only act as a hub for flights to Australia or the Pacific Islands. You may be able to travel on from one of those places to your final destinations, however.

Yet New Zealand's airports are well placed for domestic traffic. Most major destinations can be reached by air, and the main routes have frequent service for business travelers.

INTERNATIONAL FLIGHTS

Unless you're hopping "across the ditch" to Australia, flights out of New Zealand have a few main routes. From Auckland, you can find direct flights to Los Angeles, San Francisco, and Vancouver to access the rest of North America. If you're off to Europe, you can fly via Dubai, various Australian cities, Hong Kong, Singapore, and a few other hubs. Asia is well served out of Auckland, with direct flights to China, Hong Kong, Singapore, Bangkok, and other popular destinations. In 2015, Air New Zealand added a direct flight to South America that lands in Buenos Aires.

International flights from New Zealand are expensive. With such a small population to draw from, you simply don't get the same kinds of bargains that are offered to customers in the United States or Europe. There are seat sales and special offers, but you won't find prices that match those in other major centers. There are quite a few airlines flying in and out of New Zealand, so it pays to explore different options and routes if you have a major journey in mind. Sometimes a stopover in Tahiti can be just the thing to save you several hundred dollars. (And wouldn't you just love a stopover in Tahiti, anyway?)

DOMESTIC FLIGHTS

Air New Zealand is the dominant provider of domestic flights in New Zealand. It serves all of the little airports other airlines don't consider profitable. But on the main routes (between Auckland, Wellington, Christchurch, Queenstown, and Dunedin) there is some healthy competition from Jetstar (owned by Qantas).

Domestic flights can be a reasonably affordable way to save time if you are traveling for business or to a holiday destination. On competitive routes, flights can cost as little as $50, but the remoter the airport, the more you're likely to pay for your flight.

Short flights across the Cook Strait, for those who don't want to spend three hours on the ferry, can start from $99. Some fly between Wellington and Picton; others land in Blenheim or Nelson. These flights are offered by Sounds Air, Air2There, and Air New Zealand.

If you are flying into a small airport, be prepared to take a small plane. On many routes you will find yourself on a propeller plane rather than a jet.

Train

For those who feel that getting there should be half the fun, a scenic train journey in New Zealand is an ideal way to get around. It's not for anyone in a hurry, though, and there are limited intercity lines. New Zealand's train journeys are sold mainly as a tourism option, rather than a practical way to get through the country.

The most popular lines are between Auckland and Wellington, called the Northern Explorer, and between Christchurch and the West Coast, called the Tranz Alpine. There's also a trip between Picton (where the South Island ferry terminal is) and Christchurch, called the Coastal Pacific. For more practical purposes, there is a Capital Connection route between Wellington and Palmerston North. The full-length scenic journeys can cost from $140 to over $200, depending on the route. Smaller portions cost proportionately less.

COMMUTER TRAINS

Commuting to work by train in major cities is gaining popularity as fuel prices increase and global warming is on everyone's minds. Unfortunately, very few cities in New Zealand have put in the infrastructure for a commuter train system.

The best commuter trains in the country are probably those in Wellington. The city has four lines spreading out from the central train station, servicing the suburbs

Train journeys in New Zealand can be very scenic.

© NATHANIEL BEAVER

and towns along the coast, and up the Hutt Valley. In Auckland, the government has been pouring money into improved rail systems by electrifying the commuter train network and adding or upgrading stations in a number of suburbs. In 2006, three-quarters of Aucklanders went to work by car, but with improved public transportation, the number of public-transit users is on the rise.

Both Wellington and Auckland use zone-based fare systems, so the farther you are traveling, the more it costs. Both offer discounted multiride tickets, as well as monthly passes for regular commuters. The system in Wellington is run by Metlink, and in Auckland it is run by Auckland Transport.

Bus

Traveling by bus can often be the most affordable way to get where you're going, although schedules are somewhat limited and prices can be just as high as flying if discounted fares are sold out. But if you enjoy a road trip, the bus system is worth checking out. Like trains, long-range buses tend to stop in several towns along every route. You can't get anywhere in a hurry this way. So if you're planning a journey by bus, expect it to take much longer than it would to drive yourself in a car.

INTERCITY BUSES

There are a few companies that operate bus services shuttling people from one city to another. The biggest by far (with the most comprehensive routes) is InterCity Coachlines. It operates coach services all over the country, with regularly scheduled service. Its routes cover the main towns and cities where New Zealanders live, and the more touristy destinations as well. Where InterCity does not have its own service, it teams up with local operators to offer connecting buses.

Prices for a bus journey of this kind depend of course on how far you are going and how early you book. For example, travel from Auckland to Wellington can range from $30 for an online special to $100 for a full adult fare at peak time. You can expect that journey to take almost 11 hours.

TOURIST BUSES

Although they're aimed at visitors, many of the tourist buses offer affordable trips from one city to another. Several companies operate tourist coach services around New Zealand, and while some give you a pretty straightforward ride with some commentary, others are full-on tours with sightseeing stops and activities. So before you choose one of these to get you from A to B, take note of what they'll be doing in between.

Newman's Coach Lines is one operator with a range of routes available. Some of its routes combine with InterCity Coachlines. More touristy operators (popular with the young backpacker crowd) include Kiwi Experience, Stray Bus, and Naked Bus. These may not be the most practical way to travel around the country, but if you want to do some sightseeing while you travel to your destination, this can be a good way to get the best of both worlds.

CITY BUSES AND TRAMS

Most major cities in New Zealand offer bus service to help commuters get around the city, and in and out of the city from the suburbs. Auckland, Wellington, Christchurch, and Dunedin all have major bus networks as part of their public transit systems. In Wellington there are also electric trams (buses powered by electrical wires above the streets) as part of the system. Christchurch's historical tram tracks are now only used as a tourist attraction.

In many of the smaller cities, weekend and late-night service may not be available. Some places have Saturday service but don't operate buses on Sunday. Others are weekday-only. Some operate every day, but not necessarily on every route. Some cities shut down service on public holidays, and most will put out a special timetable over the Christmas-New Year's period.

Even in the big cities it can be hard to get home by public transit after a late night out. This is one of the major contributors to New Zealand's drinking and driving problem. There is no good alternative way to get home from the pub or your mate's big party without driving a car. Check the timetables for your local bus to make sure you can get home from wherever you're going, or be prepared to fork out some extra money for a taxi.

Boat

As a nation of islands, New Zealand is a country that uses boat transportation regularly. It's the most popular way of traveling between the islands and also one of the top leisure activities in the country. After all, most New Zealanders live within an hour's drive of the coast. Even landlocked cities like Hamilton are situated on rivers, so boating is not out of the question for their residents, either.

FERRY SERVICES

The largest ferries in the country operate on the Cook Strait, the body of water that separates the North and South Islands. These ferries carry large numbers of cars and passengers back and forth between Wellington on the North Island and Picton on the South Island. The trip is quite long, considering the distance. It takes about three hours to do a crossing because of speed restrictions both in Wellington's harbor and in the Marlborough Sounds. There is only a short stretch in the middle of the trip where the ferries can travel at full speed. The Cook Strait also has a reputation for high winds and rough waters, so at times the ride can be anything but smooth. On rare occasions, in extreme conditions, ferry trips can be canceled.

Two companies operate the passenger ferries across Cook Strait. Interislander has three ferries that offer 5-6 daily departures in each direction. Bluebridge also operates two ferries with four daily trips in each direction. The fare per person ranges from just over $50 to around $75, but if you are bringing a car, it jumps up to $175 or more. If you're feeling indulgent, Bluebridge has added private cabins to some of their ferry services so you can nap on a bed, get some work done at a desk (with free wireless Internet), or just escape from the other passengers.

© KATHY PHILLIPS

The Insterislander ferry carries passengers and cars between the North and South Islands.

Ferry services also operate between Auckland and various nearby islands and outlying suburbs. Fullers operates most of the ferries, which are used by commuters as well as visitors to the region. There are multitrip and monthly tickets available to regular ferry commuters, which will save a bit in fares. In fact, commuting by ferry can be just as affordable as taking the bus (if it gets you exactly where you need to go) and the timetables are just as frequent on popular routes.

Traveling to Stewart Island also requires a ferry ride. The one-hour crossing of Foveaux Strait between Bluff on the South Island and Stewart Island runs three times daily over the winter months, and four times daily over the summer. The ferries are catamarans seating 100 people, but they do not transport cars.

Smaller ferry services operate in other areas such as Northland and within Wellington Harbour. These are used by locals to get around and also by tourists looking for a scenic experience.

PERSONAL CRAFT

New Zealand has one of the highest rates of personal boat ownership in the world. Sailing isn't just a hobby in this country, it's a passion. In fact, Auckland's nickname is "The City of Sails." New Zealand is also well known for boat construction, including some of the world's most decadent super-yachts. While that may be out of your price range, the large number of boat owners in the country means that there is a healthy market for both new and used boats of every size and type.

Sailboats are by far the most popular around the country, with everything from catamarans to racing boats to leisurely yachts cruising the coastlines. Fishing boats are also big with Kiwis, with so much seafood out there to catch. Smaller watercraft like Jet Skis are growing in number, which can be good or bad depending on how loud you like your beaches. Even kayaks are popular in many areas, although open canoes are hard to come by.

There is no requirement to register a personal boat in New Zealand or to have a specific license to operate one. There are stricter rules for commercial operators.

All coastal cities and towns have marinas and other moorings for privately owned boats. Some are owned by local and regional councils, while others are privately run, so prices can vary a lot. There are also local yachting clubs with their own facilities.

Taxis

With public transportation sometimes hard to come by, taxis do a pretty good business in New Zealand, especially late at night when the crowds begin to stumble out of the pubs and clubs. If you need a taxi at a specific time, for instance to get to a meeting, it's best to book one by phone or online. Relying on hailing a taxi in the street is risky, as sometimes there aren't any around even in the big cities. Airports and hotels have taxi stands, where you can just wander up and there should be a taxi waiting.

Taxis are operated by private companies all around New Zealand in all urban areas. You should be able to identify taxis by a sign on the roof, and often some kind of other signage or writing on the sides of the car. A licensed taxi driver will have an identification card clearly displayed with a picture, name, and the name of the company. The list of charges should be displayed on the passenger door of the taxi and inside the taxi.

All taxis should use a meter to track the fare. If the driver doesn't want to use the meter, you should probably find another taxi, but that would be unusual. You are free to negotiate a flat rate with the driver, but make sure you know what would be reasonable before you agree to one. While there is no regulation of overall fares, every taxi within the same company must charge the same fares. Generally there will be a base fare, plus a per-kilometer charge. Extra charges may apply for multiple passengers and luggage.

In many cities, an Area Knowledge Certificate is required for all taxi drivers. This is meant to ensure that your driver will know where he or she is going! For anyone who has sat in a taxi in an unfamiliar city, sure that the driver is going in circles, this is a reassuring move. Drivers also have to be able to communicate in English at an acceptable level.

Driving

For some reason, otherwise laid-back Kiwis become aggressive and impatient when they're behind the wheel of a car. Speeding, street racing, and drunk driving are problems throughout the country. Car culture is huge here, and people are very attached to their vehicles—perhaps a little too attached sometimes. But most people need a car to get around, so you'll likely be behind the wheel in New Zealand before long.

On top of learning to drive on the left side of the road, there are a lot of rules in New Zealand different from the United States or Canada. The rules are all spelled out in a publication called the *New Zealand Road Code.* This is for sale in bookshops, and you can also find copies in most public libraries or read the entire text on the New Zealand Transport Agency website. I highly recommend having a read of this so you know what to expect on the streets. Understanding things like who has the right-of-way at intersections can be a matter of life and death, so don't assume that you can drive safely in New Zealand just because you've been driving for years in your home country. There is a *Motorcycle Road Code,* which contains rules that apply specifically to motorcycle drivers. New Zealand Transport Agency also has a guide called *What's Different About Driving in New Zealand,* which goes over the basics.

BUYING A NEW CAR

There are no cars currently manufactured in New Zealand, so whatever you decide to buy will be an import. Kiwis have a selection of new cars coming into the country from manufacturers around the world. Some of the more popular brands around the country

DAILY LIFE

© MICHELLE WAITZMAN

Cars from Japan and Korea are popular in New Zealand.

are Toyota, Holden, Mitsubishi, Mazda, Ford, Nissan, Subaru, Mercedes, Honda, and Volkswagen. Others are available, but they tend to show up in smaller numbers.

When it comes to car information, the New Zealand Automobile Association (commonly known as AA) can be a good resource. AA road tests cars and posts reports on its website. New Zealand Transport Agency, the government department in charge of the roads, also has a lot of information and advice for car buyers and sellers.

When you buy a new car, the price will have GST added onto it, plus there is a registration fee of around $400-600, depending on the type of vehicle. When you are quoted a price, ask whether these extras are included. The registration fee will include issuing license plates for your car. New Zealand license plates are white with black letters and numbers; they contain six characters. Personalized plates are also available at an extra charge.

Negotiating the price of your new car is expected, but you may find there is not as much room for haggling as there would be in the United States or Canada. You may be able to get a few extra features thrown into the package, but don't expect huge price reductions through bargaining.

The cheapest you can expect to find a new car is around $23,000 for a small hatchback. An SUV is likely to cost at least $40,000.

BUYING A USED CAR

Used cars are available both from dealers and individuals. Private sales may get you a better price, but if anything goes wrong with the car, it can be hard to pin down the seller afterwards. There is some legal protection regarding the sale of used cars—it's illegal to tamper with the odometer and so on. But with used cars, it's always buyer beware! You should do a search of the Personal Property Securities Register, which will tell you if there is money owing on the car. You can also have the car inspected before you decide to buy it, which may be a good idea if you're not much of a motorhead. These inspections are available through the AA.

When you're looking for a used car dealership, check to see if it has LMVD (Licenced Motor Vehicle Dealers) after its name. Membership in LMVD involves sticking to a code of ethics, and dealers must display facts including the model name, year of manufacture, number of previous owners, warranty category, and full price. By law, sellers must offer the buyer a warranty for a set period, which varies with the age of the car. You'll find a bit more bargaining room when it comes to the price of a used car as opposed to a new car. If you're a good haggler, this is the time to put your skills to use.

Imported Used Cars

Many used vehicles in New Zealand are shipped in from Japan. If you buy a used Japanese import, make sure its tires are appropriate to New Zealand conditions. These cars can be difficult to assess, as their history is tough to track outside of New Zealand. However, many people buy them and are happy with their purchases.

If you buy a used car from another country and import it into New Zealand yourself, it can be very expensive (several thousand dollars) and involve an awful lot of paperwork. Generally, unless it happens to be the car of your dreams, it's much better to leave the paperwork and shipping costs to the bulk importers and buy your car once it's already in New Zealand.

Timing Your Drive

Although New Zealand's major cities may seem like they're not too far apart, driving times can be longer than you'd expect. Most highways running through the country are not high-speed motorways; they tend to run right through the center of every town along the way, making you slow down to 50 kilometers per hour each time a residential area is near.

Below are some sample driving times between major cities. These assume an average speed of 80 kilometers per hour, and rest stops of 5-10 minutes for every hour of driving. These are idealized estimates, so allow more time for delays if the weather is bad, it's a busy time like a school holiday, or you run into unexpected problems like sheep being herded across the main highway.

Driving Between	Distance	Time
Auckland and Hamilton	127 km	1:55
Auckland and Napier	423 km	6:25
Auckland and Wellington	658 km	9:15
Christchurch and Dunedin	361 km	5:00
Christchurch and Queenstown	487 km	7:15
Hamilton and New Plymouth	231 km	4:25
Nelson and Christchurch	417 km	6:20
New Plymouth and Wellington	355 km	5:10
Tauranga and Auckland	206 km	3:20

DAILY LIFE

COST OF RUNNING A CAR

It's not cheap to own a car in New Zealand. First of all, interest rates on personal loans are quite high. So if you've borrowed money to purchase a car, you could find yourself paying as much as 17 percent interest on the loan.

Then there's fuel. Not only do prices fluctuate wildly (as they do in most countries) based on the global price of oil, but gasoline is also heavily taxed. Between 2005 and 2014 prices for gasoline ranged from $1.20 per liter to over $2. That $2 liter translates to over $7.50 for a gallon of gas. It's enough to make you think twice about that SUV.

Running costs also include an annual license fee, currently $280 per year. This provides you with a sticker, which you must display on left side of the windshield. On top of that, you will need a Warrant of Fitness (often called a WoF), which will cost $30-75 depending on where you have it done.

Most people in New Zealand also pay for insurance on their cars. In many countries insurance is mandatory in case you hurt or kill someone in an accident, but since the ACC system (see *Public Health Care* in the *Health* chapter) in New Zealand covers that, it's up to you whether you still want to insure yourself. It's estimated that about a quarter of New Zealand cars have no insurance at all. While ACC will cover the cost of medical treatment, it will not pay to fix your car or the other driver's car. That's where your insurance will kick in. There is usually a $250-300 deductible (often called an excess in New Zealand policies); for drivers under 25 years old it can be much higher, even up to $1,000. If you choose to have a higher excess, it can bring down your premiums. You may also save money by having a good driving record. Of course, your premiums will depend on the level of coverage you choose, the type of car you own, how old it is, and your driving history. The most basic third-person coverage can be as little as $150 per year, while a more comprehensive policy is likely to cost at least $600 for an inexpensive car.

RULES AND REGULATIONS

The major difference on New Zealand roads for many newcomers is the switch to driving on the left. Other differences stem from this, including the rules for passing (overtaking), which must be done on the right-hand side. You must also give way to cars coming from the right at unmarked intersections and at roundabouts. It all takes a bit of getting used to, so pay attention until staying left becomes second nature.

Wearing a seat belt is mandatory in New Zealand for every person in the vehicle. Children and infants under four years old must be in an approved child or infant seat. Approved car seats can be rented from your local Plunket office (a nonprofit society for children's well-being) if you don't want to buy one.

Driving under the influence of alcohol or drugs in New Zealand is a serious offense, not to mention extremely dangerous! The legal limit for alcohol is 50 milligrams per 100 milliliters of blood for adults. For anyone under 20 a zero-tolerance limit is in effect, so no alcohol can be consumed before driving. The 50 milligram limit would allow an average-size man to have three or four drinks over a couple of hours and still remain below the legal limit. Obviously this varies from person to person depending on their size, food intake, and other factors. Sadly, many people in New Zealand still drink and drive, and alcohol is involved in almost a third of all fatal car accidents.

Roundabouts are common at New Zealand intersections. They often keep traffic moving faster than either traffic lights or a four-way stop. At peak traffic times, however, they can get backed up and frustrating. If you are entering a roundabout, remember that traffic moves in a clockwise direction. Anyone coming from your right, whether already in the roundabout or entering it, has the right-of-way before you. If you are turning left or right, use your indicator to signal your intentions before you enter the roundabout. Then indicate a left turn before you leave the roundabout, at whichever exit you take.

Traffic lights in New Zealand are the classic red, amber, and green configuration. You must not go through the intersection on an amber light unless it would be dangerous for you to stop. On a red light, you must stay put unless there is also a green arrow indicating that you may turn in the direction shown. There are no flashing green or red signals used.

In rural areas, you may have to cross one-lane bridges. Doing this safely means understanding who has the right-of-way. When you approach a one-lane bridge, there will be a sign. If the sign is a blue circle, with a bold arrow pointing up and a thinner

Careful Crossing

Learning to drive in New Zealand offers up a few challenges, but even being a pedestrian in a new country can take some getting used to! First of all, if you're from a country where people drive on the right, you have to learn to look in the opposite direction for traffic before you step into the road to cross. It took me about six months for this to become automatic.

Crossing the road at a traffic light in New Zealand is fairly straightforward. Most intersections with traffic lights also have pedestrian signals. When the red hand is lit, don't cross the road. If the red hand is flashing, finish crossing if you have already started, but don't begin crossing. If the green person is lit, go ahead and cross. Some inner-city intersections also use sounds to indicate when it is safe to cross, to help people who are visually impaired. In Auckland, there are pedestrian signals with countdown timers. These show you how many seconds remain until the light will turn red.

Pedestrian crossings are common in major cities and towns to help you get across busy roads where there isn't a traffic light nearby. These consist of a row of thick, white lines that go across the road. On either side of the road there will be poles with orange circles or balls on the top. When a pedestrian is waiting at a crossing, cars *must* stop for them. It isn't optional, but from the behavior of some drivers you'd think it was. So make sure any cars coming your way are stopping before you take the first step.

Crossing at roundabouts can be particularly difficult. Since the traffic isn't forced to stop, or even slow down, a busy roundabout can be almost impossible for a pedestrian to negotiate. If this is the case, look around to see if any pedestrian crossings have been placed a little way down the road. If there are none, then walk a reasonable distance away from the roundabout itself, and cross the road in one direction at a time, when there is a break in traffic.

When you are on the footpath (sidewalk) and it crosses over a roadway, such as the entrance to a parking lot, you have the right-of-way as a pedestrian. Cars entering across your path *should* stop for you. Again, drivers don't always play by the rules, so make sure nobody is speeding toward you before you walk across these entrances.

It's not just the drivers who cause pedestrian accidents. You'll regularly see people in New Zealand darting across the road against the traffic lights, or where there are no crossings. I've seen more than a few close calls, so don't put yourself in that situation. Make sure it's safe to cross the road, and remember to look to your right.

arrow pointing down, you have the right-of-way. This means you may go onto the bridge as soon as any cars on the bridge traveling the opposite direction have left it. If the sign is a white rectangle and the thinner arrow points up, while the bold arrow points down, you must yield to oncoming traffic, and not go onto the bridge until the way is clear.

Converting Your License

If you already have a driver's license from your home country, or an international driving permit, you can legally drive in New Zealand for up to 12 months. This makes things simple if you're in the country temporarily and don't want to go through the hassle of getting a New Zealand license.

If you are planning to stay longer, you'll want to get that New Zealand license before time runs out on your old one. The good news is, if you're from one of the following countries and can show that you've been a licensed driver for at least two years,

Boy Racers

Once you're living in New Zealand, it won't be long before you start hearing the term "boy racers." This refers to drivers, mainly young and male, who take their souped-up cars out to race each other on the streets. Another common word used to describe them is "hoons," but this is becoming a bit of an old-fashioned term.

Boy racers are a concern because they often lose control (sometimes intentionally) and can be a danger to other drivers and pedestrians. They're also considered a menace because they modify their cars to be incredibly noisy and drive around late at night disturbing people in residential areas. The problem exists all over the country.

In 2003, the government created a "Boy Racer Act" (it's officially called The Land Transport [Unauthorised Street and Drag Racing] Amendment Act) to help police put a stop to races in their jurisdictions. Under the act, illegal street racing, wheel spins, "doughnuts," or driving a car on a road in a way that causes the car to lose traction could get you three months in prison or fines up to $4,500, as well as losing your license for at least six months. Police may impound your car for 28 days at your expense. If you injure or kill someone while doing this, you could go to prison for up to five years or face a fine up to $20,000 and lose your license for one year.

The law has been in place for several years, and while it has allowed the police to get hundreds of cars impounded, it has not seen an end to the races. In a country where car racing is hugely popular, it's difficult to get through to young drivers about the difference between a racetrack and a city street.

In an effort to increase the stakes for drivers, the government passed a law in 2009 that allows police to confiscate the cars of repeat offenders and have them destroyed. With all of the money these guys sink into their cars, losing them is a big threat.

Some people advocate bringing in compulsory insurance, which will make it more expensive for young men to drive these modified cars. Others think that raising the minimum driving age will help. However, neither of these ideas been taken up by the government yet.

you won't have to take a written or practical driving test: Australia, Austria, Belgium, Canada, Denmark, Finland, France, Germany, Greece, Hong Kong, Ireland, Italy, Japan, Luxembourg, the Netherlands, Norway, Portugal, South Africa, South Korea, Spain, Sweden, Switzerland, the United Kingdom, and the United States. People from other countries will have to pass a practical in-car test as well as a written test. Everyone is required to undergo a vision test before a license is issued. Your New Zealand license is valid for 10 years and contains your picture and signature.

If you are required to pass a written test you should get yourself a copy of the *New Zealand Road Code*. The book is available in book shops, at many libraries, and you can also read it online at the New Zealand Transport Agency website. There are even sample questions for you to practice on before your test. The written test is followed by a basic vision test, and if you pass both, you will be issued a New Zealand license. The license is valid for 10 years and contains your picture and signature. Even if you are not required to take the test, a copy of the Road Code is a handy reference for those who are unfamiliar with driving in New Zealand.

Learning to Drive

If you come to New Zealand without a driver's license, or your kids reach the age when they are ready to learn to drive, you will have to go through New Zealand's graduated licensing system. This consists of three stages of licensing with different limitations.

You can get a learner license from the age of 16. This involves passing a written test and a vision test. With your learner license, you must only drive when accompanied by a fully licensed driver, and display "learner" plates, which are yellow squares with a big L on them. This stage lasts for a minimum of six months.

After six months you can take a practical test, which (if you pass) will move you up to a restricted license. With a restricted license you can drive on your own, except between 10pm and 5am. There are also restrictions on whom you can take as passengers in your car with this type of license, but your spouse and children are allowed.

You can apply for a full driver's license after 18 months on your restricted license if you're at least 18 years old. You must pass one final practical driving test, after which you are issued a full license that allows you to drive without any restrictions.

There are a large number of driving schools around the country that can help you to learn the necessary skills and prepare for the various tests. If you haven't driven before, a course is highly recommended.

Warrant of Fitness for Cars

To ensure that the cars on New Zealand roads are roadworthy, they must all carry a current Warrant of Fitness, or WoF. Your initial inspection for a new car is valid for three years. After that, cars first registered in 2000 or later must get their WoF renewed yearly. For cars first registered before 2000, you must renew the WoF every six months.

The WoF inspection can be carried out at any approved garage or testing station. A sign will be displayed to indicate that the business is approved for this. Inspectors will check a list of items including your tires, brakes, windshields, lights, doors, seat belts, airbags, structural soundness, speedometer, steering and suspension, and exhaust and fuel systems. If your car does not meet the WoF standards, you will have to get it repaired before it is legal to drive. A WoF inspection is priced individually by the provider but is usually $30-75.

TRAFFIC SIGNS AND SPEED LIMITS

Speed limits in New Zealand are quite straightforward. On open roads and motorways, the maximum speed is 100 kilometers per hour. In built-up areas, the maximum is 50 kilometers per hour. Of course, it is possible for other limits to be put in place, in which case there will be signs indicating the speed limit. Speed limits are shown as a black number inside of a red circle.

Stop signs are less common in New Zealand than in many other countries, and you'll often see a Give Way (yield) sign at intersections instead. The Give Way sign is an inverted triangle, outlined in red, with the words "give way" in the center. If you approach an intersection with a Give Way sign, you are not required to come to a complete stop (as you are with a stop sign), but you must yield the right-of-way to traffic crossing your path.

Many newcomers are confused by New Zealand's No Stopping signs. These are solid blue circles, outlined in red with a red X through them. Sometimes there are conditions written under the symbol (times and days), which means that at other times it is fine to stop there. No Parking signs are the letter P with a red circle and diagonal line through it, as in most English-speaking countries. Other forbidden acts are also indicated with the red circle and diagonal line, such as no U-turn or no right turn.

Orange or yellow diamond-shaped signs indicate driving hazards. The yellow signs normally indicate permanent hazards, while the orange ones are used for temporary hazards, such as construction zones. A picture on the sign will illustrate the type of hazard ahead, such as falling rocks or slippery conditions.

PRIME LIVING LOCATIONS

OVERVIEW

Once you've committed to making your move to New Zealand, choosing a place to live is probably the biggest decision you'll face. New Zealand is roughly the same size as Great Britain or Japan, so you can't expect to have the same landscape, climate, or work opportunities in every part of the country.

New Zealand has a wide range of towns and cities, some bustling with business and others enjoying life at a snail's pace. You need to find the region or city that best suits your needs and the lifestyle you're hoping to achieve.

To begin with, there is the matter of choosing between the North and South Islands. The South Island is less populated and has more spectacular mountains, but with a sparser population there is less development and infrastructure. The North Island is somewhat more cosmopolitan, but if you're looking to get away from it all, it may not be the best choice.

I recommend making a list of what you're looking for in your new home. Include things like the types of work that have to be available, activities you'd like to do (such as skiing or sailing, which depend on being in an appropriate place), conveniences you consider important (such as shopping malls, multiplex cinemas, or fitness clubs), and what sort of climate you're comfortable in. Then as you consider your options, it's easier to see which places meet your needs.

© MICHELLE WAITZMAN

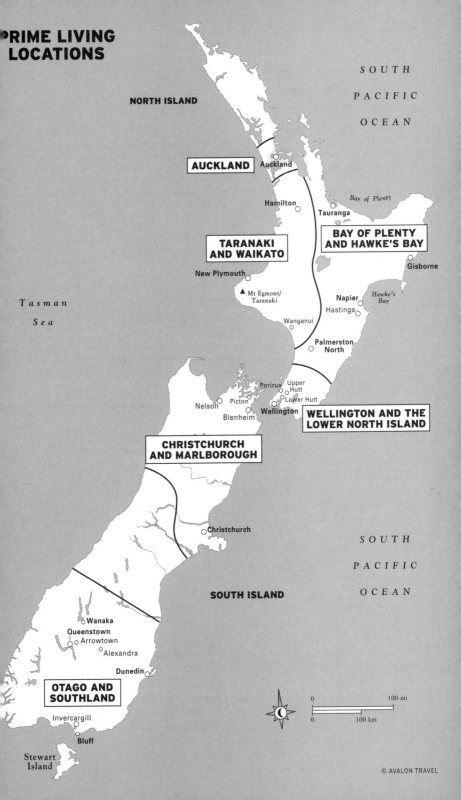

PRIME LIVING LOCATIONS

SOUTH

PACIFIC

OCEAN

NORTH ISLAND

AUCKLAND ○ Auckland

○ Hamilton

Bay of Plenty

○ Tauranga

BAY OF PLENTY AND HAWKE'S BAY

TARANAKI AND WAIKATO

○ New Plymouth

○ Gisborne

▲ Mt Egmont/
Taranaki

○ Napier

Hawke's Bay

○ Hastings

Tasman

Sea

○ Wanganui

○ Palmerston
North

○ Porirua

Upper
Hutt

Nelson ○ Picton

○ Lower Hutt

**WELLINGTON AND THE
LOWER NORTH ISLAND**

○ Blenheim ○ Wellington

**CHRISTCHURCH
AND MARLBOROUGH**

○ Christchurch

SOUTH

PACIFIC

SOUTH ISLAND

OCEAN

○ Wanaka

Queenstown ○
○ Arrowtown

○ Alexandra

○ Dunedin

**OTAGO AND
SOUTHLAND**

○ Invercargill

○ Bluff

*Stewart
Island*

0 ___ 100 mi

0 ___ 100 km

A Lifestyle Choice

Kiwis use the term "lifestyle block" to describe a rural property with a significant amount of land, but not large enough to be a working farm. Most of these are created from larger farms whose owners have sold their property, which is then subdivided into several blocks.

Lifestyle blocks are popular among retirees and others who like a taste of the country life without making a living at farming. Block owners usually keep a few animals on their properties, which can include horses, chickens, cows, and even alpacas. Others prefer to use the land to grow small crops of fruits and vegetables, or perhaps have their own private vineyard.

It sounds idyllic, but even a small farm is a lot of work. If you are thinking of buying a lifestyle block, and you've always lived in a city, do some homework. Raising crops or animals is tricky, even on a small scale, and you will be responsible for the well-being of any animals you keep.

For some immigrants, this is the perfect expression of their New Zealand dreams—getting away from the hustle and bustle of city life to relax on a sprawling property in a quiet, green valley. And with New Zealand being a relatively compact country, you're never more than a couple of hours away from a main town or city with supplies and services to make your life a bit easier.

When shopping for a lifestyle block, pay attention to the property sizes. There is no restriction on what can be called a lifestyle block; some properties are only one or two acres, while others may be over 50 acres. Depending on how you are planning to use your property and how much time you are willing to spend maintaining it, there will be a rural paradise somewhere in New Zealand that fits your needs.

AUCKLAND

The majority of immigrants end up settling in Greater Auckland, which is no surprise considering it houses about a third of the country's population. But for some newcomers, living in a city of over one million inhabitants almost defeats the purpose of moving to a small country. Immigration New Zealand would prefer newcomers to be spread throughout the country, so to stem the flow of immigrants into the city, they award extra points on visa applications for moving anywhere other than Auckland. You can improve your chances of being granted residency by accepting a job or starting a business outside of Auckland, but for many, Auckland will still be the best option.

Living in Auckland is popular because it offers the widest range of cultures, employers, and products in New Zealand. The latest figures show that more than half a million of the city's population of 1.4 million were born in another country. Due to the sheer number of consumers, many items are available in Auckland but difficult to find in other parts of the country. This can be especially important to immigrants, who are sometimes looking for familiar items from home. Many Muslim immigrants settle in Auckland for the greater availability of halal foods, and Jewish immigrants find the same advantage when looking for kosher foods (although they are still difficult to find). Other ethnic groceries are easier to buy in Auckland as well, making the transition easier on Asian, Southeast Asian, and European immigrants.

The comfort of having other immigrants from your homeland around is something that attracts a lot of people to Auckland. It is large enough to have significant multicultural communities, so that immigrants don't feel alone. If hanging out with other

Auckland is the most populated city in New Zealand.

expats is important to you, there's a good chance that you'll find a group of them in Auckland no matter which culture you're from. There are, of course, immigrant communities in other parts of New Zealand, but they are smaller and more scattered.

If you are from a smaller town or city, Auckland can be overwhelmingly large. This is a big, sprawling city, and many compare it to Los Angeles (although it's not as huge) due to the fact that most residents commute in and out of the city daily on a series of congested highways. On a more positive note, Auckland is almost surrounded by stunning bays and extinct volcanoes, making it one of the most scenic large cities in the world.

Most national offices for New Zealand companies are located in Auckland, as are the New Zealand offices of many multinational corporations. So for employment, it is by far the largest pool to draw from. The only industries for which Auckland doesn't offer the most opportunities are primary industries like agriculture, forestry, and government.

TARANAKI AND WAIKATO

For those who prefer their cities a bit smaller, and the countryside a bit closer, living in Taranaki or Waikato can give you the best of both worlds.

Hamilton is the biggest city in the region, followed by New Plymouth. While Hamilton started as a support center for the surrounding farms, it has grown into one of New Zealand's major cities, with a population of around 140,000. Situated on the banks of the Waikato River, it offers a wide range of conveniences, but with a more relaxed pace than you'd find in Auckland. Housing in Hamilton is relatively affordable, particularly compared to Auckland's soaring prices. You can buy a house in Hamilton starting at around $300,000, which puts ownership within reach for many immigrant families.

Hamilton still has close financial ties to the dairy farming industry in the Waikato and is home to several agricultural research companies. Manufacturing and retail are also growing sectors in the area, affording work opportunities for those with experience in related fields. There are a university and a polytechnic in Hamilton, offering opportunities to study or to teach.

The area surrounding Hamilton, known as the Waikato, is an agricultural center, the focus being the dairy industry. There is definitely a rural lifestyle in the area, with some wonderful recreational opportunities on the river and in the local parklands.

Taranaki is the region covering the western side of the central North Island. The region's defining landmark is Mount Egmont or Taranaki (both are official names), a volcanic cone that rises proudly above the rest of the landscape. It is surrounded by Egmont National Park, a popular hiking and climbing destination. The coastline around Taranaki is popular for windsurfing and other water activities, which makes the lifestyle here enviable.

The oil, gas, and petrochemical industry plays a major role in the economy of this region, generating about one billion dollars per year. While there isn't enough oil in New Zealand to make it self-sufficient, the hunt is still on and Taranaki is the major contributor so far. This opens up engineering and other technical jobs in the area.

Taranaki's main city is New Plymouth, which sits on the coast and is home to about 74,000 people. It's a nice size for those who want the convenience of city life without the crowds of Auckland or Wellington.

BAY OF PLENTY AND HAWKE'S BAY

Over on the eastern side of the central North Island you'll find a couple of the most popular regions in the country. The climate in the Bay of Plenty and Hawke's Bay regions is mild and sunny, drawing more and more immigrants and Kiwis to settle there.

The Bay of Plenty has grown by leaps and bounds in recent years, making its main city of Tauranga swell to 115,000 people. Farther east lies the city of Gisborne, the first city in the world to see the sunrise each day. The smaller population of 45,000 there makes it a more relaxed place to live, although with popular beaches for surfing there's not much stress in Tauranga, either.

Work in this region centers on a few areas. Agriculture and viticulture (winemaking) have a firm hold in the more rural parts of the region. Food processing employs many of the city dwellers. The growing population has opened up more opportunities in education, health care, and the retail and service industries. The region is also seeing a growing number of visitors, so the tourism sector has expanded as well.

Hawke's Bay is New Zealand's fruit basket. Everything from apples to peaches is grown in this sunny region, so locals tend to work in agriculture-related fields. Food-processing jobs are plentiful, and fruit-pickers and fruit-packers are often in demand, which can be good jobs for those just staying for a short time on working holiday visas.

The main city of this region is Napier, with around 57,000 people. Napier is a unique city, with an almost exclusively art deco downtown core. This, along with the region's wineries, draws a large number of tourists and makes tourism a significant contributor to the local economy.

Financier or Farmer?

For most immigrants, finding a good job is the main factor in whether they are able to successfully transplant their lives to a new country. In New Zealand, skills shortages in many areas provide opportunities for new immigrants to get that all-important job. But deciding where to live is closely linked with the kinds of work opportunities in the region. All regions are short of experienced tradespeople (including electricians and mechanics) and health care professionals, and most are also short of teachers in certain subjects. Here is a very simplified overview of the kinds of work you're most likely to find in each of our prime living locations:

Region	Main Industries
Auckland	technology, biotechnology, marine, film and TV, food and beverage, engineering, professional services
Taranaki and Waikato	petrochemicals, agriculture, biotechnology research, manufacturing, engineering, education
Bay of Plenty and Hawke's Bay	viticulture, agriculture, tourism, forestry, food processing
Wellington and the Lower North Island	public service, finance, IT, food and beverage, education, professional services
Christchurch and Marlborough	agriculture, aquaculture, viticulture, forestry, tourism, IT
Otago and Southland	education, agriculture, engineering, manufacturing, tourism, IT, biotechnology

PRIME LIVING LOCATIONS

WELLINGTON AND THE LOWER NORTH ISLAND

New Zealand's capital city is also its second largest, with a regional population of almost 400,000. It has a cosmopolitan atmosphere with seemingly endless numbers of cafés and restaurants, plus live theater, ballet, opera, and art galleries.

Most of the government's main departments are located in Wellington, so work opportunities in the public sector are one of the main sources of employment, even for immigrants. Other major industries include information technology (IT) and software, financial services, and Wellington's well-known film industry. Salaries in Wellington are among the highest in the country, and so is the percentage of residents who have a university education.

Housing in Wellington has become difficult to afford in many areas. This has made renting an increasingly popular option. The suburbs continue to sprawl outward from the city, where new housing is more in line with family budgets. A system of commuter trains helps to keep the main highways from getting too congested, and because

Mount Victoria in Wellington

© MICHELLE WAITZMAN

Wellingtonians do not have to enter the city center over bridges, the traffic is more manageable than Auckland's.

Outside of Wellington, small towns act as outer suburbs. The Kapiti Coast and Hutt Valley can offer a more relaxed atmosphere than the inner city, but they remain within commuting distance if necessary. Over in the Wairarapa region, things are still very rural. Farming is the main activity, with some excellent local wineries attracting visitors and customers from all over the country.

CHRISTCHURCH AND MARLBOROUGH

Christchurch is the main urban center of the South Island and similar in population to Wellington. But Christchurch has a different atmosphere, somewhat more "British." While Wellington strives to be trendy and cosmopolitan, Christchurch is prettier and more traditional. Nicknamed "The Garden City," Christchurch has lots of green space, which makes it popular for outdoor recreation. It's also a good base for skiers, with eight ski fields within 90 minutes' drive of the city.

Christchurch's economy relies on the primary industries in the surrounding region of Canterbury, including forestry and agriculture, such as wool, dairy, meat, and vegetables. There is also a post-earthquake building boom in the area that will last several more years. The region is trying to expand its knowledge-based industries as well, such as IT, research, and education. Two universities are located in or near the city.

The northern end of the South Island, known as Marlborough, is one of the most beautiful regions of the country. There are no large cities in the region, so primary industries such as viticulture and aquaculture fuel the local economy. Tourism is another driving force, with ferries from the North Island docking in the stunning Marlborough

Sounds. Outdoor recreation is extremely popular here, and those who can outfit visitors or lead trips make a good living.

OTAGO AND SOUTHLAND

Living in the southernmost part of New Zealand offers a huge range of lifestyle choices and also a huge range in cost of living. This region includes the resort areas of Queenstown and Wanaka, where property values are off the charts but the scenery is simply incomparable. On the other hand, moving down to Bluff on the south coast will make housing very affordable, but may limit your work opportunities to oyster farming and fishing.

Dunedin is the main city in Otago, and it has a rich history. Settled mainly by Scottish immigrants, it is home to New Zealand's oldest university and was at one point the country's largest city (back during the gold rush on the South Island in the 19th century). The population sits at around 120,000 these days, and the gold is long gone. However, the university is still very popular, and the many historic buildings in the city give it a Scottish character to this day. Work opportunities in Dunedin include IT, trades, engineering, and health care.

AUCKLAND

New Zealand's biggest city by a landslide, Auckland is the clear favorite when it comes to job opportunities, living near other expats, and the conveniences of big-city life. It's not just the Kiwis who will tell you that Auckland is a great place to live: It currently ranks third on Mercer Human Resources' list of the best cities in the world for quality of life.

So what makes Auckland such a world-renowned city? Lifestyle is a big factor. Situated on a narrow stretch of land between two harbors, Auckland is one of the most scenic large cities in the world. Extinct volcanoes enhance the skyline and provide recreational opportunities around the city and suburbs. The harbors themselves inspire the locals to have one of the highest rates of personal boat ownership in the world. Indeed, the city's nickname, "The City of Sails," is testament to the popularity of boating among the locals.

For New Zealanders, Auckland offers the best shopping in the country, with everything from big-box outlets to designer boutiques. People for whom shopping is a key leisure activity would probably not be happy living anywhere else in New Zealand.

The climate in Auckland is relatively good, with mild winters and warm summers. It does get quite a bit of rain, particularly over the winter months, but it is spared the gusty winds that plague Wellington, so at least, the locals will tell you, the rain falls

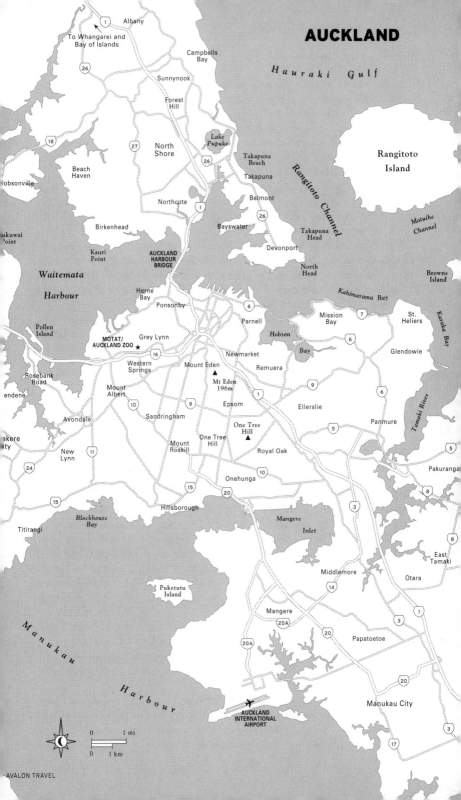

AUCKLAND

Hauraki Gulf

Rangitoto Island

Rangitoto Channel

Motuihe Channel

Browns Island

Karaka Bay

St. Heliers

Glendowie

Kahimarana Bay

Mission Bay

Hobson Bay

Tamaki River

Panmure

Pakuranga

East Tamaki

Otara

Manukau City

Papatoetoe

Middlemore

Mangere

Mangere Inlet

AUCKLAND INTERNATIONAL AIRPORT

Puketutu Island

Manukau Harbour

Titirangi

Blockhouse Bay

Hillsborough

Onehunga

Royal Oak

One Tree Hill ▲

Mount Roskill

New Lynn

Avondale

Rosebank Road

Pollen Island

Waitemata Harbour

MOTAT/ AUCKLAND ZOO ★

Western Springs

Mount Albert

Sandringham

Mount Eden

Mt Eden 196m ▲

Epsom

Ellerslie

Remuera

Newmarket

Grey Lynn

Ponsonby

Parnell

Herne Bay

AUCKLAND HARBOUR BRIDGE

North Head

Devonport

Takapuna Head

Belmont

Bayswater

Takapuna

Takapuna Beach

Lake Pupuke

North Shore

Northcote

Birkenhead

Kauri Point

Beach Haven

obsonville

kuwai Point

Forest Hill

Sunnynook

Campbells Bay

Albany

To Whangarei and Bay of Islands

akere ty

endene

AVALON TRAVEL

0   1 mi

0   1 km

vertically, not horizontally. Summer temperatures are usually around 25°C, while highs over the winter tend to rest in the midteens. It is extremely unusual for frost or snow to appear in Auckland.

Unemployment is relatively low in Auckland thanks to the wide range of businesses operating there, including the New Zealand offices of multinational corporations like KPMG, Ford, and Sony, as well as the head offices of most large New Zealand companies.

Although Auckland is the business hub of the country, most people living here still manage to maintain a good work-life balance. People from other parts of New Zealand may disagree, as they see Aucklanders as obsessed with work and money, but compared to other large, international cities, you'll find Aucklanders make more time for socializing and vacations.

With Auckland being such an important city in the New Zealand economy, you may find it surprising that it is not the capital. In fact, Auckland was at one point the capital city. Just after the signing of the Treaty of Waitangi in 1840, the capital was moved from Russell, a small settlement in the Bay of Islands, to Auckland. It remained there until 1865, when it moved down to Wellington.

At that time, Auckland was not yet growing and prospering. Wellington provided a more central location, on the doorstep of the South Island, and appeared to be the better choice. So while Auckland grew to be the economic capital of New Zealand, Wellington has remained the political capital.

The Lay of the Land

The layout of Auckland is defined by its relationship to water. With Manukau Harbour on one side and the Waitemata Harbour on the other, the city center has been squeezed onto a narrow strip of land. But as the population has grown, sprawling suburbs have taken off in every direction.

Central Auckland is only connected by land to the surrounding suburbs in two places: on the western side and the southeastern corner. This layout has kept the downtown area well contained and clearly delineated from the rest of the region. The CBD, or Central Business District, is on the northern side of this central landmass. It is surrounded by inner suburbs, which were once the homes of most of Auckland's residents. Thankfully, many of the original buildings in these suburbs have been preserved. Some continue to be used for housing, while others have become charming shops and restaurants.

To the west of central Auckland, there is an area of suburbs that ends at the Waitakere Ranges. This large parkland is filled with walking tracks, but there are roads running through it to the coast, providing access to popular surfing beaches like Piha. The west coast of the Auckland region is lined with beaches, but most of them have heavy surf and can be dangerous for swimming.

To the north, urban sprawl has taken over to house the well-to-do along the shores of the Waitemata Harbour and the Hauraki Gulf. Eventually, the population thins out as you head toward Northland, where a lot of Aucklanders go to spend vacations on the golden sand beaches in the country's warmest weather.

To the south, Manukau and the other southern suburbs practically form a separate urban center of their own. However, it is the south that connects Auckland with the rest of New Zealand. Both of the main north-south highways, State Highways 1 and 2, connect to Auckland through the southern suburbs; wherever you're heading (other than Northland), you'll be traveling through this area. It's also home to Auckland International Airport, so most immigrants arrive in New Zealand through South Auckland without even realizing it. As the suburbs sprawl farther south, there is less and less rural land between Auckland and Hamilton.

The Hauraki Gulf, east of the city, is dotted with islands large and small. Most of these islands are extinct volcanoes. A couple are large enough to be inhabited, the main one being Waiheke Island. Waiheke is a very expensive address, and commuting to the city involves a daily ferry ride. It's also home to some local wineries, with a microclimate that is well adapted to growing grapes. Most of the other islands are visited by intrepid kayakers and many of Auckland's local sailors. Very few are accessible by ferry.

CONNECTING AUCKLAND TO THE SUBURBS

Getting people in and out of central Auckland has become one of the city's biggest challenges. With a population of well over a million, a good system is necessary for getting around this largely water-locked region.

The first major bridge constructed to help commuters was the Harbour Bridge, connecting the city to the North Shore. It opened back in 1959 and was expanded from four to eight lanes 10 years later. This is the only way for residents of the North Shore to reach the city without going miles out of their way to the west along the Waitemata Harbour. Some residents prefer to cross the harbor by water, taking a ferry from one of four terminals. (There is also ferry service to Half Moon Bay in the eastern suburbs.)

© TRAVIS COTTREAU

Bridges connect downtown Auckland to the suburbs.

PRIME LIVING LOCATIONS

The ferry terminal is located at Pier 1 in downtown Auckland, and from there it's easy to walk or bus to central workplaces.

The Northern Busway is another attempt at easing congestion between the northern suburbs and the CBD. Dedicated bus lanes with several stops alongside State Highway 1 help more commuters to leave their cars behind and travel into the city by public transit.

To the south, the Mangere Bridge connects the city to the most direct route to the airport. It also provides a second option for commuters who would otherwise follow State Highway 1 toward Manukau. Having a second route is a big advantage, since the bridge could be completely closed off by just one accident.

Commuters can access the city from the eastern suburbs by land, but it involves quite a long drive through all of central Auckland to reach the CBD. For those who live near Half Moon Bay or Pine Harbour, taking a ferry to the main pier can be much less frustrating.

Daily Living

Living in Auckland can be many things to many people. Depending on your level of income, your family situation, and your lifestyle priorities, you will find a way of life in this city to suit your needs, whether it's living in the center of town in a brand-new high-rise apartment building or commuting by ferry to your suburban home on the North Shore.

Since the downtown area, or CBD, is squeezed onto such a tiny piece of land, it has not expanded much over the past several decades. Instead, some companies have chosen to locate outside the CBD, in areas with more space and lower rent. But for the main offices of many large companies, there is no substitute for a central Auckland address.

Few people can afford to live in the CBD, and most have a significant commute into town each day for work. Even if you live in a relatively close suburb, the rush hour traffic can have you spending half an hour or more to drive just a few kilometers into the city. For those in more distant suburbs, commuting can take up to two hours.

You can see why downtown living is preferred by many young professionals. Auckland now has many more apartment (condominium) buildings than ever before, catering to the upwardly mobile and childless. People who live in these apartments spend their days shopping, sipping coffee at sidewalk cafés, and eating most of their meals in restaurants. It's not a very affordable lifestyle, but those living it feel it's worth every penny.

Most people with families prefer to move out to the suburbs, where they will be able to afford (hopefully) a house of their own. Housing prices in Auckland and its suburbs are some of the highest in the country, so for some families home ownership is becoming difficult. If you can't afford to buy in the areas where you would be most comfortable, you may have to consider renting a home at first. It's something that would have been unthinkable to many Kiwis one generation ago, but the reality is that house prices have grown much faster than salaries, and not everyone can afford a big mortgage.

There are both state-run and private schools in all areas of Auckland. If you want your children to attend a specific kind of school, such as a Catholic school or other specialty school, you should strongly consider the school's proximity in deciding where to live. With the traffic being such a challenge, you won't want to be driving your kids across town every day to reach their school if you can avoid it. While in some areas you will need to drive your children to school because it is simply too far or inconvenient to walk, some neighborhoods have introduced "walking school buses," where groups of children walk to school together, supervised by a rotating schedule of parents. This reduces dangerous traffic around the schools and gives children a bit of extra exercise every day.

Unfortunately, Aucklanders do depend of their cars more than other city dwellers in New Zealand. The layout of the suburbs and city makes it difficult to get by without a vehicle, much like in Los Angeles. Public transit is convenient enough for some, but improvements are needed before Aucklanders begin to abandon their cars in large numbers.

LEISURE PURSUITS

When considering where to live in Auckland, your distance from work and schools will probably be your primary concerns. But also take into consideration how you like to spend your leisure time. Living close to your favorite activities means that you'll get to participate in them more often, and with less planning.

Beaches are a big draw for many Aucklanders and immigrants. On the west coast, pounding surf tempts local surfers. On the east coast, more sheltered beaches are great for family outings. Most people in Auckland live just a short drive from a beach, so it is part of the culture to enjoy the water.

If golf is your game, there are 23 different golf courses to choose from in the Auckland region. These range from informal, public courses with reasonable greens fees to more exclusive and luxurious clubs. Golf is popular all over New Zealand, but

© UNA HUBBARD

Auckland's many beaches make it easy to escape the city.

the concentration of courses available around Auckland is testament to the local level of participation in the sport.

Sailing is huge around Auckland, as I've mentioned. If you are planning to own a boat, you may prefer to live near one of the six marinas around the region. If your own boat is not in the cards, you can plan to be close to a sailing school or a local club instead. Other kinds of watercraft are also popular around Auckland, including kayaks for the more industrious and Jet Skis or personal watercraft for those who prefer motorized fun.

Parkland is another great part of Auckland life. There are green areas all around the city and suburbs, including some forested areas for hiking, trail running, and mountain biking. Many of the area's extinct volcanoes have become parks, including the best known, Mount Eden. Mount Eden is central, easy to access, and provides a dramatic view over the city skyline.

While there are no national parks right near Auckland, there are over 20 regional parks within a 1.5-hour drive from the city center, some much closer. For serious hikers, the Waitakere Ranges are the most popular place to lose oneself in the woods.

MULTICULTURAL POPULATIONS

The first people in Auckland were, of course, Maori, who are thought to have first settled the area around 650 years ago. Many never left, and there is a large Maori population in and around Auckland to this day. One in seven Aucklanders identify themselves as Maori, although there is often a mix of ancestry over the generations.

People from other Pacific Islands also call Auckland home in large numbers—so large, in fact, that Auckland has the highest Polynesian population of any city in the world. Their culture is evident all around the city, but most concentrated in the South Auckland suburbs.

Asian immigrants have also become a significant population in Auckland. Most come from China, South Korea, and the Philippines, although there are also immigrants from Japan, Thailand, and other Asian countries. Despite the large number of Asians living in Auckland, the city has not developed a well-defined "Chinatown" like you would find in other multicultural cities like San Francisco, New York, or Toronto.

In fact, most immigrants in Auckland are spread throughout the suburbs, rather than living in enclaves together. There are significant immigrant populations from India and Latin America, as well as various European countries.

The largest immigrant population is the least visible—people from the United Kingdom. English, Irish, and Scottish immigrants are by far the most common, but because they are not visible minorities or dealing with language barriers, Aucklanders tend not to think of them as immigrants. Those from the United States and Canada are also "invisible" immigrant populations, sometimes forgotten when it comes to getting support from the community. However, there are social and administrative groups available to anyone new to Auckland, which can help you find the services you need, meet new people, and settle in.

Coffee Talk

©MICHELLE WAITZMAN

a "flat white"

Hanging out at a local café is a big part of city life in Auckland (and other major cities in New Zealand). But before you walk in and order a mug of java, you've got to learn how to ask for what you want in Kiwi. It's simply not good enough to order a "coffee." In fact, if you do manage to find a place where American-style coffee is sold, you'll find it's called "filter coffee" or "plunger coffee," depending on what kind of coffeemaker the café uses to make it.

Most Kiwis drink espresso-based coffees, which have a language of their own. If it's any consolation, Australians use most of the same terminology, so you can feel confident on your next trip to Sydney.

Here are some of the most common coffee drinks to order at a café, and what's in them:

· **Short black:** a double shot of espresso in a small ceramic cup

· **Long black:** a double shot of espresso with added hot water, in a larger ceramic cup

· **Americano:** a double shot of espresso with more hot water than a long black

· **Flat white:** a single shot of espresso with lightly foamed, steamed milk

· **Latte:** a single shot of espresso with steamed milk, and a good layer of foam on top (more milky than a flat white)

· **Cappuccino:** a single shot of espresso with very foamy, steamed milk (in a smaller cup than a latte), sprinkled with cocoa

· **Fluffy:** a children's drink with the foam from steamed milk. It makes them think they're getting a fancy coffee, too!

Where to Live

Even after you have decided to move to Auckland, your choices are almost overwhelming. One real estate guide lists over 50 neighborhoods to choose from in the region! Each area has its own character, and since more immigrants settle in Auckland than anywhere else in New Zealand, you'll be able to find ethnic communities in this city that are difficult to find anywhere else.

Auckland is not just the biggest city in New Zealand, it is also the most expensive. Average house prices range from around $350,000 in the poorest areas to well over a million dollars in the most desirable neighborhoods. Money is certainly a big factor when it comes to deciding where in the city you will live, but lifestyle is also important, and commuting time is a key factor, too. Try to take all of these into consideration, and if at all possible, visit the suburbs you are most interested in before you decide on a home.

If you need somewhere to live right away and cannot come on a fact-finding trip before your move, consider a short-term rental until you get your bearings. Then you can take your time finding a place where you'll really feel at home in the long term.

AUCKLAND CITY

City life is preferred by young professionals, who have few financial obligations and lots of disposable income. Living in the city is great for those who hate to commute and don't mind a rented apartment. Buying a home right in the city is too expensive for most, although with more high-rises than ever before it's becoming an option for those who don't need a lot of elbow room.

City regulations impose a minimum size on city apartments, at 35 square meters (about 375 square feet) for a studio apartment, with larger minimums for one- and two-bedroom suites. At least 20 percent of the floor area must have a glazed external wall (windows), and the ceilings must be at least 2.4 meters (7.87 feet) high.

A lot of older houses in the city have been restored, and many converted into multiple apartments. These homes often have more character (and space!) than new apartments. But like other New Zealand homes, they are likely to be cold, damp, and drafty over the winter.

If you are lucky enough to live in the city, you will have the best choices when it comes to restaurants, cafés, live entertainment, and boutique shopping. On

© UNA HUBBARD

Apartments are the main housing option in downtown Auckland.

the other hand, you will have the farthest to go when it comes time to hit the beach or head for the hiking trails.

Downtown

Auckland's **downtown core, or CBD,** has few options for housing. Apartments are pretty much the only thing available, and you can't count on them coming with a parking space (although if you live and work downtown you may be able to do without a car). Some of the most popular buildings are around the Viaduct Harbour, with wonderful waterfront views. Beware of buildings constructed between 1990 and 2005 (a period of time in which poorly treated lumber was used widely in house construction) and always find out if there have been any claims made regarding leaks in the building before you buy. Even if you are renting, look carefully for signs that the walls, ceilings, or carpets have been damaged by moisture.

Renting an apartment in the CBD will cost around $360 per week for a small, one-bedroom place, or closer to $650 per week for three bedrooms. If you are thinking of buying, prices start around $200,000 for the smallest places, but something comfortable will be closer to $300,000. In a prime location like the Viaduct, prices can easily top $1 million.

Few people choose to raise kids downtown, so there are few schools around. Centrally located schools include Auckland Grammar School and Auckland Girls' Grammar. There is also an integrated Jewish school (partly funded by the government) called Kamidah College; children of all backgrounds are welcome to attend.

Ponsonby and Grey Lynn

Once home to Auckland's hippies and artists, this area just west of the CBD is now too expensive for such freethinkers. However, it still attracts those with a bit of an artistic streak, as long as they can afford to buy or rent the renovated wooden villas. Among the residents you'll find a number of local media celebrities, and in Ponsonby, Auckland's gay population gathers at trendy cafés and shops.

There are relatively few ethnic minorities in the area, and many immigrants interested in buying property shy away from the high upkeep needed on these old homes. Instead, old houses tend to be bought by Kiwis who are sentimentally attached to their character and history. Those who have invested in houses here tend to lavish attention on them.

Ponsonby is famous for its shopping, and also for people-watching. So if these are your idea of a great way to spend your spare time, this could be the area for you. **Grey Lynn** isn't quite as posh as Ponsonby, but it's so close you can hang out with your wealthier neighbors.

Schools in the area are pretty good for younger children, but there are few options when it comes to secondary schools in Ponsonby. Many parents opt to send their kids to private schools in other parts of the city or move to another area when their children reach their teens. In Grey Lynn there is a slightly better choice of secondary schools.

Living in this area comes at a price. To rent a one-bedroom flat or apartment, you can expect to pay around $475 per week. For a three-bedroom house, rent is closer to $830 per week. And if you plan to buy, you'll be looking at spending at least $850,000 for a place that has already been fixed up. Homes on the waterfront around Herne Bay or St. Mary's Bay sell from $1.5 million to over $4 million.

Parnell and Newmarket

This area could be called the Beverly Hills of Auckland. The streets are lined with glitzy shops, and few people can afford to live in this area. The homes are stately and grand, but the properties are not particularly large. **Parnell** lies just to the east of the Auckland Domain, the large park that marks the eastern border of the city center. **Newmarket** lies just south of the Domain; it is landlocked but has easy access to State Highway 1.

Schools in this area are predictably high quality. While you can expect the wealthy residents to send their children to private schools in large numbers, the state-run schools here are well funded and good performers.

While Parnell houses a lot of old Auckland families, there are a few more immigrants calling Newmarket home, including some from Asian countries. Newer townhomes and apartments are attracting retirees who are ready to downsize from their suburban homes and live closer to the city.

Buying one of the renovated older homes in the area will set you back anywhere from one million to several million dollars, depending on the size and location. If you are interested in buying an apartment, you may be able to find something starting around $400,000. Renting in the area starts at around $415 per week for a one-bedroom apartment. You can expect to pay about $850 per week for a three-bedroom house.

Mount Albert, Mount Eden, and Mount Roskill

These inner suburbs lie to the south of the CBD and are more diverse than the other city neighborhoods. You'll find Asian and Indian newcomers abundant in these areas, along with a reasonable number of Maori and Pacific Islander residents.

Mount Albert is the most diverse of these neighborhoods. It contains everything from grand mansions on tree-lined streets to student flats near the Unitec campus. However, the dominant trend is families who are comfortably well off. Ethnic groups living in the area in significant numbers include Polynesians, Indians, Sri Lankans, and Chinese, with a small Somali community as well. If you are looking for an inner suburb with a slew of different cultures, this is one of the best options.

With the focus on families, this area is well served in terms of schools. Shopping is centered on Westfield St. Lukes mall, although New North and Mount Albert Roads feature lots of Chinese shops and Internet cafés. To keep the kids entertained, there's The Mount Albert Aquatic Centre with a wave pool, waterslide, and baby pools. Or try Rocket Park, which has a popular playground.

Since Mount Albert is so diverse, it also has a big range when it comes to housing. At the lower end, two-bedroom terraced homes can be had for around $350,000. More traditional bungalows range from $500,000 to $1 million, depending on the location and how well they have been upgraded over the years. The most expensive houses in the area can cost $1.5 million or more. Renting a three-bedroom house will cost around $540 per week.

Mount Eden is the most exclusive of these neighborhoods, a family-friendly area full of SUVs and baby strollers. It has something of a village atmosphere, with friendly shops and cafés catering to parents and their offspring.

Part of the neighborhood is within the school zones for Auckland Grammar School and Epsom Girls Grammar School, and houses within that school zone can be easily $200,000 more expensive than those outside the zone. The average house price in the area is around $1 million. Renovated older homes in the Mount Eden village cost even more.

Mount Roskill is the most notably religious community in the area. Christianity is dominant in the area, although the rising number of immigrants is creating more variation when it comes to houses of worship. There are growing populations from India, Korea, and China, not to mention a well-established Samoan community.

The area is convenient for those who make frequent trips to the airport, but it is one of the farther inner suburbs from the CBD. It is well served by local schools and has a mall for your shopping needs.

House prices in Mount Roskill average around $700,000. You can rent a three-bedroom house for around $480 per week.

GREATER AUCKLAND

Inner-city living has its advantages, such as shorter commuting times, but it is very expensive and not well suited to everyone's lifestyle. Most Aucklanders live outside the city, in the outer suburbs, and most immigrants end up settling outside the city as well. The homes are more affordable (although still more expensive than most of New Zealand), the neighborhoods are mainly safe and quiet, and if you work outside the city center, you may be lucky enough to avoid commuting altogether.

North Shore

"The Shore," as Aucklanders call it, has long been synonymous with European-descent, upper-middle-class suburban living. This area began to grow as soon as the Harbour Bridge connected it to the city in 1959. It's not as homogenous here as it once was, since immigrants of various nationalities are keen to get into this family-friendly area.

There are lots of amenities, including some of the biggest shopping malls in the country, sporting facilities, and schools. There are also a lot of green areas and beaches for leisurely family time.

The closer you live to the city and/or the water, the more expensive the homes will be. Those with waterfront mansions in **Devonport** and **Bayswater** pay millions for the privilege. But there is some fairly affordable housing if you are willing to live inland and farther north. The main drawback of this is that you become one of Auckland's famously frustrated commuters.

There are so many people now living in this region that the infrastructure has grown to pretty much make it self-sufficient and independent from the city. The North Shore has a population of over 200,000. In New Zealand terms, that's a major city! Obviously a large number of shops and services are required to keep this population happy, so you may find that you are able to find work close to where you are living and avoid the dreaded downtown commute.

Massey University has a campus on the North Shore, so there is a student population in the **Albany** area. With so many families all over this area, there are tons of schools. The state-run schools have mainly good reputations on the North Shore, but for those who prefer private education, that is also available.

There are lots of restaurants and cafés to choose from around the North Shore, but only a couple of places where you can catch a movie. For real nightlife, you'll have to head into Auckland City.

The cheapest houses on the North Shore start at around $500,000 in landlocked areas like **Glenfield,** but to live near the water you'll pay much more. Even the most modest homes are selling for $700,000, and the more impressive executive houses will be well over a million dollars. It may be possible to get a smaller, older home in this area for an affordable price, but don't expect it to be full of the latest modern features. Renting a North Shore house should cost between $475 and $900 per week.

South Auckland

The suburbs south of central Auckland have a long-standing reputation as a high-crime area. It has traditionally been a less expensive area with a large Maori and Polynesian population. Most of the violent crime revolves around the drug trade and gang affiliations. But some neighborhoods bordering the more prosperous eastern and western suburbs are actually quite safe and pleasant. These are new areas that were farmland not too long ago.

Mangere is one of the areas with a bad reputation, but it is very close to the city and the airport, so the convenience and relatively low house prices make it tempting. Toward the eastern side, **Otara** is another area that has traditionally been synonymous with poverty and crime.

Manukau, the commercial center of South Auckland, has some good amenities. There is a large shopping center and several other big retailers, plus a new Events Centre and New Zealand's only major amusement park, Rainbow's End. The older areas are still run down and there is some light industrial use in certain places, but newer neighborhoods are affordable and appealing for young families, including a lot of immigrants. Manukau is ethnically diverse, and Auckland's CBD is accessible straight up State Highway 1.

The farther south you go, the more middle-class South Auckland becomes. Areas farther from Auckland, like **Papakura,** attract a lot of families who feel safer there than in the older neighborhoods.

South Auckland is by far the most affordable area of the city to buy a home, with some houses still for sale under $400,000. However, you have to choose your neighborhood carefully and have the house inspected as a condition of your offer. Many of the homes here have been rentals and may not be well maintained. If you want to get a good bargain, it will take some hard work and patience on your part to find the hidden gems. You can rent a three-bedroom house in South Auckland for $400-600 per week.

Western Suburbs

West Auckland covers a large, sprawling area from Manukau Harbour in the south to the area west of the northernmost parts of North Auckland. With such a large area, it's no surprise that there are a lot of different lifestyles to choose from here.

The reputation of the west's residents is that they are ecofriendly, artistic, and slightly hippielike. The main center for this area is **Henderson,** which has its own CBD and shopping. There are some more industrial areas in the mix, and as you get farther from Auckland, the flavor becomes more rural. It's possible to live on a lifestyle block (a property with a small amount of farmland) in West Auckland, something most Aucklanders can't even imagine. Of course, living that far from the city center makes for a long commute if you work downtown. The west is serviced by State Highway 16, which commuters can expect to be slow and frustrating at rush hour.

With the range of neighborhoods in the west comes a wide range of home prices as well. Living on any part of the waterfront is always more expensive than living inland. With areas bordering Manukau Harbour, Waitemata Harbour, and the Tasman Sea, there is quite a bit of waterfront property to choose from in the western suburbs. Much of the west coast, however, is taken up by the Waitakere Ranges in Auckland Centennial Memorial Park and the Woodhill Forest.

As you can probably guess, living in West Auckland is ideal for anyone who enjoys hiking, mountain biking, or surfing. So if you place more importance on play than on work, this could be the ideal area for you.

You may be able to find a small house in some areas for $400,000, but you will probably have to part with closer to $500,000 to get a conveniently located home. In more rural areas, lifestyle blocks cost upward of $650,000. Renting a three-bedroom house in West Auckland will cost around $375-600 per week, depending on the neighborhood.

Eastern Suburbs

The eastern suburbs are actually situated to the east of South Auckland. This area is the ultimate New Zealand suburbia. It's considered safe, clean, and family-friendly. The proximity to the calm, eastern beaches makes it a popular choice. As in other areas, the closer you live to the water, the more you will pay for your home. But if you are near the water, you can take advantage of the ferry service to the CBD, avoiding the commuter traffic.

Many groups of immigrants have taken a shine to this part of Auckland. Asian communities have grown quite large, alongside South African and English immigrants. This is also the most popular area for the small Jewish community. All of these diverse groups give the area some more interesting shops and restaurants than other suburban areas.

Those living in the northern extremities of this area may find that their children have to travel a little to get to school, but in areas like **Howick** and **Pakuranga,** schools are plentiful. So before you decide where to settle, look into the school situation in your desired neighborhood if you have children.

On top of the lovely sand beaches, the eastern suburbs contain a good range of shops and restaurants catering to the local population. So it's not necessary to head into the city every time you want to enjoy a night out.

You should expect to pay at least $500,000 for a house in the eastern suburbs, and possibly much more if you want a large home or to live near the water. Renting a house should cost around $400-550 per week.

Getting Around

The biggest complaint you'll hear from Aucklanders about their city is that there is too much traffic. Because of the city's unique layout and numerous harbors, most suburbs are connected to downtown by bridges. Those bridges, of course, get very busy during

Forget the Elevator

New Zealand has always been a bit of a breeding ground for new, extreme sports. So while most tall sightseeing towers are happy to take people up the elevator to an observation deck, then back down again, Auckland's Sky Tower has introduced a faster way to get back to ground level.

The Sky Jump allows ordinary people to get strapped into a harness and dropped 192 meters (630 feet) to the downtown streets below, reaching speeds of 85 kilometers per hour (53 mph). But don't worry, you'll slow down and stop before you go splat! It's typical of Kiwi adrenaline adventure activities, but extra scary because you're doing it in the middle of a busy, downtown area and not over a scenic river or mountain.

The Sky Tower offers visitors a harnessed 192-meter drop to the street below.

Of course, bungee jumping is the original Kiwi adrenaline rush, which was commercially launched by A. J. Hackett in Queenstown in 1988. Jumping off a bridge has never been the same.

Then extreme sports moved into the city with the invention of urban rap jumping. In this activity (also practiced in Auckland), participants walk or run face-first down the wall of a skyscraper toward the ground, attached by ropes to the roof of the building.

Obviously, some thrill-seeking Aucklanders prefer to use the elevator on the way up only and get a breath of fresh air on the way down. However, extreme descents are not mandatory: If you land a job in an office tower, you will be permitted to take the elevator in both directions!

peak traffic times. On a bad day, some commuters can spend close to two hours in their cars. And as Auckland continues to sprawl to the north and south (the only directions it can go), the commutes will just keep getting longer.

Public transit options have been shortsighted and inadequate in the past, and the city has been scrambling to catch up. Auckland has created dedicated busways and updated and electrified its trains. Now they just need to convince commuters to leave their cars behind.

DRIVING

As with most large cities, driving and parking in central Auckland can be a pain. Rush hour traffic is terrible, carparks charge outrageous sums of money, and street parking is hard to find. And yet, most Aucklanders still insist on driving to work and back every day. They are attached to their cars and the freedom to set their own schedules and routes.

The two major motorways leading in and out of central Auckland are State Highway 1, called the Northern Motorway, heading north from Auckland, and the Southern Motorway heading south from Auckland, and State Highway 16, also known as the North Western Motorway. They also create the border around the CBD, separating

© TRAVIS COTTREAU

Public transit in Auckland includes ferries.

downtown from the inner suburbs. State Highway 1 is the main north-south route used by those who live in the northern and southern suburbs. State Highway 16 extends to the west out of Auckland and continues northwest through the western suburbs. The two roads are connected north of the city by Upper Harbour Drive.

Auckland's major downtown road is Queen Street, which runs from near the Ferry Terminal at Queens Wharf straight down to the motorways. It is the main shopping street for the CBD. The CBD is basically a grid, although things quickly go wonky around Albert Park and the University of Auckland.

One positive thing about driving in central Auckland is that there are few one-way streets to contend with. There are several of them, however, around the inner suburbs.

To reach the airport from the CBD, drive south to State Highway 20, then branch off to State Highway 20A. It takes about half an hour to get there from downtown, at nonpeak times.

PUBLIC TRANSIT

With 1.4 million residents in Greater Auckland, the need to get them out of their cars and onto public transit is critical. Traditionally, public transit has not been well used in Auckland. Aging infrastructure, limited routes, and inconvenient schedules kept most commuters behind the wheel.

Millions of dollars have recently been invested in the public transit system, and so far the results are very encouraging. The main hub for public transport, called Britomart, is seeing an increase in use of trains and buses. The new Northern Busway is helping, and the electrification of the train system is complete and attracting more passengers.

The regional public transportation is run by Auckland Transport, which coordinates the various train, bus, and ferry services in and out of the city.

There are four train lines, all of which end at the downtown Britomart hub. One line runs through the western suburbs to Waitakere. Another runs south to Pukekohe. A third runs south by a different route to Manukau. The fourth runs just a short distance south to Onehunga. Instead of a train line to the northern suburbs, there is a dedicated busway, allowing buses to bypass car traffic. Local bus services connect with the trains and busway in many neighborhoods.

Train fares are based on a zone system, so the farther you travel, the more you pay. Fares start at $2 for adults and $1.50 for seniors and children. Monthly passes are available for frequent users at $140-250, depending on the zones covered.

Commuting by ferry is an option for people who live in some of the northern and eastern suburbs. These services are run by Fullers. Prices range $6-22 one-way, but better prices can be found by buying multitrip passes.

Bus services in Auckland are run by NZ Bus, while regional operators cover the various suburbs. If you need to get around the CBD and it's too nasty outside to walk, you can travel on inner-city buses for just $0.50. Other fares are based on zones and are the same as train fares for the equivalent zones.

TARANAKI AND WAIKATO

If Auckland seems just a bit too big and busy for your tastes, a short journey south changes the lifestyle choices completely. From the can't-miss-it peak of Taranaki/ Mount Egmont dominating the west to the sprawling farmland of the Waikato, the land defines this area. Hamilton and New Plymouth were built on agricultural bases, mainly servicing the dairy industry, but they have grown and expanded into cities with their own merits.

Industries like biotechnology and petrochemicals have added more diversity to the lifestyles in this region, but when it comes down to it, this is primarily a farming region. It's the home of dairy cooperative giant Fonterra, and with New Zealand's exporting 99 percent of its dairy products, this is a major industry.

If the rural lifestyle suits you and your family, this region is one of a few to consider. But this is mainly a dairy and livestock area, so if you're hoping to start a vineyard or get into the kiwifruit business, you'll be more interested in the Bay of Plenty and Hawke's Bay region.

COURTESY OF HAMILTON & WAIKATO TOURISM

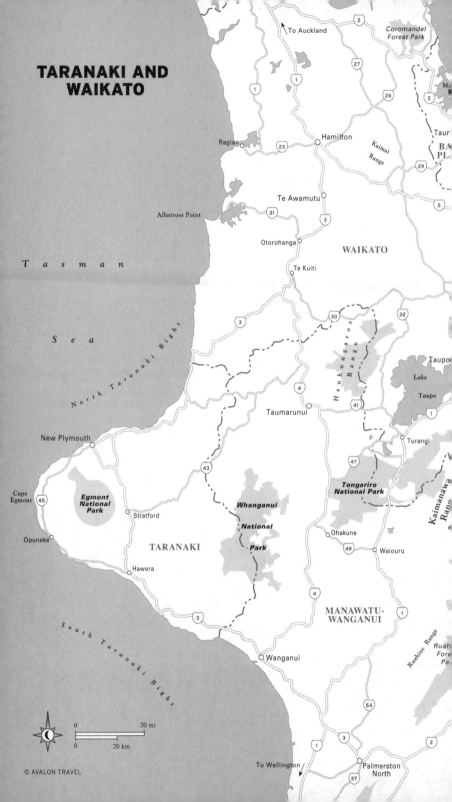

Hamilton and Waikato

Hamilton started out as a support center for the surrounding farms. It has developed into New Zealand's largest inland city, with a population of around 141,000. But life in Hamilton is still very much influenced by agriculture, with a number of research facilities and university programs aimed at that industry. Research facilities are located in and around the city, including Landcare Research, AgResearch, and Dairying Research Corporation. In fact, about 25 percent of the working scientists in New Zealand work in Hamilton. The main educational facilities in the area are the University of Waikato and Wintec (Waikato Institute of Technology).

There are also a few opportunities around for nonagricultural work (besides scientific research that supports the agriculture industry). Hamilton is home to a few niche manufacturers making things like specialty plastics, stainless steel, and aluminum, and even boatbuilding. The growing population of this region has also created new opportunity in the retail and service sectors.

THE LAY OF THE LAND

While Hamilton is an inland city, it is only a 45-minute drive from the west coast of the North Island, so visiting a beach on the weekend is not out of the question. In fact, the beach near Raglan in the Waikato has the best surfing in the country, according to locals. If you prefer the beaches on the east coast, it's about an hour and a half to Tauranga in the Bay of Plenty.

The city of Hamilton lies just over 125 kilometers (78 miles) south of Auckland

PRIME LIVING LOCATIONS

COURTESY OF HAMILTON & WAIKATO TOURISM

The beautiful Waikato River runs right through the city of Hamilton.

along State Highway 1. And just because it's inland doesn't mean you won't have water around. The city center bridges the mighty Waikato River, and just to the west of the city center is Hamilton Lake (Lake Rotoroa). There are some wonderful green areas along the shores of the lake and river to enjoy without ever leaving the city. The largest urban green area is Hamilton Gardens to the south of the downtown core.

Hamilton has grown to a size where cafés and restaurants are now plentiful, and the city is trying to become a major center for events. There's a balloon festival in April, but Hamilton's premier event (although it's actually held at Mystery Creek, just south of Hamilton) remains Fieldays in June, a national agricultural fair that has been around for 45 years.

Once you get outside of Hamilton's urban area, you'll be surrounded by farms and more farms. Most of the rural towns are of the blink-and-you'll-miss-it variety. These towns are scattered throughout the Waikato as service centers for the surrounding farmers. Most have populations of less than 5,000.

The landscape in the Waikato includes a huge number of lakes and rivers. There are also mountain ranges on both the eastern and western sides of the region. So while you may have to make your own entertainment, you'll have every opportunity to do so. And if you like your landscape more groomed, there are golf courses all along the main corridor between Auckland and Hamilton, and they continue south of Hamilton off all of the major roads.

DAILY LIVING

If you want the conveniences of the city, then you'll want to be right in Hamilton. It's a young city, with a student population of around 40,000. This means that there is a decent nightlife here, and a more vibrant culture than you might expect in an agricultural region.

One of the nicest things about living in this region is that there are so many things to see and do in the surrounding areas. Driving to Auckland for the day is not out of the question, particularly if you live in the northern parts of the Waikato. Getting to either the west coast or the Bay of Plenty to hit the beaches is also a reasonable drive. Heading south, you're within reach of the ski fields at Mount Ruapehu, making winter something to look forward to. Plus, there are all those golf courses around the Waikato to choose from.

Your lifestyle in the Waikato will depend on whether you are working on a farm or in town. The farming life is not an easy one, but a lot of dairy farmers wouldn't have it any other way. Most are part of the Fonterra cooperative, which pools the resources of dairy farmers around the country and creates products that are marketed worldwide.

The people in the cities and towns around the Waikato enjoy the conveniences of living near a major center, Hamilton, with few worries about things like traffic jams or organized crime. Even those who commute into Hamilton from surrounding towns like Cambridge and Te Awamutu have a pretty easy time of it. If you're looking for a compromise between country living and a city-based career, the Waikato might be the perfect place for you.

King Country

The Waikato also has a strong Maori history. You'll sometimes see the southern area referred to as "King Country." This refers to the Maori king (or queen) that represents all of the Maori from the region, and eventually came to represent all of New Zealand's Maori. When the British began governing—and eyeing the fertile lands of the Waikato—the Maori decided that it would be helpful to have a unified figurehead who they would consider their equal representative to the British queen. The first king was chosen in 1859, and when the surrounding Maori refused to let the British settlers take over their land, there was open warfare for around a year. Eventually the Maori were driven south, into what is now known as King Country.

I mention this because there is still a Maori king from that line today, and the culture of the Waikato is influenced by this long history of pride and struggle. The last Maori queen to die, in 2006, was mourned by the whole country, and even foreign dignitaries paid their respects. So while the position holds no official power, it is certainly something you should be aware of if you live in the Waikato.

WHERE TO LIVE
Hamilton

You'd expect that a city in the middle of an agricultural area would be pretty homogenous. But according the Hamilton's City Council, this is a melting pot of over 80 different ethnic groups. (I'm assuming that they don't consider Aucklanders and Wellingtonians different ethnic groups!) About 60 percent of the population is "NZ European" and 18 percent is Maori, so that leaves some pretty small numbers of other ethnicities to make up the rest.

Hamilton is a large city in New Zealand terms. Outside of the "big three"—Auckland, Wellington, and Christchurch—there are few other places as large and

COURTESY OF HAMILTON & WAIKATO TOURISM

Hamilton is the fourth largest city in New Zealand, with over 140,000 residents.

varied as Hamilton. The fact that there are so many students around makes the population dip by almost 40,000 over the summer, but unlike some other university towns, Hamilton does not become a ghost town when school is out. There is a steady full-time population, including a lot of young families looking for a safe place to raise their kids.

Between the Waikato River and Hamilton Lake, it's easy to forget that you're in a landlocked city. And where there's water, there are opportunities to use it for recreation. This may not be as big a sailing city as Auckland, but the lake sees its share of leisure craft. Shopping is nothing special here, but you will be able to get everything you really need without a trip to Auckland.

Jobs in Hamilton are relatively available, with everything from IT professionals to technicians to accountants in demand. So even if you aren't agriculturally inclined, there should still be a decent chance of finding yourself some work. Of course, Hamilton is only about 10 percent of the size of Auckland, so you should expect the number of job openings to be accordingly smaller.

There's no doubt, however, that Hamilton is a more affordable city for housing. You can find a three-bedroom house for as little as $280,000, but most of them fall into the $370,000-500,000 range. If you'd prefer to rent a home, you can find the same three-bedroom houses for around $350-400 per week.

Rural Waikato

To live around the rural Waikato, you have two basic options. First, you can live on a working farm. Second, you can live on a "lifestyle block" or in a small town and commute to work in a town or city.

Living on a working farm means you'll likely be in the dairy farming business. It's a good living for farmers in this region, but it means getting up early and working a long day. Most large farms use high-tech milking machines and have done away with the romantic notion of milking cows by hand. If you don't have much farming experience, you will probably want to find work on someone else's farm for at least a year before attempting to start your own. You can also take courses in farm management to help you understand what needs to be done. Farmhands and farm managers are often needed in the Waikato, so you can enjoy working in this industry without the financial and lifestyle commitments of owning a farm. If you're the sort of person who likes to take a holiday now and then, consider working for someone else.

The towns around the **rural Waikato** are mostly service centers for the farmers. They sell fuel, supplies, and food and offer services. There are also schools scattered around the region for the children living on the farms and in the towns. Some farmers, however, choose to send their kids to boarding school instead of the local school. This can save the parents a lot of driving every day to drop the kids off at the "local" school and pick them up again later.

If you're looking for just a house in a country town, with little property, you may be lucky enough to find something for under $150,000. Houses with large properties start at about $400,000. Areas such as **Raglan,** popular with holidaymakers, can be more expensive. Renting a rural property is not as common as renting in the city, so you may find that your choices are limited outside of the suburbs surrounding Hamilton. What is available usually rents for $150-250 per week.

Having a Field Day

The tractor pull is one of many Fieldays traditions.

For 45 years, Fieldays has been New Zealand's largest agricultural fair. It takes place in Mystery Creek, a Waikato town just south of Hamilton. Like any great agricultural fair, it has a lot of competitions. But the Kiwis have their own unique way of celebrating their rural heritage, so some of the competitions go beyond growing the biggest pumpkin or the plumpest pig. Here are some examples:

There is a possum fur fashion award, where New Zealand's most prolific pest is finally put to good use. Meanwhile, the AgArt awards recognize unique fashions created from items found or used on the farm, with a special category for outfits made only from plant products like grass, hay, and seeds.

Instead of comparing cows, this fair compares cowboys! The Rural Bachelor of the Year competition can be pretty heated. As well as sponsored prizes, the winner takes home the Golden Gumboot (rubber boot).

For the artistically inclined, there are sculpture competitions, with one division requiring sculptors to use materials found on the farm and another where the main material must be No. 8 wire (the size used for most fences).

If this is sounding a bit too artsy, don't worry. There are also lots of hands-on competitions, including the Festival of Logging Skills, a tractor pull, and a fencing competition (building fences, not dueling with swords).

If you thought you'd seen all there was to see at a country fair, just wait until you go to your first Fieldays in the Waikato. Farming will never be boring again.

GETTING AROUND

If you're staying close to the main highways in the Waikato, getting around by car is pretty easy. State Highway 1 takes you straight up to Auckland and down to Wellington. There are a number of other State Highways leading out to both coasts at various points and up to the Coromandel Peninsula. Most of the rural towns are also serviced by good roads, and only the most off-the-beaten-track roads may be dirt or gravel rather than sealed tarmac.

©MICHELLE WAITZMAN

Waikato is a major dairy-farming region.

Heavy traffic is extremely unusual anywhere in the Waikato. The exception is on holiday weekends, when Aucklanders may be heading for various recreational hot spots via State Highway 1 and other major roads. In Hamilton itself, traffic lights are only common in the Central Business District (CBD). You're more likely to find round-abouts at the more suburban intersections. In the rural areas, you're unlikely to see traffic lights at all. So pay careful attention to the right of way when driving around the Waikato or any rural area of New Zealand.

Public Transit

Hamilton has a good bus system, at least during the week. Their bus services are run by the Waikato Regional Council, and there are several routes leading all over the city. Some limited services also operate on Saturdays, Sundays, and public holidays. The transit company has also introduced a "Night Rider" service, offering limited bus routes late on Friday and Saturday nights. So if you happen to live along one of those routes, you can safely booze it up on the weekend and still make it home.

Hamilton's buses differ from most of the other cities in New Zealand, as they don't have different fares depending on how far you are traveling. The cash fare for one journey (including unlimited transfers onto another city bus within two hours of paying your fare) is $3.30 for adults and $2.20 for children. There are discounted fares available by using a special card called the "Busit!" card.

Hamilton International Airport is a 15-minute drive south of the city. There are direct flights to all major cities in New Zealand and also some flights to Australia plus a few other overseas destinations. The majority of international flights, however, leave from Auckland.

New Plymouth

New Plymouth sits on the north-facing coastline of the Taranaki region, which juts out into the Tasman Sea. It would probably have remained a small town if oil and gas had not been discovered in the area. Those important finds have helped New Plymouth to grow to a population of over 55,000, and if you include the whole district, it's more like 74,000. It may not be a major city, but on a New Zealand scale it is a significant urban center.

With such an industrial base for the economy, New Plymouth offers opportunities not only in petrochemicals, but also in engineering and manufacturing. But if you're expecting this to be an ugly industrial town, you'll be pleasantly surprised. New Plymouth is surrounded by magnificent scenery.

For those who like to travel around, New Plymouth is just far enough from the major centers of the North Island to be inconvenient. It takes four or five hours to drive to either Auckland or Wellington in good conditions.

THE LAY OF THE LAND

Taranaki is like a big bump on the west side of the North Island, jutting out into the Tasman Sea. This creates a lot of coastline, which makes it a scenic and enjoyable place. In the center of it all is Taranaki/Mount Egmont, an extinct volcano that dominates the skyline, surrounded by Egmont National Park, a circular area where tramping and skiing are popular with both locals and thousands upon thousands of tourists. New Plymouth is the biggest city around, and it sits on a prime piece of waterfront facing north (toward the sun).

PRIME LIVING LOCATIONS

© BOB MORRIS

the New Plymouth waterfront

The climate in New Plymouth is pretty good, although it can get more rain than the interior parts of the island. Taranaki, being the first major peak weather systems encounter as they arrive from the west, has its own microclimate. Rain clouds hit the mountain, and rain falls here before the clouds move away to the east.

Temperatures in New Plymouth tend not to reach extremes but remain moderate throughout the year. Summer temperatures tend to peak in the high teens or low twenties (Celsius), while in the winter it would be surprising to dip below freezing overnight.

DAILY LIVING

New Plymouth is a big enough city to offer all of the shopping and dining conveniences most people need. Most of this is packed into the small city center by the shoreline. There is a good-sized population to take care of there, so many jobs in retail, service industries, and education complement the main industry of petrochemicals. Outside of the city, tourism is also a pretty big employer.

The recreational activities around New Plymouth are one of its biggest draws. Along with skiing and tramping in the national park, you've got a whole lot of coastline at your doorstep. Various beaches near New Plymouth offer world-class surfing or windsurfing, and the locals often take advantage of those spots. Even in the city, there are several good parks to explore.

Most of the headline entertainment that comes to New Zealand focuses on the biggest three cities, but New Plymouth seems to get more than its share of major acts. The city's Bowl of Brooklands outdoor concert venue has seen shows like Elton John, R.E.M., and the WOMAD festival. So while New Plymouth doesn't have a particularly great nightlife, there are some very exceptional exceptions.

WHERE TO LIVE

New Plymouth is small enough that you could actually get a house right by the city center without selling your offspring to afford it. A three-bedroom house in the city can be had for as little as $400,000, and if you're willing to live another 10 minutes away, you may be able to buy a house for under $300,000.

Once you're outside the city itself, properties are larger, and you can get that rural feeling while still being able to easily drive into town for work. Some of the newer suburbs are building larger houses, so families can have a more "executive" lifestyle. It's something you might be able to afford in New Plymouth, when the same house in the better Auckland suburbs would sell for double the price.

There are fewer properties for rent in New Plymouth and the surrounding area than in major cities, so you may have trouble finding a rental to suit your needs. A three-bedroom house rents starting at around $350 per week.

GETTING AROUND

The compact city center is laid out as a grid, with Devon Street being the main road. It has a pedestrian mall halfway through, though, so it's not usually the best route for drivers to use. You can always orient yourself easily in New Plymouth by locating the shoreline, which is to the north.

Within the city and nearby suburbs there is bus service available. The main bus depot is on Ariki Street by the library. Eleven routes operate during the week, and two routes operate on Saturday. There is no Sunday service. Fares are zone-based, with adult fare starting at $3.50, while students, children, and seniors pay $2. If you use a "Smart Card," there is a significant discount.

The main highways leading out of town are State Highway 3, which takes you south or northeast, and State Highway 45, which follows the curve of the coastline around Taranaki. Unless you are going surfing, State Highway 3 will be your main route to connect with the rest of New Zealand. It eventually meets up with State Highway 1 to the south and takes you to Hamilton if you go northeast.

The airport just east of New Plymouth has direct flights to Wellington and Auckland. For business travelers it's usually the best option, since driving can eat into your valuable time. And if you're going on vacation, you can grab a flight to Auckland to catch your international connection. Flying time to Auckland is about 45 minutes.

Whanganui

At the mouth of the Whanganui River lies the city of Whanganui, or Wanganui—yes, there are two "correct" ways to spell it. This is the result of a long-standing disagreement; a compromise was made in the end, which is the Kiwi way. The city is tucked away in the bend between Taranaki and the coastline leading south to Wellington. It doesn't look like much on the map, but the district is home to about 43,000 people. Around 75 percent of them are "NZ European," while 19 percent are Maori. That doesn't leave much room for others, but there are a few scattered ethnic groups around.

There are no major industries in Whanganui that dominate the workforce. In fact, it can be a bit tougher to find work here than in other urban areas. The unemployment rate in Whanganui is about 1 percent higher than the national average.

On the other hand, the population of Whanganui is aging as more people choose it as a good, affordable place to retire. So there is not as much competition for jobs here as there is in some other areas.

THE LAY OF THE LAND

The Whanganui River is the main geographic feature of the city, with the city center occupying a bend on the west bank. State Highway 3 cuts through the city as well. To the south and west of the city center is the large estuary of the river, which is believed to be the basis of its name. (Whanganui means "great estuary," but it also means "great wait," so nobody is 100 percent sure which is the correct translation.)

To the north of the city is Whanganui National Park, and if you keep looking north, you will see Mount Ruapehu and Tongariro National Park on a clear day. Wellington is the closest large city, about three hours' drive from Whanganui. If a smaller city will do, you can always hit New Plymouth to the north or Palmerston North to the south.

DAILY LIVING

As a place gaining popularity among retirees, Whanganui may not be the best choice for people wanting an active nightlife. However, if you are nearing retirement age and want to be able to afford a nice house, it may suit your needs. If you move there with a family, there are enough local schools to send your children to at all levels of schooling, until they are ready to go to university. And then, Massey University in Palmerston North is only 70 kilometers (45 miles) away. There is a polytechnic school right in Whanganui for those more vocationally inclined, called the Universal College of Learning (UCOL).

The river itself offers some recreational opportunities. You'll see the tourists go by in historic paddleboats, but most locals prefer a canoe or kayak to explore the Whanganui. The town center is home to a golf course, several parks, a racetrack, and an indoor aquatic center.

One of the drawbacks of living in Whanganui is that it seems to have attracted a lot of gang activity. Some residents fear that intergang violence will spill over and start affecting the general population. So far incidents have been limited, but the local council is very concerned and trying to force the gangs out of town.

WHERE TO LIVE

Whanganui is one of the most affordable cities in New Zealand, with houses right in the city priced as low as $130,000 (but they may need some work). Or if living near the seaside is your thing, then suburban areas like **Castlecliff** might appeal to you. Houses there are around the same price as in the city, but if you don't need to be close to everything, the surroundings are worth the short drive from town.

Whanganui East puts you just across the river and offers everything from historic villas to brand-new homes. It's popular with families who like to have that body of water between their home and the town center. Amazingly, homes there start around $180,000, but the nicer ones are closer to $280,000.

There aren't a lot of nice rental properties in Whanganui, but the price is good for the ones that are out there. Rent for a three-bedroom house starts at about $200 per week in the city and surrounding suburbs, including the seaside area of Castlecliff.

GETTING AROUND

It's hard to get around without a car in Whanganui, as the local bus only covers four routes and has no Sunday service. Most people travel by car to work, school, and just about everywhere else. State Highway 3 is the main route heading northwest to Taranaki, and southeast toward Palmerston North and Wellington. State Highway 4 begins at a junction with State Highway 3 in Whanganui and passes through the city, heading north to Tongariro National Park (for skiing breaks) and eventually meets up with State Highway 3 in the Waikato.

Rural Taranaki

There's no doubt that the rural land around Taranaki is beautiful. The graceful volcanic peak can be seen from every direction. There is coastland all around. But what are you going to do for work if you live here? There are a few options. Sheep and cattle are kept on many rural Taranaki properties. Or you could get into forestry, working on a pine plantation or owning your very own. Or perhaps you're ready to kick back and not work so hard, and just enjoy the coastline.

THE LAY OF THE LAND

Taranaki's center is occupied by Egmont National Park, with rural land surrounding it on all sides. To the north, west, and south there is coastline on the Tasman Sea, with beaches famous for surfing and windsurfing. State Highway 3 connects the region from north to south, on the eastern side. State Highway 45 is the scenic route, following the coastline.

The many streams and rivers flowing down from the mountain have dictated the layout of many of the roads. So looking at a map, it may seem like all roads point to Egmont National Park, as roads were built in the spaces between streams. Most of these streams empty into the Tasman Sea.

DAILY LIVING

Your lifestyle in rural Taranaki will be dictated by a combination of how you are trying to make a living and your favorite activities. There's certainly a lot to do if you're outdoorsy. Between water sports, hiking, and golf, there's never a lack of leisure activities in this region.

However, if you're spending all day working on a farm, you may find it difficult to fit many of those activities into your schedule. Farming, or working in a support town for farmers, is the only game in town around these parts.

Then again, if you live toward the northern side of Taranaki, you can live in a rural area and still commute to work in New Plymouth or on an offshore rig. Driving just a few minutes outside of the urban area, you'll find life is pretty rural, but the city is close enough to reach without any hardship.

Even if you work in the rural areas, you'll probably find yourself visiting New Plymouth or Whanganui regularly to stock up on supplies. The small-town shops in other communities just won't have everything you want or need to keep your household running.

WHERE TO LIVE

There are a few towns of note in the rural Taranaki area. **Stratford** lies directly to the east of the park and is the last town before the turnoff to Taranaki's skiing area. It gets a fair bit of traffic from visitors and local outdoors enthusiasts. Most of the town's streets are named after characters from Shakespeare's plays, since the town itself is named after Stratford-upon-Avon, the Bard's home.

A bit farther south is **Eltham,** which is known for the local cheeses. It is also the

Name That Volcano

Mount Taranaki's distinctive shape dominates the skyline.

Tom Cruise casts his gaze upward toward the towering peak of Mount Fuji . . . or does he?

In fact, the scenes in the blockbuster movie *The Last Samurai* that were set in a village below Japan's iconic Mount Fuji were actually shot in Taranaki, New Zealand!

The symmetrical cone shape of Mount Taranaki (also known as Mount Egmont) is very similar to Mount Fuji, making it a perfect Hollywood stand-in. The small village set was constructed for the filming of the scenes in Uruti, Taranaki. The crew spent seven weeks filming there, and the structures built for the sets are still in place.

In fact, the movie set has become a tourist attraction, with private companies running sightseeing tours to the fake Japanese village, where photos and props have been placed in the buildings. For large groups, the horse trainers who provided the stunt horses for the film will put on a 45-minute show, where the horses and riders perform various stunts seen in the movie.

I guess the folks in Taranaki thought if so many other parts of New Zealand could cash in on their filming locations from *The Lord of the Rings,* why shouldn't they be able to cash in on *The Last Samurai?* Why not, indeed.

starting point for Eltham Road, the most direct route to the seaside center of Opunake, a favorite holiday spot.

Hawera is where the scenic route, State Highway 45, meets up with State Highway 3. It's a slightly larger town than the ones around it, so it's a popular stop for travelers. It also serves as a shopping stop for rural locals.

None of these towns is of any notable size, but that's what rural living is all about. You can find yourself a piece of land and enjoy the simpler things in life. Civilization, in the form of New Plymouth, is never too far away.

Because the beaches around Taranaki are so popular, buying a rural home here is not as cheap as you might expect. If you are looking in an area close to the sea, you can expect to pay at least $250,000 for a home without much land. If you're willing to put in the effort, however, you may be able to find a bargain. There are very few rental homes available in these rural areas.

GETTING AROUND

If you're living in a country setting, you'll most likely be driving around in your "ute" (pickup truck) or a similarly useful working vehicle. Because of all of the streams and rivers, the road layout around Taranaki can be a bit of a pain. However, the main roads are good and will connect you with the outside world.

There is rarely any traffic around, except for on the roads leading into Egmont National Park, which can get a bit too popular on weekends during ski season and on holidays. But even then, it's unlikely to affect you much.

Taranaki is a half-day drive to either Auckland or Wellington, so if you have big-city needs, you can always do a weekend trip. Trying to do the round-trip in a day is a bit much, especially if you want to spend any time doing things in the city.

BAY OF PLENTY AND HAWKE'S BAY

People who live in the Bay of Plenty and Hawke's Bay regions on the eastern side of the North Island tend to boast a lot. They'll tell anyone who will listen about their mild, sunny weather and miles of beaches—and did they mention the weather?

It's certainly easy to see why people are so keen on the area. It does get warmer, drier weather than much of the country, and most of the regions' residents live very near the coast so they can take advantage of the beaches. But before you pack your bags, including an extra bathing suit, don't forget that you'll need a job once you get there. While lots of people are able to find appropriate work in these regions, they don't have the variety of jobs you would find in the largest cities.

There's also the matter of whether you'll feel comfortable in these regions, which haven't seen as many immigrants settle in as the bigger cities have. If you're looking for a lot of other expats to socialize with, you may struggle to find them here.

Bay of Plenty

The Bay of Plenty is one of the fastest-growing areas in New Zealand. Its main city, Tauranga, has a population of 115,000 rivaling the size of Dunedin on the South Island. People were first drawn to this area as a holiday destination. The north-facing coastline is bathed in sun, attracting Kiwis all summer, relaxing in their caravans or pitching tents. If you're wondering about the name (which is also quite enticing), it was chosen by Captain Cook back in 1769. He found the area well populated with Maori, and there were lots of supplies to be traded here.

The Bay is also a great location for a port, so shipping interests developed to handle the exports of the main Bay of Plenty products, kiwifruit and lumber. It's also an import/export hub for all kinds of products coming from, and going to, various parts of New Zealand. Tauranga's port is the largest in New Zealand; it has added more traffic recently as a popular stop for cruise ships (giving visitors access to landlocked Rotorua by coach). Hospitality and tourism jobs are one growing field in the region, servicing both Kiwis and foreign visitors.

There is a lot of work here in manufacturing and engineering too, with boatbuilding being one key industry. More rural parts of the region use the plentiful sun for growing kiwifruit and other crops, and there is also a sizable forestry industry. With the population in the area growing so fast, the local council in Tauranga has become very business-friendly. So if you think you'd like to set up shop somewhere for yourself, this might be a great place to try it. The growing population has also created a need for more health care workers and professionals.

© MICHELLE WAITZMAN

Sunshine and beaches are a big attraction in the Bay of Plenty.

THE LAY OF THE LAND

I'm actually lumping in the East Cape with the Bay of Plenty to keep things simple here. The East Cape is where the coastline curves around to the south, before you get as far south as Hawke's Bay. It's the easternmost part of the country, and the main city there is Gisborne, although it is less than half the size of Tauranga.

The Bay of Plenty's western edge begins at the south end of the Coromandel Peninsula (another popular holiday destination for Kiwis). The Bay dips southward, then curves back up, and ends as the land juts northward slightly at the easternmost part of the North Island. There is then a fairly straight coastline down the East Cape until it reaches Hawke's Bay.

Aside from the coastline, the Bay of Plenty's most distinctive geographic

Desert Snowstorm

One of the favorite winter activities for people who live in Hawke's Bay and the Bay of Plenty is heading inland to Mount Ruapehu for some alpine skiing. There are two main ski fields on Mount Ruapehu: Whakapapa and Turoa. The area around Mount Ruapehu gets much more snow than the rest of the North Island, thanks to its high elevation.

While the snow is good news for skiers, it can also cause problems along the way. The stretch of highway leading to Mount Ruapehu, most often called the "Desert Road," can become impassable during snowstorms and be closed to vehicles.

If you're planning a trip to the ski fields, it's a good idea to turn on the radio and find out whether the road is open before you spend a couple of hours in the car just to get turned back in the end. And remember that things can change quickly at high elevations, so even if it's a beautiful, sunny morning when you arrive, it could be a full-on storm by the time you leave for home. Give yourself lots of extra driving time, especially if you are not accustomed to driving on snow.

Mount Ruapehu is the most popular skiing destination on the North Island.

© MICHELLE WAITZMAN

feature is Mount Maunganui. At 232 meters (760 feet), it towers over Tauranga from across a narrow channel. The mountain sits at the end of a triangular peninsula lined with a golden beach.

The mild climate of the region makes it not only the biggest producer of kiwifruit in the country but also the only place where tropical crops like avocados and citrus fruits will grow. On the eastern cape you'll find a number of vineyards.

Boiling Mud and Volcanoes

South of the coastline lies New Zealand's biggest geothermal area. Centered near the city of Rotorua, you'll find steam vents hissing out of the ground and the sickly smell of sulfur in the air. Thermal mineral pools are advertised at every hotel along the way. The underground heat is also used to generate electricity.

Right in the center of the North Island is where you'll find its highest peak, Mount Ruapehu, which is an active volcano. Its last major eruption was in 1996, and scientists are always keeping an eye on things to see when it might go off again. There are so many warning systems in place that an eruption is unlikely to cause a major disaster. In fact, people are so comfortable with this ticking bomb that they go tramping on it all summer and skiing on it all winter.

The country's largest lake, Lake Taupo, is also nearby. It was created by a catastrophic eruption around AD 400, long before any humans lived in New Zealand. A resort town of the same name sits on Taupo's shores, attracting visitors from around the country and overseas.

DAILY LIVING

Certainly lifestyle is the main reason people want to live in this region. Having so many recreational activities on your doorstep, and good weather to enjoy them in, is the obvious reward of settling in the Bay of Plenty.

Tauranga's growth has meant that services have also grown and expanded. There are no shortages of restaurants, and the nightlife is beginning to pick up, although the high percentage of retirees living in the area means that overall things remain pretty low-key.

Schools have also had to open to accommodate the local growth. The Bay of Plenty region (not including the East Cape) has 25 elementary schools, 4 intermediate schools, and 8 secondary schools. Both state-run and private education is available. Schools in the Bay of Plenty generally rate highly, but those around Gisborne and the East Cape may have more variation in their quality.

For higher education, there is a campus of the University of Waikato in Tauranga, as well as Bay of Plenty Polytechnic. The area isn't particularly known as a center for education, though, so foreign students tend to go elsewhere unless they want to take advantage of the specialized marine biology unit nearby.

The main public hospital for the region is in Tauranga, and there are also five private hospitals around. The Tauranga Hospital has a 24-hour emergency department, and some other regional medical centers have 24-hour availability for medical care that doesn't require hospitalization. Due to the high number of older residents, health care is a growing field in the Bay of Plenty, so a wide range of services are available.

WHERE TO LIVE

There are not a lot of urban areas in this region, so for those who need to be near a workplace, the options are somewhat limited. If you are working in a more rural industry, like farming, forestry, or tourism, your home could be almost anywhere in the region.

The largest city by far is Tauranga, but Gisborne and Rotorua are also significant population centers. However, the job scene in Rotorua is quite limited. Its economy relies heavily on tourism, and it has made itself the town to visit for a taste of Maori culture. There aren't a lot of opportunities there for immigrants outside of tourism and forestry, and unless you have a specific offer of employment there, I don't really recommend it as a place to settle.

Tauranga

Living in **Tauranga** offers you one of the most enjoyable climates in the country, along with a growing population that could see it become the fourth-largest city in New Zealand over the next 20 years. Getting in on the ground floor of this growth means that there are opportunities to run an expanding business, especially in the service and retail sectors.

The population currently sits at around 115,000, of which 19 percent are over the age of 65. Yes, a lot of Kiwis retire here, and who can blame them? Caring for these older residents, or selling them the products and services they need, is one of the best ways to make your living in Tauranga.

The port can also offer employment opportunities, both in the shipping industry itself or as an importer or exporter of goods. If you are in the building trade, you'll enjoy the growing need for housing and commercial real estate in the area.

The coastline around Tauranga is popular with surfers, so if you enjoy riding the waves, you will find it a convenient place to live.

All of this growth and lifestyle does come at a price, of course. With more people flocking to Tauranga, house prices have been on the increase, although they are still a bit unpredictable. A three-bedroom house in the city will probably cost you around $450,000, but in **Mount Maunganui** prices are heading higher. Some houses are still in the $450,000 range, while in the most popular spots (on the beach) they sell for well over $1 million—not exactly affordable for the average retiree.

Renting a house in Tauranga can be difficult. Beachside homes are more often rented as short-term holiday accommodations, at ridiculously high prices. Few other homes are available for rent at all. If you do manage to find a rental home, you should be charged around $340 per week for it.

Gisborne

Living in **Gisborne** on the East Cape makes you one of the first people in the world to greet the new day. With a steady population of around 47,000, it's never as busy as Tauranga. In fact, being so out of the way, Gisborne's beaches are more peaceful than those in many other regions, and it doesn't take long to escape inland into the bush, either.

There aren't a lot of major employers in Gisborne, however, which is partly why the population isn't growing. Its unemployment rate is slightly higher than the national average, and many of the residents work as skilled or unskilled laborers.

One industry that has done well in the surrounding areas is viticulture. Gisborne is where most of New Zealand's chardonnay wines are grown and bottled. However, like many agricultural industries, winemaking includes a lot of seasonal jobs, which leaves people looking for other work for the rest of the year.

The other main industries are agriculture, forestry, and manufacturing, and a wide range of products are grown or made in Gisborne. These include specialty cheeses, beer, wine, cider, popcorn, milk products, hosiery, surfboards, plastics, cashmere, and organic farming and health products from the manuka tree.

Gisborne has one of the highest percentages of Maori population in the country, at around 41 percent. As for immigrants, people born overseas make up only 8.6 percent of Gisborne's population. This may leave you feeling a bit isolated, especially if you are a visible minority. But it may also give you an opportunity to really immerse yourself in New Zealand culture and not rely on other immigrants to make you feel comfortable.

The city lies on the shores of Poverty Bay (Captain Cook didn't do so well trading with the locals here), and the Turanganui River flows through the town center. The shoreline has a lot of green space, and there are also small reserves and gardens scattered throughout the city.

Because the incomes in this area are lower than average, so are the house prices. You can buy a three-bedroom home in Gisborne in the $220,000-350,000 range. The exception would be a home right on the beach, which as always will cost a premium. Rentals in Gisborne are hard to find and average about $280 per week.

GETTING AROUND

The population increase around the Bay of Plenty has put some strain on the transportation infrastructure. In response, toll expressways were built around Tauranga to allow drivers to bypass inner-city traffic for just $2 per trip.

There is also a bus service available in Tauranga, with 12 city routes. They have even introduced Sunday service on most routes. If you are heading farther away, another bus line connects Tauranga with the inland city of Rotorua.

During the summer, you can span the distance between Tauranga and Mount Maunganui by ferry instead of driving.

For accessing the Bay of Plenty by road, State Highway 2 is the main route. It begins at State Highway 1 just south of Auckland and follows the Bay, staying near the coastline until it reaches the town of Opotiki, where it turns south and continues on to Gisborne and eventually Hawke's Bay and beyond.

State Highway 35 is the scenic route around the East Cape, which also arrives in Gisborne and joins up once more with State Highway 2.

A network of side roads connects the rural areas to the main cities and towns. Rotorua has a couple of main highways leading down to it, including State Highway 36 from Tauranga and State Highway 30 from Whakatane, which lies farther east along the Bay of Plenty.

Hawke's Bay

Hawke's Bay is a pleasant place to live by just about any definition. There's plenty of space, good weather, and a huge stretch of coastline. The main center of Hawke's Bay is a small cluster of cities: Napier, Hastings, and Havelock North. Outside of these few places, life is very rural indeed. That's all for the best, since Hawke's Bay's main industries are agricultural—growing fruit and making wine.

In addition to farming, forestry is a large industry in the area. And the offshoot of these primary industries is a significant number of jobs in food processing and wood processing. There is also work in chemicals and engineering.

Within the more urban areas, you'll find opportunities in retail, education, finance, real estate, and other service industries. Tourism has also grown in this region recently, both in the city of Napier and the surrounding vineyards.

THE LAY OF THE LAND

Hawke's Bay creates a large indent about halfway down the east coast of the North Island. There are no large towns or cities along the northern shores of the bay, but toward the south end is the city of Napier. Just a few miles south of Napier along State Highway 2, slightly inland, is its twin city, Hastings. Just southeast of Hastings is the much smaller, more rural center of Havelock North.

While the shoreline provides this region with lots of beaches, the coastal waters are mostly inhospitable for swimming. Windsurfers have better luck here, although surfers do better farther north near Gisborne.

The warm climate and dry soil make this one of the best parts of the country for growing grapes, and some of New Zealand's best red wines come from Hawke's Bay. Locals will tell you that the climate is similar to the Mediterranean. I think that's a bit of an exaggeration, but there are mild temperatures, ocean breezes from the Pacific, and an abundance of palm trees.

On the north side of Napier is an inlet and inner harbor, so the city center is bounded by water on two sides, north and east.

New Zealand's Fruit Basket

Much of New Zealand's fruit crops are grown in Hawke's Bay. The area produces huge volumes of apples, but it also has a warm enough climate to grow cherries, peaches, and other soft fruits over the summer. The fruits are transported around the country, but if you live in the local area, you'll get them fresher than anyone else. Some farms even sell fruit right on their property, so you're practically getting it right off the trees.

A lot of Hawke's Bay fruit is exported, making packaging and transportation important to the local economy. And, of course, some of the local fruit becomes wine, which is also a big export product for the area.

DAILY LIVING

If you enjoy a small-town or rural lifestyle, Hawke's Bay is a lovely place to settle. If your tastes are more urban, however, you may or may not be satisfied with what Napier has to offer. It's a city, yes, but not a very large one, although it does its best to be sophisticated. You'll find few international events coming through this region, and shopping (as a leisure activity) is limited.

What's nice about living here is that you have so much access to the local food products, including fruits, cheeses, wines, and honey. So if you believe in simple pleasures,

© MICHELLE WAITZMAN

Vineyards thrive in Hawke's Bay's dry soil.

you will not be disappointed. You also have few worries when it comes to traffic or city stress. Farmers markets take place every weekend in Napier and Hastings, so even if you can't make it out to the farms, they'll come to you.

The main centers have schools at all levels that your children can attend, but in rural areas they may face a longer trip to the "local" school, particularly toward the northern end of the bay. The main hospital for the region is in Hastings, and Napier has a 24-hour emergency medical service.

For your fix of big-city indulgence, you'll have to count on a five-hour drive to Wellington, and a bit longer than that to reach Auckland. But reaching the wilderness is much easier. Just head inland to the Ruahine Forest Park, with rugged mountains and challenging trails.

Living on the coast also means you'll be able to indulge in all kinds of water sports. Sailing, windsurfing, and kayaking are all common hobbies for those who live near the coast. And there are also many streams and rivers for inland dwellers to enjoy.

WHERE TO LIVE
Napier

Although Hawke's Bay is a primarily agricultural region, the city of **Napier** is like an urban oasis in a sea of orchards. The city is home to about 61,000 people and has a distinct look and personality, thanks to a disaster in the town center many years ago.

You can't spend more than five minutes in Napier without hearing or reading about "the earthquake." In 1931, an earthquake measuring 7.8 on the Richter scale shook Napier and the surrounding region. Napier's town center was badly damaged, and a fire tore its way through town as the broken water mains made it impossible to stop. In the end, over 250 people died and the town center was gutted.

Rebuilding Napier was a huge project, and the town planners were clever enough to do it right. They decided that Napier was to be rebuilt in the new art deco style, so that all of the central buildings would have a similar look. Today it rivals Miami's South Beach as the most concentrated collection of art deco buildings in the world. It looks quite urban and stylish, compared to other cities and towns around New Zealand.

Residential areas outside the town center have a more conventional look to them, with the standard wooden bungalows taking their place along the hilly streets. In some ways the city center is more for tourists than locals, with a string of hotels lining the waterfront, the National Aquarium by the beach, and lots of restaurants welcoming visitors.

Living in Napier means finding a local job, and most of the businesses in the city are small—with an average of just four employees! The service sector is the main employer here, in areas such as retail and wholesale, business services, construction, education, tourism, hospitality, and personal, household, or cultural services. Incomes vary quite a lot, and a large proportion of local employees still make less than the national average. With so many tourists coming into town and pushing prices up, that can make it a challenge to get by.

Luckily, housing is still comparatively affordable here. A three-bedroom house in Napier and the surrounding suburbs will cost somewhere between $350,000-600,000 depending on location, features, and age. If you decide to rent a home in Napier, you'll be paying about $330 per week for three bedrooms.

Dedicated to Deco

Napier's art deco city center is very distincitve.

Napier's reputation as an art deco capital is something the city cherishes and celebrates as much as possible. People come from all over the world to enjoy this unique architectural heritage; the bulk of Napier's town center was rebuilt in the art deco style following an earthquake in the early 1930s.

To make the most of its connection to this era, Napier's Art Deco Trust hosts a couple of annual events to draw people into the city and party 1930s-style. The annual Art Deco Weekend in February attracts both Kiwis and international tourists, and participants are encouraged to dress in the style of the period. Antiques are displayed and sometimes sold, cocktail parties lighten the mood, and live music also helps to set the scene. The mild winters in the area are also put to good use with Deco Winter Weekend in July.

For the rest of the year, the Art Deco Trust keeps the deco dream alive by providing guided walking tours of the city center and running an art deco shop.

It may have all begun with a terrible disaster in 1931, but the aftermath of Napier's earthquake has quite literally put this small coastal city on the map for New Zealand visitors. Throw in the local vineyards and the National Aquarium, and you've got a serious tourist destination—at least for the tourists who aren't into bungee jumping and jet boats.

Hastings

Some might say that Napier is the style of Hawke's Bay, and **Hastings** is the substance. Hastings is home to around 75,000 people, and you can definitely feel the agricultural influence in this area. It's the main service town for the surrounding rural areas and tends to focus on practicalities. **Havelock North,** which is practically a part of Hastings, contributes 10,000 people to the district, as does the neighboring town of **Flaxmere.**

The streets are even laid out in a very practical grid in Hastings town center. That makes it simple to find your way around. The biggest industries for local work are agriculture, manufacturing, health services, retail, and education—basically, either dealing directly with the main agricultural trade in the area or supporting the people who do.

But Hastings does offer its own ways to enjoy life. It's home to New Zealand's biggest water park, Splash Planet. For the more cultured, the Hawke's Bay Opera House is housed in a Spanish mission-style building in Hastings which has recently been renovated. In fact, a large number of attractive Spanish mission buildings were erected around Hastings after the 1931 earthquake, which badly damaged Hastings as well as Napier. Gardens are also popular in Hastings, which has everything from a traditional English rose garden to a peaceful Chinese garden.

Despite Hastings's efforts to keep up with the sophistication of the wineries and other nearby attractions, it is still a blue-collar town where most people get their hands dirty for a living. It has slowly developed over the years, adding more shops and restaurants, but it may never feel as cosmopolitan as Napier.

Housing in Hastings is relatively affordable. Older bungalows cost around $350,000 and newer or larger houses cost around $450,000. The average rental costs for a three-bedroom house is $275. Housing costs are similar in Havelock North and Flaxmere.

GETTING AROUND

State Highway 2 is the main route leading to, and through, Hawke's Bay from the north and south. However, State Highway 5 connects the bay to Taupo, and from there you can get onto State Highway 1 leading to Auckland. Either way, it's a long drive to get to the main cities. Auckland is around six hours away, and Wellington is almost five hours away.

Within the cities the roads are pretty good, and even as you head out into the rural areas, the main roads are well maintained. You'll need a local map to find the smaller side roads in rural parts of Hawke's Bay, as the road atlases won't have everything marked.

The region's airport is just to the north of Napier, servicing domestic flights to other main centers around New Zealand.

GoBay operates a regional bus service that covers Napier, Hastings, Havelock North, and Flaxmere. There are several routes, but only limited service on Saturdays and none on Sundays or public holidays. Fares are zone-based and range $3.60-5.40 for adults, while fares for children and seniors are about half as much and tertiary students save about a dollar. There are substantial discounts if you use a "Smart Card" to pay.

Palmerston North

Palmerston North calls itself "Student City" thanks to the main campus of Massey University located there, but most Kiwis just call it "Palmy." It's the home of the country's only veterinary school, a large number of agricultural research centers, a polytechnic called the Universal College of Learning (UCOL), which also has a campus in Whanganui, and International Pacific College. Aside from the education sector, the main areas of employment in Palmerston North are research, wholesale and retail, and business services. The city is also trying to attract more corporate offices, offering lower property costs and a better lifestyle for employees than the bigger cities. The city itself is home to around 80,000 people, and it is also the main service area for the surrounding rural population.

THE LAY OF THE LAND

The region in which Palmerston North lies is called Manawatu. The city is tucked into a small opening in the mountains between the north end of the Tararua Range and the south end of the Ruahine Range, making it a useful place for those who want to pass between the west and east sides of the North Island.

The city is bordered on the southeast side by the Manawatu River. So although it is one of New Zealand's rare inland cities, there is no shortage of water nearby.

DAILY LIVING

Having a young student population around most of the time has made Palmerston North a more vibrant and lively city than you might otherwise expect. There are lots of shops and restaurants servicing the students, locals, and even the rural residents who come into town to do their shopping.

The city gets noisy over the summer, even without the students, thanks to the local stock-car track. It even hosts international races, so race fans will enjoy this as a bonus of life in Palmerston North, while those looking for peace and quiet may end up running for the hills.

Palmerston North is far enough away from major cities to be quite self-sufficient in terms of shopping and other services. You'll be able to find everything from fashion to furniture without leaving town. But should you decide it's time for a road trip, you can reach Wellington in a little over two hours. Or if you head north, the ski fields on Mount Ruapehu are about two or three hours away, depending on the weather conditions.

The main hospital for the Manawatu region is in Palmerston North; it has a 24-hour emergency department.

WHERE TO LIVE

Palmerston North is a compact city, with a grid layout for the city center. The CBD is centered on "The Square" right in the middle of town, but just a few blocks away you'll be into the residential areas with local schools and parks. If you're not studying or working at the Massey University campus, it's quite convenient and affordable to live in the city itself. Houses in the inner suburbs cost around $350,000, unless you're after something brand-new. Renting a house with three bedrooms will cost around $300-350 per week.

The airport is just north of the city, so the suburbs close to it, like **Terrace End,** are likely to get some related noise. Golfers may enjoy living in **Hokowhitu,** a southeastern suburb well placed between the city's golf courses.

The main campus for **Massey University** is on the south side of the Manawatu River, outside the city center. To rent a three-bedroom house near campus, you'll pay around $300 per week, but students can share the cost by "flatting" with others. A lot of students find rooms in shared houses or flats for as little as $100 per week. Of course, the pickier you are about the state of your home and who you share it with, the more you're likely to end up paying. Students don't always take good care of their rentals, so make sure that things are relatively clean and in working order before you sign a rental agreement.

GETTING AROUND

There are a few roads leading to Palmerston North. State Highway 3 connects to State Highway 1 on the west side of the mountains, and to State Highway 2 on the east side. Within the city, State Highway 3 is called Main Street. From the Wellington region, you can turn off State Highway 1 onto State Highway 57 just north of the Kapiti Coast, and that will also take you to Palmy.

The grid layout of Palmerston North's center makes it easy to drive around, but in some of the suburbs, the grid gives way to residential cul-de-sacs. Only a few main streets have traffic lights, so there are few delays on the roads.

Palmerston North is a fairly compact city, which makes cycling a reasonable way to get around town or between the city and university. There is also a bus service available with several routes around the city and university. If you're a student or faculty member for either UCOL or Massey University, you get to ride the bus for free! Otherwise it's $2.50 per fare or $55 per month, with no zone rules. You can also buy a GoCard for discounted fares. Buses run seven days a week here, but the hours are not very long. If you're going out for the evening, you'll have to find another way home. Bus service between Palmerston North and the nearby rural towns is also available.

WELLINGTON AND THE LOWER NORTH ISLAND

The bottom of the North Island is home to New Zealand's capital city, Wellington. It may be a fraction of the size of Auckland, but Wellington considers itself every bit as urban and sophisticated, without the traffic jams and big-city attitude. Perched on the gateway between the North and South Islands, Wellington used to be a place to travel through on your way to somewhere else. But these days, people are settling in and around the capital in increasing numbers. The city is home to university students, public servants, and a significant arts community. While Wellington takes itself seriously as a financial and business center, it's still much more laid-back than Auckland.

The beach-lined Kapiti Coast attracts both retirees looking for a relaxed way of life and young families happy to compromise between small-town friendliness and easy access to a big city. Over in the Hutt Valley, commuters pass their time enjoying views of the harbor as they travel into the city. And over the hill in the Wairarapa, some of New Zealand's top boutique wineries are making this a popular place to buy land. Yes, everything from parliament to pastures can be found in this region.

©MICHELLE WAITZMAN

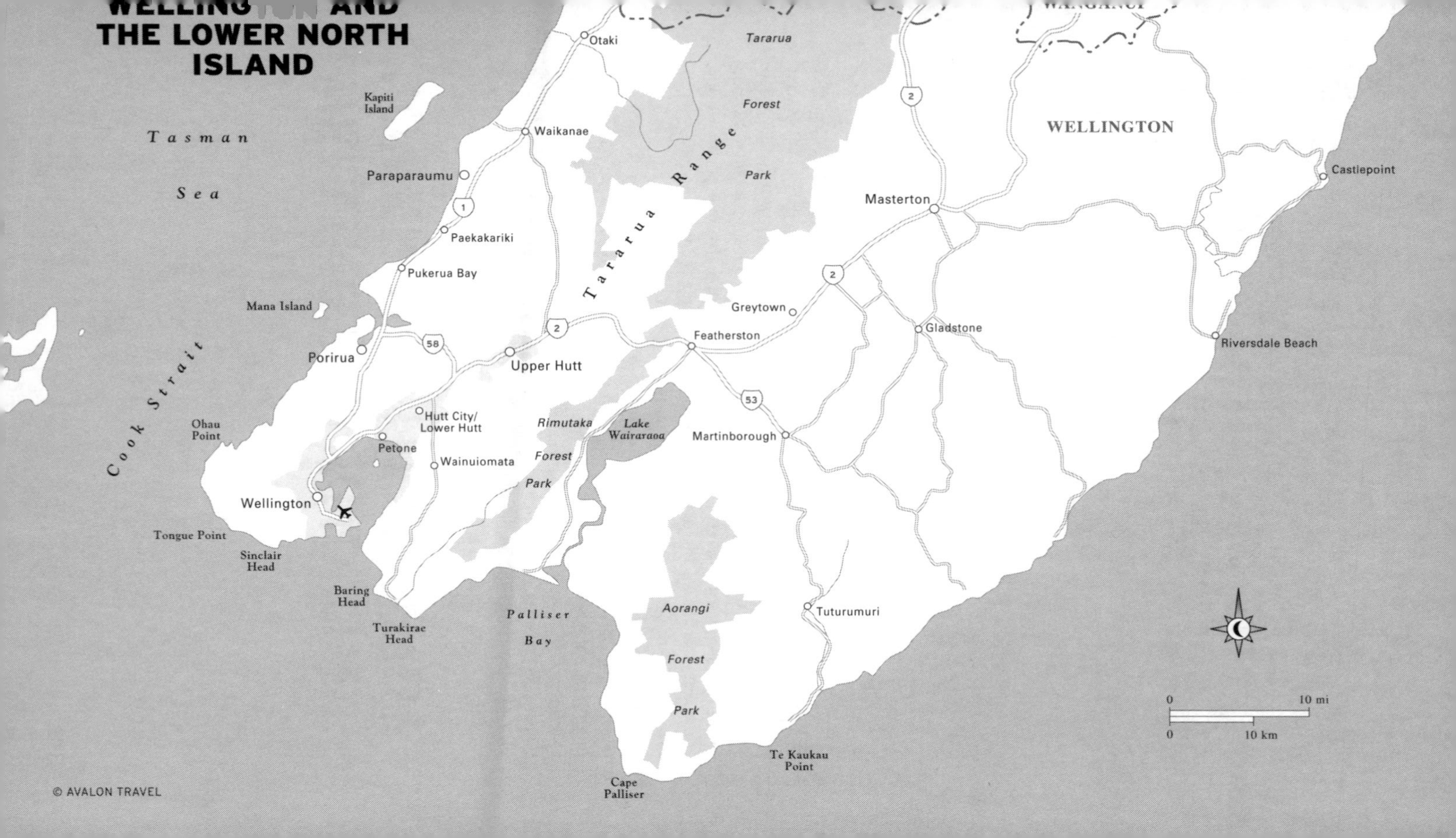

© AVALON TRAVEL

Cook Strait

Tasman
Sea

Kapiti
Island

Tongue Point

Ohau
Point

Sinclair
Head

Mana Island

Wellington

Paraparaumu

Baring
Head

Petone

Porirua

Pukerua Bay

Paekakariki

Turakirae
Head

Wainuiomata

Hutt City/
Lower Hutt

58

Waikanae

Otaki

Park

Forest

Rimutaka

Upper Hutt

1

2

Tararua
Range

Palliser
Bay

Lake
Wairarapa

Martinborough

Featherston

Greytown

Park

Tararua

Forest

Cape
Palliser

Aorangi

Forest

Park

Tuturumuri

53

2

Masterton

2

Te Kaukau
Point

Gladstone

WELLINGTON

Riversdale Beach

Castlepoint

0

0

10 km

10 mi

Wellington

New Zealand's capital city has shrugged off its reputation as a stuffy government town and undergone something of a renaissance over the last 25 years. Now it's a vibrant, cosmopolitan city with a flair for the arts, a café on every corner, and a film industry that's the envy of Hollywood. Welcome to Wellywood.

The city's residents are quick to point out that although it is one of the biggest cities in New Zealand, Wellington can almost feel like a village. There is a strong sense of community, where people get personally involved in local matters. You're likely to run into your friends and coworkers around town or when dropping into a neighborhood pub or café.

Government has a large presence in the city. The national public service has most of its offices around Wellington, not to mention the regional and city councils. Being new to the country doesn't necessarily take you out of the running for a government job, either. While certain jobs within the public sector require some knowledge of Maori language and protocol, these are relatively few of the many positions available.

The creative sector is also notable in Wellington and throughout the region, including the film and television industries, plus music, fashion, advertising, and new media. Wellington has major film studios, animation companies, and postproduction houses to meet the needs of both local and visiting filmmakers. There are large production facilities for TV and film in Hutt City and Miramar, and independent production companies are scattered around the city and suburbs.

New creative businesses are supported by a business incubator called Creative HQ,

© MICHELLE WAITZMAN

Downtown Wellington is flat and compact.

which is funded by Wellington City Council. Wellington is serious about attracting creative talent to the city, which is rare in a world that tends to value finance and industry much more than the arts. But the business of making art has been good to this city, thanks mainly to director Peter Jackson and his big-budget films, and Wellington wants to build on that relationship.

There is also business support in other areas from Grow Wellington (which is also run by Wellington City Council), so if you're looking to start up your own enterprise in New Zealand, you should check the organization's website. It provides assistance to new businesses, helps pave the way for existing businesses from overseas to set up a Wellington branch, and even helps new immigrants in the region find jobs.

Technology is also a major employment sector in this region, thanks to a very active IT industry. Almost a quarter of the information technology workers in the country work in Greater Wellington. People looking for jobs in IT will find there is a high demand for their skills here.

The region is home to two universities and a number of colleges, polytechnics, and privately run professional training schools. Over 20,000 students are enrolled in tertiary (college or university) level courses in Wellington region. Both Massey University and Victoria University offer a wide range of courses. The world-famous Le Cordon Bleu cooking school also opened a location in central Wellington a few years ago, in case you want to work on your gourmet cooking skills.

The abundance of students gives the city a bit of an edge in terms of both art and politics. You'll see the young, alternative crowd with hair every color of the rainbow on city streets. This youthful presence gives the city an energized nightlife, especially on weekends when many nightclubs keep the music pumping until dawn. In a country with a reputation for closing down at 6pm, that's something to boast about.

The suburbs provide a more conservative, family atmosphere. You'll find lots of community centers and public parks where neighborhood kids get together to play. The suburbs may not have a lot of nightlife, but some of them have movie theaters, pubs, and restaurants so you don't always have to head to the city for your entertainment.

THE LAY OF THE LAND

Located at the southern end of the North Island, Wellington is as close to the middle of the country as you can get. That makes it a perfect place for the federal government, which has been in Wellington since 1865. The city's deepwater port and sheltered harbor have also made it an important shipping center for the country. There is a dedicated wharf for container ships and a docking area for cruise ships.

The harbor is also the departure point for ferries to the South Island. This means that most tourists will pass through Wellington at some point during their time in New Zealand, much to the delight of the local tourism board.

Downtown Wellington is very compact, covering the small area of flat land between the surrounding hills and the harbor. You can walk from one end to the other in about 30 minutes. Originally the city center was even smaller, but the government undertook several land reclamation projects to push the shoreline into the harbor and make more room for buildings. The skyscrapers of downtown Wellington may seem small by North American standards, with only a couple of buildings reaching the 30-story mark. This is partly due to the possibility of a major earthquake and partly to prevent

Windy Wellington

© UNA HUBBARD

Ask people from any other part of New Zealand about Wellington, and one of the first things they'll mention is the wind. Some people blame the large number of politicians, and it's true that they certainly have hot air to spare. However, it's the Cook Strait that is really to blame for the blustery conditions. Weather systems moving across from the Tasman Sea to the Pacific Ocean have to pass by Wellington along their way, and that leaves the city exposed to winds that often reach gale force during the winter. Of course, this doesn't happen all of the time (as Aucklanders would have you believe), but it's a challenge to live in Wellington if you're obsessive about keeping your hair in place!

Wellingtonians generally take a "grin and bear it" attitude toward the wind. You won't find many of them carrying umbrellas on a stormy day, as they tend to get blown away or mangled after the first big gust. The downtown area is also designed with the strong winds in mind. There are very few tall skyscrapers, and never a lot of them in a row; this cuts down on the creation of wind tunnels, which would otherwise magnify the problem.

How bad is it? Well, I've never been literally blown away, but I have stumbled forward a few steps when a gusty tailwind caught me off guard.

the creation of a downtown wind tunnel that would amplify the already fierce winds that sometimes howl through the city.

Suburbs cover the hills and valleys around the city center until they reach the Cook Strait to the south and east, and sprawl farther north and northeast as they reach into the Hutt Valley and along the Kapiti Coast.

Like much of New Zealand, Wellington is situated on fault lines, making it prone to earthquakes. Most of the quakes are too minor even to be felt, but there is always a looming possibility of "the big one." The last big earthquake on the Wellington fault occurred in 1855. It measured 8.2 on the Richter scale, and although few people were killed (likely due to the small population at the time), it did raise the level of the land by over three feet. Scientists predict that it will be another couple of centuries before the next serious quake is due, but you never know. After a large earthquake, measuring 7.8 hit the city of Napier in 1931 and did significant damage, Wellington reassessed its own buildings to see which ones would withstand a quake of similar magnitude. They ended up knocking down several buildings that were unsafe. All new buildings have to adhere to strict requirements to make sure they don't pose a threat. While tectonic activity is not likely to interfere with your daily life in Wellington, it is always present in the back of people's minds.

DAILY LIVING
Wellington manages to have all of the conveniences of a major city, while remaining compact and very livable. People in this city are fond of their lifestyle, which puts leisure time on equal footing with work. The cafés are filled with businesspeople conducting official meetings over a cappuccino, and the waterfront plays host to a constant stream of joggers and cyclists, sneaking in a bit of exercise before or after work.

Leisure
Downtown Wellington has more going on than just politics. There are a number of professional theaters, and it is home to the New Zealand Symphony Orchestra as well as the Royal New Zealand Ballet and the New Zealand Opera. Film festivals and art galleries are also abundant. The bar and pub scene are moderately lively, at least on the weekends. Restaurants of all kinds fill the streets of the entertainment district.

Almost surrounded by water, Wellington offers a number of water sports. Lyall Bay attracts surfers from the region and is a great place to learn the sport. In 2005, an old navy frigate was sunk off of Island Bay, where it is now a destination for scuba divers. Kayaking is popular in the harbor, and rowing and dragon boat teams can also be seen practicing for competitions. There are several marinas available to sailors based in Wellington or just visiting from another town. For swimmers and sunbathers, there are beaches scattered along the city's shoreline with calm waters for cooling your feet on a summer's day.

The city center is surrounded by a greenbelt, which is crisscrossed with walking and mountain biking trails. There are several routes marked as official "walkways," and trail maps are available to point out interesting sights along the way. The city belt is also home to the Botanic Gardens, easily accessed from downtown by the historic cable car. In Wellington, both cricket and rugby are played at a professional level if you want to catch a game, but there are also local leagues playing in almost every park on weekends.

Health
Wellington Hospital is in the suburb of Newtown and has recently undergone an upgrade. The hospital is the largest in the region and should be able to meet most of your needs. The area around the hospital is where a lot of specialists and clinics have set up shop, but you should be able to find a family doctor or dentist in your own neighborhood.

Pharmacies are abundant in Wellington, but they vary greatly in size and the range of products they offer. If you can't find the medication or product you're after at the nearest pharmacy, try a couple of others or ask if it carries an equivalent product.

Wellington has the only free ambulance service in the country. By calling the 111 emergency number, you can have an ambulance dispatched to you. There is also a local ambulance contact number if your need is not as urgent.

Wellington Festivals

Wellington is New Zealand's self-proclaimed Arts Capital, so it should come as no surprise that there are a number of festivals in the city every year. Here are some of the events to mark on your calendar if you're living in Greater Wellington:

WORLD OF WEARABLE ARTS (WOW)

This popular September event combines fashion with the visual arts as participants come up with over-the-top creations that stretch the imagination. The show has been in Wellington since 2005, when it outgrew its original home in Nelson.

NEW ZEALAND INTERNATIONAL ARTS FESTIVAL

This biannual event (February-March, in even-numbered years) celebrates the best arts entertainment from around the world and within New Zealand. The first festival was in 1986, and it has continued to grow and improve ever since. It includes theater, dance, music, literature, and even circus performers. Many events are ticketed, but there are always a few free outdoor events as well.

WELLINGTON FRINGE FESTIVAL

The arts go to the edge with this festival of unusual and up-and-coming performances. These can include indoor theater, street theater, music, dance, and comedy. It's held in late February and early March, and generally ticket prices are very reasonable in order to encourage audiences to take a chance on something new.

SUMMER CITY

Wellington's City Council and Meridian Energy team up each summer to create a whole series of free events December through February. These include outdoor concerts at the Botanic Gardens and Queens Wharf, outdoor screenings of films, and other ways of enjoying the warm weather.

TOAST MARTINBOROUGH

Getting Wellingtonians to venture out to the Wairarapa can be a challenge, but Toast Martinborough has been selling out for years. This November festival of wine and food puts the spotlight on the local vineyards and their delicious offerings.

FILM FESTIVALS

It seems like there's almost always some kind of film festival happening in Wellington, particularly during the chilly winter months. Some of the most popular annual festivals include the Outtakes Queer Film Festival and the Documentary Edge Film Festival, both in June, and the New Zealand International Film Festival in July.

PRIME LIVING LOCATIONS

WHERE TO LIVE

With a population of almost 450,000, Greater Wellington is fairly small by North American city standards. But it is the second-largest urban area in New Zealand and offers many different housing choices. The real estate market in Wellington was booming for many years until the 2008 recession. The boom is still reflected in the relatively high housing costs although things have leveled off. With so many government and high-tech jobs to be had, however, there are lots of people willing to pay top dollar to live near the city.

What does this mean to you? If you're coming to Wellington without work, or with a job that doesn't pay well, finding low-cost housing will be a challenge. Renting a three-bedroom house in the city or inner suburbs averages over $550 per week. A similar house up in the Hutt Valley might rent for $400 per week. If you're looking to purchase your home, the same three-bedroom house in the city will cost at least $500,000 (and for the best locations over $600,000), but if you go far enough into the suburbs, you may find something for less than $450,000. So if money is tight, you might find yourself with a long commute, or living in a run-down old house that gets cold and damp. On the other hand, the average income in Wellington region is the highest in the country, so once you're gainfully employed, you shouldn't find yourself struggling to make ends meet.

Wellington offers a wide choice of home and lifestyle options. While many communities may look similar at first glance, they each have their own character and advantages. It is worth having a look around several areas before you decide on one, just to get a feel for your surroundings and your potential neighbors. The inner suburbs are so close to the action that it's only fair to consider them part of city living. Victorian "character" homes in areas like Thorndon and Mount Victoria, bordering the city center on either side, are being renovated to modern standards and fetching prices topping a million dollars. Waterfront houses and hilltop homes are also popular in areas like Island Bay, Lyall Bay, Oriental Bay, Roseneath, Hataitai, and Seatoun.

You will pay top dollar for a view of the water from any side, but thanks to Wellington's winding coastline and numerous hills, there are lots of options if you just *have* to live somewhere with an unobstructed view.

There's no doubt that the farther you travel from downtown, the more affordable the houses become. Most suburbs have a good infrastructure of their own, so you won't have to go into the city for your shopping or to take the kids to school.

Downtown Wellington

Like a lot of other international urban centers, Wellington's downtown became deserted and run-down during the 1960s and 1970s as families flocked to the suburbs. But the **city center** is now enjoying a revival, and older buildings are being converted into hip, new apartments. For both young singles and retired people looking for an active social life, city living offers convenience and an easy (often car-free) lifestyle.

One thing that is difficult to find in Wellington is a one-bedroom home. Most "flats" are large and shared by several people. The concept of the single person's apartment is quite new in this part of the world, and only the buildings that have gone up since the 1990s are likely to have small one-bedroom or studio apartments. So if you're on your own and you don't like the idea of having roommates, you may have trouble finding an affordable home in Wellington. This will gradually change as more new buildings are designed for executive living following the North American condominium model. Currently, small studio units are selling from about $160,000, but more comfortable, larger apartments in the city center can cost more than $300,000. Premium apartments by the waterfront can easily go for more than one million dollars.

Meanwhile, shared flats or apartments, a housing option imported from Britain, are plentiful. Large houses or spaces within buildings often have 3-5 bedrooms with shared kitchen and bathroom facilities. This can be a good choice if living in the city center

Wellinton's iconic cable car connects Kelburn to downtown.

is a priority, but renting a whole apartment is out of your price range. Students are the main renters of shared flats, but some professionals also enjoy this lifestyle and choose it over living alone. The cheapest rooms in crowded student flats rent for $100 per week, while a room in a prime location with other professionals may go for $150-250 per week.

Brooklyn, Kelburn, and Karori

North and west of downtown, you'll find a number of suburbs with old homes with character and a very residential atmosphere. The closest to the city are **Brooklyn, Kelburn,** and **Karori.** Homes here tend to be quite expensive (around $600,000-800,000), because the area is so convenient to downtown while still offering large family houses. Kelburn is also home to a Victoria University campus, so there is some student housing in the area where you can rent a room for less than $150 per week.

If you continue farther north, the suburbs get a touch more affordable. Places like **Newlands, Johnsonville,** and **Churton Park** are still a short drive to the city, but house prices go down a notch to $400,000 and $550,000 on average. Renting, however, is not a bargain at around $400 per week for a three-bedroom house.

Kilbirnie and the Miramar Peninsula

The bit of flat land connecting the Miramar Peninsula to the rest of Wellington is a bustling family suburb called **Kilbirnie.** With some of the best community facilities in the city, it has every possible convenience you could need and is just minutes away from the city center through the Mount Victoria Tunnel. Houses in Kilbirnie start at just under $500,000 and rent for $400 per week on average.

Miramar is the home of Wellington's top film studios and postproduction facilities. So if you are moving to Wellington to be part of the "Wellywood" scene, this is the most

Made in Wellywood

© NATHANIEL BEAVER

You'll find evidence of locally made blockbusters like *The Hobbit* all around Wellington.

Thanks to Oscar-winning director Peter Jackson, Wellington has become world-famous for its film production work. Prior to Jackson, Kiwi filmmakers who wanted to play with the big boys made the move to Hollywood and left their New Zealand roots behind. But over the years, some excellent facilities have developed in Wellington, allowing local filmmakers to do it all on their own shores, and even attracting projects from other countries.

Most people know that *The Hobbit* and *The Lord of the Rings* trilogies were filmed in New Zealand, with production based in Wellington. So was Jackson's remake of *King Kong*. But other blockbuster films have benefited from special effects and postproduction work completed in Wellington's facilities, including *I, Robot*, *Rise of the Planet of the Apes*, *Hellboy*, *The Chronicles of Narnia*, and James Cameron's *Avatar*.

The local council has set up Film Wellington, an agency that works to attract film and TV projects to the city and assists filmmakers who need to find crew and locations for their projects.

Wellywood may never measure up to the number of films produced in Hollywood (or Bollywood, for that matter), but the ever-growing collection of Academy Awards on local shelves can attest to the quality of work that happens there.

convenient place to live. There's also a stunning coastline around the peninsula and some popular beaches. But Miramar is becoming expensive for housing, thanks to that stunning coastline. You'll need to budget over $500,000 for a home in Miramar, but it will cost much more for a great view or a waterfront property. The well paid temporary film workers have pushed up rental prices in the area to an average of $450 per week.

Mount Victoria, Oriental Bay, and Hataitai

If you're looking for a residential area that's steps from downtown, you may want to check out Mount Victoria. This hillside location contains the suburbs of **Mount Victoria, Oriental Bay, Roseneath,** and **Hataitai.** The Mount Victoria suburb is one of the oldest neighborhoods in the city and still contains some beautiful Victorian homes. Oriental Bay is the waterfront option, with the city's most expensive apartments. The side of the hill facing away from downtown is called Hataitai, and the fact that it takes more effort to get downtown from that side makes the houses a touch less expensive. Everything around Mount Victoria (or Mount Vic, as the locals call it) is very costly, though, so this is only an option if you have at least $650,000 to spend on a house. Rentals can be found for around $460 per week, but luxury apartments along Oriental Bay will cost much more. Some rent for over $1,000 per week.

GETTING AROUND
Walking
One of the best things about living in Wellington is that it's such a pleasant place to just wander around on foot, and small enough that you can actually get somewhere that way! Whether you're strolling to work along Lambton Quay or climbing up Mount Victoria to take in the view, you're likely to do a lot more walking in Wellington than you're used to. There aren't any no-go neighborhoods, but commonsense precautions should be taken late at night. If the weather is good, do as the Wellingtonians do and get outside to enjoy the city.

Driving
Wellington tries to keep traffic flowing through the city center by using a lot of one-way streets. So until you get to know your way around, you'll have to make sure you don't find yourself driving in the wrong direction. Most intersections within the city have traffic lights, and roundabouts are rare until you get to the suburbs.

Things can get a bit backed up during rush hour as you try to get in or out of the city center. But outside of peak travel hours, traffic jams are unusual. The most common places for traffic to get heavy are the Mount Victoria Tunnel and the downtown exits from the motorway.

Street parking is available in most residential areas and on some downtown side streets, but keep an eye out for Residents Only areas marked by signs. "Pay and display" street parking is common downtown and has replaced most parking meters. Many shops and offices have their own parking lots, plus there are a few large lots for public parking in entertainment-heavy areas like Courtenay Place.

Public Transit
Wellington has arguably the best public transit in the country, incorporating commuter trains, buses, ferries, and trolley buses reaching into almost every neighborhood and suburb. The region has a higher rate of transit use than Auckland, with over one-third of Wellingtonians opting to leave their cars at home or not own one at all. Transit is subsidized by the government but owned and operated by private companies on contract. The whole train and bus system is run under the name Metlink. All transit is run on a zone system; the farther you go, the more you pay. Adult bus and train fares start at $2 and go up to $18 for the longest trips. For both bus and train travel, prepaid cards and monthly passes are available for regular users and will cut costs a bit.

To combat drinking and driving, Wellington has introduced After Midnight bus routes to get people home after a night on the town. You may have to wait a while for the next bus and routes are very limited, but it will save you a bundle over taking a taxi home to the suburbs.

PRIME LIVING LOCATIONS

Finding the Perfect Balance

Syed Shamsuddoha

AN INTERVIEW WITH IT TEST MANAGER SYED SHAMSUDDOHA

Syed Shamsuddoha was born and raised in Bangladesh. He has also lived for several years each in Tashkent, Uzbekistan, New York City, and Toronto. He immigrated to New Zealand in 2006 with his wife and three children.

What were your main reasons for moving to New Zealand?
I was constantly stressed out at work while working for a US-based company in Canada. I was made redundant by my employer after our third child Joshua was born, and we were devastated with the ruthless behavior of the organization. I was looking for a place where I could find a balance between family, work, and personal growth. We were looking for a better place, and New Zealand came to mind. So I applied for residency, and we got it.

How did you get your first job in New Zealand?
I was hired by a communications software company before I came to New Zealand. I worked at my first job for 5.5 years. This time, my organization was taken over by another US-based company and my role was made redundant as part of their cost-cutting strategy. Now I am the IT test manager for a New Zealand crown entity [government-owned organization].

What were the biggest surprises about the New Zealand workplace when you started working here?
I was absolutely ecstatic to discover the flexibility and laid-back working style of New

Zealand. I found that most of the people are absolutely genuine in New Zealand. Their work ethic is superb, and they mean what they say.

At the beginning I could not understand their English fully because I felt that they spoke very fast, plus they used certain words I had never heard. But over time it became no issue at all.

I was also surprised to know that with PAYE (pay-as-you-earn) you never need to file a tax return, which took a lot of stress away.

You have worked in both the private sector and the public sector in New Zealand. What are the main differences?
In the private sector one might get a little bit better pay or more perks, but the pressure is also higher. Also, in private organizations you have the opportunity for a lot more innovation than in public organizations. Because of the bureaucracy in the public sector, it can be a challenge to make any changes unless you are part of the senior management team.

I found, regardless of the organization, both private and public organizations are pretty much fair in their hiring process.

Outside of work, what have been the biggest changes to your lifestyle since moving to New Zealand?
I usually either ride my bicycle to work or take a train or bus or even walk/run when possible. I can freely go out during lunch and jog to keep myself fit. I have run 22 full marathons within the past three years, many as fundraisers for charity, and also done half marathons, long walks, swimming, tramping, trekking, and long-distance bicycling. I also learned to play violin, which I started in New Zealand about four years ago.

I take my family often to visit new places and enjoy the magnificent beauty New Zealand has to offer all year round. I also love the mountains and treks that are well maintained by the Department of Conservation.

What do you love the most about living in New Zealand?
It's a friendly environment, and I love it here. It's relatively a very safe place to live, work, and raise a family. It's one of the most beautiful countries I have ever visited/lived in. It does not have any ferocious animals to bite or eat me. There is no rabies in New Zealand. Gun violence is one of the lowest among the OECD countries, and most importantly it's a beautiful country all year round.

What advice would you give to potential immigrants to New Zealand?
New Zealand is a perfect place for those who want to live within their economic means. This is a country where either one can make oneself happy or sad. It's not a country to make a lot of money in, but it's a beautiful country where one can live and enjoy life. If one wants to become rich in New Zealand, it'll be a tough call, but having a reasonable and healthy lifestyle is the best reason to live in New Zealand.

PRIME LIVING LOCATIONS

Porirua and Kapiti Coast

Long before Europeans showed up, the Kapiti (CAP-uh-tee) Coast was already a popular place to live. The local Maori knew a good thing when they saw it, including accessible coastline, a river for easy transportation and freshwater, and lots of natural resources. In fact, one of the biggest challenges you might find if you live in Kapiti is pronouncing the tongue-twisting Maori town names like Paraparaumu and Paekakariki.

Early European settlers actually used the coastal beach as a road until the railway was built. Eventually the area developed into a holiday destination, with a farming community stretching farther inland. Now it is the fastest-growing area in the Wellington region, with retiring baby boomers moving away from the city to enjoy a more relaxed lifestyle. It's also attracting commuters who don't mind the longer drive into the city in exchange for living in this idyllic setting.

Local industry is growing, but the area still has a relatively small population and few large employers. It is perhaps best known as the home of Kapiti Fine Foods, a leading gourmet cheese and ice cream producer. There are some opportunities in the service sector along the coast and in tourism. You can also find your niche in the retail sector, and with the number of people looking to move to the area, it's a good spot to get into real estate.

THE LAY OF THE LAND

As you head north out of Wellington on State Highway 1, Porirua is the first city you'll reach. While not quite on the coast, Porirua is on a coastal inlet, which gives

low tide on the Kapiti Coast

© MICHELLE WAITZMAN

it a harbor feel. The city has grown significantly in recent years and is full of big-box stores and other suburban conveniences. You'll even find a Denny's restaurant there, serving real American ketchup.

As you continue north, the highway moves toward the west coast and you'll begin to pass Kapiti's resort towns, beginning with Pukerua Bay (birthplace of Peter Jackson) and continuing to Paekakariki, Paraparaumu, and Waikanae. Along this stretch, the largest of the towns is Paraparaumu, with a shopping center and other services. The land between the towns is quite rural, filled with a combination of tourist accommodations and small farms.

DAILY LIVING

The quality of life in this area is quite high. Not only is Wellington a reasonably short drive away, but most Porirua and Kapiti residents live very close to either the coast or the inlet. This gives them lots of opportunities for sailing, windsurfing, or just long walks along the beach. There are four golf courses just around Kapiti and three more near Porirua, affording a wide variety to both residents and vacationers.

Some services will be harder to come by as you head north, but the basics are all available. Kenepuru Community Hospital in Porirua has a range of services but no emergency department. Up in Paraparaumu, there is a health clinic run by the District Health Board, but not a full hospital. For serious medical emergencies, a trip to Wellington will be necessary.

WHERE TO LIVE
Porirua

The major center in the Kapiti area is **Porirua,** a city of about 54,000 people. Porirua has its own local council and is not part of Kapiti, but it is along the same highway heading north out of Wellington and resides along the same coast, so for your purposes it is part of the Kapiti Coast. It is only 20 minutes north of Wellington, which makes it a more reasonable commute. You can also take a commuter train into the city from Porirua.

Porirua is becoming a popular place to raise a family, and it has the big shopping centers to prove it. The city has a large population of Maori and Pacific Islanders. Renting a house in Porirua costs around $400 per week. To buy a three-bedroom house, the lower end of the market (older houses or less-desirable areas) starts at less than $300,000. More luxurious houses can top $600,000, but this is a comparatively affordable city.

Paraparaumu

The biggest of the towns along the Kapiti Coast, **Paraparaumu** has the bulk of the services for residents of the area. This makes it a more convenient place to live than the smaller communities. A shopping center, medical center, and other necessities are located in town.

It is possible to commute to a job in Wellington from Paraparaumu—I know several people who have done it—but it is a long drive or train ride. On a good day it takes around 45 minutes to get downtown, but it doesn't take much to slow things down.

Paraparaumu is the end of the train line, so living any farther up the coast will make you entirely dependent on your car for transportation. Housing in Paraparaumu is still reasonable compared to the suburbs south of Porirua, but as more people head out of the city, the costs are climbing. It's now rare to find a decent house for under $350,000. Rent for a three-bedroom house is around $370 per week.

GETTING AROUND
Driving
Anyone who still needs to work for a living may find most of the Kapiti Coast a bit inconvenient as a place to live. The drive into Wellington City takes about 45 minutes from Paraparaumu, assuming you don't get held up in heavy traffic; from Waikanae it's about 55 minutes, and from Paekakariki about 35 minutes.

One of the main difficulties with the roads along this area is that you are at the mercy of State Highway 1. There are only two places to get away from that road and cross over to State Highway 2 in the Hutt Valley. One is at Waikanae, and the other is just north of Porirua. An expansion to State Highway 1 is planned. This is scheduled for completion in 2020. In the meantime, every accident, flood, or rockfall has a devastating effect on traffic flow.

Public Transit
A train line stretches from Wellington to Paraparaumu, stopping at 14 stations along the way. This is a good option for commuters who don't want to risk getting caught up in traffic jams at rush hour or who just don't like the stress of a long commute in the car. The train ride from Paraparaumu takes almost one hour to the city. From Porirua, the ride is about 25 minutes.

Bus services mostly cover routes within Kapiti, between the town centers and the beach areas.

Hutt Valley

The Hutt River has attracted settlers since New Zealand's earliest days. This historically important community is still a popular place to settle down. It has become a significant urban area of its own—not just a bedroom community for people working in Wellington—boasting its own colleges, shopping districts, and entertainment. Stretching along the Hutt River, the valley is well serviced by State Highway 2 and two commuter train lines.

Today the Hutt Valley is home to the cities of Petone, Lower Hutt, Eastbourne, and Upper Hutt. Technically all of them, aside from Upper Hutt, amalgamated in the late 1980s to form one city called Hutt City, more commonly called The Hutt, but each is still worth considering separately as a possible home, as they have slightly different characters.

THE LAY OF THE LAND
The lower end of the valley is where the Hutt River empties into Wellington Harbour. This is where Petone is situated, and it was the first area in all of Wellington region to

A recreation trail runs alongside the Hutt River.

be settled by Europeans. The river comes down from the northwest, with the Rimutaka Mountains rising to the east and rolling hills to the west.

While the atmosphere is suburban in the lower valley, it becomes more rural in character as you head upstream. By the time you pass Upper Hutt, you'll be driving by farms as often as suburbs. There is a lot of parkland in this area, including a strip along most of the length of the river that features recreational paths for cyclists, walkers, and even horses.

The Hutt River

The river has its source in the Tararua Mountains. It gathers steam through the valley, fed by several tributaries, but remains a relatively small river. The Hutt River is shallow and gravelly, but parts of it are deep enough for recreational kayaking. Flooding has always been a problem for residents of the Hutt Valley, so from the early days of European settlement flood barriers have been in place to reduce the chances of damage to surrounding properties.

DAILY LIVING

With shopping, restaurants, and cinemas on your doorstep, living in the Hutt Valley is quite convenient. There are also schools at all levels for the kids to attend and a full-service hospital with a 24-hour emergency department. In fact, you could quite happily live in the Hutt Valley without ever having to make the short drive to central Wellington. Most residents, however, take advantage of their proximity to the city and go into town for a wider variety of employment opportunities and leisure activities.

The lower housing prices in this area do attract a slightly less prosperous group of residents. The area between Lower and Upper Hutt has a more working-class feel to it than the more affluent suburbs near the city. But this is by no means a dangerous place to live, and violent crime is very rare.

WHERE TO LIVE

Most people are drawn to the Hutt Valley because house prices are more reasonable there than in many other areas. The farther you are willing to live up the valley, the cheaper housing will be. But the trade-off is commuting distance to Wellington. If you don't mind a long commute, you can take advantage of the bargains to be had near Upper Hutt. If convenience is more important to you, try to find a place closer to the Hutt City/Petone end.

Petone

Petone (p'-TOE-nee) is on Wellington Harbour and the closest of the Hutt Valley locations to downtown Wellington. Just 15 minutes on the train or the motorway will get you into the heart of the city. Petone has a mix of architecture, from turn-of-the-20th-century buildings right up to boxy outlet stores, and a slightly artsy feel. Historical Jackson Street has turned itself into a bit of a tourist attraction, with cafés and restaurants scattered between quaint shops. There is a long stretch of beach along the harbor, which is a popular place for both locals and Wellingtonians to stroll on a summer's day. There is limited ferry service between Petone and Wellington, which can make for a more pleasant trip into town. But most commuters rely on cars, buses, or the train. Renting a house in Petone is not particularly cheap, around $420 per week. To buy a three-bedroom house, you'll be looking at over $450,000 for charming "character" bungalows.

Hutt City

Hutt City, sometimes called Lower Hutt or The Hutt, is more of a business center. You'll be able to do all of your shopping there and perhaps even work in Hutt City, avoiding downtown Wellington altogether. The city has a large mall for those who love to browse. Several bus routes serve the area, and two commuter train lines also head into Wellington from various stops in Hutt City. Housing in Hutt City is not a bargain, though, with a three-bedroom rental costing close to $400 per week; to buy a house you'll spend $300,000-450,000, depending on the neighborhood and how much work the house needs.

Upper Hutt

Upper Hutt is a great location for access to outdoor activities like hiking, fishing, and mountain biking. It's an affordable area for those who prefer to have a bit of property and not be able to see directly into their neighbor's windows. If you are retired or able to work or study somewhere nearby, then it does offer a quiet, small-town lifestyle while remaining within an hour's drive of a major city. It is a bit of a drag, however, if you need to commute to Wellington daily for work. Renting a house in Upper Hutt costs a bit less than in Lower Hutt, at around $350 per week. Buying a three-bedroom house can start with prices as low as $300,000, but as more old homes are replaced with newer, larger residences, the average price is climbing quickly. Most houses are now in the $350,000-500,000 range, but you'll get more for your money than you would in a closer suburb like Petone.

GETTING AROUND
Driving
The main route through the Hutt Valley is State Highway 2, which runs all the way through to Wellington. During morning and evening rush hours, it does get pretty busy. Most days it isn't a major problem, but if the weather is particularly bad or there has been an accident on the highway, you quickly see the downside of not having an alternative route into the city.

Public Transit
There are two commuter train lines that service the Hutt Valley. One stops at Hutt City, and the other continues to Upper Hutt, connecting with the Wairarapa line. There are improvements planned for the train lines over the next 10 years or so, as the current trains are quite old and the infrastructure could use some upgrading. Still, it beats sitting in traffic. There are also a few bus routes within the region and some connecting the valley to Wellington.

Ferry
For residents of Eastbourne, the Dominion Post ferry is also a transit option. With a one-way fare of $11, it may not be the most cost-effective commute, but it is a lovely and scenic one. It also saves time, taking just 20 minutes from dock to dock. For those who would rather not cross the water twice a day, there is a bus route that takes commuters around the harbor to and from Eastbourne.

Wairarapa

The Wairarapa is a fairly large rural region to the east of the Rimutaka and Tararua Mountains with a population of around 40,000. The area has become notable in recent years for producing some popular wines, particularly near the small town of Martinborough. Agriculture is the main industry here, and anyone who isn't a farmer has a business that supports farmers. This is country living, with convenient access to the Tararua mountain range for those who like a bit of adventure. There is not a single traffic light in the entire region.

Thanks to the mountains, it takes well over an hour to make it into Wellington from anywhere in the Wairarapa, and from Masterton it's closer to two hours. This is an option for those who don't feel the need to visit a big city as often and aren't too fussy about restaurants, shopping, or other urban luxuries. What you'll get in return is lots of space, peace, and quiet, and much more affordable property. Some areas now have lifestyle blocks on offer for those who like to enjoy the land without getting into farming as a business. In fact, the peaceful surroundings and affordable housing have become such a draw that some residents are actually living in the Wairarapa and commuting to work in Wellington.

Olives and Moonlight

A PROFILE OF JARED GULIAN

Jared Gulian is a self-described "expat American city boy" who now grows olives in rural New Zealand. He blogs about olives, chickens, and the expat life on his blog, "Moon over Martinborough" at moonovermartinborough.com, some of which was published in a book of the same name.

What brought you to New Zealand?

We were living in Japan, and we met a lot of really nice New Zealanders there. We also knew a handful of Americans who had traveled to New Zealand and loved it. So we decided to check it out. When we visited New Zealand, we thought, "We could live here."

Why did you decide to settle in a rural area?

We never planned to live in a rural area. It just sort of happened. We'd been living in Wellington for a couple of years when my partner, Rick, stumbled across an amazing rural property. He came home and said, "Let's move to the country!" I thought he'd lost his mind.

I agreed to visit the property, however, and I immediately fell in love with the place. Now I don't know if I could ever leave. I love the vineyards nearby, the light and snow on the mountain ranges in the morning, and the fact that we've got an olive grove with nearly 500 trees just out our front door. We sell our olive oil commercially under our own "Moon over Martinborough" label.

What do you like about the rural lifestyle?

One of the things I love most about our rural lifestyle is our neighbors. They're pure gold to us. Living in the country, everyone relies on each other in a way that I had never experienced in the city, anywhere.

Do you commute into the city for work? What is the commute like?

We both commute into Wellington for our "day jobs." It's a 10-minute drive to the bus, then a 20-minute bus ride to the town of Featherston, and then a 55-minute train ride into the city.

We used to live in Chicago. People there commute for an hour and a half and still find themselves in the middle of urban sprawl. Here the same time commute lands you in the middle of paradise. It's fantastic, and entirely worth the trip.

Do you miss anything about city life?

I miss museums, live theater, dance performances, and good, cheap Mexican food. But every once in a while we stay with friends in Wellington and see a play, or we or go on a

THE LAY OF THE LAND

The Wairarapa is bordered on the west by the Rimutaka Mountains and the Tararua Mountains. It stretches across to the east side of the island, ending along a rugged and mostly unoccupied part of the coastline. The main route through the region is State Highway 2, which emerges from the mountain pass at the top of the Hutt Valley to continue northeast toward Napier.

Once you leave the main highway, most of what you'll see is farmland stretching on for miles. There are a number of crops grown here, including vineyards and olive groves, plus some livestock farming.

small holiday "across the ditch" to Australia and visit Sydney for a big-city fix.

Can you find everything you need in your local area?

There's a small grocery store in our village. For weekly groceries we drive a half an hour to a nearby town just up the valley a bit. Pretty much everything we need isn't too far. Besides, with the Internet, nothing is ever too far away. I order gluten-free beer online, and it shows up on our front deck.

How much extra work goes into owning a large, rural property rather than an urban or suburban home?

Way more than we ever expected! We were pretty clueless about how much work would be involved. There's always something that needs to be done, whether it's fixing fences, cleaning up downed trees, tending to the garden, or looking after the olive grove and other fruit trees around the property.

© RICK

Jared Gulian

Do you have any advice for other Americans looking into buying a farm or rural property in New Zealand?

Don't be rash. Look around. Do your homework. Get a strong sense of the place before you buy. We actually stayed in accommodations nearby for a couple nights midweek and did the commute into Wellington, just to experience it before we committed to buying.

Anything else you'd like to share with those considering a move to New Zealand?

Don't expect it to be just like home. It's not. That's the point. One of the great things about living overseas is that there are always things that surprise you and remind you that the culture you're in is not your own. The food is different, the accents are different, the attitudes are different. That constant sense of the unfamiliar is what makes an overseas experience so rich and rewarding.

Always stay open to opportunity. There are open doors popping up left and right, all the time. It's up to us to have the courage to walk through them.

The Rimutaka Hill Pass

To travel between the Wellington region and the Wairarapa, you have to get through the mountains. As the Rimutaka Mountains peter out, the Tararua Mountains take over and continue northward. The Rimutaka Hill Pass is a winding, climbing road between the two sides as one range merges into the other.

The pass is well paved and includes periodic passing lanes, but there are still occasional accidents due to carelessness or poor conditions. If the conditions are particularly treacherous, the pass will be closed. The top of the pass is high enough to get the odd snowfall in winter, which is usually when closures happen. It may also be closed

PRIME LIVING LOCATIONS

if there is a landslide or rockfall blocking the road. In the case of a closure, the nearest alternate route through the mountains is at Palmerston North, almost two hours north.

DAILY LIVING

Living in the Wairarapa is not for everyone. Unless you're a farmer, employment opportunities are pretty limited. There are jobs around for retailers, schoolteachers, and other service professions, but this is definitely the rural lifestyle. But what is on offer here is that relaxed lifestyle without ever being too far away from a city. It also allows easy access to the wilderness playground of some of New Zealand's famous forest parks.

Many of the people who choose to settle in this region are past working age and buying a nice plot of land to retire on. The population of this region is aging anyway, so you'll have lots of retired Kiwi neighbors to pass the time with.

There are several primary schools available in the main towns, but secondary schools are a bit sparse, so your teenagers could have a long ride to classes each day. Correspondence school may be an option if you need your kids at home to help with farm chores.

Health care is available from local doctors, including medical clinics in Masterton, Carterton, Featherston, Martinborough, and Greytown. The region's hospital is located in a recently built facility in Masterton. The hospital includes a 24-hour emergency department with a helipad, and there is a local ambulance service.

Aside from tramping around the mountains and wine-tasting, there is not much to keep you busy in the Wairarapa. Local pubs and cafés are the best places to mingle with the locals. Some upscale dining opportunities have cropped up in Greytown and Martinborough, thanks to the tourist trade.

WHERE TO LIVE

If you're looking for a piece of farmland, you can pick just about any spot in the Wairarapa. The southern end of the region keeps you the closest to Wellington, if that's important to you. Martinborough is just over 1.5 hours from the city, and Featherston is just over an hour if the pass isn't too busy.

Toward the northern end of the Wairarapa you'll be closer to Palmerston North, a city dominated by its student population, and Hawke's Bay.

Renting a house is not common in this region, so if you're looking to try it on for size before you buy, your choices will be limited. You should be able to find a rental for $250-300 per week in the main towns.

Masterton

Masterton is the largest town in the region and the commercial center for all of the Wairarapa. Even this center has a distinctly agricultural overtone, with many of the local businesses selling farm equipment and supplies, but you'll also find the basic household necessities. On the bright side, you can at least catch a movie in town and eat at a restaurant. Masterton is about halfway up the Wairarapa, making it an almost equal distance from Wellington and Palmerston North.

A modest home in Masterton can be purchased for $250,000-350,000. If you're looking for a new home or a large property, prices will go up into the $500,000 range.

Martinborough

Martinborough has become a trendy day-trip destination for Wellingtonians, thanks to the success of its winemakers. In fact, there is a yearly wine festival called Toast Martinborough that regularly sells out within days. The town itself is very small, but if you are looking to start up a boutique winery of your own, this is a great place with which to be associated. Tourism in the area is also a growing business.

Older homes around here can still be found in the $300,000 range, but more and more people are buying property here to build their dream homes, so it's not unusual to see a larger home near the coast sell for over $500,000. Rental properties are very hard to find since most landlords can make more money renting their houses as vacation homes on a daily or weekly basis.

GETTING AROUND

Being in a rural area, residents of the Wairarapa depend on their cars to get them around. The only exception is the one train line from Wellington that makes its way through Featherston and Carterton to Masterton. The train makes it possible to commute to the city by public transport, but it only runs a few times per day. The full trip from Masterton to Wellington by rail takes 90 minutes. Service is even sparser on the weekends.

The main driving route through the region is State Highway 2, which passes directly through the middle of Featherston, Greytown, Carterton, and Masterton. There's no way to get through quickly, as the speed limit drops to 50 km/h in the towns. Side roads take you out to the more isolated farming communities. There are only a few routes out to the coast.

PRIME LIVING LOCATIONS

CHRISTCHURCH AND MARLBOROUGH

This chapter covers a large area from the northern coast of the South Island, down to Christchurch in the Canterbury Plains. Although this may seem like a lot to fit in, there are actually few cities and towns large enough to merit discussion as a place to settle. The west coast is very sparsely populated, and with few jobs outside of forestry and mining, it seems unlikely that many newcomers would choose to live there unless they were opening up tourist accommodations. So I will focus on the Marlborough region and Nelson, at the top of the island, and the city of Christchurch, the largest on the South Island.

New Zealanders call the South Island "The Mainland," which may seem strange since most people live on the North Island. But living on the South Island has its advantages, including the best skiing in the Southern Hemisphere! It's a wilderness-lover's dream come true, as long as you can find work to help support those dreams. Every lifestyle, from urban living to sheep farming to being a kayaking guide, is possible in the northern half of the South Island. It's just a matter of choosing the right spot for you.

© MICHELLE WAITZMAN

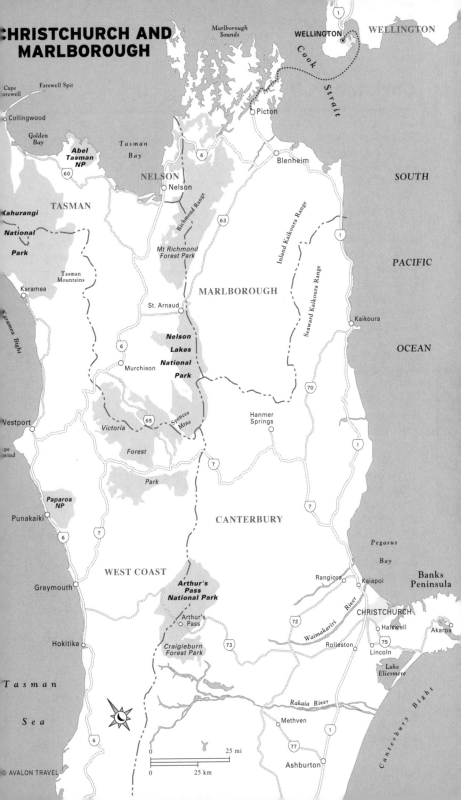

Christchurch

With around 340,000 residents, Christchurch is similar in size to Greater Wellington, but the two cities feel completely different. The largest city on the South Island has managed to retain a lot of the charm of an old English town, and not without reason is it called "The Garden City." The early settlers in the 1850s planned the city as a kind of English utopia in the South Pacific before they even arrived. They were not entirely successful, but you can see, from the planting of oaks and weeping willows, the gardens and public squares, and the now toppled cathedral in the center of the city, that they got off to a good start. The city center is undergoing a major transformation following the large earthquakes in 2010 and 2011 that damaged hundreds of downtown buildings and claimed 180 lives. Due to structural damage, more than 1,000 buildings in the city had to be pulled down, and the rebuild will undoubtedly take years to complete.

The earthquakes have made construction and infrastructure the new dominant industry around Christchurch. There is a small manufacturing sector, along with electronics and IT businesses. Retail and tourism were hit hard by the 2011 earthquake, but the construction industry is certainly benefiting from the required rebuilding. Education, health care, and service industries are also good areas for finding employment. The surrounding countryside is used extensively for farming and forestry.

THE LAY OF THE LAND

The most notable thing about Christchurch, when you compare it with other New Zealand cities, is how very flat it is. The Canterbury Plains are the largest flat area in the country, and Christchurch is the main center for the region. The flatness made it easy to lay out the city in a grid, with only the winding Avon River to break things up. Perhaps because of this flatness, the city has no strong focal point. Everything has a bit of a spread-out feeling to it.

Cathedral Square has always defined the city center, with the downtown area surrounding it for a few blocks in every direction. Emerging plans for the rebuilding of the downtown area are likely to respect this tradition, although the remains of the toppled cathedral may eventually be removed. The inner suburbs take over from there, and as you get farther from the center, you reach the outer suburbs, which were considered separate towns not that long ago.

On the western side of the city center is Hagley Park, a large green space set aside for the city's botanic gardens, a golf course, tennis courts, and other recreational uses. It also hosts outdoor concerts and other events.

Christchurch is unusual in that it lies near the shoreline, but its founders did not build the city to sit on the coast. From downtown, it's hard to imagine that you are so close to the ocean.

Despite being in the flattest part of the country, residents of Christchurch can reach eight different ski fields within a 90-minute drive of the city. And during the summer, hiking, fishing, and mountain biking opportunities are even closer.

South of the city, the Banks Peninsula pokes out into the Pacific Ocean. It is egg-shaped overall, but has bays and harbors all of the way around its circumference. This is the one place near Christchurch where you'll find big hills, so it's a popular escape from the city. In fact, many Christchurch residents have a "bach" (holiday home) on the peninsula, usually along the coast.

The Southern Alps

The landscape of the South Island plays a large role in determining the weather. The Southern Alps run most of the way down the center of the island, dividing the east and west. The western side of the Alps sees a lot of rainfall, as incoming systems from the west hit the large mountains and are forced to dump their moisture in order to rise over the tops.

The eastern side of the mountains is much drier, seeing the systems after they have dumped their rain to the west. Living in Christchurch, or anywhere on the Canterbury Plains, means that you'll get much less rain than other New Zealanders.

DAILY LIVING

Christchurch, despite its very English appearance, resembles North American cities more than you might expect. People tend to live out in the suburbs and spend their time at big, suburban shopping malls. With several years of construction planned for the city center, this decentralization is actually quite fortunate. In another city, the virtual destruction of the city center would have shut the city down completely. For Christchurch, although it was heartbreaking to lose much of the city's original character, life has gone on almost normally for most people.

Shops and restaurants are plentiful in the suburbs, and they are gradually returning to the city center. After all, this is the major city for the South Island, so whatever you're after, you should be able to find it here.

© MICHELLE WAITZMAN

The Re:START mall made from shipping containers is a popular downtown destination.

Despite being a large city, Christchurch is quite safe. There is little violent crime, aside from isolated incidents. Common sense should still prevail when it comes to wandering around alone at night, but as long as you stick to well-lit and populated areas, there is little need to worry.

Christchurch has a reputation for being a bit conservative and perhaps even snobbish. People are very particular about which school their children attend, where they live, and how their roses are doing this year. This is unusual for New Zealand, which does its best to be a classless society. It seems like that part of the old British mentality has managed to survive down here.

This is part of what makes Christchurch feel so different from cities like Wellington and Dunedin. But with more immigrants settling there, the old rules are breaking down a little. With more ethnic diversity, the city cannot hang on to old traditions and presumptions. There is now a large Asian population in Christchurch (mainly in the northwest part of the city), along with other minority groups from Southeast Asia, the Middle East, and other parts of the world. Compared with the larger North Island cities, the Maori and Pacific Islander population in Christchurch is pretty small.

WHERE TO LIVE
Downtown and Inner Suburbs

Inner-city living in Christchurch will probably have a bit of a renaissance once the rebuild is further along. In the meantime downtown apartments are few and far between. Keep an eye on emerging plans for the **city center,** which are certain to include housing within walking or cycling distance to central workplaces. Even in the closer suburbs there is currently a shortage of good housing. A large number of houses, especially on the eastern side of the city, were damaged in the earthquakes. People scrambled to find new accommodations if their homes were not fixable. New construction will take several years to catch up.

Strangely, one of the most desirable neighborhoods in Christchurch is one of the closest to the airport. **Fendalton** is an old neighborhood with large houses and tidy gardens. It's in the district for the "right" schools, and people are happy to pay a premium to live there. Although there are some lovely old homes between the airport and the western border of Hagley Park, many are now being torn down and replaced with new houses. **Cashmere,** on the southern side of the city, is also a very desirable neighborhood.

For those who like a short commute, the areas of **Merivale** and **St. Albans** on the northern side of the city are just outside the city center and feature some fun, trendy shops.

Because of the tight supply, prices for a three-bedroom house in the inner suburbs start around $500,000 but can get much higher for newer homes in the best areas. Inner-city apartments are not much cheaper, easily costing $400,000 for something family-sized. Renting in the city ranges from $400-750 per week in the city and inner suburbs.

Rangiora

If you find the homes in the inner suburbs are packed a little too tightly for you, try heading north of Christchurch to satellite communities like **Rangiora.** The sections are a bit roomier out here, and the drive into the city is still quite reasonable, about 20-30 minutes on most days.

These suburban areas are growing all around Christchurch because the land is

Temporary but Terrific

© BOB MORRIS

The temporary Christchurch Cathedral was buillt using cardboard cylinders.

The extensive earthquake damage to the center of Christchurch stole the heart of the city, but it also made its people and leaders come together to make things feel more "normal" as quickly as possible.

One of the most noticeable losses was the iconic Christchurch Cathedral. The cathedral's tower and much of its structure crumbled. While the decision to rebuild or demolish what remains is still in limbo, there is a temporary replacement that is both visually striking and innovative.

Dubbed the "Cardboard Cathedral," the building's main support structure is made from heavy-duty cardboard rolls, but also incorporates wood and steel beams. It seats up to 700 people and cost just $5.3 million to build. While a permanent building would have taken many years to fund and build, the Cardboard Cathedral opened two years after the 2011 earthquake and is already a tourist attraction in its own right.

Downtown shopping also took a hit from the earthquakes, with many shops too damaged to remain standing. To draw people back downtown the city organized the Re:START shopping district. It's a street full of shops and cafés all made from shipping containers. The project came together in a matter of months, and rather than being ugly and depressing, it's actually colorful, funky, and urban.

It remains to be seen how long these temporary attractions will be part of Christchurch. After all, there is still a fountain in central Wellington that was built as a "temporary" display in 1969! If the public becomes attached to these temporary structures, they may become a permanent sight in the new Christchurch city center.

plentiful and flat, allowing lots of expansion. Also, some of the inner suburbs east of the city center were too earthquake-damaged to rebuild, sending residents farther afield in search of new homes. As the Maori name suggests, Rangiora has a long history. But these days it's a popular place to bring up a family, as long as you're not one of those people who care an awful lot about school districts. The district where Rangiora is located has grown to around 50,000 people. The area has its own shops and services, so most day-to-day needs can be met without driving into the city.

Housing prices in this area have gone up considerably since 2011 with the increase in demand. Three-bedroom homes average around $450,000-500,000, with higher prices for larger properties. Renting is likely to cost around $300 per week.

Rolleston, Halswell, and Lincoln

West and south of the city are more satellite communities that are growing into suburbs of Christchurch. **Rolleston** is about half an hour from the city along State Highway 1 and has become something of a planned community. Developers are putting up entire subdivisions in the style of U.S. suburban development, with planned shops and parks to serve the local communities.

Halswell is closer to the city, perhaps 15 minutes away, but is being developed similarly, with lots of new housing construction. Considering the cold, drafty reputation of New Zealand homes, buying a brand-new house is very tempting, even if it means living outside of the city.

In a rural area to the southwest of Christchurch lies **Lincoln,** home of Lincoln University. Studying or working at the university is the only real reason to base yourself there. There is campus housing available for students, as well as rental flats and homestays. Lincoln Township has the basic shops and services you'll need to get by, but you may find yourself heading into the city for most of your entertainment and major shopping. If you are looking into studying in Christchurch, remember that there are two universities located here. Lincoln is outside of the city, while the University of Canterbury is on the western side of the city in **Ilam,** near the suburb of Avonhead.

Houses in Rolleston sell for around $500,000, and older houses in Halswell cost around $400,000. For a brand-new home, add another $100,000 or so, depending on the size of the home and property. In Lincoln, the homes tend to be large and built on expansive properties—after all, there's a lot of space out there. But they are no bargain, mostly starting in the $500,000 range. Renting in Rolleston and Halswell is not very common, but you may be able to find a house for rent around $400-500 per week. In Lincoln, students do most of the renting. Flatting in a shared house will cost around $130 per week.

GETTING AROUND

Because central Christchurch is accessible from every side, unlike Auckland and Wellington, there is nowhere you can live around Christchurch where there is only one route into the city. This layout helps to prevent traffic nightmares due to an accident or closure. However, for as long as the city center remains a major construction zone, temporary road closures and detours are bound to make things difficult on and off.

The flat layout makes Christchurch a great city for cycling, and the city has put in a number of bicycle lanes and paths to keep the cyclists safe. If you live near the city, cycling to work or to school is quite easy.

Driving

Christchurch is reached from the north and south via State Highway 1. The highway skirts the western edge of the city, near the airport. From the west, you can take State Highway 73, which goes through Arthur's Pass in the Southern Alps from the west coast.

The city center uses one-way roads to keep traffic moving. This system takes some getting used to, but it does seem to do the trick when there aren't too many road works going on. A series of avenues frame the city center, including Bealey Avenue to the north, Fitzgerald Avenue to the east, Moorhouse Avenue to the south, and Deans Avenue to the west. Outside of this box is basically where the residential neighborhoods begin.

Christchurch does see quite a lot of "boy racers." These are mostly young men with souped-up cars who race around the streets late at night. Mostly they are just a noisy nuisance, but occasionally they do cause accidents.

Public Transit

The original public transit in Christchurch was provided by trams, but those have now been retired except as a tourist attraction. Instead, Christchurch is served by a system of buses, which connect the city center with the surrounding suburbs.

The bus service is operated by Metro; it serves not only Christchurch but also Lyttelton, Lincoln, and Rangiora. Fares start at $3.50, or $2.50 if you use a reloadable Metrocard instead of cash. For additional fare zones you'll pay up to $6.20. Services operate seven days a week.

Marlborough

Before you thought about moving to New Zealand, the place you would most likely have seen the name Marlborough was on a bottle of sauvignon blanc wine from this renowned region. The worldwide success of the region's wineries and its popularity with tourists have put Marlborough on the map. But tourism is not the only game in town, so the possibility of settling in this wonderfully scenic region is very real for people in the right industries.

Marlborough offers a pretty nice lifestyle for those who manage to settle in. The weather is sunny and mild, the local economy is in good shape, and the coastline is spectacular, with rolling hills and golden sand beaches.

THE LAY OF THE LAND

The northern coast of the South Island features the islands and inlets of the Marlborough Sounds on its eastern side. Then Tasman Bay dips down through the center of the coast, sheltering the city of Nelson. Abel Tasman National Park juts out between Tasman Bay and Golden Bay, whose sandy beaches make a popular vacation area for Kiwis. Then at the northwestern edge of the coast, Farewell Spit is thrust out like a long, slender beak to shelter the bay.

Most of the population in this area lives near the coast. Even the inland settlement of Blenheim is only a short drive from the eastern coast and Cloudy Bay. Once you get farther inland, most of the region is taken up by protected forest and mountain parkland. Inland towns do pop up between the mountain ranges, but most are service towns for the local forestry industry.

I'm including Nelson in this section on Marlborough, although officially it is connected with Tasman region to the west. That region includes Golden Bay and Farewell Spit, and a large, forested area to the south. Marlborough includes Picton, the Marlborough Sounds, and Blenheim, and also goes down the east coast to Kaikoura.

The upper South Island is one of New Zealand's main aquaculture (seafood farming) centers.

DAILY LIVING

With the beaches, mountains, and vineyards at your doorstep, lifestyle is the best attraction when it comes to living around Marlborough. People here take their leisure time seriously, and although their work ethic is good, they emphasize a balanced life more than you might find in the more urban regions.

The biggest (and only) urban area nearby is Nelson, in the Tasman region. Blenheim acts as the main center for the eastern part of Marlborough, but with just 27,000 people it's really more of a town than a city. So if you like the trappings of city life, such as cafés, restaurants, and live music, you may find yourself drawn toward Nelson.

Marlborough has a rural sensibility to it. Small towns, farmland, and forests make it feel miles away from the traffic jams of Auckland or the government bureaucracy of Wellington. But if you do need to get to those major centers, it's not too much of a burden. The port town of Picton is where the various Cook Strait ferries depart from for the three-hour journey to Wellington. Christchurch is about a six-hour drive from Nelson or 4.5 hours from Blenheim. But if you're in a hurry, there are airports in Nelson, Picton, and Blenheim that connect you to domestic destinations.

There's no doubt this is a nice place to live, but you'll need to find out if your skills can be put to use in this region before you settle in. The main industries in the area are primary industries like forestry (there are large pine plantations), seafood and aquaculture, and horticulture in the areas of soft fruits and hops (for brewing beer). Viticulture and winemaking are also skills in demand here.

To back this up, there are secondary jobs in timber processing, food packing and processing, and so on. But many of those kinds of work are seasonal, and unskilled or semiskilled workers may find themselves switching jobs every few months to keep the money flowing.

If you're interested in taking advantage of the huge tourist market at Golden Bay and Abel Tasman National Park, you'll find work in areas like hotel and restaurant management; chefs are generally in short supply as well. More entrepreneurial types may want to set up their own tourism ventures, but do some research first as there is already a lot of competition in this field.

The region's population is growing, and this is expected to continue. There is an increasing need for professionals and service industry workers in the main centers like Nelson and Blenheim, including lawyers, accountants, architects, and health care professionals. People love to retire in this region, so any business that caters to the older population will have a good chance of growing. Construction is also booming these days, which keeps skilled tradespeople busy.

WHERE TO LIVE
Nelson
Nelson is the main city at the top of the South Island, with a population of around 46,000. The city sits at the mouth of the Maitai River, where it empties into Tasman Bay. The city trails off to the southwest toward the outer suburb of **Stoke** and the town of **Richmond.** The cathedral is the focal point of the city, with Trafalgar Street keeping the shoppers happy. Nelson has the region's main hospital, all the schools your children will need, and a polytechnic.

Nelson has a reputation as an artsy city, with lots of artisans creating and selling their wares in the area. This gives Nelson a lot of style, with more than its share of galleries, live music, and other artistic endeavors. But with the population on the rise, more traditional lines of work are crying out for skilled practitioners. The infrastructure of the city needs to keep up with its expanding numbers.

People who live in Nelson love to take advantage of their surroundings. Once you've settled in, you may find yourself tempted to take up kayaking, mountain biking, or kitesurfing, even if you were never interested in those things before. Most people live quite close to the water, and because Nelson gets more sunshine than any other city in the country, there are more opportunities to get out there and enjoy the scenery. The most popular beach in the area is called Tahunanui, with wide shores and lots of room for adventure.

With a large number of tourists passing through, the restaurants in Nelson have had to raise their standards to meet international expectations. If you live in the city, that's a bonus for you. Excellent food and wine are widely available.

Nelson's weekend market is one of the oldest in the country. A lot of the vendors are tourist-oriented now, but there are still opportunities to buy local produce and treat yourself to an authentic German bratwurst.

If you are lucky enough to live close to work, you can take advantage of the sunshine by walking or cycling to the office. The city has several cycle ways (bike paths) and is hoping to get more people to commute this way. The local bus service, called NBus, runs on six routes. Most routes operate Monday through Saturday. It connects Nelson's city center with the surrounding suburbs; adult fares are $2.50-4. There's also a Late, Late Bus operating on Friday and Saturday nights between Nelson and Richmond for $4.

The only thing lacking in Nelson is large-scale events. It was the original home of the World of Wearable Arts competition (often called WoW), but it grew so popular that it

Which Wine Where?

Marlborough is New Zealand's largest producer of wine. But good wines are being grown and produced all over the country. Each region's climate and soil lends itself to certain grape varieties, used to make a particular wine. Here's an overview of the country's wine-growing regions and the varieties they specialize in.

Region	Main Varieties
Auckland	cabernet sauvignon, merlot, cabernet franc
Bay of Plenty	chardonnay, cabernet sauvignon, sauvignon blanc
Canterbury	chardonnay, cabernet sauvignon, sauvignon blanc chardonnay, pinot noir
Gisborne	chardonnay
Hawke's Bay	cabernet sauvignon, merlot, cabernet franc, syrah
Marlborough	sauvignon blanc, chardonnay, riesling, pinot noir
Nelson	chardonnay, sauvignon blanc, riesling, pinot noir
Northland	cabernet sauvignon, merlot, chardonnay
Otago	pinot noir, chardonnay
Wairarapa	pinot noir

was moved to the larger city of Wellington. You won't get big-name concerts or national-level sporting events here. Then again, perhaps you'd prefer it that way—nice and quiet.

There are still some houses in Nelson in the $350,000 range or less if you're happy to do some renovating, but newer homes or those with bigger properties are selling for $450,000 and more. Wages in Nelson tend to be lower than the national average, so affording a mortgage can be a challenge here. Even moving out to Richmond won't help much with costs, since many of the houses there are bigger and on larger properties. Renting a house costs about $360 per week.

Blenheim

Blenheim is the main center for Marlborough's very successful winemakers. Over 50 vineyards inhabit the surrounding area. And over on the coast, the seafood industry also contributes to the local economy. The town itself features a lot of green space, mainly following the winding rivers that make their way through the town center. Recently, it has become more popular with retirees as the traditional areas for retirement such as Nelson and Tauranga get more expensive and crowded. Blenheim rivals Nelson as the sunshine capital of New Zealand.

Although Blenheim's main purpose is to support the rural population of

© MICHELLE WAITZMAN

The sand seems to stretch on forever on Nelson's Tahunanui beach.

Marlborough with services and products its population needs, the town has also become a popular tourist stop for people exploring the surrounding vineyards. This has created a demand for accommodations, restaurants, and cafés to keep the visitors happy. Blenheim is also a socializing center for the rural dwellers, with festivals of music, food, and more drawing in the hardworking locals for a bit of relaxation.

There is no public transportation in Blenheim, so residents must rely on cars to get them around. If you are planning to settle here, you'll have to quickly buy a car and get used to driving on the left. The town center is compact enough to get around by foot or bicycle, but unless you live and work right in town, you'll be dependent on your wheels.

Unfortunately, Blenheim's house prices are beginning to catch up with other places around the country. It's difficult to find a nice house for under $300,000, and most cost significantly more. Renting a house will generally cost around $320 per week.

Picton

With the ferry traffic coming and going from **Picton** every day, you would expect it to have grown into a sizable town. But Picton is stubbornly small, more a village than a town, with just 3,000 people. It services the port and local tourism industry as the gateway to the South Island. The port is mainly used for shipping forestry products but also serves the ferries and a growing number of cruise ships. There are marinas in Picton for personal boats, and many well-to-do Wellingtonians have "bachs" (vacation homes) in the nearby Queen Charlotte Sound.

It is the scenic Queen Charlotte Sound and the other parts of the Marlborough Sounds that draw people here, usually just for a short time. So accommodations, tour operators, gift shops, and car rentals do well in this gateway town. Otherwise, it's a nice place to relax if you don't actually need to work for a living.

Cultural Exchange Through Bratwurst

A PROFILE OF DORIS FAULHABER

Kiwis love a "sausage sizzle." It's as much a part of their culture as rugby or pavlova dessert. Often sausages are sold to raise money for local charities or schools, so the cheapest sausages from the supermarket are grilled and served on white sandwich bread.

That came as quite a shock to Doris Faulhaber. Sausages were also a big part of her culture back in Germany. But when she traveled to New Zealand as a 20-year-old seeking new experiences, the "cuisine" was rather disappointing.

Doris didn't arrive with big plans to bring bratwurst to the Kiwis. But when she met a local busker playing guitar on the streets of Rotorua, her plans changed forever. Doris and Andre fell in love, and he followed her home to Germany.

Doris and Andre returned to New Zealand in 1996, intending to sell Bavarian bratwurst sausages from a cart. Doris had studied as an apprentice sausage-maker and knew just what was required to make an authentic bratwurst.

The pair traveled around the South Island looking for the perfect place to launch their business. They chose Nelson, because the local city council was open to their idea. "Other councils didn't like the idea of a mobile shop selling food, because they didn't have anything like that," Doris explains. "Nelson already had the Nelson Market established, and at the time it was the only market like that in New Zealand."

At first, most of her customers were German and Swiss immigrants missing the European-style sausages served on baguettes. But as more Kiwis tried the bratwurst, it was a hit with the locals, too. Now at least half of her customers are Kiwis, but her Bratwurst Grill is still a gathering place for the expat community. "Even though I'm working, when I'm at the market, it's like a socializing day. I get to talk to the other Germans who live in Nelson. And the hotels and backpacker [hostels] always send their German guests!" she says.

The cart in Nelson was so successful that they've added a second cart in Christchurch. They have also expanded the list of meat products they make and sell. After several people from out of town asked about buying their products, they started a mail-order business.

While Doris and Andre chose Nelson for the business opportunities, she says they couldn't be happier with their new home. "The climate is wonderful—we only see the bad weather on TV. And there are lots of opportunities to go tramping and for walks. We've been here many years, but I'm still exploring!" Doris says. "This is my home now. It doesn't happen overnight, it happens gradually." She finds New Zealand a friendlier, more community-oriented place to live than Germany.

Doris doesn't think she would have been able to build a business back in Germany the way she has here. European bureaucracy would have made it almost impossible to establish her own sausage company. "It's a lot easier to start something from scratch here. You can try anything, and if it fails, you try something else!"

Picton's town center is at Nelson Square, although most of the action is closer to the waterfront on High Street and London Quay. There is a lot of room for improvement and growth here, so if the small-town life is something that appeals to you, along with just a 20-minute flight to the nearest big city, Wellington, then Picton could be an interesting place to settle. But with such a small population, don't expect too many services around. The nearest hospital is in Blenheim, and there are only two doctors in the whole town. These are the realities of small-town life in New Zealand. Houses in Picton start at around $250,000, but these are generally small homes built as vacation getaways. More substantial houses range upwards from $350,000. Rental homes are hard to find, but start as low as $150 per week.

GETTING AROUND

Most travel in Nelson and Marlborough is done by car. State Highway 1 starts right at the water's edge in Picton and can take you southward all the way down the island's eastern side. It leads right into Blenheim's town center, where it takes a turn toward the coast.

Nelson is accessed by State Highway 6, which begins at Blenheim (although there is also a more direct route from Picton). After reaching Nelson, State Highway 6 turns southwest and winds its way through the mountains to reach the west coast. You can continue westward along the northern coast from Nelson by using State Highway 60.

Nelson is the only city or town in the region with its own public transport. But with so many tourists traveling around, there are a lot of coach services that will get you from town to town if you don't want to drive yourself.

Train service is available from Picton to Christchurch via Blenheim and Kaikoura. This trip is called the Coastal Pacific and is one of the scenic journeys offered to visitors, but it's also handy if you want to get from your home in Blenheim to the bright lights of Christchurch. Fares for the train are priced more for tourists than locals, with a regular-priced fare costing $160 one way. There are sometimes special offers which can make a significant difference to the cost.

OTAGO AND SOUTHLAND

The residents of the southern end of the country consider themselves a bit tougher than their northern compatriots, especially those spoiled "JAFAs" (a commonly used acronym for Just Another...Aucklander). These are the only New Zealanders who regularly experience temperatures below freezing at night during the winter. The roads can get icy and treacherous, especially in the mountains around Queenstown. But on the flip side, summer days can be long and hot, with plenty of gorgeous places to enjoy the outdoors.

A lot of the land in Otago and Southland is dedicated to farming (especially dairy farming) and forestry, but there are other reasons to move to the south. The tourism industry around Queenstown Lakes and Fiordland is huge and seems to just keep growing. Oysters from Bluff are coveted and keep a lot of the local population gainfully employed. Education is a big employer in Dunedin, thanks to the University of Otago. And everywhere in between, creative, innovative, and enthusiastic entrepreneurs are being lured to this underdeveloped area.

OTAGO AND SOUTHLAND

Tasman Sea

Westland National Park

Mt Cook National Park

Lake Pukaki

80

8

Lake Ohau

SOUTH

PACIFIC

OCEAN

1

WEST COAST

6

Southern Alps

CANTERBURY

Lake Benmore

83

Omarama

Oamaru

Mt Aspiring National Park

Lake Hawea

8

85

Palmerston

Lake Wanaka

Wanaka

6

OTAGO

87

1

Milford Sound

Harris Mtns

Arrowtown

Alexandra

Dunedin

Mosgiel

Queenstown

Lake Wakatipu

8

Franklin Mtns

94

The Remarkables

90

Balclutha

Stuart Mtns

6

1

Lake Te Anau

Murchison Mtns

Te Anau

94

Gore

Catlins Forest Park

Manapouri

SOUTHLAND

96

The Catlins

Lake Manapouri

Fiordland

99

1

National

Invercargill

Park

Bluff

Te Waewae Bay

Foveaux Strait

Oban

Rakiura

Stewart Island

National

Park

0   25 mi

0   25 km

© AVALON TRAVEL

Dunedin

Dunedin was first settled in the early 1800s by whalers and sealers, mainly from Scotland. Dunedin's Scottish roots give the city a very distinct character. Rather than messing about with wood, the early settlers built sturdy stone and brick structures that have endured to this day. With just over 120,000 residents, Dunedin may be a small city compared to Christchurch, but it was once the largest in the country thanks to a nearby gold rush. That drew the first wave of Chinese immigrants to New Zealand, some of whom still have descendants in the region today.

The Scots also brought with them an appreciation of education, setting up New Zealand's first university. The impressive University of Otago (founded in 1869) attracts students from around the country and the world. Students dominate the area, many of them living away from home for the first time. That spirit of youth and adventure provides a lot of energy in what might otherwise be a sleepy little city.

THE LAY OF THE LAND

Dunedin lies at the innermost point of Otago Harbour. The city center was modeled after Edinburgh in Scotland (Dunedin is actually the Gaelic name for Edinburgh), with an octagon in the middle, and another, larger one surrounding it. The main street passes through the center of The Octagon and is called Princes Street going south and George Street going north.

The city is mostly flat near the harbor, but is very hilly in almost every other

Dunedin has some of the world's steepest streets.

© MICHELLE WAITZMAN

direction. The inner suburbs are scattered over the hills, giving some wonderful views and sunshine while others suffer in the shadows down below.

The Otago Peninsula stretches northward from the city's east side, providing more suburbs, lots of beaches, and some rare wildlife. Yellow-eyed penguins and the royal albatross are among the unusual birds that manage to make their home within just a short distance of the city.

DAILY LIVING

For a relatively small city, Dunedin feels more urban than you might expect. There is a lot of life and culture here, perhaps because of the university. Live theater, music, art, and nightlife are all part of the scene. Over the summer, when the students have gone (and quite a few others go on holiday too), it does get noticeably quiet.

People who live in Dunedin love the fact that it is small enough to get pretty much anywhere in the city within 10 minutes. Even those who live in the suburbs rarely sit in their cars for longer than 15-20 minutes to get to work. This is great for their quality of life, since they can use their time for more important things, like socializing or enjoying the outdoors. Some of the activities people enjoy within a few minutes of the city are swimming, surfing, windsurfing, mountain biking, and hiking. Over the winter, they are the closest major city to the country's top skiing destination, Queenstown.

They also feel that their weather is one of the country's best-kept secrets. While those up north assume that the folks in Dunedin are shivering away all winter in frost and snow, they are often enjoying clear, sunny skies, with crisp but pleasant winter days. Yes, it gets cold overnight, so you need to pay attention to your home heating situation, but if you have that under control, it can be very pleasant in Dunedin year-round.

Students in the city do get up to typical student mischief. They drink too much, get noisy on the weekends, and sometimes even light couches on fire in the middle of the road. But they are generally under control, and by no means do they make Dunedin an unsafe place to live. The students enjoy the city, and many stay on after they have completed school if they can find appropriate work.

If you're not a student, you'll be wondering what kind of work is available in Dunedin. The city currently has a shortage of engineers and IT professionals, as well as health care workers. There are also opportunities in manufacturing, agriculture, forestry, and various trades. Teaching jobs are quite competitive in Dunedin, so if you're hoping to teach, you'll need good credentials. The upside to that is that your kids are sure to have good teachers, no matter where in Dunedin you live. There is no big competition within the city to get your kids into the "right" school district, as there is in Christchurch. Dunedin City Council is actively recruiting for more skilled workers to come and live in the city, both from around New Zealand and from overseas.

WHERE TO LIVE

Dunedin houses have been described as "old and cold." They're not any more so than houses in other parts of the country, but because temperatures can dip below freezing quite often over the winters here, you'll notice it more. As a result, choosing a home in Dunedin isn't just a matter of picking the neighborhood that suits your needs. You should also pay attention to whether the house will get any sun in the winter (north-facing windows are best) and whether your potential new home has proper insulation and a heat source. While most homes here have some kind of insulation, you should always ask for details before signing a rental agreement or offering to purchase.

Downtown and University of Otago

The **University of Otago** occupies the northern end of the city center, so a lot of student housing is clustered around that part of town. This includes purpose-built high-rise apartments on campus, plus a variety of older houses that are rented out as student flats. These older flats vary from beautifully maintained villas to run-down dumps, so I strongly recommend seeing the place for yourself before you decide anything. And flatting with other students means that you may be dealing with loud parties and big messes, or you may be surrounded by people who insist on total silence while they study. Try to meet the flatmates and determine whether you are all compatible when it comes to lifestyle. Rooms rent for around $90-130 per week near the university.

Few nonstudents bother to live in the **city center,** since it takes so little time to get there from the suburbs, anyway. But there are some very central homes for those who like to live in the thick of it. Living in the city is not a big financial burden in Dunedin, with a three-bedroom house renting for around $340 per week. You can buy an older home (which may need some updating to make it comfortable) for just over $300,000.

Inner Suburbs

Dunedin's inner suburbs cover the hills surrounding the city center. There are a variety of house sizes and styles, with more brick houses down here than you would find on the North Island. Prices have risen over the past several years, as they have everywhere in New Zealand, but Dunedin has remained more affordable than many other cities.

© MICHELLE WAITZMAN

University of Otago

Beer Geography

Dunedin's historic brewery, Speight & Co. is better known as Speights.

New Zealand is known as a land of "rugby, racing, and beer." Kiwis drink an average of more than 75 liters (almost 20 gallons) of beer per person each year. Traditionally, Kiwis have been fiercely loyal to their local brew. Depending on where in the country you lived, you would be expected to drink your region's beer or get some nasty looks at the pub.

Speight's is the main brew in the south, with its historic brewery in Dunedin. Its influence stretches beyond the city though, all through Otago and Southland.

In Canterbury, the historic favorites are Canterbury Draught (CB), and DB Draught from Timaru.

The west coast is home to Monteith's brewery which originated in Greymouth, although it is now brewed in several locations.

In Nelson (which is the main growing area for hops in New Zealand) you'll find Mac's brewery. Mac's also has a brewery restaurant in Wellington.

The lower North Island is home to Tui, as famous for their clever advertising campaigns as for their beer. The brewery is near Palmerston North.

Steinlager, one of the most commonly exported New Zealand beers, is brewed in a suburb of Auckland and appeals to that city's cosmopolitan population.

While old habits sometimes die hard in New Zealand, the growing popularity of microbreweries and the increasingly wide range of imported beers mean that regional brand loyalty is fading away. Besides, many of these historic brands are now made by large, foreign-owned brewing companies. So feel free to order the beer that you enjoy, even if it is "imported" from out of town.

PRIME LIVING LOCATIONS

Most suburbs have their own local shops and services, but for major shopping, the city center is close enough to be convenient.

At the north end of the city, suburbs like **Opoho,** the **Northeast Valley,** and **Woodhaugh** house families close to the well-used Botanic Gardens. To the south are communities like the very affordable **South Dunedin** and beach suburbs like **St. Kilda** and **St. Clair.** In most of these suburbs, an older house costs less than $300,000, while newer homes or recently renovated ones can run $400,000 or more. Renting is also quite affordable at around $325 per week for a three-bedroom house.

Surfing beaches are just 10 minutes from downtown Dunedin.

Mosgiel

If you're looking for a little extra space in your home, or a larger property around it, you might consider buying in **Mosgiel.** This is technically a separate town, about 15 minutes outside of Dunedin. The flat landscape in this area means it won't be running out of space to expand any time soon; the homes are a bit more spread out. It's a bit like living out in the country, but with a very short commute to the city. Brand-new homes are going up in this area, so they are likely to be warmer and need less care than the older houses close to the city.

Because the homes in Mosgiel are mainly quite new, they tend to cost around $450,000-600,000, depending on the size of the house and the property, but you'll end up with something that in other cities might well be a million-dollar home. Renting in Mosgiel is similar in price to Dunedin, around $300 per week for a three-bedroom house.

Otago Peninsula

Dunedin natives may try to tell you that the peninsula is too far to bother commuting from, but in reality it's no more than a 20-minute drive to work for most of the folks who live out there. Quite reasonable in any other city, but for those who are used to getting anywhere they want in 10 minutes or less, it's a long way to go.

However, the **Otago Peninsula** offers some of the nicest homes and best views in Dunedin. And immigrants seem to be drawn to the place, so living here will put you in the company of many other expats. Most of the communities are close to the Otago Harbour side of the peninsula, with the far side used more for holiday homes. There are schools nearby, but few other major services on the peninsula itself.

With the great hillside views, fancy homes, and access to beaches, living on the peninsula is a bit more expensive than in other suburbs. You can expect to pay about

$50,000 more for a house on Otago Peninsula than you would pay elsewhere in Dunedin. So expect to pay at least $350,000 for a home there, but prices get much higher for the best views and most secluded lots. Renting is not a popular option here, but you may find a house for around $330 per week if anything is available.

GETTING AROUND

Dunedin lies along State Highway 1, although the highway briefly disappears through the city center itself. Following State Highway 1 south of the city, you'll reach the airport in around 25 minutes. State Highway 87 branches off State Highway 1 just south of the city and leads to Mosgiel and other inland communities as it turns north.

In the city center there are one-way streets designed to be the main through streets for traffic moving across the city near the harbor. These are the city route for State Highway 1. The general layout of the city center can take some getting used to, thanks to The Octagon in the middle and the hills interrupting any attempt at a grid pattern. But traffic is rarely a problem, so once you get your bearings, Dunedin is an easy city for drivers.

A bus network also services the city and suburbs, if you don't want to bother with your own car. They operate on a zone-based fare system, with adult fares ranging from $2-6.70. A discount "GoCard" will save you 10 percent or so off these fares. Services operate seven days a week, and there is also some limited service on public holidays.

You will notice that Dunedin is very proud of its historic train station. But if you are counting on it for train service to other areas, you're pretty much out of luck. There is only one train journey still operating out of Dunedin, a daily tourist train to Taieri Gorge. It's a lovely trip, but not terribly useful for residents.

Invercargill and Southland

Southland has a small but proud population. They're a tough bunch, and they are so independent they've even developed their own accent (Southlanders roll their r's). Not many people live down south, around 93,000 in the entire region, but it is one of the best-known and most-visited regions in New Zealand, thanks mostly to the stunning Fiordland National Park. Although most visitors want to head to Southland, most immigrants don't even consider it. International immigrants are a fairly new phenomenon in this area, so the old-timers are a little baffled by new cultures, accents, and lifestyles. But as the area becomes more diverse, it is also becoming much more interesting and lively.

Not long ago, the only types of work around Southland were fishing, forestry, and livestock farming. Things are changing rapidly down south. Now many of the livestock farms are converting to dairy, thanks to a boom in the dairy industry. Tourism is growing in this already-popular spot. And the south's gas, oil, and mineral reserves are looking like important contributors to the economy in the future. While the offshore oil and gas basins south of New Zealand were long considered too expensive to explore, the worldwide hunger for more oil may make it worthwhile after all. Even radio technology is an emerging industry down south. Its unique position toward the

The Adventure You Want, the Culture You Need

AN INTERVIEW WITH EXPORT EDUCATION COORDINATOR SARAH GAUTHIER

Sarah Gauthier moved from Ontario, Canada, to Dunedin in 2003 for an eight-month internship at the Dunedin Public Art Gallery and never looked back. She currently works at Dunedin City Council as the export education coordinator for Enterprise Dunedin.

Sarah Gauthier is the export education coordinator for Enterprise Dunedin.

How did you end up living in New Zealand?

I moved in September, 2003 after completing some tertiary studies and a road trip across Canada. My parents drove me to the airport in Montreal and saw me off on what was meant to be an eight-month adventure. I have been in New Zealand for 12 years. I have spent most of my time in Dunedin, but I have also lived in central Otago and Wellington.

Was it always your intention to settle in Dunedin?

It wasn't my intention—but it certainly seemed like a good idea once I got off the plane. I really liked Dunedin and New Zealand—the place and the people. It has been a really good fit for my personality, interests, and freedom-seeking nature.

What surprised you about Dunedin when you first moved here?

The willingness of people to welcome me to everything! Dunedinites want you to be happy and entertained—people really invited me into their homes and lives. I have super friends here who have shown and explained to me Aotearoa New Zealand—the landscape, culture, and history.

How did you find your first job in the city? Was it difficult?

My internship was arranged in Canada—so from that perspective it was easy. After that experience, and some time spent relaxing and ski instructing in central Otago, I returned to

bottom of the world has made Southland a center for rocket tracking, study of the southern ionosphere, and radio astronomy. So the local farmers and fishers are now hanging out with a few rocket scientists. Other industries making a major contribution to the local economy are mining and manufacturing.

The largest urban center in the south is Invercargill, famous as the home of Burt Munro, whose story was turned into the hit movie *The World's Fastest Indian*. The colorful mayor, Tim Shadbolt, also keeps Invercargill in the New Zealand headlines. One of his moves to attract more residents to the area was to introduce a "zero fees" scheme for the Southern Institute of Technology (SIT). New Zealand citizens or residents can study at the school without paying tuition fees.

Southland does have some cold winter nights, and it gets windy along the south

Dunedin. Within a month or so I was working at Otago Polytechnic in marketing. It was relatively easy, and Dunedin business and industry are always on the lookout for good talent.

What do you love about living in Dunedin?
I love the ease, the scenic diversity, and the combination of outdoor adventures and indoor culture. Dunedin is a uniquely intriguing and sophisticated city—with a fun nightlife, great eateries, cool arts, and stunning scenery!

It's often called the 10-minute city. You can hop in your car and be at a stunning beach with waves crashing and "surfies" riding them within 10 minutes. My dog and I love that convenience.

What are some of the drawbacks of living in Dunedin?
Here's the spoiler—it's cold and damp here at times. It's important to find a warm and sunny place to live. Unsurprisingly, winter here can be tough. Not Canadian tough, but hard. Here's why: Most New Zealand homes are not centrally heated. They still light fires or bundle up under sleeping bags. Old-school skills—and I have had to learn how to make fires last through the night!

Also, it can feel really small. Dunedin is New Zealand's oldest European-settled city. This makes it historic and claustrophobic. Everyone knows you. Eventually we are all featured in the local newspaper, the *Otago Daily Times*.

What kinds of people are drawn to Dunedin? Is the city very diverse?
Dunedin is a city for and by tertiary students. We have the youngest population in New Zealand—this makes it fun, diverse (there are lots of international students here), and really welcoming. We are used to catering to people from across New Zealand and around the world. This diversity comes to life in our varied societies, activities, and cafés. You can literally find the adventure you want and the culture you need!

What advice would you give to immigrants who are considering Dunedin as their new home?
Be willing to shift your skills and abilities into new spheres. Dunedin is growing, and there are lots of small and entrepreneurial start-ups that need people with global outlooks—so be willing to take your experience and abilities and put them into something new.

Be adaptable and willing to share your story with everyone—they will want to know you, and then Dunedinites will be willing and able to support you. I have made amazingly devoted friends here. This is what keeps me here.

coast, but overall the climate is quite pleasant most of the time. People's perception of Southland being just short of the South Pole is definitely an exaggeration! The region is so big that there are several microclimates in different areas, but overall the summers are warm and the winters see a bit of snow, but nothing like the snowbelts of the northern United States or Canada.

THE LAY OF THE LAND

Southland spans the entire width of the South Island, but goes farther up on the western side than on the east. Of course, a big chunk of that land on the western side is taken up by Fiordland National Park, so it's not among the places you can choose to live.

The city of Invercargill lies almost in the center of the south coast, with the even more southern town of Bluff sitting on a peninsula directly south of it. The other main town in the region is Gore, an inland town northeast of Invercargill. To the northwest, Te Anau sits on the edge of Fiordland, acting as a tourism center and support town for the local rural residents.

The landscape of Southland includes almost endless variety, from vast areas of farmland to the low mountains and rocky headlands of the Catlins Forest Park in the east and the famous fiords in the west. Stewart Island, home to a small population of about 400 full-time residents, is also considered part of Southland.

DAILY LIVING

Lifestyle is the big draw for people considering Southland. The low cost of living, relaxed atmosphere, the great outdoors at your doorstep, and the small population make it a great place for quality of life. But it's not the right lifestyle for everyone. If you enjoy city nightlife, lots of shopping, and large-scale events, then you may find yourself going a bit stir-crazy in the south.

The closer you live to Invercargill, the more access to shops, restaurants, movies, and other city delights you will have. Anywhere in Southland you'll have a reasonably short drive to the ski fields around Queenstown, some of the best hiking in the world in Fiordland, and plenty of space to call your own.

With only one city around, however, Southlanders need to be independent. You may be finding creative ways to fix things around the house until you get a chance to properly repair or replace them. You'll have to learn how to drive in the sometimes-icy conditions over the winter. And you may have to make do with limited selection at the local shops.

Not only do Southlanders need to take care of themselves, they also have to look out for each other. It's a place where you're likely to get to know all of your neighbors and give one another a hand when it's needed. This kind of community spirit is rather old-fashioned, in the best way possible. After all, you won't find a lot of Aucklanders willing to give neighbors a hand when their fence needs fixing or they have a leaky roof. Southland is famous for its friendly people and warm hospitality. If you thought you'd have to go back in time to find a place where people are still friendly to each other, you're in luck here.

The main towns have schools, and buses take children from neighboring communities into town. But in a lot of rural areas, it's difficult to find schools, doctors, and other necessities nearby. Some farmers homeschool their kids or use correspondence school, while others send them to a boarding school. Some find that the "local" school is close enough to drive there and back daily with their children. While Southland is a nice, safe place to raise kids, it isn't always a convenient one outside the main centers. Health care can also be a challenge. While the Southland Hospital (completed in 2004) in Invercargill offers emergency care and some shiny new equipment, the only other public hospital in Southland is over in Gore. Some Southlanders may be closer to the Lakes District Hospital in Queenstown than either of these.

WHERE TO LIVE

As always, your choice of career will dictate the best part of this region for you to live in. Rural areas take up most of the land, with dairy farms, livestock, and some food crops. If the seafood industry beckons, you'll head for the south coast. If you want a piece of the tourism industry, you can base yourself in Te Anau or one of the other small communities near Fiordland. And if you want to have all of the urban conveniences nearby, you're bound to be most comfortable in Invercargill. The rest of the region's population is spread quite thinly around the huge area. The other main center of population is the town of Gore, with 8,000 residents, which is New Zealand's country music capital.

Invercargill

With a population of 53,000, **Invercargill** is bigger than many imagine it to be. The city has Scottish roots, much like Dunedin, and the first European settlers were whalers. But Invercargill is determined to attract immigrants, offering special courses for international students and sending representatives overseas to explain the benefits of living in Southland.

It's the relaxed, southern lifestyle that draws people here. The clean air, complete absence of traffic, and proximity to the sea, fjords, mountains, and any other gorgeous scenery you could want are strong selling points. In fact, people who come to Invercargill for the free tuition often fall in love with the place and try to find work in Southland afterward. That's exactly what the city council hoped would happen, and the plan seems to be having some success.

There are a limited number of jobs in a city this size, but skilled professionals and tradespeople are always in demand. Engineers are in short supply, and anyone working in the manufacturing sector will also find work. There are also lots of small businesses around, servicing the community. Or perhaps you'd like to start your own. The unemployment rate in Southland is the lowest in the country, so don't believe those who will tell you there's no work down south.

One of the best things about living in Invercargill is that the houses are still affordable. If you're an astute shopper, you can still buy a three-bedroom house in the city for under $200,000. Of course, the newer the house and the bigger the property, the more you will pay. Be sure to find out how the house is heated and insulated before you buy or even rent anything in Southland. The average price to rent a house in Invercargill is around $230 per week.

Bluff

New Zealand's only aluminum smelter, which is a major contributor to Southland's economy, is at Tiwai Point near Bluff. There is also an active port at Bluff (first built to import sheep from Australia) as well as a fishing industry. The town is famous for its oysters, which are prized around New Zealand.

Bluff has a very close relationship with Invercargill since they are such close neighbors and their economies are also closely linked. The town of about 2,000 people is barely a blip on the map, but it is well known around the country as the southernmost town on the mainland, the jumping-off point for trips to Stewart Island, and a major player in the seafood industry.

A three-bedroom house in Bluff is a steal compared to other parts of New Zealand—some sell for as little as $100,000. There's not a lot for rent in town, but prices are around $250 per week for whatever is available.

GETTING AROUND

You'll be pretty dependent on your car in Southland, as there is little public transportation available outside of Invercargill. This means getting your New Zealand license promptly and being prepared for winter driving on occasion. If you live in a very rural area, you should also be able to take care of minor maintenance on your car, since you may be some distance from the nearest garage.

Southland is serviced by a network of State Highways. The main route is State Highway 1, which begins its journey through the country at Bluff and heads northeast toward Dunedin. State Highway 6 leads directly north from Invercargill toward Queenstown and Wanaka in central Otago. There is a turnoff from State Highway 6 that leads to Te Anau and Fiordland as well.

The city of Invercargill is basically a grid of streets, with the New River Estuary forming a border to the west. Within the city, State Highway 1 is known as Tay Street, and State Highway 6 is called Dee Street to the north of State Highway 1 and Clyde Street to the south. Their intersection is at the city center and also where the main campuses of the Southern Institute of Technology are found. The main bus terminal is only a short walk from the campus and city center.

Invercargill has a city bus service to take commuters to and from the city center. The routes are all circular, so you can catch them going either direction and eventually get to your stop. There is also a free bus that circulates around the town center to cut down on traffic congestion. For other services, the fare is $1.40-3.40 for adults depending on the distance and the time of day.

Queenstown Lakes

Queenstown, Wanaka, and the surrounding region are undoubtedly one of the most beautiful parts of New Zealand, if not the entire world! The jagged peaks of the Remarkables Range, the stunning blue lakes and rivers . . . it all seems like an impossibly perfect landscape. Who wouldn't want to live in the middle of all that? It's certainly a dream for many immigrants, and more than a few Kiwis, too.

The unfortunate truth is that the beautiful landscape is a pricey one. So much of the area has been developed for tourism that the property values are beyond the reach of the average family. In fact, this has created big problems for the people who do live there, working in the hotels and restaurants and running the adrenaline-pumping tourist activities. Many simply can't make ends meet on their small salaries, creating an underclass of struggling employees in the region.

Of course there is also farmland around, which can provide a slightly more affordable piece of paradise if you are willing to stray farther afield. Rural industries in this region include forestry and winemaking. Or you can try to make your property a business investment by opening up a fishing lodge or bed-and-breakfast.

THE LAY OF THE LAND

Queenstown Lakes is an area of mountains and lakes within the Southern Alps that stretch along the center of the South Island. It lies approximately a quarter of the way up the island, north of Dunedin and south of Christchurch.

As the names suggest, there are several lakes in the region. The main ones are Lake Wakatipu, a long, thin lake with Queenstown perched on the north shore; Lake Wanaka, where you'll find the town of Wanaka; and Lake Hawea, famous for its trout fishing.

The mountains between Queenstown and Wanaka are considered the best skiing locations in the Southern Hemisphere, so the place is popular with tourists year-round. Adventure-seekers, hikers, and anglers enjoy the summer activities, while the skiers and snowboarders take over for the winter.

Due to the altitude in the mountains, this area gets more ice and snow than most parts of the country. Some locals keep tire chains around in case of severe road conditions, and with so many tourists around all winter, there are always quite a few road accidents when the weather is bad.

DAILY LIVING

If you want to live here among the 28,000 full-time residents, you'll have to find a niche in this crowded market. Tourism is the main industry, including extreme activities like skydiving and bungee jumping, and more subdued pursuits like fishing, hiking, and just enjoying the scenery. There are lots of restaurants and hotels, and these provide the main sources of employment for local residents.

Although the local population is growing, there is not a lot of infrastructure in the region. Everything is so focused on visitors that the residents are kind of pushed aside. Affordable clothing, food, and supplies are difficult to come by. If you own the hotel, you'll probably be just fine, but if you make the beds, you will struggle to get by.

One upside of the growth in tourism is that the need for more hotels and other facilities has created a lot of jobs in the construction industry. Anyone in a building-related trade will be kept busy in the region for at least the next few years.

WHERE TO LIVE
Queenstown and Arrowtown

Living in **Queenstown** is like living at a holiday resort. There's something a bit unreal about it. It would be similar to living somewhere like Whistler, British Columbia, or Aspen, Colorado. But outside of the touristy town center, people do try to live normal lives in this town. There are a lot of temporary residents who only come for the ski season or for the summer tourist season, while others have tried to put down roots and make this a real home.

It's almost impossible to find a house in Queenstown for under $600,000, with many selling for millions of dollars. Most residents live in nearby suburbs like **Fernhill** and **Frankton,** but there is not a lot of difference in house prices no matter where you are. Everything close to Queenstown is prime real estate. Renting is the only option for a lot of people in hospitality jobs, whose wages simply can't cover a mortgage here. A three-bedroom home rents for around $475 per week, depending on how close to town it is.

Just northeast of Queenstown is **Arrowtown,** another resort area, although slightly less touristy than its neighbor. Homes are just as expensive here, and work still revolves

If All Your Friends Jumped Off a Bridge...

There are a lot of things to do and see in and around Queenstown, but one of the most popular activities is bungee jumping. This rather extreme form of entertainment is based on a coming-of-age ritual on the Pacific island of Vanuatu. Young men would leap from high platforms with vines tied around their ankles to stop them from smacking into the ground.

Impressed by the sheer thrill of such an activity, Oxford University's "Dangerous Sports Club" decided to give it a try in the 1970s, and a video of that event inspired Kiwi adventurer A. J. Hackett to develop a similar activity using latex rubber cords. The bungee jump was born.

Returning to New Zealand, Hackett set up the world's first commercial bungee jump site on the Kawarau suspension bridge just outside of Queenstown in the late 1980s. The jump is 43 meters (141 feet) from the bridge to the water and still operating today. Jumpers can choose whether or not they want to get dunked into the river during their jumps.

The jump became so popular that similar sites were set up around the country, but Queenstown remains New Zealand's bungee capital. In addition to the Kawarau bridge, you can jump from a hillside platform over the city called "The Ledge," the Pipeline Bungy (as it is spelled locally) over the Shotover River, or the 134-meter-high (440-foot) Nevis Bungy over the Nevis River.

For a bit of variety, the Shotover Canyon Swing turns the jumper into a human pendulum after a 60-meter (200-foot) free fall over the Shotover River.

Queenstown specializes in creative ways to part visitors with their money. While bungee jumping might be the iconic extreme activity, visitors also participate in skydiving, river rafting, jet-boating, and paragliding.

mostly around the hospitality industry. Some of the region's vineyards are also nearby, so if you get involved in that industry, Arrowtown may be your nearest service town. The town was formed during the gold rush in the 1860s and at one point was home to 7,000 people. These days the population is just over 2,000.

Wanaka

Perched on one of the most spectacular lakes you'll ever see, close to New Zealand's premier ski resorts, **Wanaka** is a place many of us would love to call home. Living here is expensive, but not quite as off-the-charts expensive as Queenstown. If you can afford $500,000-700,000 for a house, you may be in luck. Renting a house in Wanaka can easily cost more than $500 per week.

Hospitality is still a dominant force in this area, with holidaymakers using Wanaka as a base for skiing, hiking, skydiving, and other activities. Local vineyards are also a contributor to the town's economy. And the building boom is alive and well here, and especially in need of carpenters and electricians.

The lifestyle here is hard to beat, with Mount Aspiring National Park just a short drive away, plus of course the ski fields and lakes. But you may find that the overpriced restaurants and thousands of tourists make it an unsatisfying home. Shopping is not great here, either, so an occasional trip to Dunedin or Christchurch may be in order for those who enjoy retail therapy or just need a wider range of household supplies.

Alexandra

About an hour's drive east of Queenstown lies the town of **Alexandra.** This town of 4,800 people is the service center for the surrounding fruit orchards and vineyards of central Otago, as well as a good number of sheep farms. Besides the agriculture industry, the town is a popular stop for tourists between Queenstown and Dunedin.

Living in Alexandra is somewhat more affordable than the heart of Queenstown Lakes. There are actually a few houses available for under $400,000, which is a bargain compared to Queenstown. But you are an hour away from the bulk of the tourism business, so you'll need an income from farming, or from support industries like retail, transportation, or professional services. Since the area is mainly agricultural, renting a home is rare.

GETTING AROUND

The Queenstown Lakes region can be reached from either side of the Southern Alps. From the west coast, State Highway 6 crosses Haast Pass through Mount Aspiring National Park to reach the district. From the south, you can approach via State Highway 6 from Invercargill. From the east, State Highway 8 branches off from State Highway 1 near Timaru, about halfway between Dunedin and Christchurch. You just can't get there directly from the north, since all those Southern Alps are in the way.

During the winter, some of the mountain passes can be quite difficult to drive through, and at times you can expect roads to be closed during and after winter storms. You will have to learn how to drive in snowy and icy conditions if it's new to you, and remember to adjust your speed to the road conditions.

All of the towns in this region are small enough to find your way around without difficulty. A decent road map will get you from place to place, although the smaller roads in the rural areas may not be well marked on general maps. Only Queenstown has a local bus service.

For traveling farther away, you may want to take advantage of Queenstown's airport. It has domestic flights and a limited number of international flights to Australia. The main transportation hub to other destinations is Christchurch.

RESOURCES

Consulates and Embassies

UNITED STATES

**NEW ZEALAND
CONSULATE ATLANTA**

513 Seminole Ave. NE
Atlanta, GA 30307
tel. 404/745-4551
fax 404/525-2495
newzealand@mindspring.com

**NEW ZEALAND
CONSULATE CHICAGO**

6400 Shafer Ct., Ste. 275
Rosemont, IL 60018
tel. 773/714-8669
fax 773/714-9483
eaburkhardt@railworld-inc.com

**NEW ZEALAND CONSULATE
GENERAL LOS ANGELES**

2425 Olympic Blvd., Ste. 600E
Santa Monica, CA 90404
tel. 310/566-6555
fax 310/566-6556
nzcg.la@verizon.net
www.nzcgla.com

**NEW ZEALAND CONSULATE
GENERAL NEW YORK**

222 East 41st St., Ste. 2510
New York, NY 10017-6702
tel. 212/832-4038
fax 212/832-7602

**NEW ZEALAND
CONSULATE GUAM**

Street Address: 290 Salar St.
Taumuning, Guam 96931
Postal Address: P.O. Box 8196
Taumuning, Guam 96931
tel. 671/646-7662
fax 671/646-1061
john@jwsguam.com

**NEW ZEALAND CONSULATE
HONOLULU**

Street Address: 3929 Old Pali Rd.
Honolulu, HI 96817
Postal Address: P.O. Box 730
Honolulu, HI 96813
tel. 808/595-2200
fax 808/595-3409
plewis7777@hawaii.rr.com

**NEW ZEALAND CONSULATE
HOUSTON**

4224 W. Sam Houston Pkwy. North
Houston, TX 77041
tel. 713/501-5418
connely@nzhonoraryconsul.org

**NEW ZEALAND CONSULATE
NEW ENGLAND**

Street Address: PretiFlaherty
57 North Main St.
Concord, NH 033021-1318
Postal Address: P.O. Box 1318
Concord, NH 033021-1318
tel. 603/225-8228
fax 603/226-2637
nzconsulate@preti.com

**NEW ZEALAND CONSULATE
PORTLAND**

500 NW Hilltop Rd.
Portland, OR 97210
tel. 503/803-7129
cjs@theswindells.org

**NEW ZEALAND CONSULATE
SACRAMENTO**

44733 North El Macero Dr.
El Macero, CA 95618-1066
tel. 530/756-8013
fax 530/756-7032
starrned@msn.com

**NEW ZEALAND CONSULATE
SALT LAKE CITY**
1655 Linden Ln.
Bountiful, UT 84010
tel. 801/296-2494
iain.mckay1@hotmail.com

**NEW ZEALAND CONSULATE
SAN DIEGO**
tel. 619/988-0828
fax 619/540-0655
rob@syranuse.com

**NEW ZEALAND CONSULATE
SAN FRANCISCO**
P.O. Box 1276
Burlingames, CA 94011-1276
tel. 650/342-4443
fax 650/762-7001
newzealandHCSF@gmail.com

**NEW ZEALAND
CONSULATE SEATTLE**
P.O. Box 51059
Seattle, WA 98115
tel. 206/527-1896
fax 206/525-8104
nzconsulseattle@gmail.com

**NEW ZEALAND EMBASSY
WASHINGTON**
37 Observatory Circle NW
Washington, DC 20008
tel. 202/328-4800
fax 202/667-5227
info@nzemb.org
www.nzembassy.com/usa

NZ CONSULATE VERMONT
Street Address: 211 Ordway Shore Rd.
Shelburne, VT 05482-1103
Postal Address: P.O. Box 1103
Shelburne, VT 05482-1103
tel. 802/489-5677
georgeburrill@me.com

CANADA
**NEW ZEALAND CONSULATE
GENERAL VANCOUVER**
1050 West Pender St.
Vancouver, BC V6E 3S7
tel. 604/684-7388
fax 604/684-7333
vancouveroffice@nzte.govt.nz

NZ CONSULATE CALGARY
tel. 1844/261-1292 (toll-free)
info@nzconsulcalgary.org

**NEW ZEALAND CONSULATE
TORONTO**
tel. 1855/612-4928 (toll-free)
info@nzconsultoronto.org

**NEW ZEALAND HIGH
COMMISSION OTTAWA**
150 Elgin St., Ste. 1401
Ottawa, Ontario K2P 1L4
tel. 613/238-5991
fax 613/238-5707
info@nzhcottawa.org
www.nzembassy.com/canada

NEW ZEALAND
**CANADIAN CONSULATE &
TRADE OFFICE AUCKLAND**
Street Address: 9th Floor, 48 Emily Place
Auckland
Postal Address: P.O. Box 318
Shortland Street
Auckland, 1040
tel. 09/309-3690
fax 09/307-3111
aklnd@international.gc.ca

CANADIAN HIGH COMMISSION WELLINGTON
Street Address: Level 11, 125 The Terrace
Wellington
Postal Address: P.O. Box 8047
Wellington, 6143
tel. 04/473-9577
fax 04/471-2082
wlgtn@international.gc.ca
www.newzealand.gc.ca

U.S. CONSULATE AUCKLAND
Street Address: Level 3, Citigroup Building
23 Custom St. East, Corner Commerce Street
Auckland
Postal Address: Private Bag 92022
Auckland, 1142
tel. 09/303-2724, ext. 2800
fax 09/366-0870

U.S. EMBASSY WELLINGTON
Street Address: 29 Fitzherbert Terrace
Wellington
Postal Address: P.O. Box 1190
Wellington, 6140
tel. 04/462-6000
fax 04/499-0490
http://newzealand.usembassy.gov
Note that the embassy does not provide consular services. For those you must use the U.S. Consulate in Auckland.

Immigration

NEW ZEALAND BRANCHES
AUCKLAND CENTRAL BRANCH
Level 4
280 Queen St.
Auckland CBD, 1010
tel. c/o National call center 09/914-4100
fax 09/914-4118

AUCKLAND HENDERSON BRANCH
39 Paramount Dr.
Henderson
Auckland, 0610
tel. c/o National call center 09/914-4100
fax 09/969-3498

AUCKLAND MANUKAU BRANCH
Level 2
Epicor House
20 Amersham Way
Manukau City
Auckland, 2104
tel. c/o National call center 09/914-4100
fax 09/914-4728

CHRISTCHURCH
110 Wrights Rd.
Addington, Christchurch 8024
tel. c/o National call center 09/914-4100

DUNEDIN
Street Address: Level 3
Norwich House
1 Bond St.
Dunedin
Postal Address: P.O. Box 557
Dunedin, 9054
tel. c/o National call center 09/914-4100
fax 03/955-7606

HAMILTON
Street Address: Level 5 Westpac House
Corner of Victoria and Alma Streets
Hamilton
Postal Address: Private Bag 3013
Hamilton, 3240
tel. c/o National call center 09/914-4100

PALMERSTON NORTH
Street Address: Level 5
65 Rangitikei St.
Palmerston North
Postal Address: P.O. Box 1049
Palmerston North, 4440
tel. c/o National call center 09/914-4100
fax 06/952-6910

QUEENSTOWN
Street Address: Level 2
Dart House
Remarkables Park
Frankton, Queenstown
Postal Address: P.O. Box 2354
Wakatipu, 9349
tel. c/o National call center 09/914-4100
fax 03/441-1811

WELLINGTON
Street Address: Level 2
Kordia House
109-125 Willis St.
Wellington
Postal Address: P.O. Box 27149
Wellington, 6141
tel. c/o National call center 09/914-4100
fax 04/917-6640

U.S. BRANCHES
LOS ANGELES
New Zealand Visa Application Centre Los
Angeles
1620 26th St., Ste. N2075
Santa Monica, CA 90404
tel. 855/844-2835 (toll-free within the U.S.)
fax 310/496-7437
ttslanz@ttsvisas.com

WASHINGTON, DC
New Zealand Visa Application Centre
1120 19th St. NW, Ste. 415
Washington, DC 20036
tel. 202/223-3400
fax 202/223-3900
nz@nzemb.org

Making the Move

GENERAL WEBSITES
IMMIGRATION NEW ZEALAND
www.immigration.govt.nz
This website is your first stop for learning about the immigration system. You can check out your qualifications and look up the Short-Term and Long-Term Skills Shortages Lists. There is also information about visa requirements and background information about various cities and towns in New Zealand.

NEW ZEALAND GOVERNMENT
www.govt.nz
This government website is a good place to start for information from other government departments. From here you'll find links to government websites for health, education, housing, labor, transportation, and so on. You'll also find information on how the New Zealand government is structured and a list of elected officials.

NEW ZEALAND NOW
www.newzealandnow.govt.nz
This is Immigration New Zealand's website aimed at attracting new immigrants. It gives you basic information on the various options for work visas, study visas, and residency in New Zealand. It's much more attractive and descriptive than the regular Immigration New Zealand site, and makes a good first stop. However, once you get into the nitty-gritty of applying, you'll need to visit the official Immigration New Zealand website listed above.

NZ EDGE
www.nzedge.com
This website contains an interesting mixture of New Zealand in the news around the world and background info about exceptional Kiwis. It's worth a browse and will give you an idea of who's who in New Zealand.

100 PERCENT PURE NEW ZEALAND
www.newzealand.com/ca
A tourism site, but with lots of great general information. It has a good tool for finding travel times and distances between various locations. There are also links on the home page to business websites, study websites, and more.

STATISTICS NEW ZEALAND
www.stats.govt.nz
If you're a "facts and figures" type of person, this is your source for the details about New Zealand. Things like population, income, birth and death rates, and just about every other detail can be found here. The site's search function is not the best, but if you keep digging, you'll eventually get what you're after.

STUFF
www.stuff.co.nz
To keep on top of what is happening around New Zealand, even before you arrive, check out the news on Stuff. You'll get all of the domestic stories, plus the New Zealand perspective on international news.

EXPAT ORGANIZATIONS
AMERICAN CLUB
www.americanclub.org.nz
This club has been around since 1966, fostering a closer relationship between New Zealand and the United States. Members receive newsletters and can attend organized events.

AMERICAN WOMEN'S CLUB (AUCKLAND)

www.awcauckland.com

This club encourages expat American women to get together for networking and to celebrate American holidays and events.

ENZ

www.enz.org

This site contains an active forum that lets expats living in New Zealand and those planning to immigrate ask each other questions on a variety of topics. Registration is required to participate in the discussions. There is also a lot of general information on topics such as jobs, housing, and finances.

MEETIN.ORG

www.meetin.org

This is a worldwide social network to get newcomers out and enjoying their new homes. There are New Zealand clubs in Auckland and Wellington. They hold frequent social events and send out newsletters to their members weekly.

THE NEW ZEALAND AMERICAN ASSOCIATION

www.nzaa.org.nz

This is similar to the American Club, but it has roots back to 1939. The group holds networking events and lets members know about U.S. speakers and performers coming to New Zealand.

MOVING COMPANIES

ALLIED VAN LINES

One Parkview Plaza
Oakbrook Terrace, IL 60181
tel. 800/444-6787 (toll-free within the U.S.)
www.allied.com

NZ VAN LINES

Street Address: 19 Barnes St.
Seaview, Wellington
Postal Address: P.O. Box 38058
Wellington, 5045
tel. 04/576-1550
fax 04/568-5529
headoffice@nzvanlines.co.nz
www.nzvanlines.co.nz

RELOCATION SPECIALISTS

IMMIGRATION ADVISERS AUTHORITY

P.O. Box 6222,
Wellesley St.
Auckland, 1141
tel. 09/925-3838
info@iaa.govt.nz
www.iaa.govt.nz

Go to the website for a list of licensed immigration advisers both in New Zealand and in your home country.

ACCESS IMMIGRATION NEW ZEALAND

1st Floor, 93 Dominion Rd.
Mt. Eden
Auckland, 1024
tel. 09/630-0411
fax 09/357-6352
bmilnes@laurentlaw.co.nz
www.accessimmigration.com

BUNAC–WORKING HOLIDAYS

750 State Highway 121, Ste. 250
Lewisville, TX 75067
tel. 800/GO-BUNAC (toll-free within the U.S.)
fax 203/264-0251
info@bunacusa.org
www.bunac.org/usa/worknewzealand

ON ARRIVAL

12 Tombane Terrace
Papakowhai
Porirua, 5024
tel. 04/237-7710
contact@onarrival.co.nz
www.onarrival.co.nz

RELOCATIONS INTERNATIONAL

Auckland tel. 09/523-1612
lsvensen@reloc.co.nz
Wellington tel. 04/479-3765
julia@reloc-wgtn.co.nz
www.relocate.co.nz

SETTLEMENT SUPPORT NEW ZEALAND

Immigration New Zealand has centralized support for new immigrants and closed most of the former locations around the country. There are still a few local support services available, as listed below. For all other areas, use the national support contact information at the top of the list. They also recommend visiting your local Citizens Advice Bureau (CAB) for face-to-face advice. There are over 80 of these around the country, so check the website for the location nearest you.

NATIONAL

tel. 0800/776-948 (toll-free within New Zeland)
09/914-4100 (from outside New Zealand)
newmigrantinfo@mbie.govt.nz
www.settlementsupport.net.nz

AUCKLAND

c/o Auckland Regional Migrant Services
Three Kings Plaza
532 Mt. Albert Rd.
Mt. Roskill, Auckland, 1042
tel. 09/625-2440
reception@arms-mrc.org.nz
www.settlement.org.nz

CHRISTCHURCH

tel. 03/355-4162
fax 03/379-5454
settlementsupport@cecc.org.nz
www.settlementsupport.net.nz

HAMILTON

c/o Waikato Migrant Resource Centre
Street Address: 46G Boundary Rd.
Hamilton
Postal Address: P.O. Box 4340
Hamilton, 3247
tel. 07/853-2192
fax 07/853-0469
info@wmrc.org.nz
www.wmrc.org.nz

CITIZENS ADVICE BUREAU

tel. 0800/367-222 (toll-free within New Zealand)
www.cab.org.nz

The Citizens Advice Bureau (CAB) has over 80 locations around New Zealand. They offer free advice on legal, settlement, education, health, and other topics. If they can't help you with your questions, they can at least point you in the right direction.

Health

ACCIDENT COMPENSATION CORPORATION (ACC)

tel. 04/816-7400

information@acc.co.nz

www.acc.co.nz

If you are injured in any type of accident, ACC should pay for your medical treatments. So make sure you understand how it all works, and hope that you never need it!

EQC

www.eqc.govt.nz

This website is run by the Earthquake Commission and has a lot of good information on how to prepare for a natural disaster and what to do if one happens.

HEALTH PAGES

www.healthpages.co.nz

A good resource for finding health-related services, including family doctors, specialists, hospitals, and physiotherapists.

PHARMAC

Street Address: Level 9

40 Mercer Street

Wellington

Postal Address: PO Box 10254

Wellington 6143

tel. 0800/660 050 (toll-free within New Zealand)

enquiry@pharmac.govt.nz

www.pharmac.health.nz

PLUNKET

National Office: Level 3, 40 Mercer Street

Wellington

Postal Address: PO Box 5474

Wellington 6145

tel. 04/471 0177

plunket@plunket.org.nz

www.plunket.org.nz

MAIN HOSPITALS

AUCKLAND CITY HOSPITAL

2 Park Road

Grafton, Auckland

tel. 09/367 0000

www.adhb.govt.nz

CHRISTCHURCH HOSPITAL

Riccarton Avenue

Christchurch

tel. 03/364 0640

www.cdhb.health.nz

DUNEDIN HOSPITAL

201 Great King Street

Dunedin

tel. 03/474 0999

contactus@southerndhb.govt.nz

www.southerndhb.govt.nz

HAWKE'S BAY FALLEN SOLDIERS' MEMORIAL HOSPITAL

Omahu Road

Private Bag 9014

Hastings 4120

tel. 06/878 8109

www.hawkesbay.health.nz

WAIKATO HOSPITAL

Corner Pembroke and Selwyn Street

Hamilton

tel. 07/839 8899

info@waikatodhb.health.nz

www.waikatodhb.health.nz

WELLINGTON HOSPITAL

Riddiford Street, Newtown

Wellington

tel. 04/385 5999

info@ccdhb.org.nz

www.ccdhb.org.nz

RESOURCES

Employment

JOB SEARCH WEBSITES
CAREERS NZ

www.careers.govt.nz

This is a very helpful website that contains links to dozens of other job search and recruitment websites from the general to industry-specific. If you want to find recruiters in your field, this is a great place to start.

GOVERNMENT JOBS

www.jobs.govt.nz

MY JOB SPACE

www.myjobspace.co.nz

NEW KIWIS

www.newkiwis.co.nz

Q JUMPERS

www.qjumpers.co.nz/job-seekers

SEEK

www.seek.co.nz

TRADE ME JOBS

www.trademe.co.nz/trade-me-jobs

WORKING IN NEW ZEALAND

www.workingin-newzealand.com

RECRUITMENT AGENCIES
HAYS

Auckland office: Level 12, PWC Tower, 188 Quay St.
Auckland, 1010
tel. 09/377-1123
fax 09/377-5855
auckland@hays.net.nz, wellington@hays.net.nz, christchurch@hays.net.nz
www.hays.net.nz

A general recruitment agency covering a large number of industries with two offices in Auckland and one each in Wellington and Christchurch. Check the website for complete contact details.

THE JOHNSON GROUP

Street Address: 139 The Terrace, Level 6
Wellington
Postal Address: P.O. Box 25245
Panama Street
Wellington, 6146
tel. 04/473-6699
info@thejohnsongroup.co.nz
www.johnsongroup.co.nz

A Wellington-based recruitment agency that specializes in public sector jobs.

MADISON RECRUITMENT

Street Address: 203 Queen St., Level 6
Auckland
Postal Address: P.O. Box 105 675
Auckland, 1143
tel. 09/303-4455
fax 09/303-4452
auckland@madison.co.nz
www.madison.co.nz

A large, general recruitment firm covering everything from construction to banking. It has five offices around New Zealand, so check the website for contact details outside of Auckland.

ROB LAW MAXRECRUITMENT

Street Address: 12 Johnston St., Level 4
Wellington
Postal Address: P.O. Box 5555
Wellington, 6145
tel. 04/499-8800
fax 04/499-0955
reception@roblawmax.co.nz
www.roblawmax.co.nz
Technical and professional recruiters, mainly for the technical, infrastructure, engineering, and print & packaging sectors. See the website for Auckland contact details.

TEACH NZ

Street Address :45-47 Pipitea St.
Thorndon, Wellington
Postal Address: P.O. Box 1666
Wellington, 6140
tel. 0800/165-225 (toll-free within New Zealand)
fax 04/463-8456
TeachNZ.admin@minedu.govt.nz
www.teachnz.govt.nz
This government website contains information for teachers who want to work in New Zealand.

Education

GENERAL INFORMATION
NEW ZEALAND QUALIFICATIONS AUTHORITY

Street Address: Level 13, 125 The Terrace
Wellington, 6011
Postal Address: P.O. Box 160
Wellington, 6140
tel. 04/463-3000
fax 04/463-3112
www.nzqa.govt.nz
The NZQA is the regulatory body for all kinds of qualifications, from high school diplomas to doctorates and everything in between. Here you can find out if your degree or diploma is recognized in New Zealand and where to upgrade your skills if needed.

STUDY IN NEW ZEALAND

www.studyinnewzealand.com
This website is aimed mainly at international students (not permanent residents), but it has basic information about all levels of education in New Zealand as well as a course and institution search function to identify where you can find the courses you are looking for. It also contains information on scholarships available to non-New Zealand citizens. If you're looking for a polytechnic school or institute of technology, this is the best place to find links to all of their websites.

KINDERGARTEN AND DAY CARE
NEW ZEALAND KINDERGARTENS INCORPORATED

Street Address: Level 1, 32 The Terrace
Postal Address: P.O. Box 3058
Wellington, 6140
tel. 04/471-0775
contact@nzkindergarten.org.nz
www.nzkindergarten.org.nz
This is a good place to start if you're looking for a "kindy" in your area or just want to understand how they work. This organization represents over 400 kindergartens around the country.

NEW ZEALAND PLAYCENTRE FEDERATION

P.O. Box 218
Whangaparaoa, Auckland 0943
tel. 09/428-4851 or 0800/752-969 (toll-free within New Zealand)
secretary@playcentre.org.nz
www.playcentre.org.nz

Playcentres are parent cooperatives that provide preschoolers with early childhood education. The website contains links for the 33 local associations around the country.

PRIMARY, INTERMEDIATE, AND HIGH SCHOOLS

CATHOLIC EDUCATION OFFICE

Street Address: Catholic Centre
22-30 Hill St.
Wellington
Postal Address: P.O. Box 12 307
Wellington, 6038
tel. 04/496-1739
fax: 04/496-1734
nzceooffice@nzceo.catholic.org.nz
www.nzceo.catholic.org.nz

This website is a good place to start if you're looking for a Catholic school anywhere in the country.

EDUCATION REVIEW OFFICE

Street Address: Level 1, 101 Lambton Quay
Postal Address: P.O. Box 2799
Wellington, 6140
tel. 04/499-2489
fax 04/499-2482
info@ero.govt.nz
www.ero.govt.nz

This government department reviews all schools every three years. It's a great source of information on the schools in your area, going from early childhood education right through to high school. In addition to the head office, there are area offices in several cities. You can find contact details for all of these on the main website.

INDEPENDENT SCHOOLS OF NEW ZEALAND

Street Address: Level 16
142 Lambton Quay
Wellington
Postal Address: P.O. Box 5222
Wellington, 6145
tel. 04/471-2022
fax 04/472-4635
rochelle.quan@isnz.org.nz
www.isnz.org.nz

This is the umbrella organization for 45 independent (private) schools around New Zealand. Many of the individual schools have their own websites as well, but this will give you a good overview of what's available.

MONTESSORI ASSOCIATION OF NEW ZEALAND

P.O. Box 31461
Lower Hutt, Wellington 5040
tel. 0800/336-612 (toll-free within New Zealand)
eo@montessori.org.nz
www.montessori.org.nz

Representing Montessori schools and preschools around New Zealand. The majority are preschools, but some go right up to college level.

TKI (TE KETE IPURANGI)

tel. 0800/858-525 (toll-free within New Zealand)
fax 04/382-6509
help@tki.org.nz
www.tki.org.nz

Te Kete Ipurangi is Maori for "The Basket of Knowledge." The website is maintained by the Ministry of Education. It can help you find schools in your area, and it also has a wealth of information about the New Zealand curriculum and other education-related resources.

COLLEGES, UNIVERSITIES, AND POLYTECHNICS

NEW ZEALAND QUALIFICATIONS AUTHORITY (NZQA)

www.nzqa.govt.nz/providers-partners

The New Zealand Qualifications Authority website contains a page with links to the websites of each polytechnic and institute of technology in New Zealand. You can also find the links by searching the Study in New Zealand website under Institute of Technology and Polytechnic.

STUDY IN NEW ZEALAND

www.studyinnewzealand.com/get-started/find-institutions-and-schools

UNIVERSITIES NEW ZEALAND

Street Address: Level 9
142 Lambton Quay
Wellington
Postal Address: P.O. Box 11915
Wellington, 6142
tel. 04/381-8500
www.nzvcc.ac.nz

This is the umbrella organization for New Zealand's eight universities. It contains general information about the university system in New Zealand, lists scholarships, and links to all of the university websites.

AUCKLAND UNIVERSITY OF TECHNOLOGY

Private Bag 92006
Auckland, 1142
tel. 09/921-9999
fax 09/921-9812
studentcentre@aut.ac.nz
www.aut.ac.nz

LINCOLN UNIVERSITY

P.O. Box 85084
Lincoln, Canterbury 7647
tel. 03/423-0000 or 0800/106-010 (toll-free within New Zealand)
info@lincoln.ac.nz
www.lincoln.ac.nz

MASSEY UNIVERSITY

Private Bag 11222
Palmerston North, 4442
tel. 06/350-5701
fax 06/350-5618
contact@massey.ac.nz
www.massey.ac.nz

UNIVERSITY OF AUCKLAND

Private Bag 92019
Auckland, 1142
tel. 09/373-7999
www.auckland.ac.nz

UNIVERSITY OF CANTERBURY

Private Bag 4800
Christchurch, 8140
tel. 03/366-7001
info@canterbury.ac.nz
www.canterbury.ac.nz

UNIVERSITY OF OTAGO

P.O. Box 56
Dunedin, 9054
tel. 03/479-1100
fax 03/479-8692
university@otago.ac.nz
www.otago.ac.nz

UNIVERSITY OF WAIKATO
Private Bag 3105
Hamilton, 3240
tel. 07/856-2889
fax 07/838-4300
info@waikato.ac.nz
www.waikato.ac.nz

VICTORIA UNIVERSITY OF WELLINGTON
P.O. Box 600
Wellington, 6140
tel. 04/472-1000
fax 04/499-4601
info@victoria.ac.nz
www.victoria.ac.nz

Finance

BANKS
All of the major banks have multiple branches throughout New Zealand. To find the branch nearest you, look on the bank's main website. Some of the websites also list the locations of ATMs (automatic teller machines) throughout the country. Note: Rather than email addresses, most of the banks have online inquiry forms on their websites.

ANZ
Private Bag 92210
Victoria Street West
Auckland, 1142
tel. 0800/269-296 (toll-free within New Zealand)
tel. 04/470-3142
www.anz.co.nz

ASB
P.O. Box 35, Shortland Street
Auckland, 1140
tel. 0800/803-804 (toll-free within New Zealand)
tel. 09/306-3000
www.asb.co.nz

BNZ
Private Bag 39806
Wellington Mail Centre
Lower Hutt, 5045
tel. 0800/275-269 (toll-free within New Zealand)
tel. 04/931-8209
www.bnz.co.nz

KIWIBANK
Private Bag 39888
Wellington Mail Centre
Lower Hutt, 5045
tel. 0800/113-355 (toll-free within New Zealand)
tel. 04/473-1133
www.kiwibank.co.nz

TSB
tel. 0800/872-2265 (toll-free within New Zealand)
tel. 06/968-3700
fax 06/968-3815
www.tsb.co.nz

WESTPAC
tel. 0800/400-600 (toll-free within New Zealand)
tel. 09/912-8000
www.westpac.co.nz

FINANCIAL ADVISERS

INSTITUTE OF FINANCIAL ADVISERS

Street Address: Level 6, Technology One House
86 Victoria St.
Wellington
Postal Address: P.O. Box 5513
Wellington, 6145
tel. 04/499-8062
tel. 0800/404-422 (toll-free within New Zealand)
fax 04/499-8064
admin@ifa.org.nz
www.ifa.org.nz

TAX

ACCOUNTANTS AND TAX AGENTS INSTITUTE OF NEW ZEALAND

P.O. Box 87475
Meadowbank, Auckland, 1742
tel. 0508/829-460 (toll-free within New Zealand)
www.atainz.co.nz

This website lists members by region, so it's an easy way to find a tax agent if you don't have anyone to ask for a recommendation.

IRD (INLAND REVENUE DEPARTMENT)

Inland Revenue
P.O. Box 39010
Wellington Mail Centre
Lower Hutt, 5045
tel. 0800/227-774 (toll-free within New Zealand)
tel. 04/978-0779
www.ird.govt.nz

If you require a face-to-face appointment with an IRD representative, you can set up a meeting at nearly 100 locations around the country by calling the general phone number above.

Communications

INTERNET SERVICE PROVIDERS

Rather than email addresses, most of the ISPs have online inquiry forms on their websites.

ORCON

Street Address: Level 2, Building B
28 The Warehouse Way
Akoranga Business Park
Northcote
North Shore City
Postal Address: P.O. Box 302362
North Harbour
Auckland, 0751
tel. 09/444-4414 or 0800/131-415 (toll-free within New Zealand)
www.orcon.net.nz

SLINGSHOT

P.O. Box 108-109
Symonds Street
Auckland, 1150
tel. 09/929-0418 or 0800/892-000 (toll-free within New Zealand)
fax 0800/892-222 (toll-free within New Zealand)
www.slingshot.co.nz

SPARK NEW ZEALAND

tel. 0800/800-123 (toll-free within New Zealand)
www.spark.co.nz

RESOURCES

VODAFONE
tel. 09/355-2007 or 0800/800-021 (toll-free within New Zealand)
www.vodafone.co.nz

PHONE COMPANIES
Again, rather than email addresses, most phone companies have online inquiry forms on their websites.

SPARK NEW ZEALAND
tel. 0800/800-123 (toll-free within New Zealand)
www.spark.co.nz

VODAFONE
tel. 09/355-2007 or 0800/800-021 (toll-free within New Zealand)
www.vodafone.co.nz

TELEVISION
FREEVIEW NZ
tel. 0800/373-384 (toll-free within New Zealand)
freeviewadmin@freeviewnz.tv
www.freeviewnz.tv

SKY TV
P.O. Box 9059
Auckland, 1149
tel. 0800/759-759 (toll-free within New Zealand)
tel. 09/525-5555
www.sky.co.nz

VODAFONE
tel. 09/355-2007 or 0800/800-021 (toll-free within New Zealand)
www.vodafone.co.nz

NEWSPAPERS
DOMINION POST
Street Address: 42-52 Willis St.
Wellington
Postal Address: P.O. Box 3740
Wellington, 6140
tel. 04/474-0000
www.stuff.co.nz/dominion-post

NEW ZEALAND HERALD
P.O. Box 706
Auckland, 1140
tel. 0800/100-888 (subscriptions)
www.nzherald.co.nz

THE PRESS
Street Address: 158 Goucester St.
Christchurch
Postal Address: Private Bag 4722
Christchurch, 8140
tel. 03/364-8464 (subscriptions)
tel. 03/379-0940 (general)
www.stuff.co.nz/the-press

POSTAL SERVICE AND COURIERS
NEW ZEALAND POST
Customer Service Centre
PO Box 2349
Christchurch Mail Centre
Christchurch 8140
tel. 0800/501 501 (toll-free within New Zealand)
www.nzpost.co.nz

FASTWAY COURIERS
www.fastway.co.nz
The website contains the contact details for local franchises.

FEDEX NEW ZEALAND
tel. 0800/733 339 (toll-free within New Zealand)
tel. 09/2565 382
www.fedex.com/nz

POST HASTE
tel. 0800/106 828 (toll-free within New Zealand)
customer.services@posthaste.co.nz.
www.posthaste.co.nz

UPS NEW ZEALAND
66 Westney Road, Mangere
Auckland International Airport
Auckland 2022
tel. 0800/742 587 (toll-free within New Zealand)
tel. 09/255 4630
www.ups.com/content/asia/nz/engindex.html

Travel and Transportation

AIRLINES
AIR NEW ZEALAND
Private Bag 92007
Auckland, 1142
tel. 0800/737-000 (toll-free within New Zealand)
tel. 09/357-3000
www.airnz.co.nz

AIR2THERE
Paraparaumu Airport
231 Kapiti Road
PO Box 349
Paraparaumu 5254
tel. 04/904 5133
info@air2there.com
www.air2there.com

QANTAS
tel. 0800/808-767 (toll-free within New Zealand)
tel. 09/357-8900
www.qantas.com.au

JETSTAR
tel. 0800/800-995 (toll-free within New Zealand)
tel. 09/975-9426
www.jetstar.com/nz

SOUNDS AIR
Street Address: 3 Auckland St.
Picton
Postal Address: P.O. Box 116
Picton, 7250
tel. 0800/505-005 (toll-free within New Zealand)
tel. 03/520-3080
info@soundsair.com
www.soundsair.com
Short flights linking Wellington and northern South Island destinations.

TRAINS
KIWIRAIL SCENIC JOURNEYS
tel. 0800/872-467 (toll-free within New Zealand)
tel. 04/495-0775
fax 04/472-8903
bookings@kiwirailscenic.co.nz
www.kiwirailscenic.co.nz

BUSES
AUCKLAND TRANSPORT
Private Bag 92250
Auckland 1142
tel. 0800/103-080 (toll-free within New Zealand)
tel. 09/366-6400
www.at.govt.nz

INTERCITY
tel. 09/583-5780 (local numbers for various cities available on the website below)
fax 09/583-5774
info@intercitygroup.co.nz
www.intercity.co.nz

METLINK–WELLINGTON REGIONAL TRANSPORT
P.O. Box 11646
Wellington, 6142
tel. 0800/801-700 (toll-free within New Zealand)
info@metlink.org.nz
www.metlink.org.nz

METRO–CHRISTCHURCH REGIONAL TRANSPORT
c/o Environment Canterbury
P.O. Box 345
Christchurch 8140
tel. 03/366-8855
metro@ecan.govt.nz
www.metroinfo.co.nz

FERRIES
Auckland Region Ferries
FULLERS
Pier 1, Ferry Terminal, Annex
99 Quay Street
Auckland, 1010
tel. 09/367-9111
fax 09/367-9148
www.fullers.co.nz

Cook Strait Ferries
BLUEBRIDGE
tel. 0800/844-844 (toll-free within New Zealand)
tel. 04/471-6188
bookings@bluebridge.co.nz
www.bluebridge.co.nz

INTERISLANDER
Private Bag 39988
Lower Hutt 5045
tel. 0800/802-802 (toll-free within New Zealand)
tel. 04/498-3302
fax 04/498-3090
info@interislander.co.nz
www.interislander.co.nz

CAR RENTALS
BUDGET
Private Bag 92144
Auckland, 1142
tel. 0800/283-438 (toll-free within New Zealand)
tel. 09/529-7784
www.budget.co.nz

EZI-RENT
tel. 0800/545-000 (toll-free within New Zealand)
tel. 09/254-4397
info@ezirentcarhire.co.nz
www.ezirentcarhire.co.nz

KEA CAMPERS
tel. 0800/520-052 (toll-free within New Zealand)
tel. 09/448-8800
www.keacampers.com

THRIFTY
P.O. Box 39 010
Christchurch, 8545
tel. 0800/737-070 (toll-free within New Zealand)
tel. 03/359-2720
fax 03/940-2503
customerservice@thrifty.co.nz
www.thrifty.co.nz

VROOM VROOM VROOM

tel. 0800-141-466 (toll-free within New Zealand)

tel. 09/889-0034

www.vroomvroomvroom.co.nz

This website helps you to compare rental rates between several major car and campervan rental companies.

TAXIS
BLUE STAR TAXIS

Christchurch

tel. 03/379-9799

www.bluestartaxis.org.nz

CO-OP TAXI

Auckland

P.O. Box 8626

Auckland, 1150

tel. 09/300-3000

fax 09/303-0080

www.cooptaxi.co.nz

WELLINGTON COMBINED TAXIS

Wellington

P.O. Box 16126

Wellington, 6242

tel. 04/384-4444

admin@taxis.co.nz

www.taxis.co.nz

CAR PURCHASES AND DRIVING
AUTO TRADER

tel. 0800/800-146 (toll-free within New Zealand)

internet@bauertrader.co.nz

www.autotrader.co.nz

For buying and selling both new and used vehicles.

NEW ZEALAND AUTOMOBILE ASSOCIATION (AA)

Street Address: 99 Albert St.

Auckland

Postal Address: P.O. Box 5

Auckland, 1140

tel. 0800/500-444 (toll-free within New Zealand)

tel. 09/966-8800 (head office)

fax 09/966-8896

www.aa.co.nz

A good source of general information on driving in New Zealand, plus it offers road service, insurance, and other services.

NEW ZEALAND TRANSPORT AGENCY

Private Bag 6995

Wellington, 6141

tel. 0800/822-422 (toll-free within New Zealand)

tel. 06/953-6200

info@nzta.govt.nz

www.nzta.govt.nz

This government department handles the *Road Code* publication, licensing, and registration of vehicles.

TRADE ME MOTORS (NEW AND USED VEHICLES)

www.trademe.co.nz/trade-me-motors

New Zealand's biggest online commerce site has a large section just for vehicles.

Housing Considerations

In addition to the agencies and websites listed here, you can often find real estate and rental listings in your local newspaper. The largest selection of listings appears in the weekend editions.

This is where you'll find information about upgrading or building a house for better energy efficiency. This website also has information about subsidies for upgrading heating systems and insulation in older homes.

BUILDING AND RENOVATING
BUILDING PERFORMANCE

P.O. Box 10729
Wellington, 6143
tel. 0800/242-243 (toll-free within New Zealand)
tel. 04/238-6362
info@mbie.govt.nz
www.building.govt.nz

This department regulates the building and housing industry, so it's a good place to start if you are looking to build or renovate a home.

CONSUMER

Private Bag 6996, Marion Square
Wellington, 6141
tel. 800/266-786 (toll-free within New Zealand)
tel. 04/384-7963
info@consumer.org.nz
www.consumer.org.nz

This online resource offers unbiased information on building, renovating, and maintaining your home.

ENERGY EFFICIENCY AND CONSERVATION AUTHORITY

Street Address: Level 8, 44 The Terrace Wellington
Postal Address: P.O. Box 388
Wellington, 6140
tel. 0800/358-656 (toll-free within New Zealand)
tel. 04/470-2200
www.eeca.govt.nz

BUYING
REAL ESTATE INSTITUTE OF NEW ZEALAND

P.O. Box 5663
Auckland, 1141
tel. 09/356-1755
fax 09/379-8471
info@reinz.co.nz
www.r-einz.org.nz

This group regulates the real estate industry in New Zealand. If you have problems with a bad agent, lodge a complaint here.

REAL ESTATE AGENTS AND PROPERTY RENTALS
HARCOURTS

Street Address: 7-9 Alpers Ave.
Newmarket, Auckland
Postal Address: P.O. Box 99549
Newmarket, Auckland, 1149
tel. 09/520-5569
fax 09/524-1481
headoffice@harcourts.co.nz
www.harcourts.co.nz

OPEN 2 VIEW

www.nz.open2view.com
Listings that include virtual tours of some properties.

REALESTATE.CO.NZ

www.realestate.co.nz
Online listings for all types of property.

RE/MAX

Level 1, 70 Stanley St.
Parnell, Auckland, 1010
tel. 09/309-8478
www.remax.co.nz

SELLA

www.sella.co.nz/classifieds/property/
Online listings for both sales and rentals
from agents and private sellers.

THE PROFESSIONALS

Street Address: 383 Khyber Pass Rd., Unit S
Newmarket, Auckland
Postal Address: P.O. Box 74024
Greenlane, Auckland, 1543
tel. 09/529-0361
fax 09/529-0348
information@professionals.co.nz
www.professionals.co.nz

TRADE ME PROPERTY

www.trademe.co.nz/property
Online listings for both sales and rentals
used by agents and private sellers.

RENTING
HOUSING NEW ZEALAND

tel. 0800/801-601 (toll-free within New
Zealand)
www.hnzc.co.nz
Housing New Zealand provides affordable
housing to low-income families around the
country. There are often long waiting lists
for these homes. Visit the website or call
the toll-free number to find a local office.

TENANCY SERVICES

tel. 0800/836-262 (toll-free within New
Zealand)
tel. 04/238-4695
www.tenancy.govt.nz
Tenancy Services has lots of information
on the rules of renting in New Zealand,
current market rents for all areas, and a
dispute resolution service.

Prime Living Locations

AUCKLAND
AUCKLAND COUNCIL
Street Address, central office: 1 Greys Ave.
Auckland
Postal Address: Private Bag 92300
Auckland ,1142
tel. 09/301-0101
fax 09/301-0100
www.aucklandcouncil.govt.nz
There are several physical offices where you can find council services. See the website to find the nearest office to you.

AUCKLAND REGION
www.aucklandregion.co.nz
A great unofficial website with links for all kinds of community groups, businesses, and other useful information about all parts of the Auckland region.

TARANAKI AND WAIKATO
HAMILTON CITY COUNCIL
Private Bag 3010
Hamilton, 3240
tel. 07/838-6699
fax 07/838-6599
info@hcc.govt.nz
www.hamilton.govt.nz

NEW PLYMOUTH DISTRICT COUNCIL
Street Address: 84 Liardet St.
New Plymouth
Postal Address: Private Bag 2025
New Plymouth, 4342
tel. 06/759-6060
fax 06/759-6072
enquiries@npdc.govt.nz
www.newplymouthnz.com

SOUTH TARANAKI DISTRICT COUNCIL
Street Address: 105-111 Albion St.
Hawera
Postal Address: Private Bag 902
Hawera, 4640
tel. 06/278-0555
contact@stdc.govt.nz
www.southtaranaki.com

TARANAKI REGIONAL COUNCIL
Street Address: 47 Cloten Rd.
Stratford
Postal Address: Private Bag 713
Stratford, 4352
tel. 06/765-7127
fax 06/765-5097
info@trc.govt.nz
www.trc.govt.nz

WAIKATO DISTRICT COUNCIL
Private Bag 544
Ngaruawahia, 3742
tel. 0800/492-452 (toll-free within New Zealand)
tel. 07/824-8633
fax 07/824-8091
www.waikatodistrict.govt.nz

BAY OF PLENTY AND HAWKE'S BAY
GISBORNE DISTRICT COUNCIL
Street Address: 15 Fitzherbert St.
Gisborne
Postal Address: P.O. Box 747
Gisborne, 4040
tel. 06/867-2049
fax 06/867-8076
www.gdc.govt.nz

HASTINGS DISTRICT COUNCIL
Street Address: 207 Lyndon Rd. East
Hastings
Postal Address: Private Bag 9002
Hastings, 4156
tel. 06/871-5000
council@hdc.govt.nz
www.hastingsdc.govt.nz

NAPIER CITY COUNCIL
Street Address: 231 Hastings St.
Napier
Postal Address: Private Bag 6010
Napier, 4142
tel. 06/835-7579
fax 06/835-7574
info@napier.govt.nz
www.napier.govt.nz

TAURANGA CITY COUNCIL
Street Address: 91 Willow St.
Tauranga
Postal Address: Private Bag 12022
Tauranga, 3110
tel. 07/577-7000
fax 07/577-7193
info@tauranga.govt.nz
www.tauranga.govt.nz

WELLINGTON AND THE LOWER NORTH ISLAND
GREATER WELLINGTON REGIONAL COUNCIL
Street Address: Shed 39, 2 Fryatt Quay
Wellington
Postal Address: P.O. Box 11646
Wellington, 6142
tel. 04/384-5708
fax 04/385-6960
info@gw.govt.nz
www.gw.govt.nz

HUTT CITY COUNCIL
Street Address: 531 High St.
Lower Hutt
Postal Address: Private Bag 31912
Lower Hutt, 5040
tel. 04/570-6666
fax 04/569-4290
contact@huttcity.govt.nz
www.huttcity.govt.nz

KAPITI COAST DISTRICT COUNCIL
Street Address: 175 Rimu Rd.
Paraparaumu
Postal Address: Private Bag 60601
Paraparaumu, 5254
tel. 04/296-4700
fax 04/293-4820
kapiti.council@kapiticoast.govt.nz
www.kapiticoast.govt.nz

MASTERTON DISTRICT COUNCIL
Street Address: 64 Chapel St.
Masterton
Postal Address: P.O. Box 444
Masterton, 5840
tel. 06/370-6300
fax 06/378-8400
mdc@mstn.govt.nz
www.mstn.govt.nz

SOUTH WAIRARAPA DISTRICT COUNCIL
Street Address: 19 Kitchener St.
Martinborough
Postal Address: P.O. Box 6
Martinborough, 5741
tel. 06/306-9611
fax 06/306-9373
enquiries@swdc.govt.nz
www.swdc.govt.nz

WELLINGTON CITY COUNCIL

Street Address: 101 Wakefield St.
Wellington
Postal Address: P.O. Box 2199
Wellington, 6140
tel. 04/499-4444
fax 04/801-3138
info@wcc.govt.nz
www.wellington.govt.nz

CHRISTCHURCH AND MARLBOROUGH

CHRISTCHURCH CITY COUNCIL

53 Hereford St.
Christchurch
tel. 03/941-8999
fax 03/941-8033
info@ccc.govt.nz
www.ccc.govt.nz

ENVIRONMENT CANTERBURY (REGIONAL COUNCIL)

Street Address: 17 Sir Gil Simpson Dr.
Christchurch
Postal Address: P.O. Box 345
Christchurch, 8140
tel. 0800/324-636 (toll-free within New Zealand)
tel. 03/353-9007
ecinfo@ecan.govt.nz
www.ecan.govt.nz

MARLBOROUGH DISTRICT COUNCIL

Street Address: 15 Seymour St.
Blenheim
Postal Address: P.O. Box 443
Blenheim, 7240
tel. 03/520-7400
fax 03/520-7496
mdc@marlborough.govt.nz
www.marlborough.govt.nz

NELSON CITY COUNCIL

Street Address: 110 Trafalgar St.
Nelson
Postal Address: P.O. Box 645
Nelson, 7040
tel. 03/546-0200
fax 03/546-0239
enquiry@ncc.govt.nz
www.nelson.govt.nz

OTAGO AND SOUTHLAND

DUNEDIN CITY COUNCIL

Street Address: 50 The Octagon
Postal Address: P.O. Box 5045
Dunedin, 9058
tel. 03/477-4000
dcc@dcc.govt.nz
www.dunedin.govt.nz
www.dunedinnz.com

INVERCARGILL CITY COUNCIL

Street Address: 101 Esk St.
Invercargill
Postal Address: Private Bag 90104
Invercargill, 9840
tel. 03/211-1777
fax 03/211-1433
webteam@icc.govt.nz
www.icc.govt.nz

OTAGO REGIONAL COUNCIL

Street Address: 70 Stafford St.
Dunedin
Postal Address: Private Bag 1954
Dunedin, 9054
tel. 03/474-0827
fax: 03/479-001
www.orc.govt.nz

QUEENSTOWN LAKES DISTRICT COUNCIL

Street Address: 10 Gorge Rd.
Queenstown
Postal Address: Private Bag 50072
Queenstown, 9348
tel. 03/441-0499
fax 03/443-0024
services@qldc.govt.nz
www.qldc.govt.nz

SOUTHLAND DISTRICT COUNCIL

Street Address: 15 Forth St.
Invercargill
Postal Address: P.O. Box 903
Invercargill, 9840
tel. 0800/732-732 (toll-free within New Zealand)
tel. 03/211-2500
emailsdc@southlanddc.govt.nz
www.southlanddc.govt.nz

Glossary

afternoon tea: afternoon snack, light meal
arvo/avo: afternoon
aubergine: eggplant
bach: holiday home, cottage (also crib)
banger: sausage
barbie: barbecue
bikkie/biscuit: cookie
bog-standard: normal, average
bonnet: hood of a car
boot: trunk of a car
boy racer: young person with a loud car involved in street races
brekkie: breakfast
bring a plate: potluck
bro: buddy (also cuz)
bub: baby
bum bag: fanny pack ("fanny" is offensive, and refers to female genitalia)
bush: forest, wilderness
bust a gut: try very hard
BYO: bring your own (wine at a restaurant)
capsicum: sweet/bell pepper
caravan: trailer, RV
car park: parking lot
cheers: thanks, good-bye (casual)
chemist: pharmacy
chilly bin: cooler
chips: french fries
choice: great, cool
cotton buds: cotton swabs (like Q-tips)
courgette: zucchini
crib: holiday home, cottage (mainly in Southland)
crook: not well, sick
cuz: bro, buddy
dairy: convenience store
doco: documentary

dodgy: suspicious, not quite right
dummy: pacifier ("spit the dummy" means to throw a tantrum)
dunny: toilet
entrée: appetizer (main courses are called "mains")
flash: fancy
flat: apartment
footpath: sidewalk
fortnight: two weeks
full on: intense, busy
give it a go: try something
give way: yield (traffic)
good as gold: everything's fine
good on ya: congratulations, good for you
gumboots: rubber boots
hard yakka: hard work
heaps: a lot, tons
hokey pokey: sponge toffee
hoon: gang member, thug
hot dog: usually a hot dog dipped in batter and fried (like a corn dog)
ice block/ice lolly: popsicle
jandals: flip-flops, thongs
jelly: Jell-O
jersey: sweater
journo: journalist
keen: interested, enthusiastic
Kiwi (upper case): New Zealander, or anything from New Zealand
kiwi (lower case): small, flightless, nocturnal bird, national animal of New Zealand
kiwifruit: oval fruit with green flesh and fuzzy brown skin
knackered: tired, beat
kumara: sweet potato

lemonade: lemon-lime soda (7UP, Sprite)
lift: elevator
lolly: candy
loo (also toilet): restroom
lounge: living room
mate: buddy, pal
metal road: gravel road
mission: something that will be difficult to do
mobile: cell phone
morning tea: morning snacks with coffee and tea
motorway: freeway
nappy: diaper
no worries: no problem (also, you're welcome)
pavlova (or pav): meringue topped with whipped cream and fruit
petrol: gasoline
pie: meat pie
pissed: drunk
plaster: adhesive bandage
PMT: PMS (premenstrual syndrome)
Pom: English person
post code: postal code, ZIP code
pram: stroller
presenter: host
pudding: dessert

pull a sickie: call in sick to get the day off
ring: call on the phone
rubbish: trash, garbage
shattered: exhausted
she'll be right: everything will be OK, it'll all work out
singlet: tank top
smoko: a smoke break, although used for a break even without smoking
sweet as: great, awesome
takeaway: takeout food
take the piss: to make fun of (also take the mickey)
tea: sometimes afternoon snacks, sometimes the evening meal
tin: can
tip: trash dump, landfill
togs: bathing suit
tomato sauce: ketchup
tramping: hiking, backpacking
unwaged: unemployed
wag: skip school
wardrobe: closet
whinge: complain, whine
wop-wops: somewhere very remote

Maori Phrasebook

PRONUNCIATION GUIDE

The Maori language uses five vowels (a, e, i, o, u) and eight consonants (h, k, m, n, p, r, t, w), plus two combined consonants (wh, ng) which are pronounced as single sounds.

Each vowel has a short and a long sound as follows:

Vowel	Short	Long
a	as in "about"	as in "far"
e	as in "enter"	as in "bed"
i	as in "eat"	as in "sheep"
o	as in "awful"	as in "pork"
u	as in "put"	as in "boot"

The consonants are basically pronounced as they are in English, except for "r," which is softly rolled, similar to the sound of a cat purring. The "ng" sound is like in the word "sing." The "wh" sound is pronounced like an English "f."

HELPFUL PHRASES

Aotearoa: New Zealand, literally "the land of the long white cloud"
haere mai: welcome
haka: traditional Maori chant and dance
hangi: earth oven dug into the ground
hongi: greeting of "shared breath" by pressing noses together
hui: meeting
iwi: tribe
kai: food
ka kite ano: see you later
ka pai: great
kia kaha: be strong, give it your best
kia ora: hello (casual)
mana: power, strength
Maori: the original people of New Zealand, literally "normal"
Maoritanga: Maori culture
marae: meeting house, gathering place
moko: traditional Maori tattooing

pa: fortified buildings in historic Maori settlements
Pakeha: non-Maori people
pounamu: greenstone, New Zealand jade
tangi: mourning period involving a gathering of family and friends

te reo: Maori language, literally "the language"
waka: canoe
waka hourua: traveling canoe
whakapapa: ancestry/genealogy
whanau: family
whenua: the land

Suggested Reading

Reading New Zealand books is a great way to supplement your research and get to know the country better and faster. Tourist guidebooks have some limited value for immigrants, in that they can give you an overview of various parts of the country. Nonfiction books are probably your best resource, from history and culture books to biographies of famous Kiwis. If you're interested in flora and fauna, there are plenty of guides to native trees, shrubs, and birds available.

Reading New Zealand fiction isn't as directly beneficial, but it does provide a window into the Kiwi psyche and give accounts of how lives are lived in this country. Being familiar with the country's best-known authors also keeps you in the conversation when books come up around other Kiwis.

In this section I've included just a small sample of what is available to you. If you are interested in reading more New Zealand literature, I suggest starting by browsing the New Zealand Book Council website at www.bookcouncil.org.nz.

GUIDEBOOKS

AA Road Atlas of New Zealand. Auckland: New Zealand Automobile Association, 2005. Before you set off on your fact-finding trip, I suggest getting a good atlas like this one to help you find your way around. With so many mountain ranges and large, rural areas around, it's a good idea to have a complete guide to the highways and back roads.

Hart, Stephen. *Where to Live in Auckland.* Auckland: Barbican Publishing, 2012. If you're planning to settle in New Zealand's largest urban area, this detailed guide to the dozens of neighborhoods around the region can be a big help. The descriptions are more honest than anything you'll get from a real estate agent, although prices can change so quickly that it's best not to rely on the estimates.

Hempstead, Andrew. *Moon New Zealand.* Berkeley: Avalon Travel, 2012. A good all-around guide to traveling in New Zealand. This will give you information about transportation, places to stay during your fact-finding trip, and perhaps some more ideas about where you'd like to live.

Slater, Lee. *Lonely Planet Hiking and Tramping in New Zealand.* Oakland: Lonely Planet, 2014. This guide to the mountains and forests of New Zealand is a must if you're planning on exploring the outdoors after your move. It gives detailed descriptions of how to get to the most popular tracks, what to expect on the routes, and how difficult they are.

HISTORY AND CULTURE

Bennett, Joe. *A Land of Two Halves.* Scribner, London: Simon & Schuster,

RESOURCES

2005. After 10 years in New Zealand, English immigrant Joe Bennett decides to explore the country and figure out what has kept him so intrigued for so long. He hitchhikes through both islands and meets some very odd characters along the way.

Butler, Sue. *New Zealand—Culture Smart!* London: Kuperard, 2006. This short guide gives those unfamiliar with New Zealand an overview of the country's history and culture. At 170 pages it is a relatively fast read if you want to know the basics.

Gulian, Jared. *Moon Over Martinborough.* Auckland: Random House NZ, 2013. Jared is interviewed in the Wellington and Lower North Island chapter of this book. His entertaining and enlightening blog about living in rural New Zealand was turned into this charming book. It is difficult to find a copy outside of New Zealand, but the digital version is widely available for download.

Hillary, Sir Edmund. *View from the Summit.* New York: Pocket, 2000. Hillary is pretty much royalty to the Kiwis. His autobiography is a good way to find out what makes someone heroic to New Zealanders. From scaling Everest to working tirelessly to improve the lives of the Sherpa people of Nepal, Sir Ed lived an exceptional life. Yet he always just considered himself an ordinary Kiwi bloke, with a bit of a stubborn streak.

King, Michael. *The Penguin History of New Zealand.* North Shore, New Zealand: Penguin New Zealand, 2003. This book by the late Michael King is acclaimed for being easy to read and understand, without sounding like a textbook. This is a great way to get acquainted with the

country's history and get some insight into (relatively) current issues.

Thompson, Christina. *Come On Shore And We Will Kill And Eat You All.* New York: Bloomsbury, 2008. Written by an American who fell in love with and married a Maori man, this book combines her personal story with a historical look at the interaction between European and Maori people in New Zealand. The book is filled with lively anecdotes and substantial research.

FICTION

Rather than suggesting specific titles, I'm providing the names of some of New Zealand's favorite homegrown authors. Some of their work may be difficult to find outside of New Zealand, but once you're in the country, the bookstores are generally great at stocking the latest Kiwi novels. For older titles, check your local library.

Catton, Eleanor. Catton's epic second novel, *The Luminaries*, made her the youngest-ever winner of the Man Booker Prize for fiction. It's a Victorian-era story that brings to life the gold rush on the west coast of New Zealand's South Island in the 1860s. Although Catton is considered a New Zealand author, she was born in Canada and spent her first six years living there.

Crump, Barry. His first novel, *A Good Keen Man,* has become the iconic portrait of the Kiwi bloke. He offers a peek into the mentality of the guy who just wants to forget about the city and "go bush" with humor and style.

Frame, Janet. This Dunedin-born writer died in 2004, by which time she was a household name in New Zealand, although she spent much of her life in other places. Her books set in New

Zealand include her three-part autobiography *To the Is-Land* (1982), *An Angel at My Table* (1984), and *The Envoy from Mirror City* (1985). The novel *The Rainbirds* (1968; published in the United States in 1969 as *Yellow Flowers in the Antipodean Room*) is one of her fictional works set in New Zealand.

Gee, Maurice. Gee is a major name in New Zealand fiction. He grew up in Henderson, west of Auckland. Gee uses fictionalized New Zealand settings in his books, so you may struggle to figure out just where his characters are meant to be. He covers many topics, but for extra Kiwiana, *The Big Season* looks at the seedier side of rugby, the country's national obsession.

Ihimaera, Witi. You might know Ihimaera as the author of *Whale Rider,* which was made into a film, but he has a large collection of fiction that reflects the emotional experience of the Maori like no other writer. Some of his novels are overtly political, while others delve into the significance of the past.

Mansfield, Katherine. Mansfield is New Zealand's best-known short fiction writer. She actually left New Zealand early in her adult life, but if you have children in the school system in New Zealand, rest assured they will be reading some Mansfield before they graduate.

Shadbolt, Maurice. Shadbolt's early novels are set in contemporary New Zealand, but it's his later historical novels that are the real standouts. His masterpiece is said to be *The New Zealand Wars Trilogy.*

RESOURCES

Clothing and Shoe Sizes

Most clothing and shoes you'll buy in New Zealand will be imported from other countries. Because they are from overseas, the sizes will vary according to the company's home market. Most often you will see UK sizes, although there are also U.S. and European sizes of some products. Many (especially shoes) list the sizing for multiple regions. These charts should help you to figure out what will fit best.

WOMEN'S SHOES

UK	4 1/2	5	5 1/2	6	6 1/2	7	7 1/2
US	6	6	7	7	8	8	9
Europe	37	38	39	39	40	40	41

MEN'S SHOES

UK	7 1/2	8	8 1/2	9	9 1/2	10	10 1/2
US	8	8 1/2	9	9 1/2	10	10 1/2	11
Europe	40	41	42	43	44	45	46

CHILDREN'S SHOES

UK/US	2	3	4	5	6	7	8	9	10	11	12
Europe	18	19	20-21	22	23	24-25	26	27	28	29-30	31

WOMEN'S CLOTHING

UK	4	6	8	10	12	14	16	18	20	22
US	2	4	6	8	10	12	14	16	18	20
Europe	30	32	34	36	38	40	42	44	46	48

MEN'S SHIRTS

UK/US	14	14 1/2	15	15	16	16 1/2	17	17 1/2
Europe	35	36-37	38	39-40	41	42-43	44	45

CHILDREN'S CLOTHING

US/UK		4	6	8	10	12	14
Europe (height in inches)		43	48	55	58	60	62
Europe (height in cm)		109	122	140	147	152	157

Infants' clothing sizes may also be labeled in different ways, but usually there is an age guideline on the label as well as the size.

Index

Acknowledgments

First, I'd like to take this opportunity to thank my parents, Emile and Suzy, for their constant support no matter what I get up to—even when it involves moving halfway around the world! Even when they are far away, they are always near my heart.

Also close to my heart is my husband, Gerhard. Meeting him was the best reward I could imagine from moving to New Zealand. He was a big help during the writing of this book, diligently clipping relevant newspaper articles for me. He was also extremely patient every time I stopped us in our tracks to take pictures of strange things like cows or shipping containers.

Of course this kind of guide involves input from a lot of people. I'd like to thank my fellow immigrants for their participation, including Don and Eve Casagranda, Ross Palmer, Syed Shamsuddoha, Sarah Gauthier, Roslyn Bullas, Melanie Hirsch, Jared Gulien, Doris Faulhaber, Jason Liu, and Danzia Galinovic.

My co-photographers were very generous with their pictures, and I couldn't possibly have managed to capture it all myself. So I'm grateful for the visual contributions from Travis Cottreau, Una Hubbard, Kathy Phillips, Nathaniel Beaver, Bob Morris, Rohit Kashikar, Education New Zealand, Fieldays, Hamilton and Waikato Tourism and Whitireia Performing Arts. If a picture is worth a thousand words, then you collectively saved me an awful lot of writing!

Of course this book is also the work of the team at Avalon Travel who were kind enough to put their faith in me not just once but three times, from Elizabeth Hansen to Erin Raber, Kat Bennett, and Lucie Ericksen. You have been a real pleasure to work with. My agent, Matt Wagner, has been a big supporter and my California connection.

Moving to New Zealand was a great adventure, and the opportunity to share my enthusiasm for my adopted country with others who are interested in immigrating is a real privilege for me. If I can help a few people to make their moves go a bit smoother or make their adjustment to Kiwi life easier, then the time spent writing and updating this book will have been worthwhile. *Kia kaha,* and I'll see you in New Zealand!

Also Available

MAP SYMBOLS

▒▒▒ Expressway	○ City/Town	✈ Airfield	▲ Archaeological Site
▒▒▒ Primary Road	◉ State Capital	✈ Airport	⌂ Church
▒▒▒ Secondary Road			🯄 Gas Station
▪▪▪ Unpaved Road	✦ National Capital	▲ Mountain	Mangrove
⋯⋯ Ferry	★ Point of Interest	♣♣ Park	Reef
▬▬▬ Railroad	▪ Other Location	🎿 Skiing Area	Swamp

CONVERSION TABLES

°C = (°F - 32) / 1.8
°F = (°C x 1.8) + 32
1 inch = 2.54 centimeters (cm)
1 foot = 0.304 meters (m)
1 yard = 0.914 meters
1 mile = 1.6093 kilometers (km)
1 km = 0.6214 miles
1 fathom = 1.8288 m
1 chain = 20.1168 m
1 furlong = 201.168 m
1 acre = 0.4047 hectares
1 sq km = 100 hectares
1 sq mile = 2.59 square km
1 ounce = 28.35 grams
1 pound = 0.4536 kilograms
1 short ton = 0.90718 metric ton
1 short ton = 2,000 pounds
1 long ton = 1.016 metric tons
1 long ton = 2,240 pounds
1 metric ton = 1,000 kilograms
1 quart = 0.94635 liters
1 US gallon = 3.7854 liters
1 Imperial gallon = 4.5459 liters
1 nautical mile = 1.852 km

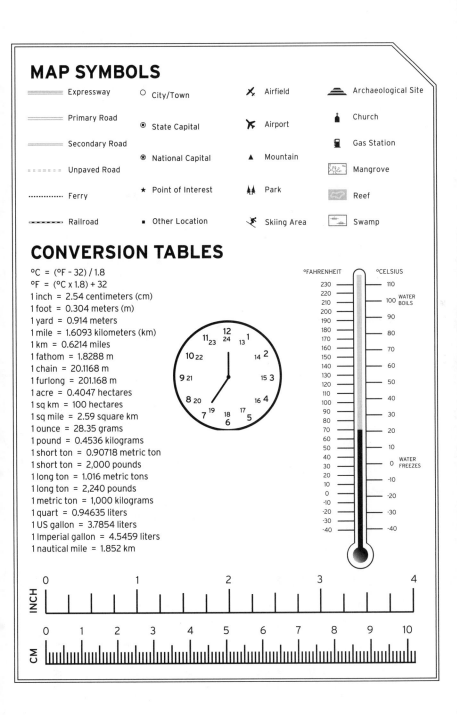

MOON LIVING ABROAD NEW ZEALAND

Avalon Travel
a member of the Perseus Books Group
1700 Fourth Street
Berkeley, CA 94710, USA
www.moon.com

Editor: Erin Raber
Copy Editor: Ashley Benning
Graphics and Production Coordinator:
  Lucie Ericksen
Cover Designer: Lucie Ericksen
Map Editor: Kat Bennett
Cartographers: Kat Bennett, Brian Shotwell
Indexer: Greg Jewett

ISBN-13: 978-1-63121-248-2
ISSN: 1943-149X

Printing History
1st Edition – 2008
3rd Edition – November 2015
5 4 3 2 1

Text © 2015 by Michelle Waitzman.
Maps © 2015 by Avalon Travel.
All rights reserved.

KEEPING CURRENT

Although we strive to produce the most up-to-date guidebook that we possibly can, change is unavoidable. Between the time this book goes to print and the time you read it, the cost of goods and services may have increased, and a handful of the businesses noted in these pages will undoubtedly move, alter their prices, or close their doors forever. Exchange rates fluctuate—sometimes dramatically—on a daily basis. Federal and local legal requirements and restrictions are also subject to change, so be sure to check with the appropriate authorities before making the move. If you see anything in this book that needs updating, clarification, or correction, please drop us a line. Send your comments via email to feedback@moon.com, or use the address above.